PUBLIC POLICYMAKING REEXAMINED

PUBLIC POLICYMAKING REEXAMINED

YEHEZKEL DROR

With a New Introduction by the Author

Transaction Books
New Brunswick (U.S.A.) and London (U.K.)

Library of Congress Catalog Number: 83-351
ISBN: 0-87855-928-0 (paper)
Printed in the United States of America

Library of Congress Cataloging in Publication Data

Dror, Yehezkel, 1928-
    Public policymaking reexamined.

    Reprint. Originally published: San Francisco :
Chandler Pub. Co., [1968] (Chandler publications in political science) With new introd.
    Bibliography: p.
    Includes index.
    1. Policy sciences.   I. Title.   II. Series: Chandler publications in political science.
H97.D76   1983   350   83-351
ISBN 0-87855-928-0 (pbk.)

To **BENJAMIN AKZIN,**
my teacher and colleague

Introduction to the Transaction Edition

Interest in the study and improvement of policymaking has been on the increase during the fifteen years since this book was first published. Multiplication of teaching programs, periodicals, and books devoted to policy sciences (never mind under what name) testifies to intense academic activity; and proliferation of improvement attempts in many governments indicates growing practical concerns.

But no breakthroughs have occurred. While somewhat better data is available on some facets of policymaking and a few useful concepts have been developed (Dunn [1981] surveys the field admirably, with comprehensive bibliographies), no major advances in policymaking theory have taken place. While some countries have engaged in interesting improvement experiments, no shift for the better in overall policymaking has occured. Regrettably, neither research in policy sciences nor changes in policymaking have antiquated this book. Dealing with policymaking theoretically, the main propositions, ideas, concepts, models, and proposals developed in the book continue to fit the real world and the continuing state of policy sciences underdevelopment.

This does not mean that I would rewrite the book as it now stands. Some parts of it are superior to what I could do at present, preoccupied as I am with other perspectives and overloaded as I am with additional acquired incapacities. Some details need revision and updating. Much more important, some perspectives, concepts, ideas, and theoretic observations need to be added. This is the task of the present new introductory essay. A different perspective is presented in *Policymaking under Adversity* (Dror 1983b).

First, let me move into a short autobiographic prelude. Time has, hopefully, provided better understanding of the impact of life history and "identity experiences" (to change somewhat a term of E.H. Erickson [1975, ch. 1]) on my intellectual and professional-scientific endeavors—a matter of special importance in as ambiguous and "existential" a subject as policymaking. The overall orientation of *Public Policymaking Reexamined* had been strongly shaped by my Israeli background; while my present approaches to policy-making have been significantly reshaped by experiences in governments, with some recent additional input provided by study of German approaches.

As a prelude to the substantive contents of this essay, I would like to share some of these insights with the reader. This, not in order to justify ideas, findings, propositions, and proposals; those have to stand on their own, supported with appropriate professional data and analysis. Neither do I fancy self-exposure for its own sake. Some responses to the book sensitized me to important background differences between many readers and myself—differences which cause some problems. Recognition of main influences shaping my professional opinions may help better understanding of my writings, though not necessarily agreement with them. Some such self-observations may also serve as raw material for a sociology of policy sciences—which is urgently needed, in view of the high sensitivities of this interdiscipline to cultural assumptions and to locality-bound mind sets.

ISRAELI LIFE IMPACTS

Israeli background and engagement influence my policy writings in at least two important dimensions (leaving aside my strategic writings [such as Dror 1980]), distinguishing them in some important respects from prevalent U.S. approaches. First, I believe in a broad ideology, namely Zionism. I therefore consider policy improvement largely, but not exclusively, in an instrumental sense, directed at achieving higher effectiveness in approximating whatever changing values a society, via its legitimate policymakers, prefers. This does not mean that value discourse is unimportant and that I have no strong opinions on various issues (Dror 1983b). But I feel no emotional need to constantly justify policymaking improvement in terms of absolute belief systems. Rather, as explained in this essay, the possibility to strive for value-free understanding of policymaking and for value/sensitivity-tested policymaking-improvement prescriptions is accepted. This may be emotionally difficult for those engaged in advocacy and semiprophetic endeavors; dangerous for those facing nihilism; anathematic and even repugnant to those searching for a faith to believe in; and impossible for those mixing up the roles of politicians, pedagogues, social activists, scholars, and policy professionals (for another view, Tribe 1972). While scholars and policy professionals must follow appropriate rules of ethics (Ad Hoc Committee of the Operations Research Society of America 1971; Dror 1971:119; Mitroff 1972; Wagner 1972), this is quite different from negating the desirability and partial feasibility of Max Weber's "value-free science" approach as an ideal to strive for within delimited worlds of scientific and professional endeavor (Weber 1949; for a different opinion, Miller 1979). In this connection, Weber's personal engagement in politics, his "ethics of responsibility" (Roth and Schluchter 1979), and his strong political beliefs are worth mentioning (Bruun 1972; Weber 1958; Mitzman 1970; Mommsen 1974).

With due appreciation of the importance of social critique and intellectuals' roles in it, I think that the functions of policy sciences have a different focus from those of the Frankfurt School (Geuss 1981), though personal overlaps and cross-fertilizations are possible and desirable. The very fact of my strong involvement in sociopolitical activities with intensely held ideologies is probably a main autobiographic feature supporting value-free policy sciences when dealing with knowledge on policymaking, as well as value restraint in making recommendations, in the sense of putting aside personal values in favor of those of the legitimate value judge, while helping the latter develop and clarify his preferences. All this, subject to overarching ethics of responsibility. My legal background may also contribute to this position, owing to the clear distinction in legal ethics and in the legal profession between legal opinions, which try to be clinical and detached, and client-serving legal advocacy, both subject to overriding moral-professional codes of behavior (Katz 1972).

Intense and direct involvement in Israeli societal architecture is a second main influence on my policy writings. Israel is a fascinating case of a society subjected to explicit molding through collective action, based on a fundamental ideology with very high aspirations. While conscious of the built-in limits of government, I tend to take an active view of policymaking as a main mode of collective attempts to influence the future. Early doubts about incrementalism (Dror 1964) definitely reflected Israeli experience. In this respect I regard the Israeli background as an advantage, because an active policymaking stance is becoming increasingly necessary in more and more countries, including the United States of America, as has become clearer during the fifteen years since the book was first published (despite Lindblom 1979). Even when attempts are made to reduce the scope of government activities, this paradoxically requires very active and high-quality policymaking, to achieve such a difficult shift; and, then, to engage in essential central societal steering with more sophisticated instruments than direct governmental management.

LEARNING INSIDE GOVERNMENT

Fifteen years ago I already had some experience with government, but from the outside and on a superficial level. This is the main cause for some missing dimensions in the book, shared with most policy sciences. Learning about government from within has become during the last fifteen years a main reshaper of my policymaking knowledge, both objective and subjective. In the last fifteen years I have spent half the time in and near governments, mostly on a full-time basis, on leave from my university: two and a half years in a major think tank working for a government on major policy issues; one year setting up a new think tank—which later foundered; two and a half years in a top-level policy-planning position within the inner core of a government; half a year as chief scientist to a political party in opposition; and an aggregate of about one year on relatively short consultative missions to diverse governments.

These seven and a half years in governments add up to some major shifts in my perceptions, to be fully developed in other writings. Here I shall mention a few main findings derived from "actor-observer" roles in government. (This term expresses full-fledged and authentic positions in government which, as a side benefit, permit study by direct observation. This is quite different in intensity and reality-involvement from participant observation as a deliberate research method.) Some of these will be further considered in this essay.

• Policymaking should be viewed as an existential phenomenon, or phenomena cluster, much too complex and dynamic to be fully caught in concepts, models, and theories.

• Western political science and public policy studies are largely inapplicable to non-Western countries. The world of discourse and the cognitive maps of Western, democracy-based political science seem especially unable to catch main realities of many Third World countries (the category "Third World" is used as a matter of convenience, with recognition of its misleading overgeneralization [Pletsch 1981]).

• Social science studies from the outside do not penetrate into the realities of central high-level decision making. Such processes are immune to usual behavioral research methods, as distinguished from special methods that can and should be developed, such as intense interviewing of top politicians (as illustrated by Boyle et al. 1971). Leaked in-house studies (such as the Pentagon Papers; Sheehan 1971), frank diaries (such as Crossman 1975-77; and Moshe Sharet, as yet published only in Hebrew), memoirs by insiders (Kennedy 1969; Kissinger 1979, 1982; Sorensen 1966), and writings by actors-observers (Schlesinger 1965)—reflect many crucial choices better than rigid research and strict data processing. Integrated case studies that rely on a multiplicity of approaches have a better chance (as illustrated by Moharir 1979). Historians have here important advantages, with serious problems of their own (D.H. Fischer 1970; Roper 1977). In short: within my limited personal knowledge, social sciences' standard research methods have been unable to uncover the realities of important decisions made at high levels of government, in those few but not trivial cases where I could observe reality and read social science studies presuming to deal with them.

• Governmental realities are both more dismal and promising than presented in much professional literature. Those governmental decision-making processes that I could directly observe are not a "garbage can"

(Cohen et al. 1972), nor an exercise in ambiguity (March and Olson 1976). Egocentric behavior models (Downs 1967), "satisficing" (Cyert and March 1963), "groupthink" (Janis 1972), and so on—are also very doubtful explanations of complex realities, even if fitting single facets of behavior and providing important insights. Policymaking is often oriented at high aspiration, distinguished by intense commitments and characterized by result-focused consideration. At the same time, policy quality is often wretched. Here lies a major task for research: to uncover the underlying causes of policymaking inadequacies. My proposition is that ominous policymaking weaknesses are built-in into core components of governance, with present policy predicaments overtaxing maximum policymaking capacities. The stronger sense for such "built-in incapacities" I gained in government has dampened my optimism about improving governance, while making the need for such improvements all the more obvious. Emphasis on "debugging" of error propensities as a main improvement approach, to be added to "optimality seeking," as considered later, is a direct product of seasoning inside establishments.

   • There is little hope to comprehend basic patterns of governance and policymaking within the thin slices of time typically considered by contemporary social and policy sciences. Historic approaches are a must for understanding policy dynamics and present realities (as illustrated by Eisenstadt 1963; Eschenburg 1976; and supported by Zaret 1980). Concomitantly, long cycles have to be taken into account for directed change of policymaking patterns, though necessarily shorter than for historic analysis.

Others may have arrived at equivalent and superior understanding of policymaking without exposure to its realities from within. But for me the learning and stimulating effects of service as an actor in the antechambers of central power have been essential for crystallization of revised views, as reflected partly in this essay. Anyone who wants to arrive at in-depth understanding of policymaking should spend some years in suitable governmental positions. This will be a sobering and enlightening experience.

Unexpectedly, exhilarating as well as deeply frustrating long days and nights in government have made me even more doubtful about both microempiric research methods and so-called practical improvement approaches. The deep roots of policymaking behavior need examination to gain valid understanding and require redesign to affect outputs. Movements in these directions, even if limited to a pragmatic level because of constraints on researchability and intervention, depends on appropriate transempiric assumptions and approaches. Policymaking reality is too complex for comprehension by shallow probing and for improvement by tinkering. Full understanding is beyond the achievable, but a middle level of comprehension and redesign may be feasible, if appropriate approaches can be developed. This makes careful concern with philosophic and theoretic issues a must for policy sciences, a conclusion paradoxically reinforced by the years spent in government since the first edition of the book was published.

GERMAN LITERATURE AND LANGUAGE CULTURE

Growing concern with transempiric dimensions of policymaking and policy sciences has been supported and influenced by another input—a long research period in the Federal Republic of Germany, mainly with the Institute for Advanced Study Berlin and partly with the Science Center Berlin. Leaving aside the moral and emotional problems of this experience, one and a half years in Germany have introduced me to many ideas and material very important for policy sciences and otherwise inaccessible. Philosophic discourse on decision making and related issues, historic studies on relevant subjects, different theoretic approaches to salient processes, and revealing and penetrating recent literature on the Third Reich—all these stimulated new thoughts on policymaking. Beyond such specific inputs, the different language-culture throws another light on the same phenomena, with untranslatable terms such as *Macht* (quite different from *power*), *Herrschaftssystem* (quite different from *regime*, not to speak of *political system*), and the absence of a modern term for *policy* itself. Hence another recommendation to the mature as well as becoming policy scientist: to devote at least a year to research and study in a different country, after fully learning its language. A phenomenon as existential as policymaking needs multiple frames of appreciation; and, living in another culture having different scientific and contemplative traditions helps provide additional important dimensions to one's cognitive maps.

POLICYMAKING AS A CONCEPT

Moving from autobiographic influences to the subject matter itself, reconsideration of the concept of policymaking serves to introduce some problems and considerations beyond the tentative definitions provided in the book. It is difficult to delimit the contents of policymaking (a term I use in this essay and book as referring to "public policymaking," though parts of the treatment also apply, mutatis mutandi, to private policymaking). The difficulty of identifying the scope of the concept of policymaking is put into sharp relief by comparison with some other subjects of political science, such as parties and voting.

When exploring the history of policymaking, one runs quickly into the question of when did political entities develop a consciousness of choice among policies as distinct from ordinary decisions. If we consider that many classical and modern languages lack any term equivalent to *policy* as distict from *politics* or *decisions* (which is a testimonial to the nonessentiality of the term for handling sociopolitical realities), serious difficulties become obvious. Conscious awareness of choice between main alternatives for steering societies seems to be unequally distributed, without clear relationships to historic successes or failures. Thus, "the foundations of both Greek and Renaissance political science are in ethnical theory coupled with the strategy of decision" (Pocock 1975:116), and in ancient Greece there existed a strong sense for choice on a "policy" level (Meier 1980b). Yet during long periods of very successful empire building, Rome lacked any awareness for "policy alternatives" (Meier 1980a, c). Moving to economic activities, economic policymaking as a conscious choice is a late phenomenon, related to mercantilism (Weber 1966:21, 24), with some beginnings in the sea trade cities (Oppenheimer 1926, pt. 4).

Reality looks quite different when policymaking is regarded as including policy formation (Bauer and Gergen 1968), with evolvement of policies through aggregation of specific and even small decisions, as a kind of cumulative side-product, never or seldom considered as such. Returning to Rome, distinct grand strategies were arrived at (Luttwack 1977), apparently without ever being selected among explicit alternatives.

Comprehensive study of policymaking must adopt the broader concept, including all processes by which policies are formed, with conscious policymaking (however multidimensional and hard to circumscribe) serving as a subcategory of policymaking as a whole. In this broad sense of the term, policymaking is a main aspect of all public life. It might best be viewed as a main existential expression of the very being of a community and as a main aspect of collective life and of historic processes. As such, policymaking poses an unsolvable dilemma to its study: on one hand, it cannot be studied as a whole, but has somehow to be broken up and divided into segments that can be conceptualized and investigated. On the other hand, nonunderstanding of policymaking as a whole casts doubts on the validity of knowledge derived from policymaking segments. Multiplicity of antinomies in policymaking and interweaving of policymaking with other sociopolitical processes further strengthen this dilemma.

APPROACHES TO THE STUDY OF POLICYMAKING

The view of policymaking as an existential feature of collective human entities has a number of implications for its study:

1. Whatever one does, policymaking must be accepted and recognized as too complex a phenomena cluster and idea to be fully grasped. Progressively better knowledge and understanding are all that can be aimed at—and this is a high ambition too. This, without falling into semimystic traps, as in some versions of German "decisionism" (Hofmann 1972; Krockow 1958).

2. A multiplicity of approaches and a variety of combinations

thereof are needed to try to grasp different aspects of policymaking. Reductionism, segment-focused research, and attempts to move toward general theories are all needed. Especially important is choice of multiple starting assumptions, in order to arrive at comprehensive general theories that can serve as explicit selection criteria and problem posers for empiric research. Albeit, no set of approaches can hope for more than growing understanding within limited worlds of interest and utility. Constant awareness of limits, recognition of much fallibility, and subjection to critical rationality (Albert 1978, 1980) are a required philosophy of science posture for policy sciences. When working on particular aspects of policymaking within defined disciplines, appropriate specific methods for that piece of work can be relatively easily designed and judged. But the study of policymaking as a whole permits and requires a large range of diverse approaches, with due attention to the potentials, limits, and pitfalls of each (Mitroff and Kilmann 1981) and of all of them together.

3. Contemporary "regular" social and political science research methods need much supplementation with additional forms of knowledge and knowledge seeking. Historic studies, broad pure constructs, anthropological-impressionistic (Leach 1982), and interpretive approaches (Rabinow and Sullivan 1979) may yield additional knowledge on policymaking, partly in the form of *Verstehen*, sometimes even approaching hermeneutics (Bauman 1978; Thompson 1981; I do not go as far as R.H. Brown 1977). This involves serious dangers of unsupported critical theory on one hand (Berg 1981) and of verbose pseudoscientism on the other (Andreski 1972). Such risks must be recognized and handled, but cannot serve as a reason to bind policy research to highly structured but partial methodologies.

4. Constant self-awareness is essential in policy sciences, with attention to sociology of policy sciences, to archaeology of policy knowledge (whether along the lines of Foucault 1976 or not), and to underlying philosophic, paramethodological, and transempiric assumptions and postures (Kruse 1979).

SHARED VERSUS SPECIFIC FEATURES

Related to the delimitation of policymaking is the question of whether there are any features shared by policymaking as such, beyond an abstract and ambiguous idea. This is a crucial issue for endeavors to move toward general theories of policymaking, as attempted in this book. Such efforts necessarily depend on the assumption that some nomographic features shared by all policymaking do exist, beyond culture-, issue-, and context-specific characteristics of policymaking subsets. Regarding this question, empiric findings permit a partial answer:

1. Many features of policymaking are specific to given issues and

contexts. Thus defense policymaking (Rohety 1980) is different in important respects from policymaking on cancer research (Chubin and Studer 1978; Rettig 1977; Strickland 1982) or on economics (Porter 1980; Shultz and Dam 1977); interorganizational policymaking (Hanf and Schapf 1978) is different from crisis policymaking (Brecher 1979; Hermann 1972; Holsti 1972); space policymaking from social policymaking (Nelson 1977); and many features are unique to discrete decisions in their historic context (Backer 1978; Rostow 1982).

2. Many features of policymaking are specific to institutional settings, such as "satisficing" to some organizations; incrementalism to consensual politics under smooth conditions; and large-scale policymaking to high-threshold technological domains (Schulman 1980).

3. Many features of policymaking are specific to types of regimes, political cultures, and societal characteristics. Thus some features of policymaking in Japan are quite unique (Hofheinz and Calder 1982; Vogel 1975, 1979; a different view in Campbell 1977; Pempel 1977, 1979). It may well be that other countries with special cultures and conditions have unique policymaking features, even if ignored by writings dominated by Western perspectives and Western-based social sciences. Some indications point to very unusual features of Indian policymaking (Dumont 1981; Lall 1981). China surely must be special in many facets of policymaking, with its culture, population size, political history, etc.—even if most available literature reveals no striking differences from Western conceptions. There is a neglect in the literature of important special features of policymaking in Nazism (Bracher 1976; Hildebrand 1980: 162-63) and less so in Fascism (Buchheim 1962; Kuhn 1973; Schulz 1974; Wipperman 1975). Albeit, comparative studies on economic preparation for war show some similarities in main policymaking modes among most countries (Forstmeier and Volkmann 1975, 1977). Within Western democracies significant differences do exist (cf. Anderson et al. 1978; Doern and Aucoin 1979; Heclo and Wildavsky 1974; Mayntz and Scharpf 1975; Obler et al. 1977; Sharkansky and Meter 1975; Steiner and Dorff 1980). The situation is in part different in Communist countries and among them (Beck and Mesa-Lago 1975; Cocks et al. 1976; Holmes 1981; Juviler and Morton 1967; Triska and Cocks 1977). Developing countries are distinguished by special policymaking characteristics, within a broad range of variance (Barkan and Okumo 1979; Brewer and Brunner 1975; Dang 1966: 245-82; Dietz 1980; Grindle 1980; Quandt 1982: passim; Rothschild and Curry 1978). Differences in policymaking can be identified in the same country and on similar issues under conditions of prosperity or scarcity, peace or international tension, before and after elections, and so on.

4. Even graver doubts arise as to whether and how the policymaking concept can be applied in other social contexts, such as feudal societies, republican Rome, historic bureaucratic states, not to speak of tribal polities.

5. Despite these policymaking specifics, there is strong evidence

that policymaking shares some basic patterns within different environments in most of the contemporary world. Shared features are brought out by processing the literature dealing with specific policymaking situations, and in the growing literature dealing with public policymaking as such (C.W. Anderson 1977; J.E. Anderson 1975; Dye 1978; Eyestone 1971; Frohick 1979; Gwyn and Edwards 1975; Heclo 1972; Hofferbert 1974; Jones 1977; Lerner 1976; Lindblom 1968; Lineberry 1977; Mitchell and Mitchell 1969; Ranney 1968; Richardson 1982; Rourke 1976; Sharkansky 1970; Simeon 1976; Wade 1972). Even though heavily slanted by U.S. situations, growing comparative or comparable literature indicates possibilities for policymaking theories of broad applicability (cf. Bobrow et al. 1979 with W. Wallace 1976; Caiden and Wildavsky 1974 with Wildavsky 1975; Elboim-Dror 1982 with Kogan 1975 and Lieberman and McLaughlin 1982; Hayward and Watson 1975; Leichter 1979; Liske et al. 1975; Rohety 1980; Rose 1973; 1976).

6. I am of the tentative opinion, on the basis of preliminary work, that the concept of policymaking, in the broader sense proposed in this essay and book, can also be use fully applied, with some adjustments, to historic states (Creel 1970; Creel 1974; Eisenstadt 1963; Goldhamer 1978; Meier 1980a, b; Wittfogel 1975). How far it can be applied to other types of body-politics (Geertz 1980; Feiermann 1974) and to the different transition stages from various prestate forms to the state (Cohen and Service 1978), such as from feudalism to the absolute state in Europe (Barker 1945; Brunner 1959; Hartung 1950; Hintze 1970; Kern 1949; Poggi 1978) remains an open question, regrettably undertreated in modern public policy literature.

To conclude observations on the nature and spread of policymaking, let me add that definitions of policymaking are a muddy affair. Distinctions between deliberate policy choices and cumulative policy evolvement, or between critical and history-shaping single decisions and choices between complex strategies, are tedious. Concomitantly, the question of whether one characterizes a choice as "policymaking" ex post facto, or by its real time features, or its image in the eyes of decision makers, or of the contemporary beholders—leads to additional difficulties. Such issues are best left for consideration in relation to particular research and study problems, such as the autonomy of policymaking with respect to society, or policymaking during revolutions—when concepts of policymaking useful for the enquiry can be further elaborated.

This book does not move into such domains, being limited to a partial approach toward a general theory of policymaking, with some movement between macroanalysis and specific structures. Adjustment of the general approach of the book to specific contexts, historic as well as contemporary, including needed reconsideration of the concept of policymaking itself, is a separate task.

VALUES, POLICYMAKING, AND POLICY SCIENCES

During the past fifteen years value schisms have exerted growing influence on policymaking and its study. *Public Policymaking Reexamined* provoked quite some reactions on this score. Some explanations and expansions are therefore in order:

To the opinion that policymaking always serves existing powers, I respond that policymaking can achieve much autonomy and can be very radical; that in democracies policymaking can be made to serve what an enlightened majority wants; and that in some nondemocratic countries there is a good chance to achieve policymaking autonomy and to use improved policymaking for the better. There *are* situations where the only hope lies in breaking the hold of some oligarchy through revolution or preferably through radical reforms from above, with autonomous policymaking often aided (but sometimes hindered) by grass-roots pressures.

To the opinion that most improvements in policymaking strengthen central authority and reduce the chances for social change from below, my replies are: (1) A lot of grass-roots initiative and localization can and often should be accommodated and encouraged by high-quality policymaking. This, because of values as well as utilitarian reasons, including beneficial effects on central policymaking itself, such as alternative innovation, overload reduction, and support. But strong central policymaking is essential and some grass-roots activities may have to be overcome to advance collective goals under harsh conditions. (2) Far-reaching expectations of solving basic policy predicaments mainly through communal and participatory action instead of central government (Bermback 1973; Vilmar 1973; Ward 1981) are somewhere between utopia and delusion—a conclusion to be fully worked out in *Policymaking under Adversity*.

Somewhat different is the claim sometimes made that policymaking deals with the "establishment" and strengthens the state against "the people." In democracies these are empty phrases, "the people" being a term misused by true believers and political charlatans. In nondemocracies, dangers of making repression more efficient do exist and need careful prevention.

An important distinction may help explain some value debates surrounding policymaking and the book, namely between "pattern values" and "output values." Pattern values refer to values to be realized by the patterns of policymaking. Participation and open government relate to policymaking patterns, namely processes and institutions. Output values relate to values to be realized by the products of policymaking, such as elimination of discrimination, growing employment, and national security. Often, difficult choices between different pattern values and output values are unavoidable. My general position is that in Western democracies, where main pattern values are substantially realized, pressures of problems may require more attention to output values. Of course, measures which increase both pattern values and output values are always preferable; and very careful mixes and balances between various pattern values and output values to be achieved in and by public policymaking are essential.

Related to the above is the important distinction between striving for positive values and trying to avoid evils. This is not the same operation with different plus/minus signs, as assumed in monodimensional utility scaling. Agreement on evils to be avoided is often much easier to achieve than for "good societies" to be achieved. Under present conditions, when many evils lurk around the corner, a lot of attention has to be devoted to avoiding bad situations, as a main output value at which policymaking is to be directed. Many growing demands for significant improvements in pattern values are very appealing, but ignore the grimness of predicaments faced by policymaking and the dire necessity to allocate priorities accordingly to avoid harking catastrophes.

To the frequent argument that better policymaking provides efficiency for wrong policies (Hoos 1972), the answer is that these are often the result of bad policymaking or of value judgments beyond policymaking itself. Recent material, such as the Pentagon Papers, reinforces the opinion that bad policymaking, in the sense discussed in *Public Policymaking Reexamined*, is much more at the root of doubtful policies than evil goals or reprehensible values (though the latter also occur frequently).

Some of the central concepts and tools of much of contemporary policy sciences introduce biases and doubtful value judgments in insidious ways. Thus, most systems models implicitly prefer systems maintenance over systems transformation (Greven 1974; Habermas and Luhman 1971) and sometimes demonstrate hostility to politics (Churchman 1979). To overcome such biases of some instruments, policy sciences should be more sophisticated about assumptions, methods, models, and tools; develop a larger repertoire of methods that mutually offset unavoidable limitations of any single approach; and make a concerted effort to overcome equilibrium-type unidimensionality and addiction to smooth curves. The fact that many of these weaknesses are shared with other social sciences, including economics, is not much of a consolation. But rejection of the very idea of policy sciences and abandonment of the whole endeavor, or its corruption through indiscriminate amalgamation with social critique functions, however valuable the latter may sometimes be by themselves—is unjustified and apt to cause much more harm than temporary and treatable failings of contemporary policy sciences. Better policymaking is not a remedy for all problems of governance, but only one dimension of required redesigns. Historic tendencies of governmental systems to decay and become "corrupt" in the Aristotelian sense (Dobel 1978), are beyond treatment through policymaking improvement, needing much stronger medicine.

Following these partial clarifications, some main value issues of policymaking and policy sciences neglected in the book can be briefly considered. Fully discussed in the literature is the issue of value-free or value-serving social sciences, especially in the sensitive context of policymaking and policy sciences (F. Fischer 1980; Geuss 1981; MacRea 1976; Miller 1979; Mitroff 1972; Schluchter 1980: passim; Thompson 1981; Tribe 1972). While recognizing the weighty moral and psychological arguments behind some contemporary resistance to seeking value-free knowledge in the study of policymaking, I nevertheless cast my vote for efforts to approximate fact/value-differentiating ideals of science, subject to caveats to be considered. In this respect, the argumentation of Arnold Brecht (1959, esp. chs. 1, 2; 1978: 184-95) seems to be accepted (see also Albert 1976: 160-91).

Given this approach, little philosophic-theoretic (as contrasted with methodological) difficulties are posed by the study of values as facts influencing policymaking. Adapting methods from anthropology, value maps can be prepared and value dynamics studied (Handy 1970; Inglehart 1977; Klages and Kmieciak 1979; Rokeach 1973). As far as metarules postulate value facts as norms for policymaking, because of utilitarian consensus-seeking or because of a possible version of democratic ideology (e.g. in the form of an overriding norm that policymaking should fit main population values)—additional ways for injecting values into policymaking can theoretically be provided.

That values influence problem perceptions and recommendations (Dillon 1979) is well known. It merges into broader problems of epistemology and cognition, all views of reality being influenced by subjective and intersubjective variables, which construct world pictures and reality images, in complex interaction with "objective reality." But there is a big difference between acknowledging such factual impact of values as a science-influencing and reality–image-shaping variable, and accepting this state of affairs as desirable and irreducible.

Based on preference for maximum approximation of value-free policy sciences, suggested treatments of unavoidable value-fact fusions include:

1. Explication of personal values by researchers and maximum personal efforts to reduce the impact of such values on findings and professional recommendations.

2. Positive redundance in having policy scientists of multiple values (and cultures) deal with main subjects and problems. This, without permitting this requirement to degenerate into a dogma legitimizing every baseless or falsified opinion as entitled to equal consideration in scientific-professional endeavors.

3. Constant search for methods containing and reducing the impact of values on findings and recommendations, such as improved value analysis, multiple value assumptions, value sensitivity testing, and perhaps psychodi-

dactic help for researchers to become more aware of values (and other factors) unconsciously influencing problem formulation, findings, and recommendations.

4. Value codes, explicitly to provide value guides and value limits to some policy sciences activities, while also reducing situations where values are especially prone to overinfluence findings and recommendations.

5. Frank acknowledgment of the limits of human endeavors, with all findings and recommendations viewed as fallible, doubtful, and conjectural.

6. Recognition of the corrupting effects of total personal engagement (Albert 1980: esp. 4ff.) and the consequent needs, in policy sciences, to preserve a stance of clinical concern and a posture of critical rationality—also in respect to intensely held values and dogmas.

In distinction from some natural sciences, policy sciences run little danger (or hope?) to stand on the verge of discoveries that may endanger basic values accepted nearly universally, such as survival of the human race. Therefore, discussion of Nietzsche's aphorism that "we prefer the ruin of humanity to giving up understanding" (*Morgenröte* 429, see Montenari 1982:66, discussion: 64-78) is unnecessary here. But the prescriptive dimensions of policy sciences are unique and require careful attention.

The concept of legitimate value judge is essential for handling prescriptive dimensions of policy sciences. Once some such entity is accepted (itself a matter for subjective moral choice), prescriptive policy sciences face many difficulties of methods and approaches, but less of moral principle: their task is to help legitimate value judges develop their choices and make them more effective, as part of policymaking improvement, without usurping the legitimate functions of value judges or encroaching on them. This involves hard analytic and psychological efforts to handle conflicting values, value inconsistency, value consequences, motives versus values, and so on, including invention of new values as an option—but not final value judgment itself, which belongs to the legitimate value judge. The fact that usually the legitimate value judge is a multidimensional collective that does not want to make many of the value judgments and is unable to do so, is a complication, but not a change in principle.

To be noted is the dynamic view of value choices and the role of improved policymaking in helping this process. The alternative opinion, to take values, as shaped in political processes, as given and to concentrate policymaking improvement on working out the consequences of these given values (Baker et al. 1975), is based on misapprehension of value choice processes. Societies can be partly viewed as value-creating and goal-seeking systems (Luhmann 1968). Policymaking, as a facet of societal problem-handling behavior, involves parts of value-creating and goal-seeking processes. Policymaking improvement is not exhausted by efforts to maximize achievement of given values and goals, but includes contributions to value creation and goal seeking. This is especially crucial in periods of transformation and in the face of policy predicaments that cannot be handled without value changes. As explained above, a strict analytical distinction should be preserved between value judgment and antecedent value consideration. The first is a matter for legitimate value judges exercising a political duty and prerogative. The second includes, inter alia, intellectual elements which can be aided by policy sciences. This leads to important consequences concerning the nature of rationality, to be viewed more as a matter of policymaking patterns than output maximization (Simon 1976a), as will be further explored.

All the more important is the problem of how to choose a legitimate value judge and what limits to place on his legitimacy. If one accepts some absolute value system, in a religious sense, a natural law sense, a basic norm sense (Kelsen 1961)—this system provides, in principle, an answer. Otherwise, professional codes can be of some help, but depend themselves on subjective value choice.

In a period of value seeking following erosion of traditional values, persons working in the sensitive areas of policy sciences and recommendations seek a way out by searching for a solid foundation of absolute value justification, preferably in the name of science. This is in vain. At some point ''dogmatic'' subjective commitment must serve as a starting premise for ethical codes and value systems. (This, in somewhat different forms, is also true for ''positivistic'' sciences—but this is another subject, though an important one for the philosophic foundations of policy sciences.)

Value philosophy can help explicate some meanings of basic norms, such as justice or equity (Ackerman 1980; Rawls 1971, and his critics, such as Barry 1973). Value dilemmas of specific policy issues and ways to handle them can be examined (Calabresi and Bobbitt 1979; Dekema 1981; Fudenberg and Melnick 1978; Rhoads 1980; Tribe et al. 1976; many articles in *Philosophy and Public Policy*). On a deeper level, no basis for categoric value imperatives exists other than subjective choice—a situation not to be regretted, since otherwise the significance of moral choices would be eliminated. Ideas such as ''survival of mankind,'' ''whatever is natural to humanity,'' ''maximum individual development,'' ''highest quality of life to all,'' ''justice,'' ''equality,'' ''maximum happiness,'' etc., may be agreeable and serve as a guide one chooses to follow and wants to see others follow. This does not make these values any more objective or scientific: not only are such values hard to operationalize (Lederer and Mackenses 1975; Meyer-Abich and Birnbacher 1979; Turner and Krauss 1978), but their justification always depends on some underlying value judgment. Hence they remain what has been called ''transscience'' (Weinberg 1972).

This conclusion also applies to attempts at deriving value imperatives from functional needs, as in some Club of Rome work (Laszlo 1977a, b). It might be possible to build a strong case that human survival depends on adopting certain values (Vickers 1968). But this makes the latter an instrument for survival, which in turn is not more and not less than a subjective value biologically widespread but not objectively compelling (despite Schell 1982; on involved politics, see Feenberg 1979).

The subjective basis of all absolute values increases the moral responsibility of policy scientists, who cannot rely on objective values as a substitute for painful personal choices. At the very least, constant reflection and soul-searching on appropriate ethical guidelines for policy scientists, especially when engaged in prescriptive engagements, are indispensable. Some tentative principles are:

1. A policy scientist should declare whether he regards himself as a value advocate or is striving for value-free knowledge. He should make his choice known to his peers, readers, students, and clients (Miser 1973).

2. A policy scientist should not help to 'improve'' policymaking which is serving values he regards as immoral (Deitchman 1976; Horowitz 1967).

3. In improving policymaking, a policy scientist should help legitimate value judges to improve their value choices, such as by making them more aware of value issues; value conflicts, hidden value dimensions (e.g. lottery values [Raiffa 1968]), value consequences, alternative values, and so on. A policy scientist can ''improve'' policymaking by supporting values he believes in and advancing their impact on policies. The same person can at different periods or in respect to different policy work adopt these different forms of policy engagement (Schalk 1979). But his role should be clear to himself, his peers, his readers and students, and his clients.

4. The same applies to improving the policymaking system, with tradeoffs between various pattern and output values being explicated to the legitimate value judge and developed for him or advocated.

5. A policy scientist should recognize the corrupting effects of total commitment to any rigid value system, dogma, or mental orthodoxy. Even when serving as a value advocate, a policy scientist must preserve a personal capacity for heterodoxy and iconoclasm regarding values he strives to advance. A delicate balance of engagement/detachment and enthusiasm/scepticism is essential for policy scientists, however hard to achieve and maintain. Some elements of stoicism have much to recommend them as part of a personal philosophy for policy scientists.

Within this ethical-professional code for policy scientists, this book strives to adopt the stance of striving for value-free knowledge, recognizing the limits of any such endeavor and the unavoidable embedment of this book in the subjective worldview and value structures of the author, as shaped by his life history.

POLICYMAKING REEVALUATED

During the fifteen years since the book was published, intense work has been going on in many units and facets of decision making and policymaking. Despite much interesting work and some important progress, few fargoing innovations in understanding policymaking have emerged, with some exceptions in decision psychology. Leaving those for later consideration, some of the main works can be summed up as follows.

On small-group decision making, recent studies have not changed main findings (Brandstatter et al. 1978; Brandstatter et al. 1982; Zander 1979). One major application to policymaking is the concept of group-think (Janis 1972), according to which group support drives out goal achievement as a main decision criterium.

On organizational decision making processes, few main new findings have emerged either. Striking, with few exceptions, is continuous focusing on organizational limits (Arrow 1974; Breton and Wintrobe 1982; Hall 1981; Inbar 1979; Kickert 1980) and decision-making disarray (March and Olsen [1976] widely acclaimed in the literature despite its one-sided view). Earlier outstanding progress in propositions and theories has hardly continued.

On policymaking as a whole, burgeoning literature supplies much new empirical data. But on the level of general theory, most of the literature repeats, in new versions and with some refinement, earlier identified theories. (In addition to already mentioned literature, specific studies of special interest are illustrated by Cox et al. 1973; Davis 1972; Derthick 1979; Greenstein and Polsby 1975; Kriesi 1980; Ramsden 1980; Schmitter 1977; Wallace et al. 1977; Warwick et al. 1975. The low marginal utility of traditional quantitative research of public policy determinants is brought out by Foley 1978). Some pat theories and concepts have emerged and been advanced significantly, such as "bureaucratic politics" (Allison 1971); "public entrepreneurship" (Lewis 1980); "honeymoon policymaking" (Bunce 1981); "larger-scale policymaking" (Schulman 1980), and some more. But overall, little new on a theoretic level has emerged during the last fifteen years, reflecting the situation in the social sciences as a whole (Bell 1982; Krusal 1982).

The situation is different in decision psychology. As reflected in proliferating literature (Janis and Mann 1977; Erickson and Jones 1978; Jungermann and Zeeuw 1977; Kahnemann et al. 1982; Kaplan and Schwartz 1977; Kozielsecki 1982; Sjobert et al. 1980; Slovic et al. 1977; different but relevant is Cranach and Harré 1982), main findings lead to a pessimistic interpretation: innate and imprinted human processes produce imposing incapacities to handle uncertainty, learn rapidly, process multiple information, and engage in other tasks inherent in policymaking. True, some findings leave scope for improvement. Thus, well-designed aids can improve performance (Cosier 1978); suitable selection of decision makers may utilize their talents (Weiss

1980); and training can overcome some mistakes (Lichtenstein and Fischhoff 1980). Some interpretations see main findings in the psychology of decisions in a more optimistic vein, viewing policymakers as "naive scientists" (George 1980: 58ff.) who pick decision strategies fitting their circumstances (Beach and Mitchell 1978; Christensen-Szalanski 1978, 1980). This is also the thrust of some work on intuition (Bastick 1982; Perkins 1982). But even when scrutinized in as hopeful a mood as possible, research in decision psychology leads to rather gloomy conclusions on policymaking and its improvement potential.

Many limitations of decision-psychological studies must be remembered, which cast doubts on their validity. Similarly to the neglect of committed and achieving organizations in most of organization theory and the downgrading of visionary governments and outstanding establishments in much of political science, a lot of decision psychology may cling to the median and underrate high-level policymaking, far away from experiments with students or armchair reconstructions. Nevertheless, the overall picture is at best harassing. Scholarly studies of policymaking during the last fifteen years pose grave doubts on the policymaking potential of human institutions and call for maximum improvement efforts, to achieve a little.

From a theoretical perspective, accumulating empirical findings combine with conclusions from ethological observation of top-level policymaking behavior within governments and result in the concept of *built-in incapacity*. The underlying idea is that main components of policymaking have maximum performance capacity. Thus, rulers, advisors, small groups, and organizations have inherent features which, within a range, determine their performance potential. Processes constituting main facets of policymaking, such as reality cognition and alternative identification, can also be analyzed in terms of performance ranges related to their structural characteristics. Different combinations of such components and processes can increase or decrease aggregate performance capacities, but policymaking with given structures has always some maximum performance range. As some features of policymaking accompany all known societies and seem inherent to human institutions, such as the importance of individual and group processes in collective decision making within various arrangements, from markets to hierarchies—broader generalizations may be possible on universal limits on policymaking capacities, at least till main features of basic components are changed or new interaction patterns overcoming such features are found. Metaphorically, and avoiding organistic connotations, the concept of inherent capacities/incapacities may be heuristically useful.

The same range of capacities and incapacities may produce different policy qualities under various conditions. Under relatively simple conditions and with social change moving in desirable directions, limited policymaking capacities may perform very well. But when aspirations for policymaking increase, conditions become adverse, and historic processes move in dismal directions—the potential of policymaking becomes overtaxed and outputs reflect incapacities more and more. A simple illustration will explain this point: Assuming that policymaking components are poor in handling high uncertainty, as strongly indicated by current knowledge, this will not impair policy quality when conditions are stable and incrementalism meets aspirations. But if and when pivotal variables move into a phase of ultrachange (in the sense of change in the patterns of change itself), with resulting ignorance, then inherent incapacity to handle uncertainty will downgrade policy quality. Such overtaxing of policymaking capacities characterizes contemporary and emerging policy predicaments, with serious theoretic and applied implications to be considered in detail in *Policymaking under Adversity*.

The concept of inherent incapacity poses sharp challenges to improvement approaches. The basic logic of prescription needs reconsideration, to supplement the treatment of metapolicymaking in the book.

THE LOGIC OF PRESCRIPTIVE ENDEAVORS

Public Policymaking Reexamined combines examination of policy realities with analysis of policymaking requisites and development of approaches and proposals for the improvement of policymaking. Avoidance of normative stances and advocacy roles makes it all the more important to explore the logic of such prescription. This need is reinforced by continuing neglect of methodlogical justifications for prescription in much of applied social sciences (Scott and Shore 1979:passim) and the oversimplicity, in underlying assumptions, of quantitative prescriptive decision disciplines, such as operations research and management sciences (Mintzbert 1979; exceptional is Checkland 1981).

Leaving aside critical writings and their possible implications for policymaking improvement (Marković 1974), it is essential to try to build bridges between reality and some preferred images of reality. Regarding policymaking, preferred images, on which improvement prescriptions can be based, are either norms on policymaking patterns (pattern values) or ideal models aimed at policymaking productivity with substantive (output) values to be maximized, one step further away. Values of free access to policymaking information or of participatory democracy serve as norms directly applicable to policymaking patterns and guiding their improvement. Rationality models, as a guide for policymaking improvement, have a radically different justification, namely the assumption that rationality maximizes policymaking productivity, which in turn increases undefined and open-ended values, as postulated from time to time for policymaking on the basis of different types of value judgment.

The selection between these two pure-type bases for improvement and various mixes thereof is a matter of choice, tempered by weighting norm patterns as compared with enhanced value production. Polar preferences are hardly tenable, as policymaking is inherently output directed; and all policymaking is contingent on basic contextual values conditioning fundamental features, such as democracy or equality as omnipresent supreme values. Sometimes the same prescription can serve both norm patterns and policymaking productivity. Thus, freedom of information is a value in itself, while in some opinions also enhancing policymaking productivity by motivating more care by decision makers (Robertson 1982). Or, participatory democracy is a value directly applicable to policymaking patterns, while perhaps also contributing to policymaking productivity by inputting information otherwise unavailable (Sowell 1980).

Within the productivity-oriented approach to policymaking improvement, various preferable images can serve as bases for prescription. In the book, a detailed general model of optimal policymaking is developed and serves as basis for improvement proposals. Anteceding growing recognition of policymaking patterns as superior to "maximization" ideas as a basis for defining rationality (March 1978; Simon 1976, 1979), the model developed in the book continues to qualify as a main basis for general policymaking theories, including prescriptive approaches to policymaking improvements. The very completeness of the model within its explicit boundaries is an advantage for theory and application, even if utilization of the model in discrete circumstances requires simplification. At the very least, the full model can serve as a basis for design of simpler versions fitting specific and more limited needs.

The robustness of the model within its boundaries does not imply exclusiveness and completeness. Thus, as considered in the book, various extrarational choices serve as essential inputs into the rationality model, raising different issues of improving choices which cannot be handled through rationality concepts in their usual meaning. This leads to the difficult and controversial question, quite neglected in most policy sciences, of whether and how additional bases, other than rationality in the usual sense, should serve as foundations for construction of preferable models for policymaking.

Related is the fundamental question of how far to go trying to improve policymaking by taking up for reconsideration choices preceding policymaking and external to it, but conditioning policymaking. This is often though inadequately done regarding the institutional settings within which policymaking takes place. But it is only a small, though important, part of the matter. Thus choices between belief systems and between metaphysical bases for science condition inputs into policymaking, such as value judgments and predictions.

An expansive approach to policymaking improvement cannot go very far without becoming unmanageable, intellectually as well as pragmatically. Nevertheless, some steps outward into policymaking-conditioning choices are necessary to achieve significant improvements in policymaking. This requires reconsideration of the models to serve as bases for policymaking improvement, because different concepts of rationality or preferability may apply to various types of policymaking choices. This is a broad subject requiring reconsideration of the boundaries of policy sciences, which can only be touched upon here. Metapolicymaking, as discussed in the book, moves somewhat in the direction of enlarging the scope of choices to be handled within policymaking improvement. Albeit, deeper penetration into underlying choices is needed and possible. To take up this need, far-reaching strengthening of the philosophic-theoretic bases of policy sciences is essential. Within the usually narrower confines of policymaking a broad range of normative models and conceptions can provide guidance for improvement, in addition to usual conceptions of rationality. Here, again, much additional work is needed, requiring a deepening of the philosophic-theoretic bases of policy sciences.

Aesthetic ideals and ideas from legal rationality illustrate possible infrastructures for additional multidimensional preferable policymaking models, to serve as anchors for prescriptive endeavors (Benn and Mortimose 1976; Elster 1978; Toulmain et al. 1979). Other approaches range from broad sociopolitical constructs (Diesing 1962; Habermas 1970) to pragmatic critique of policymaking behavior, with or without some philosophic underpinnings (Albert 1972, 1978) and various combinations, including different conceptions of rationality (Barry and Hardin 1982; H.I. Brown 1978; Elster 1979, 1979–; Gershuny 1978; Hartwig 1978; Hennen 1976; Koertge 1979; Machan 1980; Popper 1967; Wilson 1970). As long as care is taken not to slip from behavioral findings into preferable models, there is scope and need for diverse bases to serve the complex endeavor of improving so multidimensional and existential a phenomenon as policymaking. Ongoing work on nonmarket performance (Eby 1982; Wolf 1979) may add useful preferable models.

The optimality model presented in the book needs development in additional directions, such as adjustments to overriding conditions of uncertainty and ignorance and examination of functional requisites of policymaking quality. This is part of the constant need to improve models as foundations for prescriptive endeavors, adjusted to different worlds of application.

There is a fundamental difference between all model-based prescriptions on one hand and improvement attempts based on error reduction or "debugging" as their main logic, on the other. There is some convergence of these two approaches, because the very concept of error and error identification as an activity implies some underlying, often tacit conception of error-free situations. Nevertheless, error reduction is a distinct and very important approach to bettering policymaking.

The procedure in principle is straightforward, however hard to apply. On the basis of empirical research and performance evaluation, as well as relevant theoretical studies, prevalent and consequential errors in policymaking are identified. Then, with the help of examination of the causes of such errors, remedial prescriptions are developed and compared within a qualitative benefit/cost frame, leading to a number of error-reducing recommendations.

Increasingly reliable and disturbing knowledge about error propensities, partly related to the concept of built-in incapacities and their growing impact in depressing policymaking quality, serve to make debugging an important approach in policymaking improvement. This is in combination with various rationalizing approaches based on diverse explicit models. The debugging approach should be added to the logic of prescriptive endeavors, as considered in the book.

Without going into the serious problems of applying evolutional theory to sociocultural phenomena and social institutions (Langton 1979; Ruse 1974), advancement of policymaking can be viewed as a step in human history, by providing organized humanity with a little more control over environments, over humanity itself, and over human futures. Within such a perspective of policymaking as an important artifact of humanity, its study and improvement become meaningful beyond acquisition of pure knowledge of marginal application. A sense that the study and improvement of policymaking carry elements of a significant life mission, approaching a calling, has accompanied the author while first writing this book. Contemporary and emerging realities augment this feeling. I hope my readers will share it, whether they agree with the main contents of this book or not.

References

Ackerman, Bruce A. 1980. *Social Justice in the Liberal State*. New Haven: Yale University Press.

Ad Hoc Committee of the Operations Research Society of America. 1971. "Guidelines for the Practice of Operations Research." *Operations Research* 19 (September): 1123-48.

Albert, Hans. 1927. *Ökonomische Ideologie und politische Theorie: Das ökonomische Argument in der ordnungspolitischen Debatte*. Göttingen: Otto Schwartz. 2nd ed.

————. 1976. *Aufklärung und Steuerung: Aufsätze zur Sozialphilosophie und zur Wissenschaftslehre der Sozialwissenschaften*. Hamburg: Hoffmann & Campe.

————. 1978. *Traktat über rationale Praxis*. Tübingen: J.C.B. Mohr.

————. 1980. *Traktat über kritische Vernunft*. Tübingen: J.C.B. Mohr. 4th ed.

Allison, Graham T. 1971. *Essence of Decision*. Boston: Little, Brown.

Anderson, Charles W. 1977. *Statecraft: An Introduction to Political Choice and Judgment*. New York: Wiley.

Anderson, James E. 1975. *Public Policy-Making*. New York: Praeger.

Anderson, James E.; David W. Brady; Charles Bullock. 1978. *Public Policy and Politics in America*. North Scituate, Mass.: Duxbury.

Andreski, Stanislav. 1972. *Social Sciences as Sorcery*. New York: St. Martin's Press.

Arrow, Kenneth J. 1974. *The Limits of Organizations*. New York: Norton.

Backer, John H. 1978. *The Decision to Divide Germany*. Durham, N.C.: Duke University Press.

Baker, Robert F.; Richard M. Michaels; Everett S. Preston. 1975. *Public Policy Development: Linking the Technical and Political Processes*. New York: Wiley.

Barkan, J.D.; John Okumo (eds.). 1979. *Politics and Public Policy in Kenya and Tanzania*. New York: Praeger.

Barker, Ernest. 1945. *The Development of Public Service in Western Europe, 1660-1930*. New York: Oxford University Press.

Barry, Brian. 1973. *The Liberal Theory of Justice: A Critical Examination of the Principal Doctrines in A Theory of Justice by John Rawls*. Oxford: Clarendon.

Barry, Brian; Russell Hardin (eds.). 1982. *Rational Man and Irrational Society? An Introduction and Sourcebook*. Beverly Hills, Calif.: Sage.

Bastick, Tont. 1982. *Intuition: How We Think and Act*. New York: Wiley.

Bauer, Raymond A.; Kenneth Gergen (eds.). 1968. *The Study of Policy Formation*. New York: Free Press.

Bauman, Zygmunt. 1978. *Hermeneutics and Social Sciences*. New York: Columbia University Press.

Beach, Lee Roy; Terence R. Mitchell. 1978. "A Contingency Model for the Selection of Decision Strategies." *Academy of Management Review* (January): 439-49.

Beck, Carl; Carmelo Mesa-Lago (eds.). 1975. *Comparative Socialist Systems: Essays on Politics and Economics*. Pittsburgh, Pa.: Pittsburgh University Press.

Bell, Daniel. 1982. *The Social Sciences since the Second World War*. New Brunswick, N.J. Transaction. (First published 1980.)

Benn, S.J.; G.W. Mortimose (eds.). 1976. *Rationality and the Social Sciences: Contributions to the Philosophy and Methodology of the Social Sciences*. London: Routledge & Kegan Paul.

Berg, Axel van den. 1981. "Critical Theory: Is There Still Hope?" *American Journal of Sociology* 86 (no. 3): 449ff.

Bermback, Udo. 1973. *Theorie und Praxis der direkten Demokratie*. Opladen: Westdeutscher Verlag.

Bobrow, B. Davis; Steve Chan; Johan A. Kringer, 1979. *Understanding Foreign Policy Decisions: The Chinese Case*. New York: Free Press.

Boyle, Edward; Anthony Crosland (in conversation with Maurice Kogan. 1971. *The Politics of Education*. Harmondsworth (England): Penguin.

Bracher, Karl Dietrich. 1976. *Zeitgeschichtliche Kontroversen: Um Faschismus, Totalitarismus, Demokratie*. Munich: R. Piper.

Brandstatter, Hermann; James H. Davies; Gisela Stocker-Kreichgauer. 1982. *Group Decision Making*. New York: Academic Press.

Brandstatter, Hermann; James H. Davies; Heinz Schuler. 1978. *Dynamics of Group Decisions*. Beverly Hills, Calif.: Sage.

Brecher, Michael (ed.). 1979. *Studies in Crisis Behavior*. New Brunswick, N.J.: Transaction.

Brecht, Arnold. 1959. *Political Theory*. Princeton: Princeton University Press.

———. 1978. *Kann die Demokratie überleben? Die Herausforderungen der Zukunft und die Regierungsformen der Gegenwart*. Stuttgart: Deutsche Verlags-Anstalt.

Breton, Albert; Ronald Wintrobe. 1982. *The Logic of Bureaucratic Conduct*. Cambridge: Cambridge University Press.

Brewer, Garry D.; Ronald D. Brunner (eds.). 1975. *Policy Development and Change: A Policy Approach*. New York: Free Press.

Brown, Harold I. 1978. "On Being Rational." *American Philosophical*

Quarterly 15 (October): 241–48.

Brown, Richard H. 1977. *A Poetic for Sociology: Towards a Logic of Discovery for the Human Sciences*. Cambridge: Cambridge University Press.

Brunner, Otto. *1959. Land und Herrschaft: Grundfragen der territorialen Verfassungsgeschichte Österreichs im Mittelalter*. Vienna: Rudolf M. Rohrer.

Bruun, H.H. 1972. *Science, Values, and Politics in Max Weber's Methodology*. Copenhagen: Munksgaard.

Buchheim, Hans. 1962. *Totalitäre Herrschaft: Wesen und Merkmale*. Munich: Kösel.

Bunce, Valerie. 1981. *Do New Leaders Make a Difference? Executive Succession and Public Policy under Capitalism and Socialism*. Princeton: Princeton University Press.

Caiden, Naomi; Aaron Wildavsky. 1974. *Planning and Budgeting in Poor Countries*. New York: Wiley.

Calabresi, Guido; Phillip Bobbitt. 1979. *Tragic Choice*. New York: Norton.

Campbell, John Creighton. 1977. *Contemporary Japanese Budget Politics*. Berkeley: University of California Press.

Checkland, P. 1981. *Systems Thinking, Systems Practice*. London: Wiley.

Christensen-Szalanski, Jay J.J. 1978. "Problem Solving Strategies: A Selection Mechanism, Some Implications, and Some Data." *Organizational Behavior and Human Performance* 22:307-23.

———. 1980. "A Further Examination of the Selection of Problem-Solving Strategies: The Effects of Deadlines and Analytic Aptitudes." *Organizational Behavior and Human Performance* 25:107-22.

Chubin, Daryl E.; Kenneth E. Studer. 1978. "The Politics of Cancer." *Theory and Society* 6 (July):55-74.

Churchman, C. West. 1979. *The Systems Approach and Its Enemies*. New York: Basic Books.

Cooks, Paul; Robert V. Daniels; Nancy Whittier Heer (eds.). 1976. *The Dynamics of Soviet Politics*. Cambridge, Mass.: Harvard University Press.

Cohen, Michael D.; James G. March; Johan P. Olsen. 1972. "A Garbage Can Model of Organizational Choice." *Administrative Science Quarterly* 17 (March):1-25.

Cohen, Ronald; Elman R. Service (eds.). 1978. *Origins of the State: The Anthropology of Political Evolution*. Philadelphia: Institute for the Study of Human Issues.

Cosier, Richard A. 1978. "The Effects of Three Potential Aids for Making Strategic Decisions on Prediction Accuracy." *Organizational Behavior and Human Performance* 22:295-306.

Cox, Robert W., et al. 1973. *The Anatomy of Influence: Decision-Making in International Organizations*. New Haven: Yale University Press.

Cranach, Mario von; Rom Harré (eds.). 1982. *The Analysis of Action: Recent Theoretical and Empiric Advances*. Cambridge: Cambridge University Press.

Creel, Herrlee G. 1970. *The Origins of Statecraft in China*. Vol. 1: *The West-*

ern Chou Empire. Chicago: University of Chicago Press.

————. 1974. *Shen Pu-Hai: A Chinese Political Philosopher of the Fourth Century BC*. Chicago: Chicago University Press.

Crossman, Richard. 1975-77. *The Diaries of a Cabinet Minister*. 3 vols. London: Hamilton.

Cyert, Richard; James G. March. 1963. *A Behavioral Theory of the Firm*. Englewood Cliffs, N.J.: Prentice-Hall.

Dang, Nghiem. 1966. *Viet-Nam: Politics and Public Administration*. Honolulu: East-West Center.

Davis, David Howard. 1972. *How the Bureaucracy Makes Foreign Policy: An Exchange Analysis*. Lexington, Mass.: Heath.

Deitchman, Seymour J. 1976. *The Best-Laid Schemes: A Tale of Social Research and Bureaucrats*. Cambridge, Mass.: MIT.

Dekama Jan D. 1981. "Incommensurability and Judgement." *Theory and Society* 10 (July):521-46.

Derthick, Marth. 1979. *Policy-Making for Social Security*. Washington, D.C.: Brookings.

Diesing, P. 1962. *Reason in Society: Five Types of Decisions and Their Social Conditions*. Urbana: University of Illinois Press.

Dietz, Henry A. 1980. *Poverty and Problem-Solving under Military Rule: The Urban Poor in Lima, Peru*. Austin: University of Texas Press.

Dillon, Robert John. 1979. *Reality and Value Judgment in Policymaking: A Study of Expert Judgments about Alternative Energy Technologies*. New York: Arno.

Dobel, J. Patrick. 1978. "The Corruption of a State." *American Political Science Review* 72: 958-73.

Doern, G. Bruce; Peter Aucion (eds.) 1979. *Public Policy in Canada: Organization, Process, and Management*. Toronto: Macmillan of Canada.

Downs, Anthony. 1967. *Inside Bureaucracy*. Boston: Little, Brown.

Dror, Yehezkel. 1964. "Muddling Through: 'Science' or Inertia." *Public Administration Review* 24 (September):153-65. Reprinted in idem, *Ventures in Policy Sciences*. New York: American Elsevier, 1971.

————. 1971. *Design for Policy Sciences*. New York: American Elsevier.

————. 1980. *Crazy States: A Counterconventional Strategy Problem*. Milwood, N.Y.: Kraus Reprint. Supplemented ed.

————. 1983a. *Raison de Zionism*. In production.

————. 1983b. *Policymaking under Adversity*. New Brunswick, N.J.: Transaction.

Dumont, Louis. 1981. *Homo Hierarchicus: The Caste System and Its Implications*. Chicago: University of Chicago Press. Rev. ed.

Dunn, William N. 1981. *Public Policy Analysis: An Introduction*. Englewood Cliffs, N.J.: Prentice-Hall.

Dye, Thomas R. 1978. *Understanding Public Policy*. Englewood Cliffs, N.J.: Prentice-Hall. 3rd. ed.

Eby, Charles. 1982. *Performance Norms in Non-Market Organizations: an Exploratory Survey*. Santa Monica, Calif.: Rand N-1830-Yale.

Eisenstadt, N. Shmuel. 1963. *The Political Systems of Empires: The Rise and Fall of the Historic Bureaucratic Societies*. New York: Free Press.

Elboim-Dror, Rachel. 1982. "Die Erziehungspolitik Israels." In A. Aker-
man; A Carmon; D. Zucker (eds.), *Erziehung in Israel*. Stuttgart:
Klett-Cotta. 2 vols.

Elster, Jon. 1978. *Logic and Society: Contradictions and Possible Worlds*.
New York: Wiley.

————. 1979. *Ulysses and the Sirens: Studies in Rationality and Irrational-
ity*. Cambridge: Cambridge University Press.

————. 1979–. "Rationality and Society." Periodic section in *Social Science Information* (starting) 18 (no 3).

Erikson, Erik H. 1975. *Life History and the Historical Moment: Diverse Presentations*. New York: Norton.

Erickson, James R.; Mari Riess Jones. 1978. "Thinking." *Annual Review of
Psychology* 29: 61-90.

Eschenburg, Theodor. 1976. *Über Autorität*. Frankfurt/Main: Suhrkamp.
Rev. ed.

Eyestone, Robert. 1971. *The Threat of Public Policy: A Study in Policy Leadership*. Indianapolis: Bobbs-Merril.

Feenberg, Andrew. 1979. "Beyond the Politics of Survival." *Theory and Society* 7 (May):319-61.

Feierman, Steven. 1974. *The Shambaa Kingdom: A History*. Madison: University of Wisconsin Press.

Fischer, David Hackett. 1970. *Historians' Fallacies: Toward a Logic of Historical Thought*. New York: Harper & Row.

Fischer, Frank. 1980. *Politics, Values, and Public Policy: The Problem of
Methodology*. Boulder, Colo.: Westview.

Foley, John F. 1978. *A Comparative Study of the Determinants of Public
Policies: A Review of Two Decades of Multidisciplinary, Quantitative
Research*. Ithaca, N.Y.: Cornell University. Program in Urban and Re-
gional Studies.

Forstmeier, Friedrich; Hans-Erich Volkmann (eds.). 1975. *Wirthschaft und
Rüstung am Vorabend des Zweiten Weltkrieges*. Düsseldorf: Droste.

————. 1977. *Kriegswirtschaft und Rüstung, 1939-1945*. Düsseldorf:
Droste.

Foucault, Michel. 1976. *The Archeology of Knowledge*. New York: Harper &
Row. Translated from French.

Frohick, Fred M. 1979. *Public Policy: Scope and Logic*. Englewood Cliffs,
N.J.: Prentice-Hall.

Fudenberg, H. Hugh; Vijaya L. Melnick (eds.). 1978. *Biomedical Scientists
and Public Policy*. New York: Plenum.

Geertz, Clifford. 1980. *Negara: The Theatre State in Nineteenth-Century
Bali*. Princeton: Princeton University Press.

George, L. Alexander. 1980. *Presidential Decisionmaking in Foreign Policy:
The Effective Use of Information and Advice*. Boulder, Colo.:
Westview.

Gershuny, J.I. 1978. "Policymaking Rationality: A Reformulation." *Policy
Sciences* 9:295-316.

Geuss, Raymond. 1981. *The Idea of a Critical Theory: Habermas and the
Frankfurt School*. Cambridge: Cambridge University Press.

Goldhamer, Herbert. 1978. *The Adviser*. New York: Elsevier.

Greenstein, F.; N. Polsby. 1975. *Handbook of Political Science*. 9 vols. Vol. 6: *Policies and Policymaking*. Reading, Mass.: Addison-Wesley.

Greven, Michael Th. 1974. *Systemtheorie und Gesellschaftsanalyse: Kritik der Werte und Erkenntnismöglichkeiten in Gesellschaftsmodellen der kybernetischen Systemtheorie*. Darmstadt: Luchterhand.

Grindle, Merilee S. (ed.). 1980. *Politics and Policy Implementation in the Third World*. Princeton: Princeton University Press.

Gwyn, William B.; George C. Edwards, III (eds.). 1975. *Perspecives on Public Policy-Making*. Tulane Studies in Political Science. Vol. 15. New Orleans: Tulane University.

Habermas, Jürgen. 1970. *Toward a Rational Society*. Boston: Beacon.

Habermas, Jürgen; Niklas Luhmann. 1971. *Theorie der Gesellschaft oder Sozialtechnologie: Was leistet die Systemforschung?* Frankfurt/Main: Suhrkamp.

Hall, Roger I. 1981. "Decisionmaking in a Complex Organization." In George W. England; Anant R. Negandhi; Bernard Wilpert. *The Functioning of Complex Organizations*. Cambridge, Mass: Delgeschlagen, Gunn & Hain.

Handy, Rollo. 1970. *The Measurement of Values: Behavioral Science and Philosophical Approaches*. St. Louis, Mo.: Green.

Hanf, Kenneth; Fritz W. Scharpf (eds.). 1978. *Interorganizational Policy Making: Limits to Coordination and Central Control*. Beverly Hills: Sage.

Hartung, Fritz. 1950. *Deutsche Verfassungsgeschichte: Vom 15. Jahrhundert bis zur Gegenwart*. Stuttgart: K.F. Koehler.

Hartwig, Richard. 1978. "Rationality and the Problems of Administrative Theory." *Public Administration* 56 (Summer):159-79.

Hayward, Jack; Michael Watson (eds.). 1975. *Planning, Politics, and Public Policy*. London: Cambridge University Press.

Heclo, Hugh. 1972. "Review Article: Policy Analysis." *British Journal of Political Science* 2:83-108.

Heclo, Hugh; Aaron Wildavsky. 1974. *The Private Governance of Public Money*. London: Macmillan

Hennen, Manfred. 1976. *Krise der Rationalität—Dilemma der Soziologie: Zur kritischen Rezeption Max Webers*. Stuttgart: Ferdinand Enke.

Hermann, Charles F. (ed.). 1972. *International Crises: Insights from Behavioral Research*. New York: Free Press.

Hildebrand, Klaus. 1980. *Das Dritte Reich*. Munich: R. Oldenbourg. 2nd ed.

Hintze, Otto. 1970. *Staat und Verfassung: Gesammelte Abhandlungen zur allgemeinen Verfassungsgeschichte*. Göttingen: Vandenhoeck & Ruprecht.

Hofferbert, Richard I. 1974. *The Study of Public Policy*. Indianapolis: Bobbs-Merrill.

Hofheinz, Roy, Jr.; Kent E. Calder. 1982. *The Eastasia Edge*. New York: Basic Books.

Hofmann, Hasso. 1972. "Dezision, Dezisionismus." In Joachim Ritter, *Historisches Wörterbuch der Philosophie*. Vol. 2. Basel: Schwabe.

Holmes, Leslie. 1981. *The Withering Away of the State? Party and State under Communism*. Beverly Hills: Sage.

Holsti, Ole R. 1972. *Crisis Escalation War*. Montreal: McGill-Queen's University Press.

Hoos, I. 1972. *Systems Analysis in Public Policy: A Critique*. Berkeley: University of California Press.

Horowitz, Irving L. 1967. *The Rise and Fall of Project Camelot: Studies in the Relationship between Social Science and Practical Politics*. Cambridge, Mass.: MIT.

Inbar, Michael. 1979. *Routine Decision Making: The Future of Bureaucracy*. Beverly Hills: Sage.

Inglehart, R. 1977. *The Silent Revolution: Changing Values and Political Styles among Western Publics*. Princeton: Princeton University Press.

Janis, Irving L. 1972. *Victims of Groupthink: A Psychological Study of Foreign-Policy Decisions and Fiascoes*. Boston: Houghton Mifflin. New ed. forthcoming 1983.

Janis, Irving L.; Leon Mann. 1977. *Decision Making: A Psychological Analysis of Conflict, Choice, and Commitment*. New York: Free Press.

Jones, Charles O. (1977). *An Introduction to the Study of Public Policy*. North Scituate, Mass.: Duxbury. 2nd ed.

Jungermann, Helmut; Gerard De Zeeuw (eds.). 1977. *Decision Making and Change in Human Affairs*. Dortrecht (Holland): D. Reidel.

Juviler, Peter; Henry Morton (eds.). 1967. *Soviet Policy-Making*. New York: Praeger.

Kahnemann, Daniel; Paul Slovic; Amos Tversky (eds.). 1982. *Judgment under Uncertainty: Heuristics and Biases*. Cambridge: Cambridge University Press.

Kaplan, M.F.; S. Schwartz (eds.). 1977. *Human Judgment and Decision Processes in Applied Settings*. New York: Academic Press.

Katz, Milton. 1972. Quoted in *News Report* (National Academy of Sciences, Washington, D.C.) 22 (June): 4-5.

Kelsen, Hans. 1961. *General Theory of Law and State*. New York: Russel reprint.

Kennedy, R.F. 1969. *Thirteen Days*. New York: Norton.

Kern, Ernst. 1949. *Moderner Staat und Staatsbegriff: Eine Untersuchung über die Grundlagen und die Entwicklung des kontinental-europäischen Staates*. Hamburg: Rechts- und Staatswissenschaftlicher Verlag.

Kickert, W.J.M. 1980. *Organization of Decision Making*. Amsterdam: North Holland.

Kissinger, Henry A. 1979. *White House Years*. Boston: Little, Brown.

———. 1982. *Years of Upheaval*. Boston: Little, Brown.

Klages, Helmut; Peter Kmieciak. 1979. *Wertwandel und gesellschaftlicher Wandel*. Frankfurt: Campus.

Koertge, Noretta. 1979. "The Methodological Status of Popper's Rationality Principle." *Theory and Decision* 10: 83-95.

Kogan, Maurice. 1975. *Educational Policy-Making: A Study of Interest Groups and Parliament*. London: Allen & Unwin.

Kozielsecki, Josef. 1982. *Psychological Decision Theory*. Dortrecht (Holland): D. Reidel. First published in Polish in 1975.

Kriesi, Hanspeter. 1980. *Entscheidungsstrukturen und Entscheidungsprozesse in der schweizer Politik*. Frankfurt: Campus.

Krockow, Christian Graf von. 1958. *Die Entscheidung: Eine Untersuchung über Ernst Jünger, Carl Schmitt, Martin Heidegger*. Stuttgart: Ferdinand Enke.

Krackow, Christian Graf von. 1958. *Die Entscheidung: Eine Untersuchung über Ernst Jünger, Carl Schmitt, Martin Heidegger*. Stuttgart: Ferdinand Enke.

Kruse, David S. 1979. *Policy Studies: An Overview of the Contemporary Enterprise*. Private distribution.

Kruskal, William H. (ed.). 1982. *The Social Sciences: Their Nature and Use*. Chicago: University of Chicago Press.

Kuhn, Axel. 1973. *Das faschistische Herrschaftssystem und die moderne Gesellschaft*. Hamburg: Hoffmann & Campe.

Lall, Arthur. 1981. *The Emergence of Modern India*. New York: Columbia University Press.

Langton, John. 1979. "Darwinism and the Behavioral Theory of Sociocultural Evolution: An Analysis." *American Journal of Sociology* 85 (no. 2): 288-309.

Laszlo, Erwin. 1977a. *Goals in a Global Community*. New York: Pergamon.

Laszlo, Erwin, et al. (eds.). 1977b. *Goals for Mankind: A Report to the Club of Rome on the New Horizons of Global Community*. New York: Dutton.

Leach, Edward. 1982. *Social Anthropology*. Oxford: Oxford University Press.

Lederer, Katrin; Reiner Mackenses. 1975. *Gesellschaftliche Bedürfnislagen: Möglichkeiten und Grenzen ihrer wissenschaftlichen Bestimmung*. Göttingen: Otto Schwarz.

Leichter, Howard M. 1979. *A Comparative Approach to Policy Analysis: Health Care Policy in Four Nations*. Cambridge: Cambridge University Press.

Lerner, Allen. 1976. *The Politics of Decision Making: Strategy, Cooperation, and Conflict*. Beverly Hills: Sage.

Lewis, Eugene. 1980. *Public Entrepreneurship: Towards a Theory of Bureaucratic Political Power–The Organizational Lives of Hyman Rickover, J. Edgar Hoover, and Robert Moses*. Bloominton: Indiana University Press.

Lichtenstein, Sarah; Baruch Fischhoff. 1980. "Training for Calibration." *Organizational Behavior and Human Performance* 26: 149-71.

Lieberman, Ann; Milbrey McLaughlin (eds.). 1982. *Policy Making in Education*. Chicago: University of Chicago Press. 81st Yearbook of the National Society for the Study of Education. Pt. 1.

Lindblom, Charles E. 1968. *The Policy-Making Process*. Englewood Cliffs, N.J.: Prentice-Hall.

———. 1979. "Still Muddling, Not Yet Through." *Public Administration Review* 39 (November-December): 517-26.

Lineberry, Robert L. 1977. *American Public Policy: What Government Does and What Difference It Makes*. New York: Harper & Row.

Liske,Craig; Willian Loehr; John McCamant (eds.). 1975. *Comparative Public Policy: Issues, Theories, and Methods*. New York: Wiley.

Luhmann, Niklas. 1968. *Zweckbegriff und Systemrationalität: Über die Funktion von Zwecken in sozialen Systemen*. Tübingen: J.C.B. Mohr. Republished 1977 by Suhrkamp Taschenbuch, Frankfurt/Main.

Luttwack, Edward. 1977. *The Grand Strategy of the Roman Empire: From the First Century A.D. to the Third*. Baltimore: Johns Hopkins.

Machan, Tibor R. 1980. "Rational Choice and Public Affairs." *Theory and Decision* 12: 229-58.

MacRea, Duncan, Jr. 1976. *The Social Functions of Social Sciences*. New Haven, Conn.: Yale University Press.

March, James G. 1978. "Bounded Rationality, Ambiguity, and the Engineering of Choice." *Bell Journal of Economics* (Autumn): 587-608.

March, James G.; Johan P. Olsen. 1976. *Ambiguity and Choice in Organizations*. Oslo: Universitetsforlaget.

Marcović, Mihailo. 1974. *From Affluence to Praxis: Philosophy and Social Criticism*. Ann Arbor: University of Michigan Press.

Mayntz, Renate; Fritz W. Scharpf. 1975. *Policy-Making in the German Federal Bureaucracy*. New York: Elsevier.

Meier, Christian. 1980a. *Res Publica Amissa: Eine Studie zur Verfassung und Geschichte der späten Römischen Republik*. Frankfurt am Main: Suhrkamp.

———. 1980b. *Die Entstehung des Politischen bei den Griechen*. Frankfurt am Main: Suhrkamp.

———. 1968c. *Die Ohnmacht des allmächtigen Dictators Caesar*. Frankfurt am Main: Suhrkamp.

Meyer-Abich, Klaus M.; Dieter Birnbacher. 1979. *Was Braucht der Mensch um glücklich zu sein: Bedürfnisforschung und Konsumkritik*. Munich: C.H. Beck.

Miller, Richard W. 1979. "Reason and Commitment in the Social Sciences." *Philosophy and Public Affairs* 8 (Spring): 241-66.

Mintzberg, Henry. 1979. "Beyond Implementation: An Analysis of the Resistance to Policy Analysis." In K.B. Haley (ed.), *Operational Research '78*. Amsterdam: North Holland.

Miser, Hugh J. 1973. "The Scientist as Adviser: The Relevance of the Early Operations Research Experience." *Minerva* 11: 95-108.

Mitchell, Joyce M.; William C. Mitchell. 1969. *Political Analysis and Public Policy*. Chicago: Rand McNally.

Mitroff, Ian I. 1972. "The Myth of Objectivity or Why Science Needs a New Psychology of Science." *Management Science* 18 (June): B613-B618.

Mitroff, Ian I.; Ralph H. Kilmann. 1981. "The Four-Fold Way of Knowing: The Varieties of Social Science Experience." *Theory and Society* 10 (March): 227-48.

Mitzmann, Arthur. 1970. *The Iron Cage: A Historical Interpretation of Max Weber*. New York: Knopf.

Moharir, V.V. 1979. *Process of Public Policy-Making in The Netherlands: A Case Study of the Dutch Government's Policy for Closing Down the Coal Mines in South Limburg, 1965-1975*. The Hague: Institute of Social Studies.

Mommsen, Wolfgang. 1974. *Max Weber und die deutsche Politik, 1890-1920*. Tübingen: J.C.B. Mohr. 2nd ed.

Montinari, Mazzino. 1982. *Nietzsche lesen*. Berlin: Walter de Gruyter.

Nelson, Richard R. 1977. *The Moon and the Ghetto*. New York: Norton.

Obler, Jeffrey; Jurg Steiner; Guideo Dierckx. 1977. *Decision-Making in Smaller Democracies: The Consociational "Burden."* London: Sage.

Oppenheimer, Franz. 1926. *State: Its History and Development Viewed Sociologically*. New York: Arno. Reprinted 1972. Translated from German.

Pempel, T.J. (ed.). 1977. *Policymaking in Contemporary Japan*. Ithaca: Cornell University Press.

Pempel, T.J. 1978. *Patterns of Japanese Policymaking: Experiences from Higher Education*. Boulder, Colo.: Westview.

Perkins, D.N. 1982. *The Mind's Best Work*. Cambridge, Mass.: Harvard University Press.

Pletsch, Carl E. 1981. "The Three Worlds or The Division of Social Scientific Labor, circa 1950-1975." *Comparative Studies in Society and History* 23: 565-90.

Pocock, J.G.A. 1975. *The Machiavellian Moment: Florentine Political Thought and the Atlantic Republic Tradition*. Princeton: Princeton University Press.

Poggi, Gianfranco. 1978. *The Development of the Modern State: A Sociological Introduction*. Stanford: Stanford University Press.

Popper, K.R. 1967. "La Rationalité et le statut du principe de rationalité." In E.M. Classen (ed.), *Les Fondements philosophiques des systèmes économiques*. Paris: Payot.

Porter, Roger B. 1980. *Presidential Decision Making: The Economic Policy Board*. Cambridge: Cambridge University Press.

Quandt, William B. 1982. *Saudi Arabia in the 1980s: Foreign Policy, Security, and Oil*. London: Basil Blackwell.

Rabinow, Paul; William M. Sullivan (eds.). 1979. *Interpretive Social Science: A Reader*. Berkeley: University of California Press.

Raiffa, Howard. 1968. *Decision Analysis*. Reading, Mass.: Addison-Wesley.

Ramsden, John, 1980. *The Making of Conservative Party Policy: The Conservative Research Department since 1929*. London: Longman.

Ranney, Austin (ed.). 1968. *Political Science and Public Policy*. Chicago: Markham.

Rawls, John. 1971. *A Theory of Justice*. Cambridge, Mass.: Harvard University Press.

Rettig, Rachard A. 1977. *Cancer Crusade: The Story of The National Cancer Act of 1971*. Princeton: Princeton University Press.

Rhoads, Steven E. 1980. *Valuing Life: Public Policy Dilemmas*. Boulder, Colo.: Westview.

Richardson, Jeremy (ed.). 1982. *Policy Styles in Western Europe*. London: Allen & Unwin.

Robertson, K.G. 1982. *Public Secrets: A Study in the Development of Government Secrecy*. London: Macmillan.

Rohety, James M. (ed.). 1980. *Defense Policy Formation: Towards Comparative Analysis*. Durham, N.C.: Carolina Academic Press.

Rokeach, Milton. 1973. *The Nature of Human Values*. New York: Free Press.

Roper, Michael. 1977. "Public Records and the Policy Process in the Twentieth Century." *Public Administration* 55 (Autumn): 253-68.

Rose, Richard. 1973. "Comparing Public Policy: An Overview." *European Journal of Political Research* 1:67-94

Rose, Richard (ed.) 1976. *The Dynamics of Public Policy: A Comparative Analysis*. Beverly Hills: Sage.

Rostow, W.W. 1982. *The Division of Europe After World War II*. Farnborough (UR): Gower.

Roth, Guenther; Wolfgang Schluchter. 1979. *Max Weber's Vision of History: Ethics and Methods*. Berkeley: University of California Press.

Rothchild, S. Donald; Robert L. Curry, Jr. 1978. *Scarcity, Choice, and Public Policy in Middle Africa*. Berkeley: University of California Press.

Rourke, Francis E. 1976. *Bureaucracy, Politics, and Public Policy*. Boston: Little, Brown. Rev. ed.

Ruse, Michael. 1974. "Cultural Evolution." *Theory and Decision* 5: 413-40.

Schalk, L. David. 1979. *The Spectrum of Political Engagement*. Princeton: Princeton University Press.

Schell, Jonathan. 1982. *The Fate of the Earth*. New York: Knopf.

Schlesinger, A.M., Jr. 1965. *A Thousand Days: John F. Kennedy in the White House*. Boston: Houghton Mifflin.

Schluchter, Wolfgang. 1980. *Rationalismus der Weltbeherrschung: Studien zu Max Weber*. Frankfurt am Main: Suhrkamp.

Schmitter, Philippe C. (ed.). 1977. "Corporatism and Policy-Making in Contemporary Western Europe." *Comparative Political Studies* 10 (April). Special issue.

Schulman, Paul R. 1980. *Large-Scale Policy Making*. New York: Elsevier.

Schulz, G. 1974. *Faschismus-Nationalsozialismus: Versionen und theoretische Kontroversen, 1922-1972*. Frankfurt am Main: Propyläen/Ullstein.

Scott, Robert A.; Arnold R. Shore. 1979. *Why Sociology Does Not Apply? A Study of the Use of Sociology in Public Policy*. New York: Elsevier.

Sharkansky, Ira (ed.). 1970. *Policy Analysis in Political Science*. Chicago: Markham.

Sharkansky, Ira; Donald Van Meter. 1975. *Policy and Politics in American Governments*. New York: McGraw-Hill.

Sheehan, N., et al. 1971. *The Pentagon Papers as published by the New York Times*. New York: Bantam.

Shultz, George P.; Kenneth W. Dam. 1977. *Economic Policy beyond the Headlines*. New York: Norton.

Simeon, Richard. 1976. "Studying Public Policy." *Canadian Journal of Po-*

litical Science 9:548-80.

Simon, Herbert A. 1976. "From Substantive to Procedural Rationality." In Spiro J. Latsis, (ed.), *Method and Appraisal in Economics*. Cambridge: Cambridge University Press.

———. 1979. "Rational Decision Making in Business Organizations." *American Economic Review* 69: 493-513.

Sjobert, L.; T. Tyszka; J.A. Wise (eds.). 1980. *Human Decision Making*. 2 vols. Bodafors (Sweden): Doxa.

Slovic, Paul; Baruch Fischhoff; Sara Lichtenstein. 1977. "Behavioral Decision Theory." *Annual Review of Psychology* 28: 1-39.

Sorensen, T.C. 1966. *Kennedy*. New York: Harper & Row.

Sowell, Thomas. 1980. *Knowledge and Decisions*. New York: Basic Books.

Steiner, Jörg; Robert Dorff. 1980. *A Theory of Political Decision Modes: Interparty Decision Making in Switzerland*. Chapel Hill: University of North Carolina Press.

Strickland, Stephen P. 1972. *Politics, Science, and Dread Disease: A Short History of United States Medical Research Policy*. Cambridge, Mass.: Harvard University Press.

Thompson, John B. 1981. *Critical Hermeneutics: A Study of the Thought of Paul Ricoeur and Jürgen Habermas*. Cambridge: Cambridge University Press.

Toulmain, Stephen; Richard Rieke; Allan Janik. 1979. *An Introduction to Reasoning*. London: Collier Macmillan.

Tribe, Laurence H. 1972. "Policy Science: Analysis or Ideology." *Philosophy and Public Affairs* 2 (Fall 1972): 66-110.

Tribe, L.H.; C.S. Schelling; J. Voss (eds.). 1976. *When Values Conflict*. Cambridge, Mass.: Ballinger.

Triska, Jan; Paul Cocks (eds.). 1977. *Political Development in Eastern Europe*. New York: Praeger.

Turner, C.F.; E. Krauss. 1978. "Fallible Indicators of the Subjective State of the Nation." *American Psychologist* 33: 456-70.

Vickers, Geoffrey. 1968. *Value Systems and Social Process*. New York: Basic Books.

Vilmar, Fritz. 1973. *Strategien der Demokratisierung*. Vol. 1: *Theorie der Praxis*. Vol 2: *Modelle und Kämpfe der Praxis*. Darmstadt (Federal Republic of Germany): Herman Luchterhand.

Vogel, Ezra F. (ed.). 1975. *Modern Japanese Organization and Decision-Making*. Tokyo: Charles E. Tuttle.

Vogel, Ezra F. 1979. *Japan as Number One*. Cambridge, Mass.: Harvard University Press.

Wade, Larry L. 1972. *The Elements of Public Policy*. Columbus, Ohio: Merril.

Wagner, Harvey M. 1972. "Commentary on ORSA: Guidelines." *Management Sciences* 18 (June): B609-B613.

Wallace, Helen; William Wallace; Carole Webb (eds.). 1977. *Policy Making in the European Communities*. London: Wiley.

Wallace, William. 1976. *The Foreign Policy Process in Britain*. London: Allen & Unwin.

Ward, Paul von. 1981. *Dismantling the Pyramid: Government . . . by the People . . . .* Washington, D.C.: Delphi.

Warwick, Donald P.; with M. Mead; T. Read. 1975. *A Theory of Public Bureaucracy: Politics, Personality, and Organization in the State Department.* Cambridge, Mass.: Harvard University Press.

Weber, Max. 1949. *The Methodology of the Social Sciences.* Glencoe, Ill.: Free Press.

———. 1958. *Gesammelte politische Schriften.* Tübingen: J.C.B. Mohr.

———. 1966. *Staatssoziologie.* Berlin: Duncker & Humlot. Supplemented special print from Max Weber, *Wirtschaft und Gesellschaft.* Tübingen: J.C.B. Mohr, 1980. 5th rev. ed. Pt. 8.

Weinberg, Alvin M. 1972. "Science and Trans-Science." *Minerva* 10: 209-22.

Weiss, Howard M. 1980. "The Utility of Humility: Self-Esteem Information Search and Problem-Solving Efficiency." *Organizational Behavior and Human Performance* 25: 216-23.

Wildavsky, Aaron. 1975. *Budgeting: A Comparative Theory of the Budgetary Process.* Boston: Little, Brown.

Wilson, Bryan (ed.). 1970. *Rationality.* New York: Harper & Row.

Wipperman, Wolfgang. 1975. *Faschismustheorien: Zum Stand der gegenwärtigen Diskussion.* Darmstadt (Federal Republic of Germany): Wissenschaftliche Buchgesellschaft.

Wittfogel, A. Karl. 1957. *Oriental Despotism: A Comparative Study of Total Power.* New Haven: Yale University Press.

Wolf, Charles W., Jr. 1979. "A Theory of Nonmarket Failure: Framework for Implementation Analysis." *Journal of Law and Economics* 22 (April): 107-39.

Zander, Alvin. 1979. "The Psychology of Group Processes." *Annual Review of Psychology* 30: 417-51.

Zaret, David. 1980. "From Weber to Parsons and Schutz: The Eclipse of History in Modern Social Theory." *American Journal of Sociology* 85 (no. 5): 1180-1201.

CONTENTS

PREFACE

My central subject in this book is public policymaking. My objectives are (1) to advance the study of public policymaking as a major topic of the social sciences and of human thought in general, and (2) to contribute to the improvement of public policymaking.

My basic thesis is that there is a significant gap between the ways individuals and institutions make policy and the available knowledge on how policies can best be made. This gap between knowledge and practice will widen at an accelerated rate unless some radical changes are made in policymaking methods, in policymaking organizations, and in the qualifications of policymakers. Taking up the challenge of this widening gap, I attempt in this book to advance and apply to public policymaking various approaches developed in the modern social sciences, decisionmaking theories, and systems analysis.

I try to analyze and evaluate contemporary public policymaking and to identify its main weak spots by comparing it with a proposed optimal model. I next examine the possibilities for closing the gap between actual policymaking and better possible policymaking, giving special attention to policy knowledge. I explore ways to encourage a better integration of knowledge and power. Finally, I present a number of concrete proposals, based on my analysis, for improving public policymaking.

In its intellectual orientation and conceptual tools, this book belongs to "policy science." I have tried to apply a broad orientation to studying and improving public policymaking, not only by undertaking a scientific analysis and vigorous treatment of facts and theory, but also by using tacit knowledge, imaginative contemplation, and consideration of my work's implications for realization of social goals and values. This combination may cause many social scientists to cry "naive" and to ask whether my attitude is "really scientific."

I regret my differing with some of my distinguished colleagues, but in my opinion much of the practical sterility, for which many of the contemporary "modern sciences of society" are notorious, results from mistaken notions about whether "factual inquiry" should be, or even can be, divorced from social reality and social problems, from the construction of abstract theories, and from introspective contemplation. Such notions lead to an unsophisticated disregard of the interdependence of "facts," "values," and "action." Therefore, in this book I try to integrate closely my analysis of actual policymaking, my construction of normative models, and my suggestions for improving public policymaking.

The audience I would like to speak to through this book includes students and teachers of political science and of the social sciences in general, policy practitioners, such as planners, government officials, and contemplative politicians, and other persons interested in policymaking and public affairs. The basic similarities in design and structure between public and private policymaking make my central analysis significant for private (corporate or institutional) policymakers as well. I have kept the characteristics of this varied audience in mind in writing this book. In order that the book should convey its message, I have kept my language exact but non-esoteric, and have kept footnotes at a minimum. I have provided enough bibliographic notes to guide the reader to the relevant literature, but not so many as to be exhaustive (and exhausting). My various illustrations and examples are intended only to clarify the main points of my argument, not to "prove" them in any rigorous sense, and I have presented my argument in stages that are as easy to follow as possible. To be honest, I am not sure that I have succeeded in following these self-imposed prescriptions, but I have tried.

Many persons have been of immense help to me in preparing this book. I want to thank first the director and staff of the Center for Advanced Study in the Behavioral Sciences, for inviting me to spend a year there as a Fellow. My stay was a stimulating and fruitful experience, and provided me with a unique opportunity for quiet work and thought. I shall always cherish the memory of that year. I want also to thank my colleagues at the Hebrew University for their stimulating intellectual companionship. I owe special gratitude to the senior Israeli politicians and civil servants who provided me with unique opportunities to observe the practices of public policymaking and to try out some proposals for its improvement.

In the writing and revising of this book I received considerable help from many colleagues who freely offered their penetrating and productive criticism and ideas. Especially, I would like to acknowledge my debts to Edwin Fogelman, Sam Krislov, Howard R. Sacks, Aaron Wildavsky, and Harold Wilensky. I want in particular to acknowledge my gratitude to Professor Michael Polanyi for the inspiration he has provided me, both by his writings and by personal contact.

Since knowledge and systematic thought about analyzing and improving policymaking are yet very scarce indeed, exchanges of views and comparisons of data and experiences are essential. I shall warmly welcome any comments which the reader—both the student of political theory and the practical politician—would like to offer, and cordially invite suggestions and comments to be sent to me at the Hebrew University, Jerusalem, Israel.

YEHEZKEL DROR

part I

THE MISSION

chapter 1 · The Problem and Its Setting

The major problem with contemporary public policymaking is the constantly widening gap between what is known about policymaking and how policy is actually made. Contemporary societies, faced with critical problems whose solutions will require the utmost skill, rely on outmoded policymaking machinery. Corporations, private institutions, government organizations, all need to have their decisionmaking tools continually improved.

CORRELATION BETWEEN KNOWLEDGE AND POWER

Information relevant to public policymaking is becoming more and more available. How can this information be introduced into the policymaking process so as to increase the correlation between knowledge and power? This problem, in one form or another, has been known since Plato's *Republic*. Its solution is now critical because unwise policies, hastily or laboriously "muddled through" by "rules-of-thumb" or some similar time-honored method, can now have unprecedentedly grave consequences. For the first time in history, it is possible to examine the characteristics and causal variables of public policymaking explicitly and systematically, and to institute a reform of public policymaking based in part on such explicit examination and on scientific criteria. Such a reform, however, will probably have to be rather revolutionary, and will probably not be easily accepted.

For many years our technological knowledge has been rapidly outpacing our decisionmaking institutions. (This fact has often been pointed out; it has frequently been overstated.) Until the nineteenth century, society usually showed great capacity for assimilating new scientific and technological information and putting it to rather wide use. Among the novel social adjustments to new knowledge were, for example, the limited-liability corporation, central planning units, the mass-democratic state, independent regulatory commissions, and professional managers. However, the technologies and theories of most of the older scientific knowledge did not deal directly with the central institutions and values of society (perhaps partly because a lack of autonomy, or of freedom of inquiry, kept findings that contradicted such basic institutions and values from being recognized). It is modern science that has made the relationship between knowledge and social action a radical problem. It not only has made very high-quality public policymaking necessary, but has also provided some of the knowledge needed to achieve such policymaking.

SCIENCE AS CREATOR OF PROBLEMS

That modern science both creates problems and provides better means for solving them is a striking phenomenon. I will leave exploring the metaphysics of such fascinating symmetry for some other time, and limit myself here to discussing the facts that seem to be emerging. First I want to consider some questions that are raised by science's creating new and critical problems or aggravating old ones, especially the two questions: how can the potential benefits of new knowledge be put to good use, and how can the catastrophes that can follow from their misuse be prevented?

The most dramatic and obvious form of the latter question is one we are now facing: how can we prevent nuclear war? Conflict and war have always been characteristics of human society, and will continue to be so in the foreseeable future, but now they endanger the survival of modern civilization, and perhaps of humanity as a whole, because of advances in the technologies of violence. This problem will become increasingly difficult to solve in the future, when wide use of nuclear power plants, and cheaper methods of nuclear engineering, will increase the number of states (perhaps even smaller social groups) with their own nuclear or biochemical weapons, and thus the chances of universal disaster brought about by accident, recklessness, or design.

Problems posed by developments in genetics, birth control, mass communication, and production methods are less dramatic than those posed by nuclear technology, but are in the long run no less significant. The problems of space travel will also require not only much high-quality engineering, but, even more, increasingly complex organizations able to perform better policymaking. Some other critical problems are: modernizing the "developing" states, which today include most of mankind; meeting threats to world order that are shaped by technologies of violence and communication, but are rooted in deeper ideological and social issues; resolving inequities in the balance of power and in the division of functions between individuals and various organizations in modern mass societies; facing the social implications of rapid increases in production, consumption, and leisure time; and achieving a quantitative and qualitative balance between population and resources.

Many of these problems have been around since the dawn of history, but have assumed their present proportions only since the advent of modern science. Modern science has also been a major force in disjointing traditional relationships between social institutions, belief systems, and knowledge. The technological innovations that first disturbed traditional behavior patterns were changes in production technology, hygiene and medicine, and communications, but findings that have undermined the values and assumptions of basic social institutions (theories of evolution, genetics, and depth psychology, for example) have been even more disruptive. Some examples of such problems are: the imbalance between production potential and effective demand in many modern states, which may become worse as the industrial trend toward automation accelerates; fundamental issues that space travel may pose for the major religions and for human thought in general; and the acute collision between modern technology and traditional social structures in most of the developing nations.

Extrapolating from present trends, I can see only a continuously accelerating rate of innovation in most branches of science. The knowledge these innovations will create will be able either to destroy mankind physically and socially or, if it is used to our best advantage, to lift mankind to new heights of individual and social existence. The problem of integrating knowledge and social action is therefore becoming both more difficult and more critical. Conscious calculation of social direction must therefore partly replace the automatic and semispontaneous adjustment of society to new knowledge that generally sufficed in the past.

SOME POSSIBLE SOLUTIONS

There are several ways new knowledge could possibly be better integrated into society. One would be to try to achieve a working equilibrium by explicitly limiting the freedom of scientific research, so as to forestall or contain new findings that might endanger society either physically or by undermining too many of its basic values. This solution seems a priori both infeasible and undesirable. The cold-war situation demands exactly that knowledge which could be physically disastrous, and western democratic ideology favors unrestrained scientific activity. Nevertheless, the possibility of controlling scientific activity is important, and in some areas may be essential and acceptable. For instance, an agreement to control nuclear armament is not very useful if it does not also prevent the development of a technology that could enable small countries to manufacture nuclear bombs surreptitiously. Public opinion in western democratic countries may also support restraining research on doomsday machines or mass biocontrol (that is, controlling emotions and perceptions by external signals), mass hypnosis, or similar mass opinion-shaping devices.

Another possibility would be to limit the dissemination of knowledge whose widespread availability might be physically or culturally dangerous. This solution is also formally rejected by contemporary western ideology, which regards all knowledge as being nearly always "good." Nevertheless, and luckily enough, knowledge is in fact often disseminated in channels that tend to keep it from persons who might misuse it or be harmed by it. Information about toxicology is not now readily available to criminals. Another case in point is that many assumptions of mass-democratic ideology have been rather clearly refuted by most studies of political behavior. The myth of the intelligent and autonomous voter does not square very well with empiric studies of voting behavior. Knowledge of such studies is still (in 1967) limited to specialized groups. Widespread knowledge of these studies' findings might well undermine beliefs that help maintain democracy and might generate a mass cynicism that could only be dissipated if the people could be led to accept a more sophisticated theory of democracy.

The last remarks point to a third solution, namely, to reform social institutions and culture in the light of new knowledge. This solution is the one most acceptable to contemporary ideologies, but it presents a major difficulty. How much do the characteristics of the new knowledge and of contemporary society allow them to be successfully integrated by changes in social institutions and in culture?

One conclusion seems inescapable: the problems faced even now by modern society, to say nothing of the problems scientific progress and social evolution will raise in the foreseeable future, require very high-quality public policymaking for even minimally satisfactory solutions.

TOWARD A POLICY SCIENCE

Modern science creates both problems and means for solving them, if (and this is a big if) those means are put to their best use. Science cannot answer the spiritual problems of human life, eliminate conflict and personal suffering, determine final values and beliefs, or solve problems "once and for all."[1] Furthermore, I make no claim that science will completely replace intuition, hunches, tacit knowledge, insights born of experience, or bathtub "Eurekas." All I claim is that in the future much more scientific knowledge will be available, that it will be directly relevant to policymaking about social issues and to social self-direction, and that it will have to be used to the fullest if present and future social problems are going to be adequately solved.

This new knowledge will not be limited to the instrumental aspects of social action, as the physical sciences and most of the life sciences are, but will deal with the core processes and structure of public policymaking itself. One of my major hypotheses is that we can develop a *policy science* that will significantly improve the quality of public policymaking if it is fully used. That this new discipline is becoming possible is shown by the increases in knowledge about the very processes by which human beings and human society grow and operate, about decisionmaking processes, decisionmaking systems, and systems analysis and design, and about complex decisionmaking and intelligence-amplifying machines.

The word "science" here carries certain positive connotations that the reader should not allow to impair his critical consideration of my subject matter. I would almost prefer to use the term "study," which might better describe both the inherent nature of, and the present state of knowledge in, the social "sciences," the decisionmaking "sciences," and policy "science."

To clarify my argument, I must distinguish between knowledge that is relevant to devising a given *policy,* and knowledge that is relevant to *policymaking.* Certain types of knowledge are relevant to substantive policy issues. For instance, some medical knowledge is relevant to policies about public health; some sociological knowledge is relevant to policies about social segregation; some historical knowledge is relevant to policies about external relations; and so on. Hereafter I will use the term

---

[1] For an illuminating discussion of why it is impossible to "eliminate disease" despite tremendous progress in medicine, see René Dubos, *The Dreams of Reason* (N.Y.: Columbia Univ. Press, 1961), pp. 63ff.

policy-issue knowledge to refer to knowledge pertinent to a specific policy.

Policymaking knowledge is one step further removed from discrete policy issues. It deals with the policymaking system, with how it operates and how it can be improved. Available policymaking knowledge deals, for instance, with: how organizational structures operate (organization theory); ways to improve the quality of the people engaged in policymaking (personnel development); collecting and using information (intelligence studies and information theory); coordinating and integrating different policymaking units (political science); designing better decisions (operations research and decision sciences); analyzing, improving, and managing complex systems (systems theory). To cover the complex of theory and information dealing with policymaking as a process (as distinct from that relevant to specific policies), I will use the term *policymaking knowledge*. In essence, policymaking knowledge deals with the problem of how to make policy about making policies. That is, policymaking knowledge dealing with *metapolicy*. For convenience, I will use the term *policy knowledge* to refer to both policy-issue knowledge and policymaking knowledge. *Policy science* can therefore be partly described as the discipline that searches for policy knowledge, that seeks general policy-issue knowledge and policymaking knowledge, and integrates them into a distinct study.

The major problem at which policy science is directed is how to improve the design and operations of policymaking systems. A major component of this problem is how to increase the role of policy-issue knowledge in policymaking on concrete issues. For example, new sociological knowledge is relevant to more and more social problems, such as containing social aggression and using leisure time. But if the policymaking system is to use this policy-issue knowledge, changes must be made in the system. For example, sociologists might have to be appointed to staff positions in most of the main policymaking organizations, and new process patterns would have to be introduced to assure that these advisors actually participated in policymaking.

Another major component of the problem is how to increase the role of policymaking knowledge in the operation of the policymaking system and in improving it. For example, modern decision sciences establish the best methods for dealing with certain quantifiable problems. To use that information in policymaking, other changes would have to be made in the policymaking system; policymaking activities would have to be systematically screened to identify those that could even partially be handled by quantitative methods, and personnel and an organization able to use these methods would have to be set up. Even more complicated changes in the policymaking system could be required, for example, by new knowledge from psychology and organization theory about conditions that encourage creativity.

BASIC THESES

Although I will continue discussing the central problems I have mentioned above throughout this book, I can now set forth my basic theses about such problems in the form of five propositions:

1. The scientific revolution, and the transformations it has caused in social structures and in the heights to which men can aspire, together with other changes in culture and society, have made continual improvement of public policymaking necessary if such policymaking is to lead to satisfactory results and progress, or, perhaps, is even to assure survival.

2. The amount of available policy knowledge is increasing, and so is its quality.

3. The quality of the best possible policymaking increases as a function of increases in available policy knowledge.

4. The quality of actual public policymaking improves much more slowly because there are barriers against the improvement of policymaking reality.

5. As a result, actual public policymaking falls farther below both what it could be and what it must be. (See Fig. 1.)

The development of policy science must be speeded up, and this advanced policy science put to its fullest use, if critical problems are to be adequately solved. But the many changes that will have to be made in the structure and process of public policymaking in order to use this new knowledge will involve rather substantial departures from present working methods, assumptions, and cultural biases. For instance, the new knowledge will be somewhat monopolized by new organizations and professional groups, which will have to be integrated into the policymaking process. Toward this end not only will the functions of political, administrative, and policy-science personnel and units have to be divided up differently, but novel controls and check-and-balance systems will have to be set up to avoid some of the dangers that must follow from using more scientists in government. New qualifications may be demanded from politicians and from other public policymakers such as senior civil servants. New types of agencies with autonomous staffs may also be needed for high-level policymaking.

The new policy knowledge will affect not only public policymaking, but all decisionmaking, institutional and individual. (Until now its main

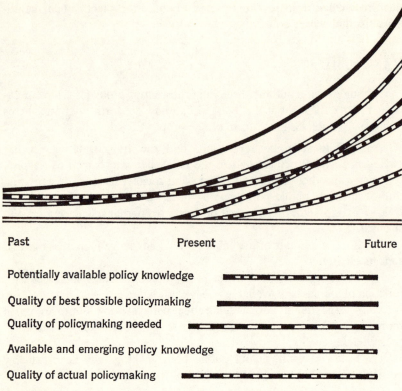

FIGURE 1. BASIC TRENDS AFFECTING POLICYMAKING QUALITY

impact has been on business corporations and military organizations, which are often more eager to seize new opportunities to improve their operations than the public administration is.) Also, some rather drastic changes in education generally may be needed to bring the individual into policymaking and to escape some of the defects of mandarinism that a meritocracy (that is, rule by persons selected only by merit) is almost always subject to.

It is not easy to put this general view of the future into more concrete terms, and any effort to do so may well be premature. Policy science is only in its infancy, and changing established institutions is a very difficult task. Nevertheless, if democratic government is to survive its competition with other forms of government, it must not lag behind in using new knowledge, no matter how difficult and painful the needed adjustments may be.

To assimilate new knowledge into policymaking machinery quickly and skillfully, the situation must be analyzed, the changes in it that are both feasible and needed must be pointed out, and steps must be taken to ensure that when changes become possible or needed, they will be made. It is up to academicians, who are one of the few social strata having the necessary time and detachment, to undertake the first part of this task, analyzing the present and, as far as possible, the future, and pointing out the main directions in which change and innovation are likely to be needed. It is my purpose in this book both to try to furnish some such help and to lay a foundation for the methods and theories of policy science.

chapter 2 · The Scope,
Significance, and Method
of the Inquiry

Public policymaking is a very complex, dynamic process whose
various components make different contributions to it. It decides
major guidelines for action directed at the future, mainly by governmental organs. These guidelines (policies) formally aim at achieving what is
in the public interest by the best possible means.

The twelve main characteristics in the above definition of policymaking require more detailed comment, as follows.

1. *Very complex.* Policymaking involves many components,
which are interconnected by communication and feedback loops and
which interact in different ways. Some parts of the process are explicit
and directly observable, but many others proceed by hidden channels
that the actors themselves are often only partly aware of and that are
very difficult, and often impossible, to observe. Thus, guidelines are
often formed by a series of single decisions that result in a "policy"
without any one of the decisionmakers being aware of that process.

2. *Dynamic process.* Policymaking is a process, that is, a continuous activity taking place within a structure; to be sustained it requires a
continuing input of resources and motivation. It is a *dynamic* process,
which changes with time; the sequences of its subprocesses and phases
vary internally and with respect to each other.

3. *Various components.* The complexity of public policymaking
is the obverse of another of its characteristics, namely, the multiplicity of
its components. Nearly all public policymaking involves a great variety
of substructures. The identity of these substructures, and the degree of
their involvement in policymaking, vary among different issues, times,

and societies. The respective influences of the President and of the Congress of the United States on policymaking in certain areas (control of the economy and the military, for example) have changed significantly during the last century. Military elites play an important role in policymaking on civilian issues in many South American states, but scarcely participate in such policymaking in western democratic countries. The substructures most involved in public policymaking constitute the "political institutions" or "political system" of a society.

4. *Make different contributions.* This characteristic suggests that every substructure makes a different, and sometimes unique, contribution to public policy. What sort of contribution substructures make depends in part on their formal and informal characteristics, which vary from society to society. In the western democracies, for instance, some aspects of different substructures' contributions to public policy could be generalized (though much oversimplified, and intended only to exemplify what I mean by "different contributions to public policy") as follows:

The *representative parliament* is highly sensitive to public opinion and pressure groups, is low or medium in "expertness," takes short- or medium-range points of view, and shows low or medium consistency in its decisions. The *merit-selected civil service* is moderately insensitive to public opinion and pressure groups, has a high level of expertness (within limits that depend on educational qualifications and experience), takes medium-range and sometimes longer points of view, and shows medium or high consistency in its decisions. The *courts* are highly insensitive to public opinion and pressure groups, have a high level of limited (legal) expertness, take short- or medium-range points of view, and show high or very high consistency in their decisions.

5. *Decides.* Policymaking is a species of decisionmaking. This point is very important, because it lets us use decisionmaking models for dealing with policymaking. Indeed, these models will be some of my main tools, although they must be used with care, since public policymaking is an aggregative form of decisionmaking, and differs in important respects from the discrete decisions that most decision-theory literature deals with.[1]

---

[1] For a different view, see James G. March and Herbert A. Simon, *Organizations* (N.Y.: John Wiley, 1958), who state on a comparable problem, "Planning, broadly defined, is of course indistinguishable from other kinds of decisionmaking" (p. 200). Such failure to discriminate among various kinds of decisionmaking may be an important reason why decisionmaking theory has contributed relatively little to the study of policymaking, planning, and similar aggregative and complex decisionmaking processes.

6. *Major guidelines.* Public policy, in most cases, lays down general directives, rather than detailed instructions, on the main lines of action to be followed. It is thus not identical with the games-theory definition of *"strategy"* as a detailed set of decisions covering all possible situations. The military definition of "strategy," as a general guide for action in contrast to *tactics,* is closer to what I mean by "policy," and is what I will mean when I use the term "strategy."

After main lines of action have been decided on, detailed subpolicies that translate the general policy into more concrete terms are usually needed to execute it. However, what often happens, to use another perspective, is that the general policy is built up by a complex, interacting set of secondary policies and decisions. In many cases, these two flows of decisionmaking, from the top down and from the bottom up, proceed simultaneously, and even partly overlap; policy is often partly "formed" and partly "executed" by the same subdecisions. For instance, if a developing country has declared a policy "to encourage all private investment," but in its day-to-day decisionmaking provides incentives mainly to private investments in heavy industry, its actual policy is to "encourage private investment mainly in heavy industry." This policy results from high-level decisions interacting with middle-level operational decisions. How "specific" or "general" a public policy seems to be depends on differing conditions. Also, the same process can often be viewed from a higher level as execution of a policy by subdecisions, and from a lower level as policymaking (or as metapolicymaking); this ambiguity makes it impossible to draw clear lines between "policymaking," "policy execution," and "administration."

7. *For action.* Decisionmaking can result in external action, in changes in the decisionmaker himself, or in both or neither. Suppose a scientist decides to accept some hypotheses as provisionally true; he may then set up a new experiment, change his view of the subject matter, or do both. The policies of most socially significant decisionmaking, such as most public policymaking, are intended to result in action. Also policies directed at the policymaking apparatus itself, such as efficiency drives in government, are action-oriented.

A special case is policies whose intent is to have someone other than the policymaker take action. For instance, a policy may be made in order to recruit support. Thus, aggressive declarations against an unpopular, but militarily stronger, neighbor may be intended to make the internal population render support to the policymakers. Another special case is policies directed at preventing some action by an adversary, such as the policy of developing second-strike capacity in order to "deter" aggression. Or such a policy may be declared in order to mislead an opponent, reassure a partner, or be a trial balloon that will test the intentions or reactions of some actors. An even more special case is "policies" made and promulgated mainly to let the policymakers themselves vent their emotions; declaring that it will be policy "to emancipate women" in an East Asian country will probably result neither in any action that might lead to such emancipation nor in any additional support, but doing so expresses the beliefs of the policymakers and helps them feel better. These very important and frequent special cases use the term "policy," but are not policymaking in the substantive sense I am mainly concerned with.

8. *Directed at the future.* Policymaking is directed at the future. This is one of its most important characteristics, since it introduces the ever-present elements of uncertainty and doubtful prediction that establish the basic tone of nearly all policymaking. In particular, because the future is so uncertain, actual policymaking tends: to formulate policies in vague and elastic terms; to be continuous, so as to adjust policy to whatever the new facts may be; to seek defensibility, and therefore to adopt policies that will probably not have unforeseeable results (this tendency often leads to "incremental policy change," i.e., trying to increase predictability by deviating only by small increments from past experience); and not to make any policy about many issue-areas (a phenomenon I call *zero-policymaking*). That policies must always deal with an uncertain future not only significantly shapes actual policymaking, but is also a major problem that must be faced by the best possible ("optimal") policymaking. The solution will require extensive use of methods for reducing uncertainty and compensating for it, and such methods must therefore be a main subject of policy science.

9. *Mainly by governmental organs.* One of the differences between making private policy and making public policy is that the latter mainly concerns actions to be taken by governmental organs. Of course, this is a matter of degree; public policy is also directed in part at private persons and non-governmental structures, as when it calls for a law prohibiting a certain type of behavior or appeals to citizens to engage in private saving. But public policy, in most cases, is primarily directed at governmental organs, and only intermediately or secondarily at other actors.

10. *Formally aim at achieving.* One characteristic of all contemporary political systems is that their *formal* aim is to achieve what is in the *public interest*. Even regimes whose real aim is, for example, to enrich a small oligarchy or to perpetuate the power of some dictator try to establish their legitimacy, and gain the support or at least the acquiescence of the population, by presenting and explaining their policies in terms of the public interest. The only contemporary exceptions are occupation regimes based on brute force during periods of war, though

even the Nazis tried to present their occupation policies in the west (but not in the east) in terms of the ultimate "public interest" of the occupied population.

11. *What is in the public interest.* However difficult it might be to find out what the "public interest" may concretely refer to, the term nevertheless conveys the idea of a "general" (as opposed to "sectoral") orientation, and seems therefore to be important and significant. Furthermore, there is good evidence that the image of "public interest," as held in good faith by the major policymakers, has a tremendous influence on the public-policymaking process, and is therefore, at least (though not only) as conceived by the various public-policymaking units, a "real" phenomenon, and an important operational tool for the study of policymaking.

12. *By the best possible means.* Public policymaking formally aims not only at achieving what is in "the public interest," but at doing so by the best possible means. In abstract terminology, public policymaking aims at achieving the maximum net benefit (public interest achieved less cost of achievement). Benefits and costs take in part the form of realized values and impaired values, respectively, and cannot in most cases be expressed in commensurable units. Often, quantitative techniques can therefore not be used in this area of public policymaking, but neither the qualitative significance of "maximum net benefit" as an aim nor the necessity to think broadly about alternative public policies in terms of benefits and costs is therefore reduced.

The interdependence between ends and means is most important. Often ends, that is, both operational and general values (though perhaps not final values), change because of innovation in means. For instance, eliminating poverty by social action became a widely accepted goal when science began to be regarded as making it possible to eliminate poverty. Reaching the moon and penetrating space were adopted as main targets of public policy in the United States and the Soviet Union after developments in technology put those targets within the image of the possible.

A less direct but not less important relationship between means and ends depends on the implications for power of changes in means. When means change, power distribution often changes also, so that to some degree different ends are stipulated for policymaking and different values motivate the components of the policymaking system. Thus, when our optimal model proposes more use of policy analysts, the goals of policymaking are somewhat changed, even though the optimal model and the recommendation are instrumental in nature. Conscious or tacit recognition of this unavoidable, though reducible, effect of changes in means is one cause of strong opposition to "instrumental" improvement. The interdependence between means and ends is most important in shaping the dynamics of public policymaking over time, and must be explicitly emphasized, since it could easily be forgotten during our preoccupation with the instrumental aspects of public policymaking.

These twelve main characteristics of public policymaking are largely shared with other related processes, especially with decisionmaking, which is a broader concept and includes policymaking, and with planning, which is also a species of decisionmaking and often overlaps policymaking. Sometimes planning is a major means of policymaking, characterized by being relatively more structured, explicit, and systematic, and by presuming to be more rational. My discussion will focus on public policymaking, but most of its points will apply, *mutatis mutandis,* to private policymaking, decisionmaking, and planning. From time to time I will mention some main differences between these related processes to help the interested reader apply the analysis to them.

REALITY AND SIGNIFICANCE IN PUBLIC POLICY-MAKING

The main characteristics of our subject of inquiry having been explored, some remarks on its reality and significance are in order. A specific characteristic that distinguishes *Homo sapiens* from even the higher primates is that he can make conscious and rational decisions, at least part of the time. The institutional decisionmaking processes of various human societies, of which public policymaking is the most complex, radically differentiate human society from animal society. No animals, to the best of our knowledge, indulge in any comparable group decisionmaking processes.

Both the importance of decisionmaking in shaping history and its moral significance as an exercise of free choice have been discussed intensely by different philosophies, ranging from the completely deterministic view, which minimizes the significance of decisionmaking or even denies its very existence, to extreme belief in "free will," which assigns human decisionmaking the determinative role in individual, social, and sometimes even cosmic history. Since belief systems are essentially immune to scientific examination, I can only point out that most of the contemporary ones, including nearly all the major religions, believe human decisionmaking to be important in shaping individual and social destinies. For our purposes, not much needs to be said about those schools that claim to base their determinism on science; I include here Marxian dialectical materialism, the biological determinism of schools of evolution, genetics, and neurology, and, more recently, the cultural and sociopsychological determinism to which some social scientists who regard the individual as predominantly shaped by social forces seem inclined.

It could be that in the long run human destiny is highly determined by environmental factors, perhaps by such a basic phenomenon as entropy, the tendency of the universe to run down to a state of undifferentiated chaos. However, it is more relevant for me to discuss the apparent fact that, in the short run, environmental factors limit the range of alternatives, though even a very few alternatives, such as between marrying suitor A or B, voting for candidate C or D, or sending diplomatic note X, Y, or Z, may sometimes be very significant for the persons and societies involved.

Indeed, the risk of dangerous consequences is often highest for decisions that must be made among a few alternatives, within a limited time, and without the resources needed to make possible good decisionmaking. Command decisions during military operations must often be made under such conditions, which is why military general staffs take care to establish standing orders, plans, and doctrines. Such decision-structuring methods are used to try to minimize the dangers inherent in decisions that must be made under intense stress; by transforming them into longer-term issues, they can be dealt with by policies adopted under conditions that permit more freedom of choice and more careful consideration.

Generally speaking, from a societal point of view, plans for shaping the future seem to work best for periods of three to fifteen years ahead, depending on the natural cycle of the subject matter and how much is known about it, on how stable or at least predictable the environment will be, and on what resources will be available to implement the plan. Even within this span, the possible choices may be very limited. For instance, in the developing countries, policymakers who are trying to accelerate their technological and socioeconomic modernization may have available only one or two basic strategies, neither of which can achieve much modernization in less than, say, two generations, in which case the many secondary, tactical decisions will often make no significant social difference either way. Similarly, a person's individual predisposition and social environment may limit his choice of spouse or political candidate to one limited type of person, so that often no real social difference can be made by his choice between persons A and B (though, as I have said, the marginal difference is often highly significant for the *individuals* involved).

Later I will touch on some limitations on free choice in public policymaking. Here it is sufficient to note that such limitations do exist, and that the significance of policymaking, decisionmaking, and planning should therefore not be overestimated. But however small the range of free choice, and however limited the significance of many decisions may look to an uninvolved retrospective observer, decisionmaking is a main way in which individuals and societies can consciously try to influence their future. After one rejects (or, I suspect, also after one formally adopts) a purely deterministic and fatalistic attitude, decisionmaking becomes for the actor a most critical activity. Similarly, once a society comes to believe in goal-oriented collective activity—as all modern societies and the policymaking strata in most developing societies do—public policymaking necessarily becomes a focal social activity. Hence the actor feels that the quality of his decisionmaking process is most significant and should be one of his central concerns. (We should keep in mind the existence of other methods used to try to influence the future, such as appeal to the supernatural by prayer. Culture and beliefs determine the extent of reliance on such methods.)

True, from the outside we must see that decisionmaking is not quite that important, and that its effects are sometimes only marginal. But even if this were so, and on this level little can be proved either way, policymaking would still be one of the most important individual and social processes; even marginal effects are often critical. The difference between the views of the involved actor and the outside observer is only one of degree, the outside observer being perhaps more reserved and skeptical, refusing to believe that better public policymaking can create apocalyptic social transformations. Both actor and observer must agree that decisionmaking in general and public policymaking in particular must be regarded as real and highly significant activities, well worth intensive efforts to study, understand, and improve them.

METHODOLOGICAL ISSUES

Having described the scope of my subject and having examined its reality and significance a little, I am left with some methodological issues. My main job is to analyze and evaluate the facts about public policymaking, and to identify ways in which it might be improved. To do even part of that, I must develop an optimal model of public policymaking on which I can base my analysis and evaluation, and my proposals for improvement. In doing so I shall rely greatly on functional-structural tools and concepts developed in the social sciences, and even more so, on systems analysis and management sciences. The functional-structural approach developed in the social sciences shares with the systems approach developed by the management sciences the central concept of "system" as an integrated structure and process. The main differences between the two are:

1. In the aim, explaining real systems vs. improving old systems and constructing new systems;

2. In the abstractness of the models employed, verbal vs. mathematical;

3. In the concreteness of what most of the models refer to, primitive (and, lately, complex) societies vs. formal organizations;

4. In the implied or explicit standards of evaluation, survival vs. optimality.[2]

I shall try to resolve these differences and develop a systems approach that applies qualitative ideas and methods from modern management sciences to a complex social phenomenon, namely, public policymaking. My main instruments will be an optimal qualitative model (that is, in modern systems-analysis terminology, a "preferred model") of public policymaking, and certain supplementary models, concepts, criteria, and standards. Aside from such formal analytical tools, I will have to rely on extrapolation and inference from present tendencies, on various social-science theories, and on my personal impressions and predictions. Thus, as far as possible, this book is based on "science." My personal hunches and feelings are also present, but such feelings, after all, are one of the most important sources of new knowledge.[3]

Using models has certain dangers: concentrating too much on the model, mentally identifying the model with reality, and so coming to oversimplified conclusions that apply to the model but not to reality and that are therefore incorrect. Such dangers would be lessened if models that are fully isomorphic with reality were used, but such a model would hardly be a model, and would be much too complex to be of any use. I think I should therefore point out the main shortcomings in models of public policymaking, so that both the reader and I may be put on guard against them.

1. The policymaking system is exceedingly complex and variegated. Its many elements are interconnected by a highly developed,

---

[2] Compare, for instance, Marion J. Levy, Jr., *The Structure of Society* (Princeton, N.J.: Princeton Univ. Press, 1952), and Leonard Binder, *Iran* (Berkeley: Univ. of California Press, 1962), on the one hand, with Donald P. Eckman, ed., *Systems Research and Design* (N.Y.: John Wiley, 1961), and Arthur D. Hall, *A Methodology for Systems Engineering* (Princeton, N.J.: Van Nostrand, 1962), on the other.

[3] The importance of "tacit knowledge" and subjective feelings for new discoveries has been emphasized by Michael Polanyi; e.g., see his *Personal Knowledge* (London: Routledge and Kegan Paul, 1958) and *The Study of Man* (London: Routledge and Kegan Paul, 1959). See also Carl R. Rogers, *On Becoming a Person* (Boston: Houghton Mifflin, 1961), pp. 22–23.

dynamic communication and feedback network. The models are relatively simple, being partly verbal and partly two-dimensional analogues structured as a flow chart.[4]

2. The policymaking system is nondeterministic.[5] It is partly a probabilistic system and partly an "arbitrary" system. In other words, we cannot predict what many, or perhaps most, of the changes ("transformations") in the systems will be in advance with much certainty. Some of them can be assigned certain probabilities (that is, they are "stochastic processes"); but others will seem "arbitrary" and not predictable by any means whatsoever.[6] The models make a much more "ordered" impression, leaving the mistaken feeling that a high degree of predictability might be achieved by using them.

3. The policymaking system is closely interconnected with other systems. It is a subsystem of the social system, whose subsystems, such as the power subsystem, partly overlap the policymaking subsystem, which itself has a number of subsystems, such as the foreign-policymaking subsystem and the economic-planning subsystem. Furthermore, none of these systems and subsystems are static; they change constantly. Strictly speaking, the public-policymaking system is therefore a dynamic and open system constellation.[7] The model is much more closed and static, though I will try to overcome these limitations in my discussion. (The model would be less misleading in these ways if I concentrated on the inputs and outputs, and regarded the public-policymaking system itself as a black box, but for the purposes of this book such a technique is too complex. The reader can easily transcribe my models into such a form if he likes.)

4. Most of my models are normative, whereas behavioral models

---

[4] On the use of flow charts for studying decisionmaking, see James G. March, "Some Recent Substantive and Methodological Developments in the Theory of Organizational Decisionmaking," in Austin Ranney, ed., *Essays in the Behavioral Study of Politics* (Urbana: Univ. of Illinois Press, 1962), pp. 203–204.

[5] In the following paragraphs, cybernetics terminology is used, with some simplified explanation of its meaning. See W. Rose Ashby, *An Introduction to Cybernetics* (N.Y.: John Wiley, 1955). A good non-technical introduction is Stafford Beer, *Cybernetics and Management* (N.Y.: John Wiley, 1959).

[6] "Arbitrariness" does not mean just "randomness" in the sense of "equiprobability," as used for instance in W. Rose Ashby, *Design for a Brain* (N.Y.: John Wiley, rev. ed., 1960), p. 150, or "uncertainty" as used in mathematical decision theory. It implies that we cannot know in advance anything about what the future state of the system might be, besides not knowing the probability that a certain state will occur.

[7] This apt term was coined by Bertram M. Gross in his paper for the Society for General Systems Research meeting in New York, September 1967.

aim at representing reality. To be more exact, my models are *instrumental-normative*. They do not state what the substantive values of a system should be, but instead show methods for increasing net output, whatever the values prescribing that output may be. For convenience, I will call my models "normative," but I ask the reader to remember that I am really dealing with instruments, as do nearly all "normative" models in management and decision sciences. This normative nature is basic to most of the models I will develop, so that extreme care must be used in transferring to them ideas and concepts derived from behavioral models.[8]

Besides the dangers we get into by using the methodological tool of a "model," we are also faced with the dangers introduced by using the very concept of "system," since our discussion may be infiltrated by connotations from various other disciplines that use the same term, but with different meanings. For instance, the reader familiar with cybernetics may read into the concept of "system" an expectation of homeostasis (a tendency to preserve equilibrium) that I am not necessarily implying. Perhaps some of these other connotations do indeed apply to the public-policymaking system, its embracing systems, and its subsystems, but that they do needs to be explicitly stated and proved, not sneaked in through the back door by the choice of certain words. Without a semantically pure, connotation-free language, such dangers are unavoidable, especially when concepts are borrowed from one discipline to be used in another, as they must be from time to time. Therefore the reader, especially the reader with a professional background in any of the disciplines I will borrow from, must be on his toes so as not to be misled by denotations or connotations that I don't in fact mean.

---

[8] The instrumental-normative character of my models distinguishes them from the mixed descriptive-normative models of Herbert Simon and his associates, and from the mainly descriptive-predictive frame of reference of Richard C. Snyder and his associates. My approach is closer to Snyder's, who pioneered in using decisionmaking models to study policymaking, and who explicitly recognized the possibilities of reform-directed models. See Richard C. Snyder *et al.*, "Decisionmaking as an Approach to the Study of International Politics," in Richard C. Snyder *et al.*, eds., *Foreign Policy Decisionmaking* (N.Y.: Free Press, 1962), pp. 27–31 *passim*.

part II

A FRAMEWORK
FOR
EVALUATING
PUBLIC
POLICYMAKING

chapter 3 · The Evaluation
of Public Policymaking

Trying to evaluate complex activities involves one in a series of difficult problems that have not yet been solved. It is particularly difficult to deal with public policymaking, which not only is complex, but also involves many values. Nevertheless, we can develop a rigorous approach to analyzing, evaluating, and improving public policymaking if we start by developing explicit criteria and standards that will replace the implicit assumptions, one-sided views, and halo effects we all use for lack of anything better.

ASCERTAINMENT AND APPRAISAL

In principle evaluation involves two main steps: (1) a *criterion* is used to ascertain the actual level or quality (including both quantitative and qualitative aspects of "quality") of a process; and (2) a *standard* is used to appraise the ascertained quality. For example, by the criterion of output we ascertain that the level of road construction this year is x miles per \$1,000,000, and by standard of comparison with the past we appraise this level as "better" if the ascertained level last year was $x - n$ miles per \$1,000,000. Often these two steps are fused into one, but evaluating public policymaking demands a clear distinction between them and an explicit examination of the problems they involve. While undertaking such an examination, I will try to illustrate the various difficulties of analyzing and evaluating policymaking by using the relatively simpler issues involved in evaluating a more concrete activity, namely, primary education.[1]

---

[1] I am indebted to Dr. Rachel Elboim-Dror for working out this illustration.

Net Output as the Primary Criterion

The first and most straightforward approach to evaluating a process is to take *net output,* defined as output minus input, as the primary criterion. However, such a criterion cannot be used outside very narrow limits, because it is often hard to measure, conceptualize, or even identify the output of a social process. For instance, the output of primary education includes knowledge, skills, mental abilities, values, and character, freeing parents to work by keeping children in school, changing the social structure by providing channels of mobility, and many more results that will come to the reader's mind.

These different outputs occur at different times, some occurring immediately, others—such as providing educated mothers who will in turn motivate their children to study—occurring in the next generation. Many of these outputs are intangible and cannot be quantitatively measured; some of them even defy qualitative formulation. Furthermore, even if a certain result could be measured, and the specific contribution of the schools, as such, could be identified as their output, the net output still could not be computed, because the input and the output could not, in most cases, be stated in commensurable units. These difficulties in evaluating social processes often cause the measurable outputs to be selected as representative of all the outputs. Such biased selection leads to incorrect evaluation, and, worse, distorts the evaluated process itself, since it motivates a concentration of the process on measurable outputs, such as factual knowledge.

Secondary Criteria

The second approach to ascertaining the quality of a process is to use *secondary criteria* (sometimes called "approximate criteria"). A secondary criterion is applied to an aspect of a process (for example, a partial output) that is chosen because it is considered, for good reasons, to be positively correlated with, and more measurable than, the net output. Secondary criteria may be applied to elements of output, process pattern, structure, or input.

Secondary criteria can be classified, more or less, into four main groups: (1) independent variables which shape the quality of the evaluated process; (2) dependent variables, shaped by the quality of the evaluated process; (3) interdependent variables, which interact with the quality of the evaluated process; and (4) variables related non-causally to the quality of the evaluated process by an interconnecting variable that shapes both the process and the criterion variable.

The relationship between the causal criteria (groups 1, 2, and 3) and the quality of the evaluated process can be either direct or indirect, that is, through intervening variables. For example, the input of qualified manpower can be used as a secondary criterion, because the quality of manpower is, in the short run, an independent variable that directly shapes the quality of public policymaking. But input into training of senior staff can be used as a secondary criterion only because of an indirect relationship—training (independent variable) influences the quality of manpower (intervening variable), which in turn shapes the quality of policymaking (dependent variable).

To return to my illustration, the quality of elementary education can also, in part, be ascertained from process patterns. The basic assumption here is that a certain patterning of the educational process, such as the global method of teaching reading, influences the net output, and can therefore be used to ascertain the quality of the process. Structure can also be used as a secondary criterion, to ascertain in part the quality of primary education. Elements such as the degree to which the school system is decentralized and subjected to local control, the amount of money put into the system per pupil, or the number of pupils who graduate (these are elements of structure, input, and output, respectively) can easily be assumed to measure the quality of the education provided by the system.

Of the secondary criteria, the most important are the process-pattern criteria. These are nearest of the phenomenon up for evaluation, the *process* of public policymaking. The other secondary criteria, which concern output, structure, and input, are in a sense derived from process-pattern criteria. Consequently, the validity of process-pattern criteria is of critical importance to the evaluation as a whole.

The major weakness of relying on secondary criteria is the assumption that they are positively correlated with the net output. If this assumption is based on sufficient evidence, the conclusions drawn from the secondary criteria are valid and reliable, but to the extent that the assumption is based on doubtful or mistaken evidence, the conclusions will be doubtful or wrong, and will lead not only to incorrect evaluation, but also to distortions of the evaluated activity itself. Explicit criteria, based on the best available information, and on consciously considered evidence and assumptions, are therefore essential.

Standards

Once the quality (past, present, or expected future) of an activity has been ascertained by primary or secondary criteria, it must be appraised by means of standards. Is a vocabulary of 1,500 words at the end of the first grade, achieved after x teacher-hours and y pupil-hours, "good" or "bad"? Is the quality of an educational process, measured in terms of process patterns, output, structure, and input, good or bad?

The seven main standards for appraising an ascertained quality are:

1. How does the achieved quality compare with that in the past? How good is education in 1967 compared with that in 1966?

2. How does the achieved quality compare with that of similar institutions? How does the quality of a primary school in Newton, Mass., compare with that of a primary school in Durham, N.C.?

3. Does the achieved quality meet the various demands of the population? Are parents generally satisfied with school x? Are the pupils in general satisfied with school y?

4. Does the achieved quality meet accepted professional standards? How is school x rated by the local branch of the National Education Association, or by the school of education of the local university?

5. Is the achieved quality high enough to assure survival? Does it meet minimum standards? Is school x in danger of parents' refusing to let their children attend it or of the superintendent's demanding radical changes in its staff?

6. Is the achieved quality as high as the quality planned for? Are there as many pupils as the planning commission had planned for?

7. Is the achieved quality as good as it could be according to an optimal model? Education should and can be of quality y. Is the actual quality, x, as good as y?

Policymakers tend to rely on comparison with the past, either directly or by setting down planned goals that are in fact extensions of the past. But comparison with the past (or with other systems) is, in many respects, most misleading, because it does not provide any "zero point" for reliable conclusions. If education this year is x units higher than last year, I do not know whether it is actually "better" or "less bad." These two conclusions are logically identical, but they have totally different implications as to what can and must be improved in the evaluated process, and as to whether members of the organization are going to feel self-satisfied or inclined to introduce changes.

Even more important is the possibility that, despite higher achievements than in the past, the organization may be worse off when evaluated by significant outside standards. Thus, although an air-defense system has tripled its capacity to intercept enemy missiles from x to $3x$, it may now be in more danger than ever if in the meantime the enemy's attack capacity has increased from $x - n$ to $3x + m$. A hospital that now heals 70 per cent of patients with a certain disease, and that healed only 45 per cent in the past, may have become less efficient if in the past only 48 per cent of the patients could possibly be cured, but now, with modern medicine, 85 per cent could be.

Appraisal by comparison with the past is particularly misleading in our generation, in which rapid increases in applicable knowledge have, in most areas, made it possible to achieve much more than in the past. Furthermore, what people want, and what is needed to sustain progress, are also increasing. Comparison with the past is in many ways not only irrelevant but especially misleading in the developing nations, which want and need a radical break with the past. In sum, even when achievements are higher than in the past, they often lag increasingly behind what is possible, needed, and demanded, and they should therefore often be evaluated as "worse."

ASCERTAINING AND APPRAISING THE LEVEL OF PUBLIC POLICYMAKING

Public policymaking is incomparably more complex than primary education, but the same difficulties and solutions apply to evaluating it. The best method for ascertaining the achieved quality is by means of the primary criterion, net output. When the best method is impracticable, which it usually is, secondary criteria must be developed that can ascertain the achieved quality by measuring elements of process pattern, output, structure, and input. Because each of these secondary criteria will raise problems, policymaking evaluators will have to use all of them simultaneously. Even then it will be doubtful just how valid any ascertained quality of policymaking is. Similarly, various standards must be used for appraising the ascertained quality.

To illustrate, I will take another case from education, this time on the level of policymaking. To evaluate the policymaking process in education directly, I would have to identify the output and the input, calculate the net output, and appraise the net output by some standards. If I cannot carry out this sequence, then I must use secondary criteria, and to do so I must elaborate reliable assumptions about the relationships between the quality of educational policymaking and the elements of process pattern, output, structure, and input used as criteria. For instance, if I assume a positive correlation between the professional qualifications of policymakers and the quality of the policy they make, then, to ascertain the quality of educational policymaking, I must, among other things, survey the educational backgrounds of the senior officials in the Department of Education.

This illustration makes clear some of the difficulties of evaluating policymaking. Outputs of educational policy usually cannot be identified. Single secondary criteria may not be valid. Standards are hard to come by and to apply. For example, it is not easy to prove that the professional qualifications of policymakers have anything to do with the quality of the policy they make. Even if some studies show such a correlation exists, their validity may well apply to only a few educational problems, professional qualifications, and environmental conditions, so that their conclusions must be subjected to the constraint "other things being equal," which other things never are. The best possible professional background may be useless if other values in the particular system— values, for example, for segregation or for teaching religion—control the formation of educational policy. In such a case, reliance on professional background alone as a secondary criterion may be very misleading. Even if professional qualifications are a reliable criterion in most cases, there are problems involved in trying to appraise a quality ascertained through them: qualifications in the past or for other institutions are not comparable in many important respects; the qualifications that are aspired to or are professionally demanded differ from one school system to another; many systems lack planned qualifications or any survival (minimum) qualifications; and there is no widespread agreement on what the optimal qualifications for educational policymakers are.

TOWARD AN OPTIMAL MODEL

The next chapter explores the tools of analysis and evaluation as applied to policymaking. At this point it is clear that to construct valid and reliable secondary criteria, and, especially, to establish significant standards, one must have a model of what the evaluated activity can be at best. Such an optimal model: (1) permits one to identify secondary criteria that are reliably correlated with net output and thereby measure the achieved quality of the activity correctly; (2) provides one with a clear and significant standard for appraising the ascertained quality (that is, enables one to measure the distance between the achieved quality and the optimal quality); (3) permits one when feasible to carry out the two steps of evaluation simultaneously. (For instance, if an element of the optimal model for primary education is decentralization or teaching reading by the global method, then measuring the degree of decentralization or the degree to which reading is taught by the global method simultaneously ascertains and appraises the quality that the educational process has achieved.)

Although evaluating public policymaking is a formidably difficult task, it is not hopeless. Secondary criteria and standards need not be used one at a time. Instead, a set of such criteria and standards, based on an explicit optimal model, can allow for different variables and different conditions, and can therefore reliably identify the ways in which public policymaking needs to be improved. At least, evaluations based on explicit optimal models, and on carefully derived criteria and standards, will provide conclusions that are relatively more reliable and valid than conclusions provided by any other presently known method of evaluation.

Contemporary literature in the fields of systems analysis, economics, decisionmaking theory, management sciences, and political science, as well as in other disciplines, already includes much material relevant to constructing an optimal model of policymaking. Most of this material relies too much on quantification and rationality, or is diluted by fuzzy thinking; but by reprocessing and supplementing it, and by adjusting it to the characteristics of the public-policymaking system, much of it can be used to help develop better analytical frameworks, secondary criteria, standards, and measures of needed improvements that can be applied to policymaking. I will undertake some of this work in the following chapters.

I will develop and discuss the basic tools for evaluating policymaking in two stages. In the rest of Part II, I will first examine in detail the ways in which net output might be used to ascertain the actual quality of policymaking. Then, relying on the optimal model that will be constructed in Part IV, I will detail the set of secondary criteria to be used to ascertain the actual (present, past, or expected future) quality of public policymaking. Next I will present an expanded discussion of the major standards to be used to appraise that ascertained quality. Finally, I will construct an integrated scheme, including the primary criterion, the secondary criteria, and the standards, for evaluating policymaking. In Part III, I will use the tools developed by this discussion to evaluate public policymaking systematically and diagnostically.

In Part IV I will return to the second stage of the examination and finish constructing our basic tool for evaluating policymaking, namely, the optimal model. The optimal model is used not only to evaluate public policymaking as a whole, but also to identify main weaknesses in the process and to point out where it is most in need of improvement. My discussion will therefore be sequential, moving from evaluation of the facts, through the optimal model, to proposals for improvement. This movement will familiarize the reader with the major concepts and operations of the model, as expressed in the secondary criteria and applied to public policymaking, before he has to face the model itself in the abstract. He will thus be better equipped, when he meets it, to examine it critically and decide what and how well it contributes to the analysis and evaluation of public policymaking.

chapter 4 · Net Output as the Primary Criterion for Ascertaining the Quality of Public Policymaking

The idea of quality is analytically and conceptually the same as the idea of net output. "The higher the net output, the higher the quality" is basically a statement of identity, not of correlation. Nevertheless, it is more convenient and quite correct, though less exact, to regard net output as the primary criterion for ascertaining the quality of policymaking, as if the two were merely correlated. This looser and less demanding terminology is more useful when output cannot be quantified in terms of utilities (that is, units for measuring desirability and satisfaction) and when the opportunity costs (that is, costs in terms of other possible uses that are forgone) of input cannot be calculated.

Despite the crucial importance of this criterion, there are many blocks that make it difficult to use. In this chapter I will look more closely at these blocks and at the means for dealing with them. I will go into more concrete detail about the general observations on the primary criterion I made in Chapter 3, and I will apply these observations to evaluating public policymaking. While doing so, I shall emphasize issues and problems that will be important for our later proceeding, even when doing so involves digression outside the formal topic of this chapter.

Breaking the analysis into convenient parts, I will deal with net output in three stages, by discussing separately output, input, and output minus input. I will then summarize the problems involved in using net output as the primary criterion for ascertaining the quality of policymaking, and present my ten major findings on this question.

OUTPUT

The direct output of public policymaking is "public policy," which can be thought of as a continuous flow of more or less interdependent policies dealing with many different activities. The indirect output of public policymaking is how it affects real situations, which range from behavior involved in secondary decisionmaking and policy execution to society as a whole. All these forms and effects of output are significant for different purposes and could very well be subjected to evaluation.

The direct output, "policy," is the easiest to deal with, at least insofar as it takes some shape, which could be that of a statute, a statement, a directive, or at least a semiformal briefing. The main yardsticks for evaluating such a policy by itself are: its clarity; its internal consistency; its compatibility with other policies; its scope, in terms of the values and time-span it is concerned with; its comprehensiveness, in terms of the variety of activities it deals with; and its operationability, in the sense of its being concrete enough to be a meaningful guide for action.

Using these yardsticks is impeded by two major, interrelated blocks. First, many policies are not formally stated, either because they have never been sufficiently crystallized, or because their explicit statement is tactically undesirable (as when the policymakers want to surprise an opponent or hesitate to impair their freedom of action and the defensibility of their activities in the future). Second, sometimes policies that are ambiguous, inconsistent, narrow in scope, etc., are best for their purpose, as for instance, when such characteristics make the policy more likely to be accepted and thus more likely to significantly affect the real situation it concerns. In other words, ambiguity, inconsistency, narrow scope, etc., are often helpful and sometimes essential in making a policy politically feasible.

A more important difficulty with using the yardsticks is that how good policy *looks* may not have much to do with how good it *is*. A policy may look wonderful in terms of its form, but may still be a mere facade that hasn't a chance of affecting the real situation it is supposedly aimed at, or that could have a negative net output, an effect opposite to its apparently intended effect. Indeed, because of the compromises that are often necessary to make a policy politically feasible, because of the difficulties that hinder high-quality policymaking about complex issues, any policy that presents too good a facade, such as "comprehensive long-range plans," "overall government programs," and so on, can often be suspected, with good reason, of being a public-relations showpiece with little if any merit. Judging by external "halo effects" is an almost universal fallacy that must be carefully avoided by anyone trying to do a reliable and valid evaluation of policymaking. For these reasons, evaluating policymaking only in terms of the policy's external characteristics must be considered to be of little validity, even though it can be a useful secondary method if it is used with great care.

The real test of policymaking is its effect on real situations, or, as I will explain shortly, its probable effect on real situations. (In the case of those policies whose real purpose is to release the internal tensions of the policymakers, such release can, for analytical purposes, be regarded as the real output of the policymaking process.) The first question that should be asked about a policy is "What are its chances to affect reality?" Or, in different words, "What are its political and economic feasibilities?" The *political feasibility* of a policy is the probability that it will be sufficiently acceptable to the various secondary decisionmakers, executors, interest groups, and publics whose participation or acquiescence is needed, that it can be translated into action. Political feasibility depends on the power structure of the involved systems, and on the ability of the policymakers and of the policy itself to recruit support. The *economic feasibility* of the policy is the probability that the resources, both general (money) and specific (trained manpower, raw materials, and information), needed to execute it will be available.

Political feasibility and economic feasibility are partly interdependent, in that the political support enjoyed by a policy determines the amount of resources that will be allocated to its execution out of all the transferable resources available in that society. The scarcer the resources needed for a certain policy are (that is, the higher their costs in terms of what else could be done with them), the greater the political support needed to ensure allocation of the resources necessary for execution of that policy will have to be. (In general, in affluent societies, the constraints imposed by political feasibility are more stringent than those imposed by economic feasibility.) Policymaking must therefore be evaluated in terms of the degrees to which its policy output meets the requirements of both political and economic feasibility.[1]

Estimating the feasibility of public policy is necessary for evaluating public policymaking, but is not by itself sufficient, since doing so does not squarely examine the policy's substantive merits; a policy may be perfectly feasible, but still have a substandard effect on the real situation

---

[1] There are important differences between the basic characteristics of political and economic feasibility. For instance, political "resources" are much less fixed, often their utilization has no opportunity cost, and they cannot be invested with continuous, concave, production-possibility frontier curves. One of the negative results of the modern tendency to analyze political variables in economic terminology is to ignore such main differences between economic and political phenomena.

it is aimed at, and it is that effect which counts most for evaluating policymaking. Public policymaking is no more, and no less, than an instrumental activity, a tool, to shape social reality. Therefore the significant output on which evaluation must focus is neither the policy nor its feasibility, but its substantive effect on some real social situation.[2] (On a deeper level of analysis, policy, like all other means of action, is intended to satisfy motivations and achieve goals. For my present purposes, however, I can continue to analyze policy in terms of its effects on social reality, while keeping the level of motivations and goals as an underlying set of standards for appraising those effects.) I will refer to the form of the policies arrived at as the *nominal output* of policymaking, to the degree of feasibility of the policies (both political and economic) as the *output feasibility,* and to the substantive effects of policymaking on real social situations as the *real output* of public policymaking.

Besides the problem of the output-input relationship, which I will leave until later, evaluating policymaking in terms of its real output involves two main problems, namely, identifying the real output and examining the validity of using real output as the primary criterion.

Identifying the Real Output

Identifying the real output of any discrete policy is hindered by such problems as that:

1. It is hard to conceptualize, describe, or even qualitatively identify many elements of real output.

2. It is impossible to quantify many other elements of real output.

3. There are additional variables that interfere and make it difficult, and often impossible, to isolate the specific effects of any policy.

4. The real output tends to be dispersed over time.

5. There are frequently chain results and spillover effects in many spheres of social activity.

Let me take two policies to be worked out by the interested reader, namely, "to leave the development of television up to private enterprise .but control it by a special regulating agency" and "to support developing countries by bilateral and multilateral technical assistance." It becomes

---

[2] Similarly, the significant output of planning is not the plan itself but the plan's effect (if any) on social situations. A misplaced emphasis on plans, which are mistakenly regarded as a substantial output instead of an instrumental device (however important), is a major weakness in the contemporary study of planning. See Bertram M. Gross, "When is a Plan Not a Plan?" *Challenge,* Dec. 1961.

apparent that only a few immediate results of these policies are known. We don't even know where to look for the main body of their effects, let alone how to measure or even conceptualize them.

It's easy enough to explain why it is hard to measure real ouput or even, in many cases, to conceptualize it, but it is more difficult to do anything about the problem. Educational policies, defense policies, welfare policies, foreign policies—these and most other areas of public policymaking demonstrate why it's hard to state what is and what is not their main output. In lieu of a defined output, we have terms such as "national security," "the public good," "the cultural level of the population," "the image of the United States abroad," and similar verbal symbols, all of them far too broad and general to be of much use for evaluating policy. True enough, significant progress is being made, especially by modern utility theory and welfare economics, toward methods for measuring national welfare. Parts of the concepts of "national security," "the public good," "the cultural level" or "the national image abroad" can be translated into operational concepts that can be measured on some scale, nominal, ordinal, interval, ratio, or multidimensional.[3] Thus, "national security" can be partly measured by first and second nuclear-strike capability, recuperation ability, or available forces for limited war. "Cultural level" can be partly measured by the statistical distribution of students at the different levels of education, uses of leisure time, or the content of the mass-communication media. "National image abroad" can be measured by sophisticated public-opinion surveys, and so on. But even when such measurement is possible, and often it isn't (for instance, "the public good" cannot be measured unless more specific terms are substituted), important parts of the real output are still left out. For instance, "national security" includes the subjective readiness to strike first under various conditions; "cultural level" includes creativity, critical thinking, and aesthetic sense; and "image abroad" includes tacit feelings. None of these elements are readily measurable or even very describable.

A very serious danger with such partial measurement is that attention might be paid only to those output items that can be measured, while those that cannot be will be disregarded during evaluation and conse-

---

[3] Nominal scales are qualitative, and provide no common denominator for comparison. Ordinal scales permit the phenomena to be ordered. Interval scales permit the distances between the phenomena to be compared in terms of the scales. Ratio scales are additive and permit mathematical operations. Multidimensional scales combine different dimensions and form vectors. See Arthur D. Hall, *A Methodology for Systems Engineering* (Princeton, N.J.: Van Nostrand, 1962), pp. 244–251. Professor Louis Guttman is working on non-metric measurement scales, which may well provide a breakthrough that will permit more rigorous treatment of some such phenomena.

quently during the course of policymaking and policy execution. When those parts of the output that can be measured, or at least conceptualized, are used to ascertain the level of policymaking, then we have moved from the primary criterion of net output to the secondary criterion of aspects of output. In this case all the conditions for using the secondary criteria apply, especially the need to show that the aspects of output used as indicators of achievement are positively correlated with the net output as a whole.

Beyond the problem of conceptualization and measurability lies the problem of relating specific results to specific parts, or at least the whole, of public policymaking. What I have in mind are the many variables that shape social reality, of which policymaking is only one. For example, changes in national security, in cultural level, and in the economy are only in small part due to public policymaking. Such changes are shaped by many other variables, such as action by other states, scientific discoveries, and perhaps sheer accident. In most cases the effects of public policymaking cannot be isolated from those of other variables, and the real output of public policymaking therefore cannot be identified.

The third type of difficulty in identifying the real output is that it is dispersed over many varied social activities and over a long time; this dispersion is what concepts such as "chain results" and "spillover effects" refer to. Thus, a purely economic policy may have significant immediate effects on foreign relations, defense capability, labor mobility, rates of consumption and investment, floating-vote behavior, and so on. It may also affect important research and development activities over a much longer period. Since monitoring all such aspects of the real output of policymaking is impossible, we must find it hard to use real output as the primary criterion for ascertaining the quality of policymaking.

One way to deal with this problem (and with some of the other difficulties in identifying real output) is to set down a set of cutoff points, or a horizon, in terms of time, territory, and spheres of social activity, beyond which the effects of a policy can be ignored. For example, a municipality that establishes a policy of attracting industry is interested in the actual increase in local industry, not in effects on the locations from which industry moves, nor in possible increases in its attractiveness as a target in case of war. This illustration clarifies the conditions under which the cutoff method is valid. If most of the policy effects that are important to the evaluator fall within the horizon, the conclusions of the evaluation are valid. But if effects important to the evaluator fall outside the horizon, the conclusions are misleading. The optimal cutoff points therefore depend in part on the scope of values of the evaluator. The Council of Economic Advisers will find that the effects of the municipality's policy on other locations will often be significant and must be included within its own horizon, whereas the municipality itself is justified in ignoring these results in evaluating its policy. The problem in part can be reformulated as: In terms of what system should policy results be evaluated? In this form its close association with such concepts as "social cost" and "external economies and diseconomies" is brought out. Another variable determining the optimal horizon is the proximity or remoteness of the effects and the evaluator's ability to foresee them. Although the increased danger of attack is clearly relevant to the municipality's values, it may be so remote and unpredictable that it can justifiably be excluded from the municipality's horizon.

There are many cases in which one can establish a valid horizon that will permit the time, territory, and spheres of social activity within which the effects of policymaking must be monitored to be limited to manageable dimensions. The more we know about the time, territory, and spheres of action through which the effects of the policy will probably be distributed, the easier it is to establish a valid horizon. Also, when there are clearly dominant values, as there are in many developing countries or during periods of crisis, it is easier to draw the horizon, since many other effects will be regarded as so unimportant as to be negligible. For instance, the goal of industrialization is accepted in some of the developing countries as the dominant value for policymaking; effects on traditional family structure and culture, which are regarded as more expendable, do not have to be heavily considered by the policymakers in evaluating the industrialization policy. In many other cases, such factors as pervasiveness of a policy's effects, the inclusiveness and complexity of the values that must be considered, and not knowing where to look for the real effects make it impossible to draw a valid horizon, to identify the significant elements of public policy's real output, or to use them for ascertaining the quality of the public-policymaking process.

One characteristic of public policymaking, especially at the central-government level, is the wide scope of values and the long span of time that must be considered in order to identify the real output. Public policy is, in principle, directed at meeting many different future needs at least as well as it meets present needs. Therefore, the horizon for public policymaking as a whole must cover many values, almost all social activities, and a long period of time; these in turn make it nearly impossible to identify the real output, since it is dispersed over so large an area of inquiry. In such a case it is often useful to allocate the responsibility for discovering the effects of a policy on each different main value and sphere of activity to a different unit. This is a main justification of "suboptimization" (that is, trying to arrive at the overall optimum by dividing it into suboptima for which different units are responsible), and it is a most important principle of the public-policymaking system; I will discuss it at length later on. For now, let me just note that suboptimization is only a partial solution to the problem of too broad a horizon, and it sometimes raises more difficulties than it solves. In many cases the effects of a discrete policy that deals with an issue for which a given unit is responsible cannot be limited to a field approximating that unit's area of responsibility. For instance, transportation policies have important effects on production, defense, recreation, and population mobility. If we rule that the agency in charge of transportation policy (such as the Interstate Commerce Commission and the Civil Aeronautics Board) should take into account only effects on the internal efficiency of transportation, then very important policy results will be ignored. If we require that all results be taken into account, then the principle of suboptimization is broken. This dilemma holds for most instances of public policymaking: suboptimization is often both essential and inadequate.

At this point it becomes clear that output often cannot be used to ascertain the quality of policymaking and that consequently other criteria must be looked for. We can also see that deciding to reduce the horizon to whatever point will permit easy monitoring of the real output and fast ascertainment of policymaking quality in terms of the results left within the narrowed horizon is often a step in the wrong direction.

If a narrowed horizon is carefully established and constantly monitored, examining the policy results it covers can indicate the quality of policymaking to some degree, especially for limited and specific policies that are explicitly directed at narrow goals. Also, when overall policymaking is systematically subdivided into subpolicies, it is easier to establish narrow horizons for some of these subpolicies. But in practice policymakers now tend to establish narrow horizons merely because they are convenient and do not set up the safeguards needed to prevent serious errors in the evaluations that are arrived at in this manner.

The conclusion I am coming to, that real output is of little practical use as a criterion for ascertaining the quality of public policymaking, is reinforced by the following consideration of some other difficulties.

Validity of Real Output as the Primary Criterion

Another difficulty in evaluating policymaking arises from the fact that even the best policy can fail. This problem is not the same one raised by the interfering variables that keep the causal relationships between policies and social changes from being easily recognized, even though the two have similar effects.

Because every policy has a certain chance of failing, there is no one-to-one relation between the quality of policymaking and its real output, assuming the latter is identifiable. Even the optimal policy must often be based on predicted probabilities (though not on average expectations, which may lead to recklessness on individual policies) and can therefore fail. A purely rational policy to grow grain in a certain area can lead to disaster if a very unlikely crop failure in that area, correctly foreseen and ignored after careful consideration, should nevertheless happen. This example not only shows that "the proof of the pudding is in the eating" is a fallacy, but also throws doubt on most evaluation processes that rely on conclusions drawn from non-serial (single or few cases) feedback, and on the reliability of public opinion, which seems to be overly influenced by the results of single, dramatic policies. We may conclude that the effects of single policies, even when clearly identified, are not sufficient for reliably ascertaining the quality of policymaking, because of the elements of probability involved.

It follows that we must deal with policies in series and must apply statistical significance tests to their results, and this is nearly always impossible. Or we must substitute "probable real output" (with due allocation of price to risks) for "real output" as the relevant criterion for policymaking. This last suggestion is extremely important because it overcomes the above-mentioned fallacies involved in judging policymaking by actual results, permits policymaking to be evaluated before the main real output occurs, which is very important for long-range policies, and provides the key that will allow policymakers to try to find out in advance, rather than by hindsight, what the best possible (or at least a highly preferable) policy is. The second and third points are closely related, because once we can dispense with waiting for results before evaluating a policy, we have a way to evaluate alternative policies before definitely adopting one, during policymaking itself.

At this point, my analysis of the problems involved in ascertaining the quality of policymaking by its real output has led us directly back to the policymaking process. We see that in principle, and not only because doing so is more practical, the tests of policymaking must be applied to the policymaking process itself, and not to its results alone. The main criterion of policymaking quality then becomes: "How much does the policymaking process lead toward adoption of the policy that has the highest probable net payoff?" Notice that this probability cannot, in most cases, be deduced directly from any observed real output.

Focusing evaluation on the policymaking process instead of on the results of past policymaking has another very important advantage. In most cases, we are interested in evaluating a process in order to predict its quality in the future, and to identify the improvements it needs to achieve more in the future. When the relevant variables are changing rapidly, predictions based on extrapolation from the past are very often wrong. Therefore, future-oriented evaluations of policymaking cannot be validly based on the probable net real output of past policymaking. What we would like to know is what we can objectively expect the probable net real output of the policymaking system to be in the future, but we cannot ascertain that from direct observation of output, unless extrapolation from past output is known to be a reliable base for prediction, which it usually isn't. Therefore, using *secondary criteria* that indicate what we can objectively expect to be the probable net real output of future policymaking is in general not only the one feasible method, but also the only correct one.

For instance, a budgetary policymaking unit has performed excellently in the past, but most of its senior policymakers are approaching retirement age, and no second echelon has been prepared to take over. Also, the unit has failed to assimilate new knowledge that will probably become critical for policymaking in five years. Evaluation of the unit's past policymaking in terms of probable net real output will ascertain a high quality; extrapolation will incorrectly conclude that the future quality of the unit's policymaking will also be high. In order to ascertain correctly what we can expect the probable net real output of this unit's future policymaking to be, we must examine such secondary criteria as whether young, highly qualified candidates will be available to take over the senior policymaking jobs, and whether new knowledge that may be needed in the foreseeable future has been assimilated. These secondary criteria will ascertain that the future policymaking capacity of the unit is low, and will pinpoint the improvements that are needed to increase that capacity.

This very important point exposes the critical difference between policymaking achievements in the past and policymaking capacities in the future. The business of evaluating and improving policymaking in principle looks to the future, but many current methods of evaluation look instead to the past, ignoring the fact that predictions based on extrapolation from the past are often misleading.

The primary criterion of net output has by now taken the form of an objective expectation of what the probable net real output of future policymaking will be. This form of it cannot be used directly to ascertain the quality of policymaking, but is still valid and important, since it explains what "policymaking quality" means and has operational significance as the basis for the secondary criteria. We will therefore explore its components further. However, our next step is to clarify the concept of "input," so as to open the way for calculating or estimating net output or at least for similarly clarifying the idea of "net output."

INPUT

In discussing input into policymaking, we must carefully distinguish between input into the policymaking process as an activity, on the one hand, and input as the flow of problems, values, and data that are the raw material processed by policymaking, on the other. A machine analogy helps clarify this distinction, which is confused because in common usage the one word refers to both kinds of input indiscriminately. On the one hand we have the input into operating and maintaining the machine; this input consists of energy, lubricants, spare parts, operating and maintenance personnel, and so on. On the other hand we have the materials being processed by the machine; they flow into the machine on one side and come out in a different form on the other side. For some purposes, such as calculating the total costs of the final product, both inputs are correctly lumped together. For other purposes, such as ascertaining the quality of the machine, we are interested in the input into the operation and maintenance of the machine, in the value that is added to the raw material by the machine processing (output) and in the net added value (output minus input).

Similarly, what we are interested in when we evaluate policymaking is the input into the policymaking process as such on one side, the output of policymaking, in terms of the policy's probable effects on reality on the other side (including the expected benefits and costs), and the net output, that is, the resources contributed to society by the policymaking process less the resources (including their opportunity costs) consumed by it.

Having clarified what I mean by "input into policymaking," I must mention some problems involved in identifying and measuring that input. In general, input into policymaking is easier to describe and measure than output from it. Inputs such as manpower and equipment can be rather clearly categorized, and can be measured in terms of their costs, but it is not as easy to identify and measure some of the other inputs.

First of all, most public-policymaking units also engage in other activities, such as executing policy in the case of administrative agencies and, in the case of elected bodies, recruiting popular support and votes. It is very difficult to allocate all the elements of input to their proper activity and so arrive at a "costing" of the policymaking process as such. An occasional estimate may be derived from the distribution of manpower among different ranks and professions, but policymaking and other activities are usually so intermingled that the accuracy of such attempts is usually very doubtful.

Second, many qualities of the input are difficult to measure, and some of the more important ones cannot even be meaningfully or operationally defined. For instance, we do not know how to measure inputs of energy or intelligence. We can partly compensate for this lack of knowledge by using certain simplified assumptions that will probably be close to the facts when enough persons are involved that we can expect statistical averages to apply to the situation. Thus, we can assume that energy is equal to man-hours, and that intelligence is reliably indicated by rank and education. These assumptions are very important and useful, but it is not clear how much they apply to such elusive and important inputs as "intuition" and "foresight," neither of which we can describe at present. Also, they do not apply to small numbers of people, which is a very serious limitation, considering the important role of exceptional individuals and small elites in policymaking.

Third, from the overall point of view, inputs into policymaking should be measured not by their nominal costs alone but mainly by their opportunity costs. The characteristics of government budgeting and determination of salaries, and of the labor market in all contemporary societies, mean that we cannot use market price as a simple equivalent of opportunity cost. In societies with a freer market, the price may better measure the opportunity cost of some parts of the input, but even there we do not have reliable information on the opportunity costs of other parts of the input.

Despite these and other limitations, to some of which I will return, useful specifications of input can often be made for the purposes of an overall evaluation of public policymaking. Thus, that the quantity and quality of the manpower active in public service and of the available data-processing equipment can be estimated has some important implications for deriving the net output.

OUTPUT MINUS INPUT

Even when both output and input are satisfactorily specified, it is nearly impossible to calculate the net output of public policymaking. The output and input are usually incommensurable, so that input cannot be subtracted from output. Only in a few (by themselves very important) exceptional cases can output and input be expressed in commensurable units, usually monetary, so that net output can be calculated. For instance, in the case of that municipal policy to encourage industry to move into the town: if most of the outputs fall within a validly established horizon (including both negative and positive outputs, such as increase in employment vs. sale of public land at below-market prices), then both outputs and inputs can be translated into annual dollar values, and the net output of policymaking can in this case be approximately calculated.

Even when net output cannot be calculated as a numerical sum, the concept is still of central importance, since it focuses our attention on the necessity of considering both input and output in evaluating policymaking. Even when input and output are incommensurable, we can at least set up a balance sheet showing the separate outputs and inputs of policymaking. Most of the items on the sheet may be qualitative, incommensurable, and followed by a question mark, but it should still make us less likely to form superficial impressions by neglecting parts of the input or output. If only for this reason, the validity of ascertaining the quality of policymaking is increased if it is based on the criterion of net output. Of course, in many cases trying to construct such a balance sheet may quickly lead one to despair of using net output as a criterion, but this too is a valuable conclusion, since it gives one a reason for searching for better criteria, and helps expose the comfortable illusions that depend on the incorrect conclusions which misleading use of inappropriate criteria can lead to.

It is especially important to recognize that quality must be ascertained by net output and not by output/input ratios (total or marginal output divided by total or marginal input, respectively). The often fatal weakness of ratios lies in their neglect of the absolute sums involved, which should often be our main concern. As a very simple illustration, compare a taxation method that yields $10,000,000 output from an input of $500,000 with a taxation method that yields $100,000,000 output from an input of $10,000,000. Assuming all other effects to be equal, the second is clearly a better method, since it yields a net output of $90,-000,000 (less the annual cost of the input, which in this illustration is negligible) as against $9,500,000, even though the output/input ratio is higher in the first method (20:1 as against 10:1).

The same is true in policymaking. In principle, we should increase input into policymaking as long as doing so increases the net output, even when the total output/input ratio decreases. In marginal terminology, we should increase the input as long as there is a positive marginal net output (marginal output minus marginal input), not just to the point of maximum marginal output/input ratio. (For this last statement to be correct, input must be measured in opportunity costs and output in utility units.)

Such refinements are very important in theories of value and in quantitative decisionmaking, but are secondary to the operational problem of how to evaluate and improve the quality of policymaking. What is important for solving that very concrete problem is net output (and net benefit), not output/input (or benefit/cost) ratios.

To complete my analysis of output minus input and its implications for evaluating policymaking, I should mention two more points. Often, input into policymaking can be neglected because it is very small compared with output (and with the total costs of the operations). Often, input into policymaking is also an output of policymaking, and can therefore be neglected when we deal with the primary criterion, net output.

In much policymaking, the costs, compared with the potential and actual outputs and with the value of its subject matter, are extremely small, especially in affluent societies, where most of the resources needed as inputs for policymaking are available in relatively large quantities, and where the opportunity costs of these inputs are therefore not extraordinarily high. (However, one input, the time of top-quality manpower, is scarce in all societies.) Thus the costs of the inputs into policymaking on military, educational, economic, and most other issues are a very small fraction indeed both of the costs of executing the policies and of the improvement in real results that can stem from better policies (that is, of the "output of better policymaking"). In such cases, neglecting the input into policymaking while ascertaining the quality of policymaking in terms of output does not affect the accuracy of the estimate, which is still, in a way, rather rough. But in other cases, such as when the opportunity costs of some resources needed as an input are very high, or when one is trying to compare policymaking quality between countries or periods with radically different inputs, input cannot be omitted from consideration. To be on the safe side one should always undertake an explicit investigation to find out whether input is relatively insignificant before omitting it from consideration.

The relationship between input and output is complicated by the fact that input frequently depends on output, in the sense that demands for changes in input are an important output of policymaking. As I will show in more detail when I analyze the intermediate-feedback process in policymaking, if the policymakers think the expected real output is not good enough, they often demand the additional input that they think will bring the expected real output up to their standards. The demand for additional inputs thus must be considered an important part of output.

Admittedly there are some important limitations to this generalization, for instance, when it is clear in advance that demands for additional input will not procure any. Nevertheless, in modern societies at least, the allocation of resources depends largely on the public-policymaking system itself. Therefore, taking either that system as a whole or most of its central structures as separate entities, the input into its policymaking is in many respects self-determined, so that the input can also be regarded as an output. Thus, Congress is free within large margins to determine its research budgets. The Office of the President has large discretion in its internal division of labor. And most administrative agencies are able to influence the input into their policymaking processes, especially since the resources involved are relatively small when compared with their total budgets. To put the matter in even simpler, but not less significant, terms, it is largely up to each person to determine how much time he should spend thinking, and it is largely up to each policymaking unit to determine, within definite but broad limits, what the input into its policymaking processes should be. A lack of resources and the constraints of superior bodies can set external limits, but before limited input can be used to justify poor policymaking, the burden of proof is on the policymaking system to show that as far as possible its output includes measures for increasing its input. In many, perhaps in most affluent societies, a low output indicates low-quality policymaking, even when the low output can be sufficiently explained by a low input, because the low input is *itself* an indication of weak policymaking. Therefore, whenever input into policymaking depends significantly on the policymaking units themselves, one can regard a low output as indicating poor policymaking without referring to input at all (that is, a low output is a reliable secondary criterion). On the other hand, when output is high, input must be examined because it is possible that part of the input is being wasted; that is, net output may be low even though gross output is high.

SOME CONCLUSIONS ON USES OF NET OUTPUT

A complete and rigorous theory of policymaking requires much more refinement, but I have said enough so far that I can present some conclusions about how net output can be used as the primary criterion for ascertaining the actual quality of policymaking, as well as about some related issues.

1. Net output is conceptually equivalent to the quality of policy-making, and can be used as the primary criterion for ascertaining that quality. As such it is the real basis for evaluating policymaking.

2. To the degree that the net output cannot be ascertained, secondary criteria must be substitute tools for ascertaining the quality of policymaking.

3. Identifying net output involves, ideally, three steps: identifying the output, identifying the input, and calculating the net output by subtracting the input from the output.

4. The output of policymaking falls into three interrelated classes: (a) the policy arrived at, which is the "nominal output"; (b) the probability that the policy will be executed, which depends on its political feasibility and its economic feasibility, together called its "output feasibility"; and (c) the effect of the policy on social reality, which is the "real output." Of these, the real output is the most significant one, and is central to the use of output as a criterion (though the nominal output and the output feasibility may also be used as subsidiary primary criteria or as secondary criteria) for ascertaining the quality of policymaking.

5. Identifying and measuring the real output of policymaking are made difficult because: it is hard to recognize or conceptualize some aspects of output, and there are no measuring instruments or scales for most of them; aspects of the output are spread out over much territory and time, and over many different spheres of social action; and various interfering variables prevent one from seeing clear connections between discrete policies and specific social phenomena. Both establishing cutoff horizons and suboptimization limit the space that must be surveyed for effects of policies on real situations to manageable dimensions, and so partly answer these difficulties, but they also increase the risk of reaching an incorrect evaluation because of too narrow horizons and because values that are not assigned to any suboptimizing unit may be affected.

6. Most policymaking proceeds under conditions of uncertainty, so that policies are based at best on probable results. Therefore, "probable real output" must be substituted for "actual real output" as the dominant component of the criterion, and doing so turns the whole evaluation away from external events and toward examination of the policymaking process itself.

7. Evaluation is more interested in policymaking's capacity in the future than in its achievements in the past. Therefore, the correct primary criterion is "what we can objectively expect the probable net real output of policymaking to be in the future." Often, future capacity

cannot be extrapolated from past achievements; the quality of future policymaking must, in these cases, be ascertained by secondary criteria.

8. Assuming the probable output can be determined, to ascertain the quality of policymaking one must identify the input and calculate the net output. The input is somewhat easier to determine than the output, though measuring it in terms of opportunity costs is difficult.

9. Even when input is measured, it is often incommensurable with probable real output, so that net output cannot be calculated. Nevertheless, considering all input and output items at the same time, as in the form of a balance sheet, can be useful for arriving at a qualitative view of output minus input that will facilitate ascertaining the quality of policymaking.

10. In many cases, input into policymaking is very small compared with output. Also, in many cases, input into a unit's policymaking is itself determined by that unit's policymaking, that is, is itself also an output. When either of these two conditions applies, input can be neglected for most purposes.

These findings clearly show that policymaking cannot be evaluated by means of the primary criterion of net output alone, but they also show how net output and its components can be of some use for ascertaining the quality of policymaking. The findings, and the analysis on which they are based, also clarify some basic issues that are involved in trying to evaluate policymaking, and supply a number of concepts that will be useful for constructing my optimal model. They also reemphasize the acute need for secondary criteria on which the evaluation and improvement of policymaking can be based, since they show how inadequate net output is as a tool for these purposes.

chapter 5 · Secondary Criteria for Ascertaining the Quality of Public Policymaking

Since net output is not an adequate tool for ascertaining the quality of public policymaking, we must develop a set of secondary criteria for doing so. As I explained in Chapter 3, secondary criteria are phenomena that can be measured or estimated, at least qualitatively, that are positively correlated with net output, and that are based on such aspects of a process as a process pattern, an output, a substructure, or an input.

The secondary criteria that I present in this chapter are based on the optimal model I will construct in Part IV. For now I will limit myself to briefly presenting the secondary criteria themselves. I will then be able to use them for evaluating public policymaking in Part III, which will make them more concrete for the reader, and put their usefulness to the test, before I present the full discussion of their theoretical basis and their intellectual justification during the construction of the optimal model.

SECONDARY CRITERIA BASED ON PROCESS PATTERNS

To arrive at an operational set of secondary criteria based on process patterns, we must transform the main phases and subphases of optimal policymaking (as analyzed in Chapter 14) into a series of more compact categories, designed to meet two conditions: that they can be used to ascertain the quality of real public policymaking, taking into account available information and research methods, and that they are congruent with the optimal model and can be used as a simplified version of it. The secondary criteria based on process patterns are such a subset of all the phases of the optimal model, and include the following:

1. The first criterion concerns how much metapolicymaking there is about the basic characteristics of the policymaking process. This criterion (based mostly on phases 5 and 6 of the optimal model) is directed at ascertaining how much of the various phases of actual policymaking have been determined by precedent or tradition, and how much by sporadic or systematic reexamination and redesigning of parts of the policymaking process. Conclusions based on finding that there is no such metapolicymaking are more reliable than conclusions based on finding that there is some. A lack of metapolicymaking about the basic characteristics of the policymaking process indicates poor policymaking, but finding that such metapolicymaking takes place does not by itself indicate whether the metapolicymaking is causing improvements or distortions. The metapolicymaking must itself be examined for its contribution to be evaluated.

2. The extent of learning feedback (based on parts of phases 17 and 18) is another critical and reliable indicator of the quality of policymaking as a whole. It permits both negative and positive conclusions, since the existence of learning-feedback phases almost always indicates that the quality of policymaking is improving.

3. How much determination of policy strategy there is, and how good it is both on the metapolicymaking level (phase 7) and on the policymaking level (phase 11), is one of the most important secondary criteria, since policy strategy is critical in shaping specific policies. This criterion is hard to use for ascertaining the quality of whatever determination of policy strategy there is, since such determination is complicated by the need to consider the values built into the specific system. Nevertheless, considering the relevant variables does sometimes permit rather reliable conclusions about whether specific strategies are correct or not, given the basic values of the policymaking system in question.

4. The next secondary criterion (based on phases 6 and 9) concerns how much detail the descriptions of operational goals go into, which is one central phase of policymaking that can be examined relatively easily.

5. The degree to which alternatives are searched for (covering in effect phases 11 and 14) can be a secondary criterion, since it reflects the degree to which the policymaking moves toward being as good as possible.

6. The characteristics of the cutoff horizon within which expected results are identified and considered, especially the extent to which a broad frame of reference is adopted for defining the relevant

outputs and the extent to which long-range results are taken into account (these elements cover parts of phases 10, 12, and 13), indicate the quality of a basic feature of policymaking, and are therefore reliable as secondary criteria.

7. An overall estimate of the degree to which rational techniques have been developed as part of the public-policymaking process cuts across all other phases of that process, and partly overlaps the first six criteria. Such estimation can therefore check up on the other criteria and complete the picture arrived at piecemeal by their use. In particular, this secondary criterion is directed at estimating the degrees to which knowledge, systematic programming, and rational techniques are used for improving policymaking (which includes developing extrarational capacities by rational means).

8. Like the seventh criterion, this one, the degree to which extrarational techniques have been developed, overlaps all other phases of policymaking. Particular points at which this secondary criterion is directed are whether the policymaking process is innovative enough to assimilate extrarational techniques and whether persons who can form intuitive judgments based on wide experience are available to it.

No secondary criterion based on process patterns can by itself provide information adequate for reliably ascertaining the quality of policymaking. But taken together and used carefully, they do provide, in my opinion, a basis for such ascertainment that is at least better than an incidental impression, on which most policymaking evaluation is now based. Ascertaining the quality of policymaking can be made an even more reliable business if the secondary criteria based on aspects of output, structure, and input are also used. Although these other criteria are in principle derived from the optimal model, and so, in a sense, from the secondary criteria based on process patterns, they reveal additional facts about actual policymaking, and therefore are also valuable as tools for ascertaining the quality of policymaking, especially when all four types of secondary criteria are used simultaneously.

SECONDARY CRITERIA BASED ON OUTPUT

In Chapter 4, while discussing how net output could be used as the primary criterion for ascertaining the quality of public policymaking, I mentioned the three aspects of output that can be used as highly significant secondary criteria. To recapitulate, these three aspects of output are:

1. Nominal output, the policy itself, insofar as it is formalized or at least identifiable. The subcriteria for ascertaining the quality of the policy include clarity, internal consistency, compatibility with other policies, scope, comprehensiveness, and operationability.

2. Feasibility, both political and economic.

3. Probable real output, which includes the objectively probable results in terms of the policy's or policymaking system's effects on real social situations.

SECONDARY CRITERIA BASED ON STRUCTURE

Just as the main set of secondary criteria based on process patterns is identical to the phases of the optimal model of public policymaking, so the main set of structural secondary criteria is identical to the structural implications of the optimal phases. Those implications will be elaborated in Chapter 15, but that elaboration is somewhat too refined to be operationally applied to ascertaining the quality of policymaking, given the present dearth of relevant, detailed, and empiric information about policymaking. We must therefore use a simplified set of structural secondary criteria derived from the main set. This simplified set of structural secondary criteria parallels, in the way it is constructed and in the reasons for it, the simplified set of secondary criteria based on process patterns. It is in part a transcription of the specifications contained in the optimal policymaking model, and in part is based on projections from the structural implications of the phases of the model, both of which are developed in Chapter 15.

The secondary criteria based on structure that are included in the simplified set are as follows:

1. The existence of structural units explicitly in charge of periodically and systematically evaluating and redesigning the policymaking structure. This secondary criterion (no. 9 of the optimal specifications) is critical for the long-term quality of the policymaking structure. Like the first of the secondary criteria based on process patterns, it is a more reliable indicator when there are no such units than when there are.

2. The existence of units explicitly in charge of thinking, long-range policymaking, surveying knowledge, and research and development about policy. This secondary criterion (based on optimal specification no. 3) is also more reliable when there are no such units than when there are.

3. The existence and the extent of organizational and social distance between the units that make policy, those that execute it, and

those that motivate the carrying out of the execution. This secondary criterion is based on specification no. 5 of the model. It is just as reliable when there is such distance as when there is not.

4. This secondary criterion concerns the characteristics, role, and contribution of the various major substructures that make up the policymaking structure. The quality of aggregative policymaking depends in part on the quality of the discrete policymaking carried on by these substructures, which are of three main types: individuals, small groups, and organizations. Organizations, whose roles are central in public policymaking, include such subtypes as legislative bodies, the executive and the civil service, courts, parties and other interest groups, and universities. In some societies still other organizations, such as the military, are significant for policymaking, and therefore the quality of their policymaking can be a secondary criterion for ascertaining the quality of public policymaking. Two types of individuals, besides the private citizen, also deserve special attention: political leaders and intellectuals. The characteristics of the separate contributions of these substructures and their relative weights greatly determine the quality of public policymaking; therefore, they constitute an important secondary criterion of great practical usefulness.

5. The last secondary criterion based on structure concerns the major forms of the aggregative function. These are hard to use as a secondary criterion, but they are too important to be ignored because they are the glue that holds the various contributions to policymaking together and makes them public policymaking (see pp. 198ff). Some of the elements of this criterion are, insofar as they can be identified, the overall structure of the policymaking system, its redundancy, and its disturbances and costs.

SECONDARY CRITERIA BASED ON INPUT

Since the secondary criteria based on input into public policymaking are not derived as directly and obviously from the optimal model as those based on process patterns and structure are, they must be discussed at somewhat greater length, with some consideration given to the principal issues involved in using them.

Relying on criteria based on input into public policymaking involves both a general assumption about how input affects the quality of public policymaking, and specific assumptions about how significant specific types of input are in determining its quality. Input can be wasted on the sort of proliferation of staff and equipment that is described by Parkinson's Law and that actually decreases the quality of public policymaking. Improper balance between different components of the input, such as buying large electronic computers without hiring good programmers, may also prevent increased input from improving policymaking. To be able to use specific inputs as reasonably reliable criteria of quality, we must therefore look closely at the components of the input rather than at general budget figures. For instance, an input that includes much highly qualified manpower, or includes electric data-processing equipment and a competent operations-research staff to run it, creates a presumption that public policymaking will improve, though this presumption could easily be rebutted by facts. Examining the input should be followed up by sampling the actual uses to which the additional input is put, and by observing the effects of the input on output, process patterns, structure, and, if possible, net real output; such examination will make the secondary criteria based on input much more reliable and valid as indicators of quality.

The possiblity that input may be wasted often makes any positive conclusions based on input criteria somewhat less valid and reliable than we would like them to be. Even with large, balanced inputs, policymaking may be poor. On the other hand, input criteria permit rather reliable negative conclusions, since the lack of a certain input is nearly conclusive proof that policymaking is making do without that resource. For instance, if no books are bought, we can be sure (except for individual officials who buy books on their own) that the new knowledge in books is not being brought to bear on public policymaking; however, if books are bought, we still have to find out whether they are being read, or are just decorating executive offices, before we can draw any valid conclusions. To take a more important case, if highly qualified manpower is not flowing into politics and government service, we can be fairly sure that policymaking will tend to be mediocre. But, given a political regime that depresses individual initiative, even very highly qualified people in government service may not be able to accomplish much, and their presence is therefore not a reliable *positive* secondary criterion.

The reliability of a lack of important inputs as a criterion that always reveals definite weaknesses in policymaking makes secondary criteria based on input of great practical importance for ascertaining and improving the quality of policymaking. (This conclusion also holds when input into policymaking can be regarded as an output; the only difference is that the same discrete criteria may be classified under "output" as well as under "input.") In this light, we can easily see why the widespread tendency to try to reduce the costs of government by cutting input into policymaking (that is, there is a general preference to cut headquarters staff but not field staff, since the latter are regarded as doers of "real" work, but the former as do-gooders and loafers) is nonsensical; it is a fallacy that ignores the significance of input for the quality of policymaking.

Having accepted in principle the validity of secondary criteria based on input for ascertaining the quality of policymaking, I must now specify in more operational terms the main components of input that can be used as significant secondary criteria. There are four of them, as follows: qualified manpower; knowledge and information; equipment; and energy and drive.

The quality of the persons engaging in policymaking, in terms of their knowledge, experience, and personalities, is the most important of the inputs that determine the quality of all phases of policymaking (including both rational and extrarational components). Detailed data on the manpower input, broken down by types of experience, education, and personality, are therefore one of the most important secondary criteria for ascertaining the quality of policymaking. The very important time input can conveniently be included in the qualified-manpower category, since the input of manpower into policymaking is estimated in terms of the time that different types of personnel devote to it.

The input of knowledge and information into policymaking partly overlaps the input of qualified manpower, which is a central channel for introducing knowledge and information into policymaking, but there are some other inputs of knowledge and information, such as professional libraries, consultation services, research subcontracting, and so on. The amounts and kinds of knowledge and information relevant to policymaking are constantly increasing, thereby forcing up the optimal amounts of knowledge and information that should be put into policymaking. Measuring, or at least estimating, the amount of knowledge and information put into policymaking thus becomes more and more a critical secondary criterion, since it indicates how much a policymaking system is using new opportunities to improve its policymaking.

Equipment includes both the traditional types of work space and office equipment and the modern types of communication and data-processing equipment. The latter, especially heavy computers, are an increasingly important input into some types of policymaking, such as economic policymaking. Therefore, their presence or, especially, their absence is a significant criterion for the quality of some phases of policymaking.

Among the most important and most intangible inputs are energy and drive, without which policymaking becomes over-routinized and stagnant. In principle, they are an important secondary criterion. The trouble with them is that they are very hard to use as a secondary criterion, since they depend on tertiary criteria, such as the influx of new manpower into the senior ranks of policymakers and the existence of external pressures and demands (which stimulate internal energy and drive). Despite such practical difficulties, cautious estimation of the input of energy and drive can help ascertain the quality of policymaking.

Besides these four specific inputs, the overall input of money can also be used as a secondary criterion, though a much less reliable one; the uses of money are so diverse and depend on so many factors that an increase in a policymaking unit's budget cannot by itself indicate better policymaking. To reach such a conclusion, we must know what the money is spent for; that is, we must translate the general input of money into inputs of specific resources. For instance, both across-the-board increases in the salaries of present personnel and hiring more and better personnel for the expert staff increase the budget; the former option does not increase the probability of better policymaking (however justified such an increase might be for other reasons), but the second one does, and is therefore a significant secondary criterion.

There are still a few more problems with using input as a secondary criterion. For instance, let me mention again, first, that the way the various inputs are mixed lends them a significance much greater than the sum of their individual significances, and, second, that there are technical difficulties in trying to distinguish those parts of the input going into policymaking from those going into other activities of the same unit.

To summarize, input, especially changes in input, can be useful, if uneven, secondary criteria for ascertaining the quality of public policymaking, if three conditions are met:

1. The general input must be broken down, and a differential significance allocated to each different specific input, depending on its specific significance for policymaking under given conditions.

2. Negative conclusions, based on the absence of specific inputs, must be accepted as being more valid as indicators of weaknesses in policymaking than positive conclusions, based on the presence of specific inputs, are as indicators of policymaking strengths.

3. Positive conclusions based on input criteria must be checked by sampling the actual effects of specific inputs on the quality of public policymaking.

chapter 6 · Main Standards for Appraising Policymaking

A s I explained in Chapter 3, criteria are tools for ascertaining what the actual quality of policymaking is, whereas standards are tools for appraising, or grading, the ascertained quality. Both kinds of tools are necessary, and together they are sufficient, for evaluating policymaking. Such evaluation proceeds in principle from ascertainment to appraisal, but the two steps may often be fused.

In the last two chapters I dealt with the problems of ascertaining the quality of policymaking. Now, I turn to the problems of appraising the quality of policymaking after it has been ascertained. Here we will meet some major fallacies of the "common sense" and "muddling through" varieties, critical examination of which will carry us far beyond technical points and into consideration of some cardinal issues of analyzing, evaluating, and improving policymaking, issues that are a major focus of interest for policy science.

The operative rationale for appraising a quality involves comparing it with some yardstick or standard. There are seven main standards for appraising the quality of policymaking, namely: (1) past quality; (2) quality of other systems; (3) desired quality; (4) professional standards of quality; (5) survival quality; (6) planned quality; and (7) optimal quality. Let us examine these standards one by one, in terms of their content, their significance, and the problems involved in using them.

PAST QUALITY

The first is the simplest and most widely used of these standards. This standard is commonly used in the form of a time series, so that the progress or regress of present as compared with past performance is what is relied on for deciding whether the present quality is "good" or "bad."

Indeed, past performance can be a useful standard, but only within a carefully delimited domain in which it may be valid. More specifically, relying on past performance as a standard for appraising present performance is often misleading, mostly because of three widespread errors: (1) neglect of relevant variables; (2) insufficient time perspective; (3) bias toward over-optimistic interpretation.

Neglect of Relevant Variables

Comparison with the past, as well as with other systems, is based on the assumption that "all other things (that is, relevant variables) are equal," which they seldom are. Over short time-spans most variables are often similar enough that past quality can be put to some valid use as a standard; also, sometimes statistical techniques permit one to compensate for changes in variables (for instance, by substituting a fixed-price basis for current prices), and so somewhat enlarge the domain in which comparison with the past can be valid. But in general, the more dynamic are the variables relevant to policymaking, the less can the present be compared with the past. The present high rate of social change, and the even higher rate of innovation in policy knowledge, put definite limits on the validity of relying on the past as a standard for evaluating the present.

In extreme (but in no way unusual) situations, the changes in relevant variables are so radical that in fact no "relevant past" exists. A clear case is provided by such new states as Ghana, Nigeria, and Israel; the continuity between such new states and both their pre-independence colonial regimes and their pre-independence liberation movements is so thin, and the changes in relevant variables so far-reaching, that any comparison between post-independence and pre-independence policymaking is nearly meaningless. Similarly, though this example is not as clear-cut, revolutionary changes in government make comparisons with the past difficult to the degree that the changes in relevant variables caused by them are also revolutionary.

Another reason why there may not be a comparable past is that the problems dealt with by policymaking have themselves changed radically, as has happened, e.g., in military policymaking about nuclear weapon systems, and in social policy about birth control and segregation. Another reason, as noted above, is the rate of innovation in policy knowledge, which is an important input into policymaking. Indeed, the learning from past policymaking itself provides knowledge and insights that are a new variable in future policymaking.[1] For these reasons, comparisons between past and present policymaking are, in most cases, useless, and even meaningless, for appraising the quality of present policymaking.

Insufficient Time Perspective

Another widespread error in making comparisons with the past is insufficient time perspective, especially for the future, which is one of the most critical dimensions of a system. A change between past and present net output is insignificant and misleading unless it indicates a trend that can be extrapolated into the future. If it can't be, because a change in the net-output curve is to be expected, conclusions based on comparisons of past and present will for most purposes be fallacious.

A case in point is investments in research and development and in personnel training, which decrease present net output but make sharp increases in future net output much more probable. A contrary illustration is crash programs, which allocate all available manpower to current problems, but neglect preparations for the future and long-range programs.

Bias toward Over-Optimistic Interpretation

The most insidious and endemic of all the errors one can get into by making comparisons with the past is the danger of making an incorrect interpretation, especially of an improving time curve, which is almost always read as saying that the present situation is "good" or at least "better," whereas in fact the situation, as the curve actually shows, may be "bad" or at best "less bad," particularly when the past situation was "very bad." The most serious consequence of wrongly reading a time curve as "good" or "better" is that it impedes innovations and paralyzes efforts at reform, because it tends to generate a feeling of satisfaction. As I will show later, this phenomenon is of focal significance both for explaining actual policymaking and for reforming it.

Not only should an improving time curve often be read as "the present

---

[1] The famous argument that nuclear war is statistically inevitable if a long-enough series of crises, each with a low risk of nuclear war, is permitted to occur, ignores this learning process, thanks to which each new crisis may be handled better. The improvement in U.S. policymaking between the Bay of Pigs crisis and the later Cuban missile crisis well illustrates such learning from experience.

situation is a little less bad than it used to be, but it is still very bad," but in many cases the present situation may be worse than the past, despite apparent improvement in the quality of policymaking. The key to this paradox lies in inherent limitations of comparison with the past that stem from such comparisons' neglect of both needs and possibilities. When needs and possibilities for improvement increase faster than the actual improvements in the quality of policymaking, then the situation is becoming worse, any improvement over past quality notwithstanding. This is a common situation in policymaking, both because in many areas the need for better policymaking is increasing and because new policy knowledge makes better policymaking possible. To use more exact terminology: both the minimum quality needed for survival and the optimal quality of public policymaking are increasing rapidly, and so are making appraisal by comparison with the past fallacious more often than not.

For instance, assume that the probability of world wars is now smaller than it used to be, and that this decreased probability is due to improvements in international policymaking; nevertheless, the output of policymaking is now worse than it used to be when compared with needs, because survival nowadays requires much more effective prevention of large-scale wars. Or, assume policymaking about transportation is now better than it ever was in the past; nevertheless the gap between the achieved quality and the optimal quality may now be greater than ever, because such tools as quantitative simulation models and computers have introduced new possibilities for making better transportation policy.

The dangers of incorrect interpretations and conclusions based on comparison with the past are inherent in it, and severely limit its significance for evaluating policymaking. Additional standards are necessary for valid evaluation, the most important ones being the qualities needed for survival or to satisfy people's aspirations, or that are the best possible. But before I take up those standards, I must discuss another commonly used standard that shares most of the errors involved in making comparisons with the past, namely, the quality of other systems.

QUALITY OF OTHER SYSTEMS

The standards of past quality and quality of other systems overlap, in that the past quality of system x can be regarded in many respects as the quality of another system than the present system x. Therefore, the standard of the quality of other systems shares most of the problems found for the standard of past quality, including neglect of relevant variables, insufficient time perspective, and bias toward over-optimistic interpretation. To illustrate: comparing qualities of policymaking between modern and developing states is in most, but not all, respects meaningless; comparing the present qualities of the policymaking in two systems without taking into account the expected future qualities of their policymaking is misleading. There is also a universal tendency to misinterpret the finding that system x has higher-quality policymaking than system y, as meaning that the situation in system x is "good," whereas in fact it may be merely "less bad," or even "worse" when needs and possibilities are taken into account.

In one important respect the quality of the policymaking in another system is of even less use as a standard than the past quality of policymaking in the same system is; it is most difficult to find systems whose relevant variables are similar enough to permit meaningful comparison, especially in terms of policymaking. Also, there is always the danger that the systems compared will be selected so as to support whatever conclusion is desired. Nevertheless, if comparisons with other systems are carried out with due caution, and as part of a systematic effort at evaluation that uses a complete set of standards, they can be of some use as a standard. For example, comparing United States and British policies during World War II about invading the Balkans does permit some tentative conclusions about the relative qualities of the respective policymaking processes, despite all the differences between the two public-policymaking systems and their environments.[2]

DESIRED QUALITY

The third standard for appraising the quality of policymaking is the desired (or "level of aspiration") quality. This standard includes many sub-standards that help appraise activities, and that can be classified in terms of their publics, scope, and rank. These sub-standards have other dimensions, of course, but for my purposes I can ignore them.

Classification in terms of publics refers to the social groups that want certain qualities, such as senior politicians or Negroes in Chicago slums. Scope refers to the subject matter at which a certain desired quality is directed, such as personal income, achievement of children at school,

[2] See Hanson W. Baldwin. *Great Mistakes of the War* (N.Y.: Harper, 1949), pp. 25ff.

and national development. Rank refers to the position of a specific desired quality on the spectrum between what would be ideally desired and the minimum that would be accepted without some defensive reaction such as revolt or withdrawal. In any society many qualities can be desired simultaneously, and can be and are used as standards for appraisal. For example, when I regard a particular increase in my salary as "nice, but it could be better," I use as my standard of appraisal the quality (1) that I (and my wife) want, (2) as directed at my standard of living and social status, and (3) that is rather idealistic.

The subjective nature of desired qualities and their rich variety may lead to confusion in using them as standards for appraising social reality. Desired qualities are also dynamic, some of them changing quite quickly because of external or intrapersonal change. Nevertheless, they are a major standard for evaluation, and significantly shape behavior.

One desired quality is of dominant importance for evaluating policymaking; this is the image of quality desired by the main policymakers for what they consider satisfactory policymaking (is the situation more or less "satisfactory" or not?); I will call this the "satisfactory quality." However undefined, difficult to measure, and heterogeneous that quality may be, it largely determines the policymaking system's propensity to change, and so is worth intense attention. (On a different level, most standards are related to various desired qualities, but the implications of this interpretation, though important, would take us outside the scope of this book.)

The satisfactory quality, as I just hinted, shapes real public policymaking to a great degree. In general, the more the image policymakers have of their policymaking's quality approaches the satisfactory quality (and, *mutatis mutandis,* the desired qualities of other publics, scopes, and ranks), the less effort they will make to improve their policymaking. However, too large a gap between their image of the quality they have achieved and the satisfactory quality tends to lead to series of reactions that obstruct improvement in their policymaking. These reactions include frustration, apathy, cynicism, and convulsive change. Still, sometimes convulsive change, such as revolutions, may be the only feasible alternative to continuing to put up with a very unsatisfactory stagnant situation.

The major use of the satisfactory quality as a standard is to explain actual policymaking and the images various persons and publics have of it, rather than to help evaluate it and suggest improvements in it. The tendency to adjust, after the fact, the goal to what was actually achieved, halo effects, the effects of singularly dramatic results, the lack of pressures to make policymaking as good as it could be—such behavioral phenomena can be partly explained with the help of the concept of desired quality, but for a more objective improvement-oriented appraisal of policymaking, we must rely on other standards.

PROFESSIONAL STANDARDS OF QUALITY

Professional standards, which are based on the tacit judgments of highly developed professionals and on the implicit agreements between them, are very important for appraising operations that are intensely professionalized, such as medicine, law, and scientific research. Although professional standards are often biased toward conservatism and trained incapacities, they are nevertheless most useful for evaluating situations to which they apply. Our difficulty in evaluating public policymaking is clearly going to be worse than usual if there happen to be no professional policymakers whose standards we can use. Fortunately, there are professional standards for some areas of the public-policymaking system. For example, experienced politicians often have a good feeling for how well the Presidency, or some particular Congressional committee or executive department, is working, and senior public officials and public-administration experts have significant professional standards for evaluating administrative agencies. But the lack of "policy scientists" and trained "policy professionals," and the necessarily biased views of officials, have up to now prevented the development of professional standards for appraising policymaking in general. A gradual evolution of such professional standards is one of the benefits to be expected from policy science's advancing as a discipline and profession. Until then, this standard cannot be widely used to evaluate public policymaking.

SURVIVAL QUALITY

Under some circumstances, the minimum quality needed for survival—or, to be more exact, needed to achieve a high probability of physical and social survival—can be an important standard. In appraising military policymaking in the United States, a second-strike capability with a high probability of being able to deter nuclear aggression is the survival-quality standard, and is central to such appraisal. Similarly, the survival-quality standard specifies the minimum defense capability that must be achieved by military policymaking in, for example, Israel.

Using the standard of survival quality sometimes leads to the interesting and different conclusion that allocating resources to policymaking (and policy execution) about certain issues is wasteful; this is the case when survival quality cannot be achieved, or even approached, by any practical means. For instance, no matter how good military policymaking in the Netherlands is, it cannot be good enough to ensure survival in case of nuclear or large-scale conventional war. The military capacity of countries like the Netherlands is rather irrelevant to their military security, and is at best a membership fee in NATO. It may therefore, from this point of view (which ignores the internal and symbolic roles of the military), be quite rational for such countries to eliminate almost all input into military policymaking and its execution, the output of which is going to be all but useless no matter what the input is.

In most cases, the subjective survival quality (that is, the image of the survival quality held by a defined group, in this case, the policymakers) is also the minimum desired quality, and is the first objective of policymaking. In general, all resources will be mobilized to achieve the subjective survival quality. This is true even in organizations that supposedly have other goals, as is shown by the readiness of almost all organizations to compromise and even to change their formal goals in order to assure their survival as organizations. It is certainly true for states; all legal orders recognize the supremacy of existence itself over any other considerations when survival is at stake.

At the same time, we should recognize that often people who subscribe to certain transcendental values and ideologies regard survival as secondary, and give freedom, moral integrity, service of God, or similar precepts priority over life and society. Thus, someone who holds that freedom is more important than life will probably prefer a policy that increases the risks to survival but preserves freedom to a policy that increases the chances of physical survival at the expense of freedom. In this case, the survival quality includes "survival plus freedom," so that physical-social survival by itself loses much of its significance as a standard for appraising the quality of policymaking. Neglecting this point is a serious oversimplification that invalidates some anthropological-sociological analyses based on "functional-dysfunctional" concepts, which often implicitly refer to merely physical-social dimensions of survival.

Another point worth mentioning concerns the relationships between the subjective and objective survival qualities: if the subjective quality is significantly higher than the objective one, huge resources may be wasted. This is a critical issue nowadays in policymaking on military issues, and explains why large resources are spent on intelligence activities that are directed at finding out what the objective survival quality is.

The degree to which the subjective survival quality deviates from the objective survival quality is itself a significant secondary criterion for appraising the quality of policymaking, though it is difficult to estimate. In any case, it is the objective survival quality that must be used as a standard for appraisal, insofar as it is identifiable.

PLANNED QUALITY

All the standards considered up to now exist objectively even though they are often hard to identify. Some freedom of choice can be exercised in selecting another system for comparison, but basically the existences of past performance, performance of other systems, desired qualities, professional standards, and survival quality do not, in the short run, depend on policymaking itself, and are not directly derived from it even in the longer run. The standard of planned quality is totally different in this respect. Setting down planned targets is itself an important output of policymaking, since planning is one of the main species of policymaking. Appraising policymaking in terms of planned levels thus involves, in essence, appraising policymaking in terms of its own expectations, although the situation is rather more complex, since often different units in the policymaking system are in charge of setting down the planned qualities, of trying to achieve these targets, and of evaluating the policymaking. Nevertheless, all these units are more or less integrated in one system, and close interaction between them is often essential to their operation. As a result, planned qualities often lose much of their significance as a standard for appraising policymaking. The tendency is for planned qualities to be least significant as a standard exactly when policymaking evaluation is most important, namely, when the policymaking quality is poor. The two most common dangers of planned qualities are a tendency to "plan" whatever is going to happen anyway, and to set down targets that cannot possibly be achieved. When the planned quality approximates extrapolated predictions, appraising the achievements in terms of the degree to which planned qualities were achieved becomes a tautological exercise, the results of which depend on the quality of the extrapolation, not on the quality of the policymaking. For example, if national income is expected to grow by 4 per cent under current practices, achieving a "planned" 4 per cent growth in national income does not permit any conclusions about how good economic policymaking is. Indeed, in some countries the tendency is to "plan" a 3 per cent increase in national income, whereupon the predicted 4 per cent growth is hailed as a 133⅓ per cent achievement of the plan! However useful such "planned qualities" are as a means for manipulating mass opinion, they are not a useful standard for evaluating policymaking.

Similarly, planned qualities that cannot be achieved serve important political and administrative functions, but are not usable as a standard. For example, assuming that the maximum feasible increase in national income is 5.5 per cent, a "planned increase" of 7 per cent may be a useful device to stimulate maximum effort or to recruit popular support, but it would be misleading if it were used as a standard for appraising the quality of economic policymaking.

These remarks indicate that the more the planned qualities deviate from the optimal qualities, the less useful they are as standards for appraising an activity. In other words, planned qualities are a very significant standard when, and only when, they approximate optimal qualities.

OPTIMAL QUALITY

The single most important standard for evaluating an activity is its optimal quality, that is, how good it could possibly be. When net output is used as the criterion, it must be compared with optimal net output; when facets of process, output, structure, and input are used as secondary criteria, they must be compared with optimal models of these facets.

In theory, my conclusion is above reproach, even though for some purposes other standards are useful even when the optimal-performance standard is practical, for instance, for predicting the probability that a system will survive. But the difficulties of transforming the concept of optimal quality into a practical and usable standard are very great indeed. It is not enough to translate optimal quality into abstract conceptual or even mathematical formulations of marginal utilities, payoff curves, linear or nonlinear equations, and so on. Logical, semantic, and mathematical elaboration and manipulation of concepts are often useful for clarifying and systematizing ideas, and for applying them to concrete problems, but more is needed if we want to use the standard of optimality for evaluating and improving real policymaking about real problems. What we need is an optimal model of policymaking whose terms are sufficiently concrete that the model can be applied to actual policymaking. The optimal model should permit us to reliably derive usable criteria for ascertaining the quality of policymaking and equally usable standards for appraising that quality. The model should at the same time be optimal in the sense that it approximates the best that can be achieved, at least qualitatively.

To what degree can such an optimal model actually be constructed? How should it actually be constructed? These are problems I will try to face in Part IV of this book, but first we must continue developing some concepts related to the criteria and standards for evaluating policymaking in concrete terms, by applying them to real policymaking in Part III.

Having considered in this chapter the seven main standards for appraising policymaking one by one, I find that the following central findings emerge from the discussion:

1. The most important standard for appraising an ascertained quality of policymaking is the optimal quality. The practicality of this standard depends on constructing an optimal model of public policymaking that is close enough to reality that the optimal qualities for the different criteria can be derived in relatively usable forms, and at least in qualitative terms, by means of simulation, estimation, or an informed guess.

2. Even if the optimal quality can be stated in operational terms, other standards will continue to be significant for appraisal. Two especially important standards are (a) the survival quality, which permits one to predict the probability that a system will survive, and (b) the desired qualities, which provide one with a key for understanding actual policymaking, and permit one to predict the propensities of different systems to improve their policymaking.

3. Optimal quality will be, even in the most favorable cases, rather difficult to use as a standard. In general, the best possible appraisal of policymaking will require the use of a set of standards that includes all seven of the major ones discussed in this chapter insofar as they are available.

4. In using standards, care must be taken to avoid misleading errors, especially neglecting relevant variables, using insufficient time perspective, and being over-optimistic, in interpreting comparisons with past performance and the performance of other systems. Comparisons with planned qualities, unless they approximate the optimal qualities, can also be very misleading.

5. The relative weights to be given to different standards in appraising policymaking depend both on how operational and valid the standards are and on what the purposes of the appraisal are. For appraisal oriented toward improvement, the most important standard is

the optimal quality. For other purposes, survival quality and desired qualities are very important.

AN INTEGRATED SCHEME FOR EVALUATING REAL PUBLIC POLICYMAKING

The criteria and standards presented above in Part II are not an eclectic collection of indicators that may be used individually. They are integrated by the optimal model with itself and each other, and are one multidimensional instrument for evaluating and improving real policymaking. They should be used as an integrated scheme, since only by doing so can one be reasonably sure that the conclusions based on them are valid and reliable enough to be a dependable guide for analysis, diagnosis, and action.

Tables 1, 2, and 3 in Appendix A (pp. 307, 308, 309) demonstrate how the various criteria and standards can be combined into an integrated scheme for evaluating real public policymaking. This scheme will be the framework for the diagnostic evaluation of contemporary public policymaking that I will attempt in Part III.

part III

A DIAGNOSTIC EVALUATION OF CONTEMPORARY PUBLIC POLICYMAKING

chapter 7 · The Empiric Study
of Public Policymaking

From the beginnings of human thought, public policymaking has been a central subject for study and discussion by social philosophers and practical politicians alike. Their writings include many moving exhortations, profound insights, fascinating descriptions, and stimulating ideas that not only are of much theoretical significance, but also have been of great practical import in shaping contemporary policymaking. It is enough to mention Plato, Aristotle, Machiavelli, Burke, Bentham, the Cameralists, and the Federalists to illustrate what such discursive writings have contributed to the study and practice of policymaking, or Babur, Richelieu, Frederick the Great, Metternich, Bismarck, and Churchill to illustrate how important the autobiographies and writings of practical politicians have been as a source of data and impressionistic generalizations about policymaking.

Although I fully recognize what such writings have contributed to an understanding of policymaking, I must point out that almost all premodern thinking and writing on social affairs lacked any systematic empiric underpinning, without which they could not provide a reliable basis for descriptive generalizations, or prescriptive suggestions. One of the main tasks faced by the modern behavioral sciences is to engage in an empiric study of policymaking, and to integrate the findings of such a study with insights and abstract thought to form a comprehensive, systematic, and reliable theory of public policymaking.

This task has hardly been begun. At best, the empiric study of policymaking is just now emerging. A significant and increasing amount of work is being done on minor decisions and secondary policies, but most of it suffers from its lack of comprehensive, theoretical frameworks. Very little empiric work is being done on the macrosystem of public policymaking. At present, even suitable research methods for such a job are conspicuous by their absence.

THE PRESENT STATE OF PUBLIC-POLICYMAKING STUDY

To understand the present state of the study of public policymaking, one must consider the following points.[1]

1. Considerable empiric research and theorizing is being done on the basic components of public policymaking, namely, individual and small-group decisionmaking. Some is also being done on decisionmaking in other basic social units, such as the family.

2. Some work is being done on organizational decisionmaking, but as yet few generalized findings have emerged. Most of this empiric work is in the form of case studies. Only in one instance has a series of cases been collected within a systematic framework and in order to reach generalizations about organizational decisionmaking.[2]

3. An increasing number of studies deal with community decisions, and with single cases of public policymaking on the national level. Most of these studies are monographic, and use theoretical frameworks that do not bring out the "decision" aspects of policymaking. Some especially interesting studies are, for example, on the decision to intervene with massive force in Korea, on fluoridation, and on the Bay of Pigs invasion of Cuba.

4. Some studies of specific facets of public policymaking are available, including studies of the characteristics of some policymakers, of behavior patterns in policymaking units, and of the structuring of policymaking units.

5. With a few exceptions, most of the studies on public policymaking do not have a rigorous theoretical framework, and are not significantly related to current work in decisionmaking theory. Tentative

---

[1] Full citations illustrating and supporting these points are provided in Appendix D, Bibliographic Essay (pp. 327ff).

[2] This research was carried out in a seminar conducted by John M. Pfiffner at the University of Southern California. The method and sample cases are presented in Beatrice G. Markey and Nicholas G. Nicolaidis, *Selected Policy-Decision Cases* (Los Angeles: Univ. of Southern California Bookstore, John W. Donner Publication no. 10, 1960). The theoretical framework and generalized findings are presented in Nicholas G. Nicolaidis, *Policy-Decision and Organization Theory* (Los Angeles: Univ. of Southern California Bookstore, John W. Donner Publication no. 11, 1960). This study is concisely discussed in John M. Pfiffner, "Administrative Rationality." *Public Administration Review*, XX (1960), 125ff.

conceptual frameworks for systematic empiric study of public policymaking have been developed only recently. As yet, again with a few exceptions, these conceptual frameworks have not been systematically applied to the study of real policymaking.

6. Much interesting and significant material that is relevant to the study of public policymaking continues to appear in biographies, memoirs, journalistic descriptions, and similar literary sources. This material, which could offer very important insights and understanding, is neglected by nearly all the behavioral-science students of policymaking.

7. Almost no work is being done on analyzing and reanalyzing historical material in terms of decisionmaking concepts. This is a great pity, because both the theories of decisionmaking and policymaking and the study of history might benefit greatly from the attempt to apply decisionmaking-oriented analytical frameworks to the study of history.

8. Almost all empiric studies of public policymaking explicitly reject an orientation toward reform, since they aspire to be "value-free" and "factual-behavioral."

9. Reflecting the general situation in the behavioral sciences, most of the available studies deal with modern countries. Only a few of them focus on policymaking in the developing countries, or include material directly relevant to the study of policymaking in them.

10. Few studies have been done on high-level public-policymaking processes. Decisionmaking at the Cabinet level is almost always surrounded by secrecy, and no access to it is granted for research purposes. The most important sources of information on these critical policymaking activities are books written by insiders and occasional public hearings. Both the importance and the limitations of writings by active participants in high-level policymaking are well illustrated, for example, by the increasing number of books on the Kennedy administration by "insiders."

11. Research methods suited to studying complex phenomena, including public policymaking, are very underdeveloped. The more sophisticated tools, such as multivariable analysis, facet design, and non-metric measurement, fit complex systems in theory, but most of these tools require detailed information that will not be available in the foreseeable future. The most promising ideas for analyzing complex systems are today being developed mostly outside the main stream of the behavioral sciences, by the new interdisciplines of management science, operations research, and systems analysis. These ideas have not yet been assimilated and put to use by the behavioral sciences.

12. Integrated treatises on public policymaking as a

decisionmaking process, which could be based on what little data are available, have not been published. Only a very few attempts have been made to develop a comprehensive theory of the public-policymaking system as a decision-producing system.

THE FEATURES OF DIAGNOSIS

This not very bright picture of the state that empiric study of public policymaking is in sets some conditions on the diagnostic survey I undertake in the following chapters. Considering the dearth of relevant material and the dubious reliability of what is available on the one hand, and what I have said I want to try to do on the other, my treatment of public policymaking in this part of the book is subject to the following six restrictions:

1. I will not try to set forth a comprehensive, systematic description of real public policymaking as a whole; I will only point out those features of it that are directly relevant to analysis, evaluation, and reform.

2. Even within this limited field, the available material does not permit one to draw reliable conclusions. The degree to which I will be able to penetrate into the various aspects of public policymaking, and the significance of my findings, will depend on the rather accidental availability of relevant material.

3. My findings will be based on a survey of both "literary" and scientific literature and on my own subjective impressions. Since such findings are not susceptible to quantitative reliability tests, I will regard them as being in the range between "suggestive" and "highly probable" according to the particular kind of evidence on which each finding is based.

4. The sets of criteria and standards, and their integrated scheme, for evaluating real public policymaking that I developed at length in Part II are the framework and tools I will use for my diagnostic evaluation.

5. Basically, this diagnostic evaluation I am going to attempt is closely tied in with the optimal model I will construct in Part IV. The reader will meet some terms in practice before he learns how and from where (and why) they are derived, and what their place is in the optimal model, and so will be better prepared to understand the basic assumptions of the optimal model and the reasoning behind its details when we reach it.

6. Given my declared purpose and basic strategy in writing this book, I am not going to keep my factual findings and evaluation formally separate. I will present my findings in a concise, generalized form, without paying what would usually be the necessary amount of attention to exceptions, deviations, and subvariations. I will not try to provide a scholarly list of supporting references, nor will I go through the usual monotonous hedgings required in classical scholarly presentations.

My order of procedure will be to deal first with decisionmaking by the basic subunits of policymaking, that is, by individuals, small groups, and organizations (Chapter 8). Next I will analyze and diagnose the actual public policymaking in modern states and in developing states (Chapters 9 and 10). Finally, I will draw all my threads together in an overall evaluation, and will try to provide some exploratory explanations of the state contemporary policymaking is in (Chapter 11).

chapter 8 · Decisionmaking by Subunits

Policymaking is an aggregative process, whose quality depends significantly on the quality of the decisionmaking and subpolicymaking done by the various units that make up the public-policymaking system. These units are of three main types: individuals, small groups, and organizations. I will briefly describe the realities of decisionmaking in these basic social units, insofar as they are relevant to our concern, in this chapter as a prelude to describing public policymaking as a whole.

INDIVIDUAL DECISIONMAKING

1. The individual is often unaware of the processes (or at least of parts of them) by which he reaches his decisions. Neither current verbalization nor post-decision exploration gives much reliable information on the decisionmaking process or on its significance to the individual.

2. Nearly all decisions involve some subconscious and tacit processes; how much seems to depend on the particular decision. It seems that in most cases the more complex and creative a decision is, the more important the subconscious processes are.

3. The decisionmaking process is significantly influenced by such characteristics of the decider as his social status, sex, intelligence, education, motivations, beliefs, and degree of self-direction. These characteristics constitute most of the "pre-decision set."

4. The decisionmaking process is significantly influenced by the emotional-physical state of the decider while he makes the decisions; that is, by such things as anxiety, pain, anger, fatigue, and how involved he is in the decision.

5. The decisionmaking process is significantly influenced by such aspects of the decider's social environment as opinions expressed by friends and work-colleagues and by communication media.

6. The decisionmaking process is influenced by whether relevant data are available, but the perception of data is itself significantly shaped by the other variables, especially by the pre-decision set.

7. The decisionmaking process seems in most cases to follow the line of least resistance. Innovation and creativity seem to be rare, and are distributed unequally among individuals.

8. When making decisions, individuals almost never *spontaneously* use such elements of "rational" decisionmaking as searching widely for alternatives, elaborating operational goals, and setting down explicit expectations, or such rigorous concepts and tools of optimal decisionmaking as probabilities, logic, information search, and randomization.

9. In experimental situations in which payoff probabilities and operational goals are given explicitly as part of the problem, individual decisionmaking tends to be clearly irrational, that is, tends not to adopt the alternatives that maximize the payoff. However, many of the experiments from which these findings emerge are rather artificial game-theory situations, and the general validity and reliability of their results must be doubted.

10. Many decisions fulfill personality functions that are not directly related to the issue ostensibly to be decided. Consequently, the full significance of a decision often cannot be understood without depth analysis, and the "effectiveness" of a decision in serving such deep needs is very difficult to evaluate.

11. The quality of the decisions, all other things being equal, differs from person to person.

12. The decisionmaking process changes with time, and can to some extent be influenced (a) by establishing formal schemes for problem solving such as the military "estimation of the situation," (b) by indoctrination in terms of classifications and conceptual frameworks such as "judicial doctrines" that partly condition decisionmaking by judges, and (c) by psychotherapeutic personality development such as sensitivity sessions and T-Group experience.

Many authors go farther, and try to specify the nature of the thinking process and of its basic components by distinguishing the main stages of "problem solving." Most of these efforts follow in Dewey's footsteps, and accept in principle the distinctions between (1) feeling a difficulty; (2) locating and defining it; (3) suggesting possible solutions; (4) developing, by reasoning, the implications of the suggestions; and (5) making further observations and experiments that lead to acceptance or rejection of each suggestion. Another famous classification of the phases of thinking is by Graham Wallas, who distinguished between (1) preparation, (2) incubation, (3) illumination, and (4) verification. Despite the influence these classifications have had, they are more normative analytical models than empiric descriptions of real individual decisionmaking. More recent and ambitious work has tried to construct simulation models of individual thought, but as yet has produced no validated findings relevant to our interest beyond those enumerated above.

SMALL-GROUP DECISIONMAKING

It is very difficult to arrive at any meaningful and reliable generalizations about small-group decisionmaking. The experimental setups of most studies have been rather unique and artificial, the results contradictory, and the conclusions doubtful. Only the following five findings seem justified in their light.

1. The results of small-group decisionmaking cannot be deduced from the participants' individual characteristics alone, but are a function of both these characteristics and the group interaction process.

2. Small-group decisionmaking processes are significantly influenced by the structure and history of the group, the social relationships between the participants, the behavior of the formal and informal task- and social-leaders, the formal role-definitions of the group, and the nature of the issue to be decided (its complexity, urgency, technical features, and other specifics), as well as by other variables.

3. Participating in group decisionmaking leaves residual traces in the participants that influence both their future individual decisionmaking and their orientation toward the decisions arrived at by the group. For instance, the decisions made by the group tend to become more acceptable to them.

4. Comparing the quality of group decisions and individual decisions leads to ambiguous conclusions. For some tasks and conditions, group-decision processes yield better decisions; for others, worse decisions. The various authors and studies tend *not* to agree as to the conditions under which small-group decisions are superior (or inferior) to individual decisions. Some findings seem to indicate that when the task requires some creativity, broad information, division of labor, and reduction of random error, then groups tend to be more effective. The greater effectiveness expresses itself both in the individual productivity

of group members and in an "assembly product," that is, a group product that could not have been achieved by any member working alone or by a "synthetic group" (a total of the outputs of all the group members working as separate individuals).[1]

5. Small-group decisionmaking can be improved by preparing background material, carefully selecting the group members and discussion leaders, manipulating the interaction pattern, and shaping the "group climate" in general.

ORGANIZATIONAL DECISIONMAKING

Findings become more complex (and more important for our subject) when we reach the level of organizational decisionmaking, perhaps because the variety of organizational situations makes valid generalizations about them nearly impossible. Organizational decisions are the most important element in public policymaking; it is all the more regrettable that reliable findings and tested suggestions for improvement are very few indeed. The available material does permit some tentative and suggestive findings that, despite their vagueness, are striking in their significance:

1. Organizational decisionmaking processes are in most cases not structured by formal rules and doctrines, except for a few dealing with such specific facets as data processing and communication channels.

2. Insofar as there are official rules or verbally accepted organizational opinions on the way in which decisions should be made, these are in most cases a myth; decisions are really made by means of channels and patterns other than the official or verbally accepted ones.

3. In general, most officials do not consciously know how decisions are made or what the forces shaping them are, but the more sophisticated officials have a tacit feeling for these processes, and the more successful of these are able to manipulate these processes to a significant degree.

4. Organizational decisionmaking is partly structured by traditions, power relations, formal division of work, and so on. In other words, despite characteristics 1, 2, and 3, organizational decisionmaking is not the result of random phenomena, but follows semistructured, though mainly informal, channels and modes.

---

[1] The terminology follows Barry E. Collins and Harold Guetzkow, *A Social Psychology of Group Processes for Decisionmaking* (N.Y.: John Wiley, 1964), esp. pp. 24 and 58.

5. Organizational decisions are formed by a large variety of subdecisions made at differing locations in the organization. These subdecisions make different contributions to the decisionmaking process, such as types of expertise, values, and subjective probabilities. ("Subjective probability" is the probability for different payoffs as seen by various persons, whereas the "objective probability" might be very different.)

6. The influence that each subdecision unit has on the organizational decision is determined by such variables as the unit's relative power, the image of the issue (for example, if it is regarded as an engineering matter, the engineering division will have dominant influence), the effectiveness of communication between the units and of central control units, and the units' image of their interest and involvement in the decision.

7. The decisionmaking process includes much bargaining and coalition formation, in which exchanges of favors, power calculations, personal relations, and similar variables are often the most important influence.

8. Organizational decisionmaking usually proceeds without clear operational goals, with little data, and with very limited search for alternatives. Insofar as special units for decision techniques, operations research, and systems analysis are set up, they apparently (to judge from the very little available material) tend in the large majority of cases to deal with secondary issues, not with the main policymaking issues.

9. Organizational decisionmaking tends to follow the line of least resistance, innovation and originality being rather scarce. The quality of decisions does not in most cases reach a quality higher than "satisfactory."

10. Decisionmaking resources are concentrated on acute and pressing issues. Long-term considerations are neglected, unless specialized units are in charge of looking after them (and often are neglected even when there are such units).

11. Organizational decisionmaking tends to try to minimize risks and achieve defensibility. Except in young "crusading organizations," organizational decisionmaking tends to follow precedent and to adopt implicitly the strategy of incremental change (which is more fully discussed in Chapter 12).

12. There seem to be strong biases against uncertainty and ambiguity. Decisionmaking therefore tends to demand clear-cut subjective expectations, which provide a much more secure and certain view of the world than is justified by objective expectations.

13. Decisionmaking in organizations that survive is adaptive,

adjusting itself slowly to new needs and technologies, and to the feedback of its activities. These adjustments have an uneven rhythm, and are snail-paced most of the time. In most cases, only a shock such as perceiving an imminent crisis or catastrophe seems to lead to far-reaching reform. Other variables that have some effect on the rate of adaptivity and innovation include external pressure, the traditions and values of the organization itself, the drives and personalities of the organization's higher officials, and the presence of special units that have a vested interest in change.

These are the findings that emerge from the available behavioral studies of organizational behavior, but they seem to me rather one-sided. They ignore that the crusading spirit and immense success of many public and private organizations testify to the strength of these organizations' devotion to organizational goals and to the high quality of the decisionmaking directed toward achieving them. The preoccupations and methodologies of modern research on organizations seem to make for unduly pessimistic evaluations of organizational decisionmaking, even while they underestimate the more "idealistic" countervailing forces within decisionmaking processes. Similarly, the high quality of many "intuitive" phases of decisionmaking is also neglected by modern research methods, which often cannot deal with extrarational phenomena. Most studies have been carried out on "execution" organizations, there being available as yet very little significant material on either "creative" or "thinking" organizations, such as research units, planning units, universities, television and radio networks, movie studios, publishing houses, and advertising agencies. Also, most studies have focused on the lower or middle echelons, while the higher echelons, where the more important decisions are made, have generally escaped their scrutiny.

Despite these and other shortcomings in behavioral studies of organizational decisionmaking, their general findings that organizational decisionmaking is often (though by no means always) rather poor seem to be well supported, not only by the empiric studies, but also by the observations of the few participants who have analyzed their own experience. This poor quality does not contradict those who hold, like Max Weber, that organizations are the social units with the best decisionmaking. Relatively speaking, this seems to be true; individuals and less-structured social units, for many (but not all) types of tasks, make decisions more poorly, since they do not enjoy the advantages of extensive division of labor and specialization.

The above findings on decisionmaking by the subunits of public policymaking are relevant to evaluating public policymaking as an integrated and aggregative process, but they do not determine what conclusion that evaluation will reach. The aggregative characteristics of public policymaking are not a simple sum of the characteristics of the subunits' decisionmaking. Public policymaking has system properties conditioned by, but different from, those of its component units.

With this reservation in mind, the characteristics of the subunits' decisionmaking are among the main variables shaping the public-policymaking process as a whole. The findings on decisionmaking by individuals, small groups, and, in particular, organizations, give one reason to suspect that present public policymaking is very far from being as good as it could be. This suspicion will become certainty when we examine the realities of public policymaking as a systems process in the following chapters.

chapter 9 · Public Policymaking in Modern States

In evaluating public policymaking in modern states, we must guard against two a priori biases: one is toward being hypercritical, and regarding human history as an unbroken series of mistakes and inadequacies; the other is toward being complacent, and regarding human history as a rather successful "muddling through."[1] The only way we can escape such generalizations, and replace them by findings more concrete and more useful for our purposes, is by breaking public policymaking down into its main components, and dealing with these in terms of explicit criteria and standards. Thanks to the integrated evaluation scheme developed in Part II (and the optimal model), we can do so, using the criteria and standards presented there to try to pin down some main characteristics of real public policymaking in modern states. Of course, trying to do this job, given the present state of empiric knowledge, must be of doubtful validity. Also, to compress the relevant findings into a few pages, I must indulge in much overgeneralization, neglecting differences between various countries and skipping over the finer nuances of the investigated phenomena. But since I am interested in overall diagnosis as a basis for analysis and therapy, I prefer to deal in bold outline with the main gestalt of public policymaking, rather than lose the overall view in a wealth of secondary details.

In this chapter, I shall follow the integrated scheme developed in Part

---

[1] This is an interesting term; as Ramsay Muir, one of its early users, pointed out, it has the positive connotation "that in the end we *do* muddle through." See Ramsay Muir, *Peers and Bureaucrats* (London: Constable, 1910), p. 4; emphasis is in the original. The depressing effects that such expected and desired qualities must have on actual public policymaking are obvious.

II, first ascertaining the actual quality of policymaking by means of the criteria, and then appraising the ascertained quality by means of the standards. I will refer to the various criteria and standards by the numbers given to them in Tables 1–3, so as to permit easy cross-reference.

ASCERTAINING THE ACTUAL QUALITY IN TERMS OF THE PRIMARY CRITERION

Available material and methods do not permit one to directly estimate the net probable real output in enough cases to generalize from. Therefore, we must rely on secondary criteria to ascertain the actual (present and predicted future) quality of public policymaking.

ASCERTAINING THE ACTUAL QUALITY IN TERMS OF THE SECONDARY CRITERIA

A. Criteria Based on Process Patterns

1. Contemporary public policymaking as a whole, and most of its aspects and components in particular, are the result of historical evolution as tempered by conscious renovations that have been, in most cases, improvisations directed at imminent crises and/or reforms that followed crises or radical changes in the political order or the social values. All in all, systematic efforts to improve public policymaking have been shallow and ineffectual, though these efforts are now growing in importance and their effects are beginning to add up to a significant total effect. In respect to some components, especially the civil service, a number of significant, though insufficient, reforms have taken place from time to time.

2. Systematic institutional arrangements for learning feedback are all but absent. Some learning takes place by trial and error, but, in general, such learning is sporadic and slow. Recently, learning has been somewhat better in a few fields to which special attention is devoted, especially in crisis management.

3. There is very little explicit and conscious determination of policy strategy. What little there is mostly concerns military policy, and a few other issues about which there is a strong demand for an explicit strategy (e.g., the demand for more innovation in dealing with segregation in the U.S.A.). In most democratic countries, public policymaking tends to follow an implicit strategy aimed at maximum security, so

that "daring" action is often condemned as "brinkmanship." Since democratic countries lack militant ideological goals, and since their populations are generally satisfied with their actual achievements, incremental change is their favorite method for public action, unless they are challenged by competition from the ideological dictatorships, by novel problems, by dramatic new opportunities, or by some crisis. Dictatorial countries tend to be adventurous during their ideological periods, but when they settle down, they tend to adopt policy strategies aimed at security and not to innovate as much.

4. There are many differences between different societies, and between different policy issues within any one society, in the degree to which operational goals are elaborated. In most cases, such elaboration is tied in with "planning"; insofar as planning is a programmed organizational activity, it tends to define its operational goals. This is true for all types of planning, including: national economic planning, as in France and the U.S.S.R.; physical planning, as in the Netherlands; town planning, as in most modern countries; administrative annual and multiyear programming (generally associated with "program budgeting") and project planning, as in different government departments in the U.S.A. and other countries. Besides such islands of elaboration, there is the sea of policy issues that lack even middle-range operational goals. Policymaking is shaped in many cases by non-operational values, by generalized abstract goals, and by pragmatic considerations that have no "goal" element (other than to survive and "to carry on").

5. Most public policymaking tends to follow the line of least resistance, and to limit searching for alternatives to finding one of "satisfactory quality." Creativity, imagination, and innovation in policies are generally rare, and are called up only by some new challenge, such as a technological innovation or crisis. It seems clear that the external pressures imposed by acute problems, rather than any self-motivation, have been the main cause of innovation in public policymaking. A militant ideology can sometimes be such a stimulus, leading to much innovation of often doubtful quality and high risks.

6. In most public policymaking, only implicit cutoff horizons are established, and these are in general very narrow and exclude almost all but the more immediate and obvious results. Policymakers particularly tend to ignore both long-term results and spillover effects in spheres of social action other than the one at which the policy is explicitly directed. Some exceptions to this generalization are caused by public pressure (as for timber conservation in the United States), by relying on systematic knowledge (as for some economic activities that are based on advanced economic theory), and by the obviousness of some long-range and spillover effects (such as those caused by building hydraulic works).

These exceptions are important as far as they go, but they cover only a few cases of policymaking.

7. Rational components are dispersed throughout the policy-making process. They are relatively more developed for issues on which policymaking is professionalized and on which internal or external demands and competition press for improvements in quality (this is true, e.g., for parts of military policymaking), but for the policymaking process as a whole, rational components are few and play a minor role.

The use of knowledge, as a main rational component, takes a number of forms. Technical and scientific knowledge is significantly autonomous in its own sphere, but is hard to integrate into general policymaking because of communication barriers. Politicians and civil servants, unable to judge the merits of scientific issues, must often decide, on the basis of personal impressions and a priori bias, between different schools of scientists. This problem is coming to be recognized, and various special structural arrangements are being developed to solve it, at least partly. Economic theory is used rather widely, often by means of special planning and advisory units, but the other social sciences are regarded as marginal, and very little is being done to integrate them into policymaking. Modern systems approaches, simulation techniques, decision sciences, and the like are used a little for military and macro-economic policymaking, but are otherwise unknown and ignored (with some recent exceptions, such as the efforts to introduce some systems analysis into U.S. federal administration). It is particularly unfortunate that no real efforts are being made to put them to good use in the critical metapolicymaking phases.

8. Extrarational components play a tremendous role in public policymaking in all modern states. Some regimes explicitly regard intuition as superior to knowledge, as the Nazi and Fascist *Führer* ideologies did. All regimes, including democratic ones, largely depend on the extrarational processes of senior policymakers. The criteria for recruiting and promoting policymakers in most societies assure, in fact, a rather high level of spontaneous extrarational capacity based on much experience. However, rational action to stimulate and encourage extrarational processes is almost never engaged in.

B. Criteria Based on Output

1. The characteristics of the nominal output of policymaking—that is, of the "policies" as such—are not a very valid indicator of the quality of policymaking, as I explained in Chapter 4. Nevertheless, it is worthwhile to point out that policies in modern

countries tend to be quite inconsistent and incompatible with other policies, and non-comprehensive in scope, though perhaps they must be so because modern societies are so complex and heterogeneous. Also, democratic ideology holds that some inconsistency or limited scope in policymaking helps prevent monopolization of power. Furthermore, such policymaking is believed to be technically preferable because it takes advantage of suboptimization and reduces the risk that single mistakes could disrupt the system. However, the degrees to which policies are uncoordinated and do not cover important issues go far beyond what is unavoidable or desirable, and are instead to a significant extent a function of the weakness of mechanisms for integrating policy, of the lack of central units to oversee policies, of not using overall systems analysis, and of similar failings that are neither unavoidable nor required by democratic ideology.

2. In western democratic countries, policies are usually "realistic" in that they are economically and politically feasible. In some respects, feasibility is perhaps even over-emphasized; policies are sometimes based on over-strict interpretations of "the stubborn facts of reality" that strengthen the bias toward incremental change and against innovation. There are issues on which non-realistic values are intensely supported, and which sometimes lead to infeasible policies, such as some directed at strengthening small farmers in some European countries. Such exceptions become the rule in ideologically non-democratic societies, for instance, the modern Communist states. Driven by ideological beliefs, these countries have a strong bias toward policies, especially about economic development, that cannot be put into practice.

I may tentatively conclude that some countries tend to make policies which are often not imaginative enough, while other countries tend to make policies that are not realistic enough. Only in a few cases do policies seem to achieve the desired combination of "realistic idealism."

3. Available material and methods do not permit one to directly ascertain the probable real output in enough cases to generalize from.

C. Criteria Based on Structure

1. In most countries, there are some units charged with looking after micro-aspects of the government organization, e.g., the Organization and Methods Division of the Treasury in England. In some countries such units also penetrate into major policymaking structures in the government, e.g., the Bureau of the Budget in the U.S.A., and the Central Office for Organizational Problems of the Federal Government

in Switzerland. In many countries, some sections of the policymaking structure are reexamined from time to time by special governmental or public ad hoc bodies, such as the First and Second Hoover Commissions in the U.S.A. and the Glasgow Committee in Canada. Such structure-evaluating bodies are very useful, but they are isolated and of limited coverage and penetration. In no modern country is there a specific unit in charge of systematically and periodically evaluating and redesigning major parts of the policymaking structure.

2. Few units are explicitly established for thinking, doing long-range policymaking, surveying knowledge, and handling research and development about policymaking. A few such units have been set up, especially after World War II, to deal with policymaking about military, economic, and scientific issues. The military was the first type of governmental organization to establish such units, beginning with the Prussian General Staff. The Central Planning Bureau in the Netherlands and the Office of Science and Technology in the United States are also such units.

A number of semi-independent and non-governmental units, such as the RAND Corporation and Resources for the Future, Inc., in the United States, fulfill a similar function, as do a number of university departments. Also, within some organizations, there are staff units in charge of thinking, long-range policymaking, etc., though there is always strong pressure for such units to "climb down from Olympus," become involved in current problems, and thus lose their specific function. Despite these exceptions, the dearth of developed machinery for carrying out these long-term thinking functions is striking in, apparently, all modern countries.

3. Most modern countries seem to have little difficulty in maintaining a reasonable distance between the units that make policy, those that execute it, and those that motivate the executing of it. The major exception has been during some periods in Soviet planning when there was too wide a gulf between policymaking and policy-executing units. There have been similar gulfs, though on a much smaller scale, in western democratic countries, for instance, between the National Resources Planning Board and the United States Congress, and between some of the new town-planning units and the policy-executing units in England. But, in general, this secondary criterion seems to uncover no critical impairments of central policymaking.

4. The characteristics, roles, and contributions of the different major units that make up the policymaking structure are central to determining and indicating the quality of policymaking, and must therefore be examined in some detail. The policymaking quality of each of the

major policymaking units for each of the different criteria is outlined concisely in Tables 1 and 2 (pp. 307 and 308). For now, I will make a few comments on some of the central features of these major units in modern countries.

In general, one similarity between the public-policymaking structures of all modern societies is the central role of the "executive," which is composed of the high-level politicians who constitute the cabinet (or, in some dictatorial countries, the highest organ of the state party) and of the top civil servants who occupy the higher levels of the government bureaucracy. Also, in all modern countries, interest groups play an important role in public policymaking. The main difference between the public-policymaking processes in democratic and dictatorial countries is that private individuals and elected legislatures play a bigger role in the democratic countries. Although the results of this difference are important, they do not make for radical differences in the structures and process patterns of public policymaking. (Of course, the content of public policy is very different in the two types of systems because of different values and goals, but this is another matter.) There are also many differences between democratic countries in the details of the public-policymaking systems; compare the policymaking structures of the United States, Great Britain, the Netherlands, and Switzerland, all fully democratic countries. Even among the rather more homogeneous modern Communist states, there are very important differences between policymaking systems; compare those of the U.S.S.R., Poland, Bulgaria, and Yugoslavia.

Having made a few points about the major policymaking units as a group, let me now discuss them one by one.

a. In democratic countries, the private individual has more opportunity to shape public policy, since as a voter he can, in the aggregate, critically influence the careers of politicians. In particular, the voter exerts influence by choosing between the different general tendencies and "styles" of the competing parties and candidates. The specific contribution of free voters to public policymaking is that they increase the influence of popularly held values, interests, and opinions, which tend in most countries to be inconsistent, contrary to fact, and of very short range, but which also include a feeling for "where the shoe pinches," and (in some, but not all, democratic countries[2]) a deep devotion to liberty, freedom, and democracy.

---

[2] The belief that people always want democracy, freedom, and liberty when they are free to choose seems to be one of the most deeply rooted images of public opinion (and is shared by many policymakers) in the United States. The

In all modern societies, the individual is subjected to communications that are intended to influence his political activity, and that differ widely in the degrees to which they appeal to reason or to emotion; factual information and brain-washing illustrate the extremes. Democratic ideology emphasizes the need for appeals to reason, but both mass society and the increasingly more effective "engineering of consent" techniques tend to produce apathy and/or emotional politics, both of which make reason less important in what private individuals contribute to policymaking. A higher average educational level may somewhat offset this tendency, or perhaps even reverse it, but then again it may not. (As Toynbee, for one, points out, a major effect of the introduction of compulsory education in nineteenth-century England was the creation of "yellow" journalism. A similar trend might be indicated by the relative popularity of various television programs, despite constant upgrading of educational standards. But perhaps the "critical mass" needed for education to be effective has not yet been reached.)

Decisions by individuals have all the general characteristics of individual decisionmaking that were outlined in Chapter 8. It would be especially significant to know what personality needs of the particular individuals involved are satisfied by taking an active role in policymaking. Despite some most interesting hypotheses, nothing definitive is known about the personality functions involved in political activity.[3]

b. The intellectual fulfills a special role in public policymaking. In democratic countries he has more opportunity than professional policymakers have to contribute new ideas to public policymaking, since he is less restricted by political and ideological barriers. The important contributions of individuals to policymaking are well illustrated by the impact of Rachel Carson, author of *Silent Spring,* on the control of pesticides, and of Ralph Nader, author of *Unsafe at Any Speed,* on car-safety laws. Universities are especially important in this area insofar as they provide conditions that encourage serious thinking by freeing it from acute pressures. Insofar as intellectuals do propose new alternatives for policies and do engage in long-range thinking about social problems, they help compensate for the narrowness of the policymaking process in political and administrative units. However, the degree to which intellec-

---

experience of the Weimar Republic and, to some extent, of France, does not bear this belief out. See also Erich Fromm, *Escape from Freedom* (N.Y.: Rinehart, 1941).

[3] For some especially interesting hypotheses, see Harold D. Lasswell, *Psychopathology and Politics* (N.Y.: Viking, 1960). For a summary of available ideas and material, see Robert E. Lane, *Political Life* (N.Y.: Free Press of Glencoe, 1959), Chaps. 8 and 9.

tuals participate in policymaking in these ways depends on such variables as how much they are oriented toward policy problems, how much access they have to policymakers, how much prestige and power they enjoy, and how disposed the central political and administrative units are toward innovation.

The increasing complexity of policymaking issues, the alienation of many intellectuals from public affairs, social pressures for conformity, and the internal characteristics of many academic professions combine to limit intellectuals' contributions to innovation in public policymaking in most modern societies. This decrease is partly offset by institutionalizing such semi-autonomous "intellectual thinking units" as the RAND Corporation, the Council of Economic Advisers, or the Stanford Research Institute, and by employing more professionals in the central policymaking organizations. Under some conditions the role of a few selected intellectuals increases significantly, as happened in the Kennedy administration.

c. Central individuals in executive policymaking and, *mutatis mutandis,* in other policymaking units are particularly important. Nearly all modern countries have their central policymaking system headed by one person (Prime Minister, President, Chancellor, Secretary of the Party, etc.) who has great influence in most democratic countries and often overwhelming influence in dictatorial countries. Although the role of such individuals should not be exaggerated, a quick look at the contemporary international scene will illustrate how important their role is. Their influence is circumscribed by the limits on policymaking set by the facts the policy must deal with and by the power and interests of other persons and policymaking units. Nevertheless, such persons greatly influence not only policymaking in discrete cases, but also the general style of policymaking and metapolicymaking. The personal qualities of such leaders and their working methods are therefore important determinants of public policymaking. The same is true, on a smaller scale, for the second and third tiers of policymakers.

The screening mechanisms that condition advancement into the highest policymaking positions should be noted here. For the main political positions, the most important screening device is competition to gain support by voters and/or power centers, which puts a premium on the individual's abilities to get votes and/or build coalitions. These abilities depend largely on extrarational processes, though rational components are coming to play an increasing (and marginally very important) role in how these abilities can be best used, especially in mass societies, where techniques for engineering consent are becoming as important as natural charisma. One characteristic that very successful politicians seem to share is a highly developed political instinct that is accompanied by strong self-confidence in their own judgment and intuition. Different leaders dampen their tendency to rely too much on their own extrarational capabilities, by integrating them with rational techniques, to different degrees. In most modern countries, there are strong institutional pressures for them to do so, but the central leaders still enjoy considerable freedom to determine their own unique styles of operation.

d. Legislative bodies in dictatorial countries tend to contribute almost nothing to public policymaking. In democratic states they contribute much more, but how much varies from country to country, and tends to be relatively smaller for cabinet-parliamentary systems (like Great Britain's) than for a system of checks and balances between President and legislature (like that of the United States). Despite the many differences between democratic states, their elected legislatures seem to contribute to policymaking more or less as follows:

First, the legislator influences policymaking largely in terms of his "anticipated reaction"; that is, the expected reaction of the legislature is one of the key factors that the executive takes into account when he is considering alternative policies, particularly when the legislature must provide some of the motivation and support for executing the policy. As a result, legislatures restrain policymaking more than they initiate it.

Second, the main contributions by legislatures to public policymaking in democratic countries seem to be (a) their high sensitivity to the opinions of the various "publics" that have access to the political arena; (b) their protection of contextual goals and values; (c) their highly developed intuition for "the art of the possible"; and (d) their being a main channel (and location) for bargaining and coalition building. Legislatures operate mostly by extrarational processes, and make little use of scientific knowledge and rational techniques, aside from what is supplied in this line by the executive. The U.S. Congress relies more on its own professional staff than do legislatures in other modern countries, which often operate without having any professional staff of their own.

Third, legislatures in democratic countries often develop very high-quality extrarational capacities and acquire a vast store of pragmatic knowledge, especially when there is both considerable continuity in the body's membership and periodic screening of the members by competitive elections. The U.S. Senate is a good illustration of such a body.

e–f. The two most important policymaking units are the political executive and the government bureaucracy. Their policymaking roles are highly integrated, so that it is more convenient to discuss them together. Because their role in public policymaking is so central, I discuss their characteristics as policymaking units, as well as ways to improve the bureaucracy, at several opportune points later on, and can therefore limit myself for now to a few very general observations.

In all modern societies, both the relative influence and the absolute influence of the political executive and the government bureaucracy as an integrated structure are increasing, mainly because there are so many complex issues, because the policymaking by specialized organizations is getting relatively better, and because certain characteristics of modern mass societies and communication media tend to force such an increase.

In all modern societies, there is some (and often a very clear) differentiation between "politicians" and "civil servants." The earmarks of the civil service (the "merit system" and the "career service" pattern) hold for most modern states. In dictatorial countries, the situation is more complex, because some functions of the party bureaucracy overlap and compete with functions of the government bureaucracy.

The political executive and the government bureaucracy (and sometimes the party bureaucracy in single-party states) form a symbiosis whose details depend on the particular country and period. The executive may control the operations of the bureaucracy very closely; the bureaucracy may enjoy extensive de facto and even de jure (e.g., in Sweden) autonomy from the executive. The general tendency is toward the bureaucracy's becoming more influential for most policy issues, because the issues are becoming increasingly complex and because government tends to depend more and more on organizational decisionmaking processes. At the same time, the political executive's authority over issues regarded as "highly political" is not impaired. Also, the personal style of central political leaders has a widespread effect on the operational patterns of the bureaucracy. It may well be that the much-improved central-control methods are increasing national political leaders' influence on the operation of government bureaucracy, despite many predictions to the contrary.

Finally, both the policymaking processes of government bureaucracy and what they contribute to inter-unit policymaking have most of the features of organizational decisionmaking discussed in Chapter 8. (For further details, see Tables 1 and 2, pp. 307 and 308.)

g. The courts' role in public policymaking is minor, except for the judicial review of the constitutionality of legislation that is institutionalized in some countries. The courts that have the most far-reaching public-policymaking functions are those (especially the Supreme Court) in the United States. Some policymaking functions are also carried out by special administrative courts when they enjoy extensive authority over the government bureaucracy; the best example of such courts is the Council of State in France. In England the courts nowadays play no very important role in public policymaking.

The decisionmaking processes of courts differ in many ways from those of most other policymaking units and from most behavioral models of decisionmaking. The most important differences are that courts have available in general only a few pre-defined, dichotomous alternatives (such as "guilty" or "not guilty"); are under pressure to make their decisions unambiguous (one side wins, the other loses); must observe highly artificial limits in their search for facts (stipulation by parties, doctrine of judicial notice, rigorous rules of evidence); and are oriented toward applying given rules rather than maximizing payoffs. This is an interesting subject, and more attention should be paid to it by the decision sciences, but it would lead me too far away from my central concerns.

h. Parties play in all modern countries a central role in public policymaking, but their roles vary so much that one can hardly generalize from them. There are extreme differences between the role of parties in dictatorial, single-party states (in which the party bureaucracy is in effect a central part of the governmental structure) and that of parties in democratic states. Within democratic states, there are extensive differences between two-party and multi-party systems, and between different types of parties (mass party, ideological-elite party, religious party, and so on). Within dictatorial states, there are also such differences, as between the Fascist, Communist, and Nazi parties, though the fact that these are all the single legal party leads to some similarities in their policymaking roles.

For our purposes, the following few generalizations will supplement Tables 1 and 2 without presuming to exhaust a very complex, dynamic, and heterogeneous subject.

In democratic countries, the function of parties as a major mediator between the voters and the government tends to make their contribution to policymaking that of a sensitivity to public opinion. Large parties tend to become highly bureaucratized, so that their decisionmaking processes have the general features of organizational decisionmaking discussed in Chapter 8. There have been some very interesting efforts to prevent such bureaucratization, by setting up special inner-party cadres that are expected to preserve certain unique characteristics of the party's contribution to policymaking (e.g., the S.S. in the Nazi party was expected to make "ideologically pure" contributions to policy). In modern states, such efforts seem to have failed almost universally, perhaps because they contradict basic inherent organizational and rational features of all modern societies. The Hitler regime was the most recent attempt in a modern country, and even during the short life of Nazi Germany, many internal strains and contradictions developed, which, some people think, indicate that a modern technological society cannot be combined with a Nazi-type "culture" and policymaking structure. However, the available evidence is inconclusive on this point.

Some parties operate mainly as narrow interest groups; all parties operate to some extent as interest groups. Most parties have highly developed extrarational (but not rational) components. In some countries, including the U.S.A., there is a strong tendency for parties to use more and more knowledge about voting behavior and opinion formation as a tool to achieve one of their main goals: to increase their power.

   i. While I was discussing the role of intellectuals in policymaking, I mentioned universities and the peculiar characteristics of what they do or could contribute to policymaking. It is interesting to note how varied different countries are in how much universities do contribute to public policymaking by policy-oriented thought, research, and training. In most European countries they contribute little. In the U.S.S.R. more contributions to policy come from the "higher research institutes" than from the regular universities; in the United States universities seem to be relatively more oriented toward policy issues, and to contribute more to policymaking, than they do in other countries.

   j. Interest groups play a very important role in public policymaking in all countries. Dictatorial and democratic countries differ in how the interest groups are constituted and in how legitimate they are, but not in how important they are. The contributions of most interest groups are rather narrow, being conditioned by and oriented toward a few values and targets that each interest group tries to establish as part of the operational goals and decision criteria of public policymaking. Interest groups also contribute information and alternatives that support their respective interests; these data are a meaningful part of the knowledge put into public policymaking.

The relative power of interest groups is determined by such factors as how large the available resources are, how much access the group has to policymakers, how organized the group is, and how involved the group feels in the outcome of concrete policy issues. Diffuse interests that are shared by many people are usually not expressed by effective interest groups; consider the absence or weakness of consumer groups in modern societies.

Not all social interests are represented by interest groups, whose relative strengths may have little to do with the merits of their case for the society as a whole. Interest groups thus introduce distortions into public policymaking, although these distortions can be restrained by the multiplicity of opposing interest groups, by the autonomy of policymaking units, and by legislation (e.g., that regulating lobbying in the U.S.A.). The official public-policymaking units in all modern societies enjoy much autonomy in their policymaking, though they are significantly influenced by interest groups. How autonomous they are depends on the particular society and on the particular policy issues.

5. The last secondary criterion based on structure is the overall aggregation function. It is mixed; its main patterns include hierarchic suboptimization in the government bureaucracy, inter- and intra-unit bargaining, and certain quasi-market patterns among the individual voters. (These concepts will be discussed in detail in Chapter 15.) Bargaining seems to be the most important inter-unit pattern, and it leads in general to compromise policies, "muddling through," a tendency to minimize risks, incremental change, and achievements of satisfactory quality.[4]

That there are many disturbances and much waste of resources in the operation of the public-policymaking structure has been shown by nearly every study in depth of a case of public policymaking. Much of these redundancies and frictions seem to have a positive overall effect insofar as they reduce mistakes, protect values, and put suboptimization and inter-unit competition to good use. For instance, this is true for many check-and-balance mechanisms. Nevertheless, the public-policymaking process seems to waste many valuable resources in all societies.

D. Criteria Based on Input

1. One can distinguish between two major occupations of the manpower input: politics and civil service. How differentiated these two policymaking occupations are, and how much turnover there is in them,

---

[4] One of the more perceptive analyses of American politics sums up the consequences of bargaining as a means for arriving at public policies, as follows:

1. Public policies are seldom purely intellectual creations based on tidy, logically consistent, and empirically derived generalizations.

2. Public policies tend to be empirical and pragmatic rather than messianic and universalistic.

3. Policy alternatives, if there are any, are not likely to be very divergent.

4. Bargainers frequently become more concerned with minimizing their budgets than with maximizing their abilities to achieve their goals.

See William C. Mitchell, *The American Polity: A Social and Cultural Interpretation* (N.Y.: Free Press of Glencoe, 1962), pp. 297ff.

depend on the country. They are more integrated in some of the dictatorial countries, and more segregated in most of the democratic countries; the U.S.S.R. and Great Britain are near the two extremes. In most modern countries they are generally rather distinct. The quality of the manpower going into both occupations also depends on characteristics of the particular society, mainly on how much prestige and income the policymaking occupations and vocations bring with them, on what the public image of these jobs is, and on how men are recruited for them. For instance, the British Higher Civil Service seems to attract relatively more high-quality manpower than parallel levels of the federal civil service in the United States.

In the democratic countries, the only conscious efforts to make the policymaking occupations more attractive have been, usually, to pay civil servants a little more. Only such special crises as war have led to wholesale transfers of manpower into the making and executing of policy. Most dictatorial countries try to draw high-quality candidates into political activities by systematic training of cadres, but democratic ideology does not consider entry into political activity a legitimate area for social planning and direction, except for the basic rules about the operation of the electoral mechanism. Special training for politicians in democratic countries, beyond on-the-job learning, is almost unknown.[5]

For higher civil servants, there are educational entrance qualifications, as well as some post-entry training. These qualifications are usually either narrowly professional or very general, and are almost nowhere oriented toward policy knowledge. Proposals to set up "policy colleges" and to provide senior civil servants with broad backgrounds by means of rotation, sabbaticals, and the like have been regularly made and almost as regularly rejected. Among the few exceptions have been special National Defense Colleges in some countries (such as Canada and France); provisions enabling a few senior officials to attend a university (for instance, in the U.S.A.); and the unique Ecole Nationale d'Administration in France.

2. The amount of knowledge and information put into public policymaking is large, and is often more than the policymaking structure can absorb, but inputs of many types of information and knowledge, especially of social-science and decision-sciences knowledge, are generally conspicuous by their absence. Indeed, their scarcity is particularly striking compared with the tremendous increase in the input of natural-

---

[5] The main exceptions are schools run by labor parties for political cadres; these are made necessary by the low educational level of many trade-union and labor-party activists. The Russell College in Great Britain is such a school.

science knowledge that has taken place (mainly after World War II). In most modern countries, special bodies have been established to assure extensive input of natural-science knowledge into public policymaking; these are usually special agencies and ministries in charge of looking after the input of this type of information and knowledge. There have been no parallel arrangements made to encourage an input of social-science and decision-sciences knowledge. There are a few exceptions, especially for economic theory, but they are so narrow they do not change the overall picture.

3. The available material shows no scarcity of inputs of equipment. In general, it seems that what limits the use of modern data-processing equipment is the dearth of qualified manpower, rather than of equipment. In some cases, the input of heavy computers seems larger than can be absorbed, but this phenomenon may well be transitory.

4. Energy and drive are very elusive, and can therefore be identified and measured (even by guess) as an input only with great difficulty. There seem to be tremendous differences between different countries, and between different periods in the same country, in how much energy and drive goes into policymaking. War and other crises mobilize energy and drive, whereas balanced progress seems to stifle them.[6] Similarly, a strongly held ideology mobilizes energy and drive that are often unavailable in affluent societies except when they are drawn out by crisis or strong leadership—the latter being a very important variable, and not subject to conscious social direction.

One important conclusion that can be drawn from the available material is that the energy and drive needed to improve policymaking are in general scarce unless people believe a crisis exists. This is a major reason why there has been so little change in the public-policymaking machinery in most modern countries despite the accelerating transformations in policy issues, in social environment, and in the availability of policy knowledge.

All in all, input into public policymaking tends to be strictly limited, and is determined rather haphazardly. Although many countries are paying more and more attention to allocating their resources to substantive operations, and have introduced various techniques, such as performance budgeting, for that purpose, they still often consider policymaking a type of "overhead cost" or "administrative expense," and so

---

[6] Albert Hirschman's suggestion, which is very important for policymaking, that *unbalanced* economic growth may be optimal, can be justified by such an assumption. See Albert Hirschman, *The Strategy of Economic Development* (New Haven: Yale Univ. Press, 1958).

tend to try to save money by cutting down on this expense. This tendency is reinforced by the fact that no measurable, or at least obvious, changes in output are caused by cuts in policymaking expenses. This situation makes input into policymaking a favorite target for the axe of budget examiners, narrow-minded efficiency experts, and appropriation committees.

More specifically, most public-policymaking systems seem to lack the following inputs: resources (a) for policy research; (b) for comprehensive collecting, storing, and retrieving of policy information; (c) for thinking units; and (d) for policy training. Units that enjoy budgetary autonomy can somewhat overcome these shortages if they want to, but they are under almost no external pressure to do so, and are in most cases not aware that these shortages exist.

APPRAISING THE ACTUAL QUALITY BY MEANS OF THE STANDARDS

When we apply the seven standards elaborated in Chapter 6 to the actual quality of public policymaking in modern countries that has been ascertained by the secondary criteria, the following picture emerges.

1. Compared with the past, public policymaking in all modern states is continually improving. Among the most important advances are that the professional civil service is becoming a major contributing unit to public policymaking, that the role of knowledge and information is growing (in particular, knowledge of the natural sciences), that better structures are being set up, and that the use of data-processing equipment is increasing.

2. The qualities of public policymaking in different modern states cannot be very well compared, because there are so many variables involved and because no relevant research has focused on this problem.[7] The major relevant variables are the scope and objectives of public policymaking, the input into it, and the value environment it works in. The available facts, especially on the Nazi regime, show clearly that dictatorial states have no advantage over democratic states and are unable to make public policy of better technical quality. Insofar as any general differences between democratic and dictatorial states can be

---

[7] For a proposal about how decisionmaking and policymaking might profitably be compared internationally, see Roy C. Macridis, *The Study of Comparative Government* (N.Y.: Random House, 1955), pp. 37ff. As of 1967 few such studies have been published, one of the exceptions being Zbigniew Brzezinski and Samuel P. Huntington, *Political Power: USA/USSR* (N.Y.: Viking, 1964).

identified, democratic states seem to make relatively better policies, overall, than do dictatorial states. That dictatorial regimes can make top policy decisions at high speed often merely encourages hasty decisions, and although a compact ideology helps order goals, it often leads to infeasible policies. Many of the advantages in policymaking that dictatorial regimes are alleged to have are in fact an illusion built up by halo effects, the inferiority feelings of some democratic writers, a lack of objective data or informed critique, and differences in the scope of goals. This last is especially important, because concentrating resources on selected areas, which dictatorial-ideological regimes can do more easily, may result in higher output in these areas, and this may be an advantage if these areas are of critical international or internal importance. This, for instance, was how the U.S.S.R. carried out the development of Sputnik.

3. What most of the population considers a more or less satisfactory quality is achieved in all western democratic countries by public policymaking. (This seems to be, in fact, an essential prerequisite of democracy.) The modern dictatorial countries tend in the same direction, but their achievements lag farther behind the satisfactory quality, which is therefore directly manipulated by the policymakers.

Every modern society has particular issues for which the achievements of public policymaking do not come up to what segments of the population consider a satisfactory quality. A striking illustration of this phenomenon, one which also demonstrates the dynamic nature of desired qualities and how changes in the latter can affect policymaking, is segregation in the U.S.A.

4. There are as yet no professional standards for policymaking that can be used effectively for appraisal.

5. In all modern countries, policymaking is at present of survival quality, except possibly for the problem of international control of nuclear armaments. At the same time, there are important problems that are far from solution. Furthermore, we may expect increasingly difficult and critical problems to arise in the future. As I pointed out in Chapter 1, there are strong reasons for suspecting that both the present and the extrapolated qualities of public policymaking will become less and less adequate for solving these problems.

6. Some countries plan targets for parts of their policymaking, especially for their economic activities. These targets are partly an effort to stimulate optimal output, are partly a statement of what is really expected, and are partly a psycho-political device to mobilize support. Because the content of this nominal "planning" is so mixed, achievement of the planned targets is not a valid standard for evaluating the quality of

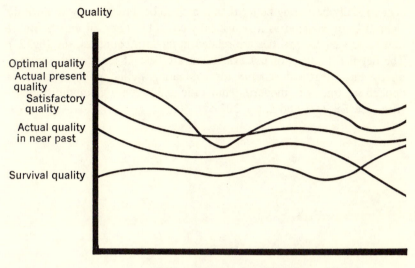

Quality

Optimal quality
Actual present
quality
  Satisfactory
  quality

Actual quality
in near past

Survival quality

Different areas of public policymaking

FIGURE 2. AN APPRAISAL OF PUBLIC POLICYMAKING IN MODERN COUNTRIES

the policymaking, not unless one has good reason to believe that the planned quality is based on an effort to identify the optimal quality. The available material is not enough to allow one to undertake a reliable analysis of planning on this level, and planned targets are therefore too unreliable a standard to be used for our present purpose.[8]

7. In all respects, public policymaking falls short of what it could be with only a little more effort, and very far short of what it could be at its best, as comparing it with the optimal model makes clear for almost every point.

To sum up, public policymaking in modern countries is generally good enough to ensure their survival and to satisfy their populations, and

---

[8] For instance, the "Annual Plans" prepared by the Central Planning Bureau in the Netherlands are forecasts of expected levels, not "planned optimal targets," a fact that is not clearly recognized in parts of the professional planning literature. Worse, if there are such extensive misunderstandings of processes that are taking place in countries that are open to study, then I must have grave doubts about just how much we do know about planning, particularly planning in the Communist countries. I hope that the comparative studies of planning now being pursued by such institutions as INTERPLAN (International Group for Studies in National Planning) and Syracuse University will provide some reliable findings on this important type of policymaking.

is continually becoming better than it used to be, but it is nowhere within sight of being as good as it realistically could be. (For an impression of how these various qualities are related in modern countries, see Fig. 2.) The detailed findings of my evaluation are best, if tentatively, summed up by the integrated scheme for evaluating public policymaking, as applied separately to modern democratic and modern Communist countries (see Tables 1 and 2, pp. 307 and 308).

chapter 10 · Public Policymaking in Developing States

Developing states vary so much, in the degrees to which any of their aspects may be underdeveloped, in their history, in their ideology, in their resources, and in their political regimes, that few generalizations about developing states as such can be considered valid. The dearth of empiric or other relevant data also makes it hard to decide which are the significant findings about such countries. Despite these problems, public policymaking in developing states is becoming so important, for both their own fates and that of the world as a whole, that we must try to identify at least some of the unique characteristics of their policymaking.

I shall try to do so by discussing a model or "pure" developing state that will have all of the more interesting features of one main type of such countries. I call this pure type an "avant-garde developing state." Its characteristics are: (a) very low technological development; (b) a once strong tribal or communal structure that is now slowly disintegrating; (c) a mass leader and a small political elite, who are aspiring toward a rapid and radical socio-economic transformation by means of centrally directed social change, the leader maintaining a strong grip on the masses by both charisma and force, but depending on support by the military; (d) nearly no middle class; (e) a long history of colonial rule that terminated recently after a period of militant nationalism; and (f) wide-scope public policymaking that covers most economic activities.

This model fits various real developing states to different degrees. The characteristics of public policymaking I will present describe real developing states to the extent that they approach this composite, synthetic avant-garde developing state. Henceforth, whenever I say "developing state," please remember I am actually talking about this model "avant-garde" developing state, although its various characteristics are shared to some extent by many differing developing states (but not by all of them).

In summing up the main specific features of public policymaking in developing states as follows (again in the order of the integrated scheme for evaluating public policymaking), I will not emphasize the characteristics they share with modern states, in order to avoid repeating my earlier findings.

ASCERTAINING THE ACTUAL QUALITY IN TERMS OF THE PRIMARY CRITERION

The dearth of reliable data on developing states and of suitable methods for dealing with such data makes it even less possible to estimate the net probable real output of policymaking in developing states than in modern states. We must therefore again turn to the secondary criteria.

ASCERTAINING THE ACTUAL QUALITY IN TERMS OF THE SECONDARY CRITERIA

A. Criteria Based on Process Patterns

1. The basic characteristics of the policymaking process are shaped by inherited, pre-independence patterns, by imitating modern countries, and by the personal work patterns of the new policymaking elite. The policymaking system is sometimes radically changed by ideological revolutions or by personal take-overs, but not by systematic and rational evaluation and redesign.

When there are no revolutionary changes in the policymaking personnel, a basic paradox in nearly all developing countries is that they are strongly conservative about the patterns of public policymaking, but intensely predisposed toward radical social change. The same people who do not hesitate to uproot whole tribes and to change patterns of social action that go back many generations often cannot change their own work patterns and reorganize their small circle of collaborators in ways that will improve the real quality of policymaking. (They may make formal changes in structure and procedure, but these have little, if any, effect on policymaking.)

2. Learning feedback is dampened because the developing countries are so young as independent policymaking systems. This objective

difficulty is reinforced by the intensity with which some of the fruits of modernization are desired and with which ideologies are held, as well as by internal socio-political tensions. These factors distort interpretation of facts and hinder feedback; a strong defensive reaction, for example, may lead to blaming some internal or external "enemy" for all failures.

As a result, learning by trial and error is generally restricted to extreme errors, whose negative results are immediate and obvious. Also, unrealistic expectations cause incorrect learning feedback; sound policies are sometimes changed because their results do not come up to the unrealistic expectations, although, objectively speaking, they approximate the best possible results.

3. The optimal strategy of public policymaking in the developing states is often one of maximax, with low security level and higher risks. In other words, achieving accelerated development often requires a sharp break with the past. Since very little experience with accelerated and directed large-scale social change is available, neither the strategy of incremental change nor that of "muddling through" (in the sense of cautious marginal action, accompanied by slow learning from experience) applies to the situation. "Planning the improbable," to use Bertram Gross's phrase, requires a strategy based on extensive innovation. Much of what experience humanity has had with extensive "social engineering" has been concentrated in the U.S.S.R. Also, Communist experts are more predisposed to radical action which as a strategy (though not in terms of the particular ideas proposed by Communist experts) often fits the needs of developing countries better than the strategy of incremental change usually favored by western democratic experts. This situation seriously challenges the western democratic countries in the struggle over what the future political orientation of the developing states will be. Imported experts must take much care not to try applying ideologies and strategies based on totally different conditions to the developing states. Experts who come from democratic countries that do engage in large-scale directed social change, such as, in some respects, the Netherlands and Israel, may have a significant advantage in some areas because their background better suits the needs of many developing countries.

The only strategy of public policymaking that promises to fit the goals and conditions of developing states is usually one of far-reaching and risky change. The weight of such risks is much reduced by the facts that developing countries have little to lose and their populations will survive anyway; a maximax strategy in developing countries is thus much less dangerous than it would be in modern, more risk-sensitive states.

Developing states do little conscious determining of policy strategy.

Their implicit policy strategies tend to that of maximax by means of radical innovation, and thus generally fit their needs. But without explicit strategy considerations, the risks involved in radical innovations are not adequately recognized, and not enough steps are taken to reduce them as much as is feasible within the radical-innovation strategy. This failure leads to a set of predictions that is unrealistic because it does not take into account that the policy is sure to have many unpredictable and undesirable results.

4. The priorities of values and, to some extent, the operational goals are rather more spelled-out than in modern countries, because clear predominance is given to technological and economic development. There are still some inconsistent values; e.g., wanting to raise the educational level of the masses ("primary education for all") conflicts with cadre education directed toward economic development. But, in general, developing states regard as expendable many values that are taken for granted in modern states, and can therefore concentrate their resources on fewer goals and simplify their public policymaking.

5. Search for alternatives is somewhat more intense than in the modern countries because there are no "policy precedents" and because the quality considered satisfactory is so much higher than the actually achieved quality that the policymakers are under pressure to improve. However, the rational components are of such poor quality that they impair the search for alternatives, as do the strong ideologies, which reduce the field of alternatives that are considered "permissible."

6. Cutoff horizons are almost never explicitly established. The implicit cutoff horizon is indeterminate and inconsistent; both long-range and short-range effects are considered without being clearly distinguished. This state of affairs is perhaps caused by a generally fuzzy and inconsistent sense of time that allows long-range effects to be regarded as just around the corner.

These weaknesses of the cutoff horizon are not necessarily dysfunctional for developing states; innovating policies make reliable predictions impossible anyway. Furthermore, it might be undesirable if too many people really understood that last point, since such understanding might result in an inappropriate "playing safe" strategy.

7. The cultural ecology within which the public-policymaking system operates, and which conditions its basic characteristics, is not conducive to rationality. That there is no orientation deeply rooted in the culture in favor of rationality, as there is in western societies, is particularly problematic. The aftereffects of the trauma of becoming an independent nation also tend to lead to highly emotional patterns of activity and/or to apathy. Both patterns interfere with the optimistic, matter-

of-fact approach that is needed for optimal development of the rational (and extrarational) components of public policymaking. Also, the behavior patterns and structural characteristics of the main policymaking individuals and organizations were conditioned by pre-independence needs and situations, which allowed relatively little scope for rational components.

The resulting poor quality of the rational components in policymaking is largely unavoidable, though it starkly contradicts both the desire often declared by developing states to base their operations on "science" and their verbal predisposition toward "planning."

Certain forces are at work, slowly strengthening the rational components. Among them are: (a) pressures from external sources of aid, which demand some rationality in policymaking as a condition for granting loans; (b) the rational contribution by foreign experts; and (c) the intense efforts by leaders in some (but not all) developing countries to improve the quality of policymaking by strengthening the rational components. These pro-rationality forces have so far had only small, though significant, effects. The poor rationality of public policymaking in most developing countries continues to be striking, as, for similar reasons, do most of the other characteristics of policymaking in these countries.

8. The extrarational components are relatively better developed than the rational components, but also show their pre-independence roots quite clearly. Extrarational components are usually of high quality for policy issues that have a parallel during the pre-independence period, but are of poor quality for the many novel issues, with which no one has had experience on which extrarational components could be based. This unavoidable weakness is only partly compensated for by the high intelligence and quick intuition of many of the senior policymakers.

B. Criteria Based on Output

1. The nominal output of public policymaking (the policies themselves) in developing states in many ways makes a better impression than that of modern, especially western democratic, countries: the policies seem to be clear, consistent, of wide scope, and very comprehensive. But here one must distinguish sharply between policies that are actually to be executed and policy declarations that are a device for recruiting support, not a guide for future action. The policies that are to be executed, which are the ones that interest us, are much less impressive. In general, the more action-oriented policies are, the less clear and

consistent they tend to become. Also, they are not comprehensive, even though some comprehensiveness is both needed and feasible in developing countries. It is thanks to the fact that policies need be fewer and less complex, and that more attention is paid to their facades, that even the policies that are to be executed often look better than those of many modern countries.

Also, public policymaking in the developing countries penetrates into social activities to different degrees than it does in modern countries. It penetrates more into the selected issues with which it deals, because it aims at radical change, and because public policymaking almost monopolizes all dealing with social problems (there being both little private policymaking and an ideology that favors centralized public policymaking). Because public policymaking concentrates on a few clusters of issues, mainly those involving economic development, it penetrates less into, and in fact neglects, many issues that modern countries deal with.

2. The feasibility yardstick cannot legitimately be applied to "policies" that are not really supposed to be executed, for example, a "policy" to redistribute land that is declared by a conservative oligarchic leadership interested only in using the declaration as a slogan to recruit support among the destitute rural population.

Even after such policies are excluded, we must observe that many of the remaining policies in many developing countries cannot possibly be put into practice. Developing countries seem to make such policies because of these five factors, jointly and severally: (a) poor rational components; (b) distortions of their interpretation of facts caused by their dogmatic ideologies; (c) the very high achievement considered satisfactory by widely held levels of aspiration; (d) internal political demands; and (e) scarce resources.

In considering this situation, one should not ignore the positive function such infeasible policies sometimes have in mobilizing aid from abroad and in helping to create a national self-image. Also, one must never forget how strong the human spirit can be in realizing ideals that are infeasible by conservative scientific standards. Human ideals and aspirations have often been more "realistic" than human knowledge; one must not stifle human energy by imposing judgments based on what was feasible in the past. Nevertheless, the conclusion that developing countries tend to undermine some of their potential by adopting definitely infeasible policies seems inescapable to me.

3. Available material and methods do not permit one to ascertain probable real output directly.

C. Criteria Based on Structure

1. There are no units in charge of periodically and systematically evaluating and redesigning the policymaking structure, though developing countries tend rather strongly to undertake extensive (and often useless) formal reorganizations based on a superficial feedback and unsuitable recommendations by foreign experts, or after changes in the political power elite.

2. Most developing states have special planning units. These planning units often have relatively better rational components than the other policymaking units, but even if they do, their policymaking quality is still often poor, partly because the dominant ideologies do not permit feasible intermediate-range highly rational planning and partly because the needed inputs are scarce.

3. It is impossible to generalize validly about the organizational and social distance between the units that make policy, that execute it, and that motivate the execution. In some developing countries the relatively highly centralized and monolithic governmental structure provides for formal inter-organizational relationships that look as if they would be effective, but so far there are no available data on how these formal relationships work out in practice. In other developing countries, there are obvious weaknesses in organizational distance; in the extreme (but not unusual) cases, the planning units are almost completely isolated from the regular governmental apparatus.

4. That public policymaking in developing countries is unique is best brought out by certain of the characteristics, roles, and contributions of the various units that make up the policymaking structure. The following will also clarify some of the facets of policymaking I have already mentioned while applying other secondary criteria.

In general, the public-policymaking structure is much simpler than in modern states. Individual and small-group decisions play a relatively greater role than complex organizational processes, and the aggregation function is less heterogeneous and easier to observe. Private individuals and legislatures influence public policymaking much less; they are more a passive material to be manipulated, or channels for recruiting support, than they are active contributors. Private intellectuals, if there are any, often do not contribute to public policymaking, especially when they are without influence and are politically apathetic. Interest groups are active, but are fewer in number, and are often integrated into the political institutions; they tend to operate more as cliques than as autonomous social units. Leaders are dominant, and are aided by small cadres of followers. In most developing countries the civil service is rather weak, and makes only small contributions to rational policymaking.

To elaborate these comments, I will discuss the major policymaking units one by one, focusing on the features that distinguish developing countries from modern countries, so as to supplement the detailed ascertainment in Table 3 (p. 309).

a. Private individuals as voters play a small role in policy-making, since free elections with meaningful alternatives are unusual.

b. Intellectuals as such play a very small role in public policy-making, since they are very scarce and tend to become either alienated from politics or absorbed in it; in the latter case they become political leaders or senior civil servants.

c. Most of those who occupy the central policymaking positions are predisposed toward improvisation and extrarational decision-making. This predisposition was carried over from the pre-independence period, during which the politicians of the independence movement operated mainly by means of improvisation; one of their major skills had to be an ability to improvise in rapidly changing circumstances, and to take advantage of every small opportunity without delay. Their qualifications for success were their highly developed political acumen and their charisma; they had little chance to be systematically rational or undertake intermediate-range policymaking. These behavior patterns were tremendously reinforced by being followed by independence, and so were brought along by the pre-independence leaders when they took over the new policymaking positions. However, these strongly ingrained behavior patterns differ in many ways from those that objectively are needed for optimal public policymaking in a developing state after it gains independence. Some outstanding politicians do change their patterns of behavior, but most of them neither feel the need to nor can do so.[1] Time is needed to allow the natural and/or violent turnover of leaders to bring to the main policymaking positions persons whose

---

[1] In some developing countries the pre-independence type of leader continues to be essential for building up a unitary nation, a task for which improvisation and quasi-mystic modes of operation may be optimal. Given such conditions, my model of optimal public policymaking is not yet relevant, and the problems that will arise, because the actual behavior patterns of the senior political stratum are not the needed ones, will be delayed but not avoided. In general, in developing countries the imbalance between capacities to acquire and maintain political power and capacities to govern is especially pronounced. On this antinomy, see Milton Katz, *The Things That Are Caesar's* (N.Y.: Knopf, 1966).

patterns of action are those needed for policymaking in a developing state that is trying to accelerate and direct its social change.

d. In developing states, legislative bodies play a secondary role in policymaking, however important they may be for communication, recruiting support, and building up a consensus.

e. The political executive in developing countries exerts even more influence on public policymaking than do cabinets in modern countries. Because there are fewer policy issues, a larger proportion of them can reach the cabinet level in developing countries; because there is often no professional civil service, the executive plays a larger role in forming public policies about most issues; because power is more highly concentrated, the political executive is free to establish policies on many more issues without worrying as much about having to build coalitions. (This is not so for those policy issues that involve strong local and traditional power centers, at least not until these power centers are broken up. I will mention constraints imposed by the military later.)

In its internal composition and in its modes of operation, the political executive in developing countries tends to follow the pattern of "court politics": much power is concentrated in one leader, for whose favor various cliques engage in struggle with each other.[2]

f. In general, the government bureaucracy in developing states is weak, cannot supply very many rational components to policymaking, and so fails to counterbalance the main weaknesses of the other public-policymaking units. With a few exceptions, most of the senior administrative positions had been occupied by foreigners during the pre-independence period. When independence was achieved, these positions were taken over in most developing states by persons who were often highly intelligent and devoted, but who had never had the opportunity to acquire the knowledge and experience needed to fill the positions properly. The insufficient contribution of the government bureaucracy to public policymaking is aggravated by the bureaucracy's being overloaded with new problems and programs. Also, in some developing countries, the new indigenous civil service had adopted their patterns of social behavior from those of the former senior class of expatriate foreigners. These patterns do not fit the new conditions and seriously impair contact between the civil servants and both the new political leaders and the masses. The cumulative result is that in most developing countries the senior civil service contributes much less to public policymaking than it does in the modern countries, and reinforces the weaknesses in the behavior patterns of the politicians instead of compensating for them.

---

[2] See C. P. Snow, *Science and Government* (London: Oxford Univ. Press, 1961), p. 63.

g. Courts in nearly all developing states play no significant role in public policymaking.

h. The role of parties in public policymaking in developing states is shaped both by the ideological nature of these states and by their stage of social development. In almost all such states, the parties function as a means for recruiting cooperation and active participation by the population in executing the policies set down by small groups of leaders. There is usually only one party; no inter-party competition is permitted. The party sometimes fulfills governmental functions, though often has not a highly developed bureaucracy. Intra-party activities also tend to follow the pattern of "court politics," which somewhat shape public policymaking by imposing limits on what is politically feasible for the leaders; beyond these limits they face increasing dangers from conspiracy and palace revolutions. The details of these limits depend on the particular circumstances of each country at the particular time.

i. Universities, as such, seem to play little, if any, role in public policymaking. They are apparently too overloaded with routine teaching assignments to be able to contribute any of their very scarce resources to policymaking. The alienation of many intellectuals from the political elite in some developing countries is another reason why the role of universities in policymaking is very slight. However, student bodies in some developing states sometimes exert a significant and often highly emotional influence on policymaking.

j. As I have already mentioned, interest groups in developing states tend to be fewer and less pluralistic than in modern states. Their behavior patterns tend to be those of "court politics," and their influence is exerted mainly by means of personal relations and overlapping elites. What they contribute to policymaking lacks the information content of interest-group arguments in modern countries, since it is less rational, has narrower goals, and is more short-sighted.

k. A special feature of the public-policymaking structure in many developing states is the influence of the military, which often contributes a sense for order and procedure, but not necessarily in terms of highly developed rational components. In more and more developing states the military in effect rules the country, policymaking being shaped by a few officers. In nearly all developing states the military at least imposes active constraints on policymaking: a policy that is not acceptable to the military is not feasible.

These few comments on policymaking units raise more questions than they answer; but I cannot give a more detailed discussion of the politics of developing countries without getting far away from the overall evaluation of policymaking I am trying to do.

5. The last secondary criterion based on structure is the aggregation function. Its main forms in developing states are (a) bargaining between a few units, and (b) a simple hierarchy. The bargaining processes are simpler in most developing states than they are in modern societies because there are far fewer units involved and so there are far fewer possible coalitions. Policymaking is more concentrated, and the national leader and his personal staff, who operate as a relatively simple hierarchy, often exert a more detailed and penetrating influence on policymaking than do leaders in any modern country, including the more totalitarian ones. Complex hierarchy plays a relatively smaller role in aggregating policymaking in many of the avant-garde developing states.

D. Criteria Based on Input

1. Qualified manpower in the developing countries is the scarcest resource of all. That there are few professionals in most of the policymaking occupations, and few educated and experienced candidates for the central policymaking roles, puts a strict specific limit on how good policymaking can be. This dearth of qualified manpower is compensated for a little by foreign aid, in the form of foreign experts who can fill advisory or executive positions. These foreign experts, some supplied by the various international agencies under the auspices of the Technical Assistance Board of the United Nations, and some by bilateral and multilateral agreements, present an unprecedented effort to import policymaking resources, but their over-all contribution to improving public policymaking in the developing countries, though impressive, is limited for two reasons. First, it is harder to use foreign experts in policymaking than in the more technical areas of policy execution, because many policy issues are more sensitive politically and because many foreign experts know very little about the socio-political situations in the developing countries. Second, no number of foreign experts can compensate for a lack of data or for non-rational patterns of behavior. The result is that, though in some developing countries the better-qualified manpower tends strongly to go into public policymaking, the absolute scarcity of qualified manpower forces most developing countries to place underqualified persons in many important policymaking positions.

2. Knowledge and information are another very scarce resource, partly because of the lack of professionally qualified manpower, but more importantly because the knowledge, both factual data about the

respective countries and scientific theories that could help accelerate development, often does not exist. Physical, demographic, economic, climatologic, and similar data are not available for most developing states, and are very difficult, time-consuming, and expensive to collect. Scientific theories that could be applied to development processes are scarce because scientists have not been interested in such phenomena; even when scientists become interested in them, the complexity of the issues and their own lack of experience hinder them from coming up with reliable findings about such processes. In other words, this scarcity of knowledge and information is not a transitory or accidental phenomenon; it may continue to exist for much of the period during which these countries will be most in need of reliable knowledge and information as inputs for their policymaking.

3. Equipment poses no special problems, except that some developing countries tend to waste resources on types of equipment that are more sophisticated and sensitive than they need or could possibly use.

4. Energy and drive for policymaking are readily available; this is almost part of the concept of "avant-garde developing state." However, energy and drive are not as available for executing policies, since the execution often requires active participation by large segments of the population. Stimulating mass enthusiasm is a major preoccupation of the policymaking elite, because active participation by large (or at least defined) segments of the population is essential in many ways for accelerated social change.

5. The overall input into policymaking is very limited. Money, though it is scarce, is still the most easily obtained resource. But money cannot be easily converted into qualified manpower or into knowledge and information. That manpower and knowledge are not available is decisive in shaping all public policymaking in the developing countries, and is the reason why both the actual quality and the optimal quality of policymaking in such countries are low, both absolutely and compared with the actual and optimal qualities, respectively, of public policymaking in modern countries.

APPRAISING THE ACTUAL QUALITY BY MEANS OF THE STANDARDS

1. Comparison with the past is inapplicable: the pre-independence period is too different in most variables, and the independence period too short. Nevertheless, strictly in terms of achieving accelerated modernization, public policymaking in the developing coun-

tries seems much superior in most cases to that of the preceding colonial regimes.

2. Both the optimal quality and the actual quality of public policymaking in the developing states are much lower than those in the modern states. The optimal level is lower because there are not enough resources, even if they are used optimally, to achieve a high quality in most of the phases of public policymaking. The actual quality is even lower because of all the various factors I've already mentioned that keep the available resources from being used optimally. Thus, although the actual quality of public policymaking could be improved with the available resources (if they were used optimally), the unavoidable conclusion is that, even under the best conditions, the overall quality of public policymaking in the developing countries will be significantly lower than that in modern countries for quite a while, and will generally continue to be lower even if resources for public policymaking are transferred on a large scale from modern to developing countries.

3. In most modern societies the gap between the actual quality of policymaking and the satisfactory quality is not very large. In the developing states the situation is much different: the elite have imported from modern countries an aspiration for very high-quality results from their policies, and this aspiration is quickly being taken over by the population. This desired quality, though it is not defined in detail, includes a standard of living and level of economic activity that is patterned on the most highly developed western societies and is to be achieved in "the near future." Not only are the outputs of the actual policymaking nowhere near this high satisfactory quality but such a quality cannot possibly be even approximated in the foreseeable future, not even with optimal public policymaking and tremendous assistance from the modern states.

This large gap between what is wanted (and often promised) and what is possible is a very serious source of tension that may well lead to social explosions when it becomes clear to the populace that their expectations have been frustrated. True, creating an aspiration for such a high quality is an essential lever for recruiting mass support and for mobilizing energy and other resources needed for development. But unless a more realistic satisfactory quality is soon substituted for the utopian one, the resulting frustrations and social disturbances will cause lower actual achievements, which in turn will increase apathy and disturbances, and so on, and will possibly create a chain reaction that can lead many developing states into stagnation.

4. There are no professional standards that can be used as standards for public policymaking in developing countries.

5. One of the most interesting features of public policymaking in all developing countries is the relationships between the optimal and actual qualities of policymaking and the objective survival quality. The basic finding to be noted is that however low the actual quality of public policymaking is, the objective survival quality is almost always achieved (the exceptions concern possible aggression from outside).

It is easy to explain this finding: the basic social structure of the developing countries is still independent of public policymaking, and localities (though not necessarily the "state" as such) would survive even if all central public policymaking were to break down. A complex modern society cannot survive any basic breakdown in public policy-making; that is, to put it simply, most of its population would die if its very complex network of services (that depend on, among other things, very high-quality public policymaking) were not maintained. The less complex developing societies are not as sensitive, and most of the population can very well survive the worst public policies or even a total breakdown of public policymaking. Therefore, in some (but not all) respects, the non-modern countries are less sensitive to nuclear warfare. Adopting what I think is a reasonable opinion, that radioactivity would not wipe out all life, but that most central activities would be disrupted, most of the population in modern countries would die because of lack of food, water, energy, and medical services (unless extensive civil-defense and other facilities for recuperating after an attack were prepared). Nothing quantitatively comparable would happen in the developing countries, where most of the population still lives in almost self-sufficient local units. (However, the regimes as such would disintegrate in most cases; this fact is completely ignored by those who make the fallacious assertion that Communist China would be insensitive to nuclear attack).

6. Despite their being predisposed toward planning, developing countries do not engage in comprehensive planning as a form of public policymaking, because they concentrate their public policymaking on limited clusters of issues. Some of the relatively more advanced developing countries, such as India, do set meaningful targets for some sectors of the economy. Most developing states lack both the necessary knowledge and the necessary behavior patterns for realistic planning, which is more often imposed from abroad as a condition for financial assistance than practiced because of local initiative. For these reasons, planned levels of performance are not now a significant standard for evaluating the quality of policymaking in most developing states.

7. To repeat a point I've already made several times, the optimal quality of policymaking in developing countries is much lower than that in modern countries. The actual quality lags behind the optimal quality

in many ways, but because the optimal quality is so low, the *distance* between the two in some developing countries is perhaps smaller than the distance between the two in many modern states.

To sum up, public policymaking in developing countries is clearly of survival quality, which makes few demands on their policymaking. On the other side, actual public policymaking lags very much behind the satisfactory quality, which cannot be achieved even by optimal policymaking (see Fig. 3).

Although the actual quality of policymaking is significantly lower than the optimal quality in both modern and developing states, this lag is a more serious challenge to the policymakers of the developing states, especially because the difficulties and dangers of directed accelerated social change require optimal policymaking in order to have any chance of success. The detailed findings of my evaluation of policymaking in developing countries is best, though tentatively, summed up by Table 3 (p. 309).

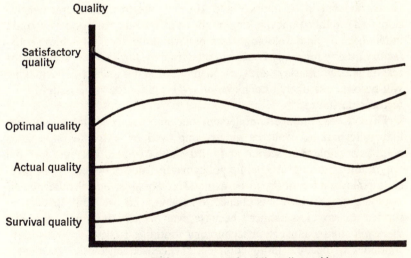

FIGURE 3. AN APPRAISAL OF PUBLIC POLICYMAKING IN AVANT-GARDE DEVELOPING COUNTRIES

chapter 11 · An Evaluation and Diagnosis of the Present State of Public Policymaking

The examination of public policymaking in contemporary states that I carried out in Chapters 9 and 10 leads me to three major conclusions: (a) public policymaking in all countries is not as good as it could in fact be; (b) in developing states policymaking does not achieve satisfactory quality for many issues (in modern states this is the case only for certain specific issues); and (c) in modern states public policymaking will become less likely to achieve survival quality for some issues in the foreseeable future.

These three findings complement one another. The first establishes that policymaking could be greatly improved by trying to make it as good as possible. The second and third emphasize that we must take the opportunities to improve public policymaking, not only because in principle policymaking ought to be as good as possible, but also because if we don't, we will have less chance to achieve what we want, or even to survive. (I say "less chance" because even with optimal policymaking, there will still be dangers; as technology continues to develop and society continues to become more complex, the consequences of "accidents" and unavoidable mistakes may become more disastrous.)

A COMPARISON OF THE PRESENT AND BEST POSSIBLE SITUATIONS

The shortcomings of current public policymaking are made clear by the comparison of actual and optimal policymaking that I carry out in the following list, in which the quality of current policymaking, as ascertained by the secondary criteria, is appraised by the standard of optimality.

Optimal Policymaking	*Current Policymaking*
1. Much metapolicymaking about basic characteristics of policy-making system.	1. There is almost none.
2. Much learning feedback.	2. There is very little.
3. Systematic and explicit determination of policy strategies.	3. There is very little.
4. Operational goals should be somewhat elaborated and ordered.	4. They are insufficiently elaborated and ordered.
5. Much search for alternatives.	5. There is very little.
6. Explicit, systematic establishment of a cutoff horizon that covers a medium range of time.	6. There is little such establishment of cutoff horizons; in modern democratic countries a short range of time is preferred.
7. Highly developed rational components.	7. They are little developed.
8. Highly developed extrarational components.	8. They are quite highly developed but are below the optimal.
9. Special units explicitly in charge of periodically and systematically evaluating and redesigning policymaking structures.	9. There are almost no such units.
10. Special units explicitly in charge of thinking, long-range policymaking, surveying knowledge, and carrying out research and development relevant to policymaking.	10. There are only a very few such units.
11. A suitable, carefully adjusted social and organizational distance between units that make policy, that execute it, and that motivate the execution.	11. The need for such distance is often not appreciated or handled properly.
12. The characteristics, roles, and contributions of the different units that make up the policy-making structure add up to those required for optimal policymaking.	12. They do so only to a limited degree.
13. The aggregation function approximates optimality at low cost and with few distortions.	13. It does so only in part.

Optimal Policymaking (Continued)	*Current Policymaking (Continued)*
14. Highly qualified manpower and much knowledge and information for policymaking.	14. Available manpower usually has median qualifications, and input of knowledge and information is medium at best.
15. Sufficient equipment available.	15. In modern countries, available equipment is almost sufficient; in developing countries, it is often unsuitable.
16. Sufficient energy and drive available.	16. In developing and some Communist countries often more energy and drive are available than in many modern democratic countries, but it depends greatly on the leadership's personalities.

The shortcomings of contemporary public policymaking brought out by the list are very formidable; but in many respects it still presents too optimistic a view because it neglects the future. Most of public policymaking's weaknesses boil down to not being able to adjust to new needs, especially those created by social and cultural changes, or to new possibilities opened up by new knowledge. You will recall that my basic thesis, which I formulated in Chapter 1, is that the quality that policymaking must achieve, if it is to meet the standards of survival quality, satisfactory quality, and especially optimal quality, is increasing at an accelerated rate, whereas the quality of actual public policymaking is improving much more slowly. The gap between the best possible (and the necessary) quality of policymaking and the actual quality of policymaking is not only large, but constantly widening, and will continue to widen unless significant improvements in actual policymaking are made (see Fig. 1, p. 10).

In Parts V and VI, I will take up some of the problems involved in improving public policymaking after I develop our central tool, the optimal model, in Part IV. But first I must step outside the evaluation of current policymaking I have already done, in order to try to point out some of the factors that have created the current situation.

Given the features of contemporary public policymaking my analysis has revealed so far, one must ask why policymaking lags so far behind what it could be at best despite all the needs there are for it to be as good as it can be. That is, considering the features of public policymaking as symptoms, we want at least a preliminary diagnosis that will throw some light on these symptoms in terms of basic social dynamics.

FACTORS CAUSING THE GAP BETWEEN THE ACTUAL AND OPTIMAL QUALITIES OF POLICY-MAKING

The available data and theories suggest to me that the gap between the actual and optimal qualities of public policymaking can be explained by four main sets of factors, namely: (a) substantive difficulties in improving public policymaking; (b) ideologies that are opposed to innovation; (c) vested interests; and (d) the general inertia of individuals and social units. I discuss the first factor throughout this book, and an adequate discussion of the other factors would require another book by itself, so I will limit myself here to pointing out some relevant issues.

1. Ideologies that are opposed to innovation take a number of forms; a few are based on deterministic beliefs, according to which every effort to change reality is vain. Some regard the present order as expressing some higher will, and any conscious effort to change it as being sacrilegious. A different conservative ideology follows Edmund Burke, and holds that social institutions embody the accumulated wisdom of many generations, and should not be endangered by rash action. These various ideologies are often (though not necessarily) closely tied in with both vested interests and the general bias that most human beings and social units have against innovation and that is well expressed in the old platitude, "What was good enough for my father is good enough for me."

2. In most concrete situations, much of the resistance to innovation, including improvements in public policymaking, is at least partly inspired by much more prosaic and less idealistic reasons, that is, by vested interests in the status quo. Those who have vested interests almost always rationalize them in terms of some conservative ideology, but, contrary to the Marxian view, not all such ideologies are necessarily created by those who have vested interests.

Improvements in the policymaking system are not a technical matter, and are never neutral in terms of social power or of the allocation of benefits and costs. Every change in input, stipulated output, structure, or process involves changes in the influence and rewards enjoyed by some persons and groups who therefore resist any change that they think will have what they consider undesirable effects on their positions.[1]

---

[1] For an excellent discussion of the effects on political power caused by budgetary reforms which appear to be purely technical in nature, see Aaron Wildavsky, *The Politics of the Budgetary Process* (Boston: Little, Brown, 1964), pp. 127ff.

3. Far more important than either of the first two factors is the general inertia of individuals and social units. Many studies have indicated that most people in most cases strongly resist change, especially when the changes would be in institutions that have an emotional and ideological significance, as most components of the public-policymaking system do.

Of course, some exceptional persons and social units are strongly in favor of change. Such persons and units have gained the upper hand for short periods of history, as in ancient Greece and during the Renaissance. They emerge as whirlpools of radical (and, up to now, mainly undirected) social change in the slow stream of history. In terms of our technology and of some other aspects of our culture, we are now in an epoch of radical social change, but in modern countries it has not yet affected the public-policymaking system, to which "crisis theory" (according to which a system almost never engages in large-scale directed self-change except after serious perceived crises) still seems to apply.

As I explained in Chapter 1, most men cling to the few social institutions, including the public-policymaking system, that seem to be stable. Among the factors that strengthen such clinging are (a) a widespread feeling of being lost in the "lonely crowd"; (b) feeling helpless in the face of possible catastrophe, whether from modern barbarism (as practiced by the Nazis), from terrorism (as launched by Stalin), or from nuclear war; and (c) the uncertainty induced by such rapid changes in the material environment as technological innovation is now causing. If a man identifies himself with traditional political structures, this identification is also reinforced by the perception of external pressure from Communism (or from "Capitalism" in Communist countries); he embraces the attacked institutions even more fervently.

For somewhat different reasons, which I mentioned in Chapter 10, most developing countries also have this general inertia about changing the basic mode of policymaking, even when their formal structure and basic culture are undergoing revolutionary convulsions. Furthermore, even when some avant-garde developing countries are prepared to change their policymaking system, their dogmatic preconceptions keep the changes from doing as much good as they should.

Even though it seems clear that poor current policymaking is being caused by conservative ideologies, vested interests, and the general inertia of men and society, we must not conclude that policymaking cannot be improved, though we must realize there are strict limits on how much it can be improved. These three factors cannot (and, perhaps, should not) be simply swept away, and so do set limits on the feasibility, that is, "optimality" (as correctly defined) of improving policymaking. But to the extent that they can be overcome (and they all can be, to one degree or another), policymaking can in fact be improved. To carry out such improvement, we must know what needs to be improved, and how in fact it can be improved. That is, it is finally time, after much hinting and many references, to construct the optimal model of policymaking.

part IV

AN
OPTIMAL MODEL
OF
PUBLIC
POLICYMAKING

chapter 12 · A Critical Survey of Normative Models of Public Policymaking

There are two ways in which I could try to analyze and improve public policymaking: (1) I could begin with a subjective impression of what public policymaking is all about, and try to improve it (when I am forced to by external pressures or when I believe that its output is unsatisfactory), given whatever limited experience and haphazard bits of scientific knowledge I might have, but without looking very hard for new alternatives or making more than incremental changes in present policies if I can help it; (2) I could try to analyze the main characteristics of public policymaking comprehensively, identify its central weaknesses and strengths systematically, and innovate alternatives that will correct the weaknesses.

The first method is typical of most practical policymakers. Although they have some idea of what "better public policymaking" would be, this idea usually consists of the present situation less some disturbances, plus some incremental changes. They have no systematic set of criteria and standards for evaluating public policymaking, since most of them believe that their feeling for "where the shoe pinches" and their personal experience give them enough information. (Most students of politics have until recently gone along with such beliefs, when studying policymaking, and have in most cases been satisfied with incidental impressions, or at best with models that dealt with only a few components of the public-policymaking system.) This method of evaluating policymaking requires no abstract models, which may be one of its important advantages. Indeed, most politicians and policymakers, being practical men, regard attempts to construct normative policymaking models as a waste of resources and idle daydreaming at best, and as some kind of subversive activity at worst.

The second method must have a normative model of public policymaking, as a tool for systematically analyzing public policymaking, as a basis for the criteria and standards needed to evaluate policymaking, and as a guide for formulating effective proposals for any improvements that are found to be desirable. Such a model must satisfy certain conditions (some of which I have already discussed) including these three, which are the most relevant to this discussion: (a) it should match reality well enough that an action-oriented analysis and evaluation of policymaking, leading to feasible proposals for improvements, can be based on it; (b) it should be systematic and comprehensive enough that it can be used for significant and penetrating analysis; (c) it should be normative, not in the sense of setting forth final goals, but in the instrumental sense of establishing processes and structures whereby a maximum net output of whatever goals and values are desired can be achieved.

A non-normative behavioral model is good enough for analyzing policymaking, but to make improvements in policymaking, one needs a model which is suitable not only for scientific analysis of actual behavior, but also for evaluating that behavior, and for deriving suggestions for improving that behavior. The normative model must therefore also be idealistic enough that it can stimulate consistent, thorough-going proposals for innovative improvements based on the best available knowledge.

Insofar as the normative model used to evaluate public policymaking is either too utopian or too realistic, it will lead to a picture that is either too dark or too bright, respectively, neither picture being much good for deciding how to improve the situation. These two extremes are well illustrated by two case studies of the Dixon-Yates episode in the U.S.A., both of which were done with commendable scholarliness. Although the two authors agree more or less on the facts, one author evaluates them by means of a pure-rationality model, and of course concludes that the decision process in the Dixon-Yates case was of very poor quality.[1] The second author adopts a bargaining model (which regards achieving final agreement on any policy a success), and so concludes that, overall, public policymaking in the Dixon-Yates episode was successful.[2] Neither model

---

[1] Jason L. Finkle, *The President Makes a Decision: A Study of Dixon-Yates* (Ann Arbor: Univ. of Michigan, Institute of Public Administration, 1960), pp. 162ff.

[2] Aaron Wildavsky, *Dixon-Yates: A Study in Power Politics* (New Haven: Yale Univ. Press, 1962), pp. 310ff. Especially striking is the standard implied on p. 322n15.

permitted a systematic, action-oriented evaluation, which would lead to innovative but non-utopian proposals for improvements based on learning feedback from the investigated case.

The optimal model of public policymaking I present in this part tries to avoid both extremes, by rejecting pure rationality on the one hand, and by providing an optimal goal that is more than an incrementally improved extrapolation of the present situation on the other hand. I intend the optimal model to be both an analytical tool for understanding policymaking and a goal that actual public policymaking can approximate if the policymakers are willing to try. It should be judged not as an end in itself, but only as an operational tool, that is, by its usefulness for analyzing, evaluating, and improving public policymaking.

Since prescriptive discourse is unfashionable among social scientists these days, little of the social-science literature has been devoted to normative models of public policymaking. Modern political science has been especially disappointing in this respect, succeeding as it does in avoiding the subject almost completely; the few exceptions have been scattered suggestions for reform that lack any systematic basis. Most of the systematic normative models that are available and applicable to policymaking have come from economics and from such new "interdisciplines" as administrative science, planning studies, decision theory, systems analysis, computer sciences, operations research, engineering economy, regional sciences, defense economics, research and development management, development studies, and conflict theory, to mention only a few. In general, these models concern specific types of decisionmaking or policymaking, but some of them can be applied to policymaking as such.

I will take up in Chapter 15 a few models that deal with the optimal *structure* of the public-policymaking system, such as the hierarchy model, the adverse-procedure model, the market model, and various bargaining and collusion models. For now, I will concentrate on six main normative models that deal with phases of policymaking: (1) the pure-rationality model; (2) the "economically rational" model, as I call it; (3) the sequential-decision model; (4) the incremental-change model; (5) the satisfying model; and (6) the extrarational-processes model.

In this chapter I will describe and critically analyze these six normative models one by one, paying special attention to the assumptions on which they are based, to their domains of validity, and to their major limitations. The conclusions I draw from this critical survey will be the raw material from which I will construct my own optimal normative model of policymaking, designing it to integrate and supplement the strengths of these various available models, but to avoid their weaknesses.

THE PURE-RATIONALITY MODEL

Most contemporary thought about decisionmaking and policymaking is based on the pure-rationality[3] model, which is often presented as the universally ideal pattern for decisionmaking that should be approximated as closely as possible. That human action approximates pure rationality, or, to be more exact, can be explained as if it did, is assumed by certain economic and political theories, for example, by most free-market models and by some theories of democracy. The pure-rationality model goes further than most other models in systematically breaking decisionmaking down into phases and in analyzing its own components. Its assumptions are deeply rooted in modern civilization and culture, and are consistent with rationalism, positivism, and optimism. Since the pure-rationality model contributes so much to understanding most of the other normative models, as well as to the optimal model, I shall examine it at some length.

Following the accepted analysis, I find that the pure-rationality model includes six phases:

1. Establishing a complete set of operational goals, with relative weights allocated to the different degrees to which each may be achieved.

2. Establishing a complete inventory of other values and of resources, with relative weights.

3. Preparing a complete set of the alternative policies open to the policymaker.

4. Preparing a complete set of valid predictions of the costs and benefits of each alternative, including the extent to which each will achieve the various operational goals, consume resources, and realize or impair other values.

5. Calculating the net expectation for each alternative by multiplying the probability of each benefit and cost for each alternative by the utility of each, and calculating the net benefit (or cost) in utility units.

6. Comparing the net expectations and identifying the alternative (or alternatives, if two or more are equally good) with the highest net expectation.

---

[3] I am using "pure rationality" here as a technical term for a specific model of decisionmaking, and not in the usual and rather undefined meaning of "rational."

The six phases are interconnected, their cumulative output being the pure-rationality policy, or policies, if there are several "best" alternatives (see Fig. 4). The policy achieves "rationality" to the degree that these six phases in actual operation approximate the characteristics of the pure-rationality model.

With a few exceptions (some very important), pure-rationality policy-making is in fact impossible. The exceptions are problems that are susceptible to quantification, such as some concerning inventory or replacement policies, allocation policies, communication-network designs, product mixes, and search patterns.

Such problems and solutions of them by techniques that approximate pure rationality are the main subject matter of operations research.

Constructing complete, weighted inventories of values and resources, identifying all alternatives, making valid predictions of the costs and benefits of all alternatives—these tasks are far beyond our knowledge and capacity. Only a start has been made at developing units of measurement and methods of evaluation that would allow net expectations to be calculated and compared. In the following discussion of the six phases I will examine such problems more closely, introducing some additional material that will be relevant later on, especially to my discussion of the aggregative nature of public policymaking.

Phase 1. Establishing a Complete Set of Operational Goals, with Relative Weights Allocated to the Different Degrees to Which Each May Be Achieved

Here there are three subphases: (a) making a list of all direct goals of the policy; (b) stating these goals in operational form; and (c) providing a "rate of exchange" between the different goals. In all but the simplest cases, carrying out these subphases runs into serious trouble, which becomes more serious when the aggregative nature of public policymaking is taken into account.

Listing all direct goals of a policy would seem to be the easiest part, but only if one leaves all the difficulties of such a listing until the second phase, for which one must list all the indirect goals and values the policy should achieve or avoid. Since all these goals ultimately appear in the model, the distinction between "direct" and "other" goals is not very important for pure-rationality decisionmaking.

To be guides for action and yardsticks for evaluating different alternatives, the goals must be stated in a sufficiently concrete form to be operational. Thus, it is not enough to establish "economic development"

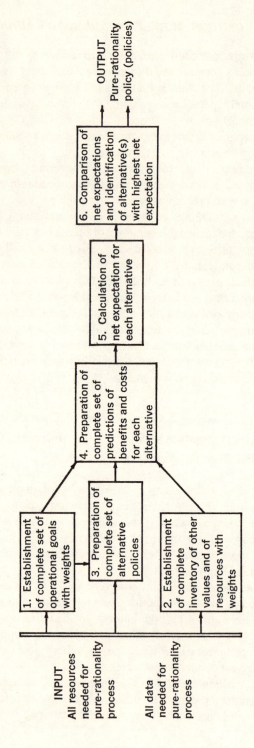

FIGURE 4. THE PHASES OF PURE-RATIONALITY POLICYMAKING

INPUT
All resources
needed for
pure-rationality
process

All data
needed for
pure-rationality
process

1. Establishment of complete set of operational goals with weights

2. Establishment of complete inventory of other values and of resources with weights

3. Preparation of complete set of alternative policies

4. Preparation of complete set of predictions of benefits and costs for each alternative

5. Calculation of net expectation for each alternative

6. Comparison of net expectations and identification of alternative(s) with highest net expectation

OUTPUT
Pure-rationality
policy (policies)

as a goal; one must establish a more concrete goal, such as "achieving an increase of x per cent per year in net per capita income for the next five years," or "increasing the qualified human resources in defined categories by y per cent (or absolute number z) in the next fifteen years." Please note that these two goals compete with each other, and are only two out of the many possible operational goals that fall in the general category of achieving "economic development."

Final goals depend largely on the values and beliefs of the policymakers. Science can point out various implications of trying to achieve specific goals, can examine the conditions under which they can be achieved, and can deal with the relationships between different goals, which can, for example, exclude, compete with, or support one another. But the values and goals themselves are outside the domain of science, and are in principle axioms that are given for the process of pure-rationality policymaking.

Formulating operational goals is one of the most difficult tasks, because the values and goals must be stated explicitly. The tremendous political advantage of a highly abstract goal lies in its non-operational character, which permits it to be perceived in as many different ways as are convenient for various purposes, and which saves the considerable costs (in terms of support, good will, possibilities for coalition, etc.) that explicitly rejecting such possible interpretations often leads to. Policymakers who need external support, such as managers who need the support of subordinates, and politicians who need the support of various interest groups (and, indeed, all policymakers), find unspecified goals an effective aid in bargaining and in recruiting such support. Since operational goals often meet resistance, policymakers tend to be reluctant to define their goals operationally, and often leave the operational definitions of their goals to be worked out by day-to-day decisions instead of setting down clearly formulated targets for policymaking to guide the day-to-day decisions. The way that some of the independent regulating agencies in the United States operate, the Federal Communications Commission or the Civil Aeronautics Board, for example, well illustrates this widespread tendency (though it may under some conditions be the optimal strategy, as I will show later). The difficulties of evaluating the results of such policymaking in the absence of goals that can serve as readily available standards are also often very convenient for the policymakers, because they increase organizational defensibility.

Sometimes, though, the situation is different. Defined goals may also be a very useful device for recruiting support and arousing mass enthusiasm; a good example is the use of production targets in organizations and in national-planning politics. In such a case, formulating operational goals is often complicated by the conflict of interests between the central policymakers, who want to encourage maximum efforts, and the units responsible for achieving the goals, which want to play safe and have a low operational goal. This difficulty is well illustrated by economic planning in the U.S.S.R.

Here, a related and very important point must be explained. In decisionmaking about concrete problems, it is often much easier to agree on pragmatic, short-range operational goals than on the overall values to be aimed for. This very important phenomenon explains much political and organizational behavior that hinders policymaking, which, by definition, deals with a longer period of time and with more alternatives. An important factor that makes for zero-policymaking is policymakers' expectation (which is usually correct) that when problems become acute, fewer feasible alternative solutions will be available, so that they find it much easier to agree on smaller and pragmatic solutions, whereas attempts to foresee problems and to deal with them well in advance by policymaking raises difficulties in forming and maintaining coalitions. It is much easier to agree to cross a bridge when it is reached, rather than to decide what bridge to reach and what new bridges to build and how.

Insofar as "agreement" is indeed the major value to be achieved, such a zero-policymaking strategy may be optimal. But when the cost of not achieving other values is taken into account, zero-policymaking is clearly optimal in many fewer (but still a large number of) cases than it is used in. In many cases in which it is feasible to undertake some policymaking, zero-policymaking may be both more convenient and easier, but will be neither optimal nor unavoidable. Whatever the best way of getting around this difficulty in a specific case may be, the difficulty is a very real one, and is another barrier to pure-rationality policymaking.

In many cases, goals for public policy cannot be defined operationally because the situation is constantly changing and unpredictable, as it is in some areas of foreign affairs. Here a general goal can be postulated, for instance, "to contain Communism." Also certain more concrete, semi-operational goals can be set down, for instance, "to preserve the military advantage of the western countries" and "to strengthen NATO." But such semi-operational goals must be able to undergo perpetual change.[4]

Setting down a complete set of operational goals is simply impossible in many cases, because policymaking requires many compromises of interests and considerations, so that the public-policy goals may be based

---

[4] The dangers of rigid fixation on such secondary goals after they become outdated are well discussed in Henry A. Kissinger, *The Necessity for Choice: Prospects of American Foreign Policy* (N.Y.: Anchor, 1962).

on a wide consensus and so be politically feasible. Exceptions to this rule are: (1) during crises, such as war, when consensus is much easier to achieve; (2) issues on which there is a general consensus on operational goals, for instance, the policy of free Jewish immigration in Israel, or protection against the sea in the Netherlands; or (3) the very important cases where public-policymaking power is concentrated in a small, relatively homogeneous elite, as it is for some issues in developing countries, and for certain problems of scientific and military policy in some modern countries.

Translating vague public-policy goals into operational goals is usually allocated—often implicitly—to the administrative apparatus in general. Administrative agencies, by determining the operational goals, exercise a most important discretionary function. The Federal Reserve Board and the Agency for International Development well illustrate this case.

Establishing a "rate of exchange" between different goals is nearly impossible, unless they are clearly subgoals of (or "means to") a measurable central goal, such as "maximizing profit during the next five years." Modern economics and parts of the new decisionmaking sciences devote much attention to creating units of measurement that will allow comparative evaluation of different goals, but as yet without much success. Beyond the often nearly unsolvable technical problem of trying to assign different marginal rates of exchange to different amounts of the various operational goals, the basic problem is still that different final values cannot be reduced to a common denominator. For limited purposes various comparative indices may be helpful (say, for budgeting), but there seems to be no possible way to assign exact weights. It is somewhat easier to set up a relative system of priorities, but this is much less than is required for pure-rationality policymaking, and is also often very hard to do.

The aggregative nature of public policymaking introduces some more very hard theoretical problems: how can you add up the values held by the different participants in public policymaking? The Arrow Paradox claims that one cannot arrive at a social-welfare function that satisfactorily sums up the heterogeneous values of the members. Leaving aside problems of welfare theory, we still face the cardinal political difficulties involved in explicitly ordering policymaking goals by priority. We have now no conceptual tools for putting many policymaking goals (including their chronological distribution) into quantitative terms that would allow us to formulate an exchange rate among them. This is the final reason why we cannot allocate weights to the different goals in aggregative public policymaking.

The combined effect of all these presently unsolvable problems with constructing any of the subphases of phase 1 is that we cannot, in most cases, construct a set of weighted operational goals or even approximate this ideal. (The few exceptions are cases in which one operational goal receives a clear priority).

Phase 2. Establishing and Weighting a Complete Inventory of Other Values and Resources

Besides the operational goals and final values at which a certain policy is directed, there are many other values (sometimes called "contextual goals") that the policymaker wants to advance, or at least not to impair. These include conserving available resources, and (with infinite weight) not consuming unavailable resources, which excludes alternatives that require resources the system does not have. All the problems I pointed out for phase 1 apply just as much to this phase, which is even harder to carry out because of the much greater variety of "other values," and because there is no way to be sure that the list of "other values" is complete.

Phase 3. Preparing a Complete Set of Alternative Policies

Having to list all alternatives (including the policy of doing nothing) is an impossible task, both quantitatively and qualitatively. There are often simply too many of them, and even the major alternatives may be so abundant that all of them cannot be considered. Qualitatively, it is even harder to imagine all relevant new alternatives for action, since this task requires amounts of creativity, initiative, time, knowledge, and energy, and a bias in favor of innovation, that cannot be mobilized.

Phase 4. Preparing a Complete Set of Valid Predictions of the Costs and Benefits of Each Alternative in Terms of Operational Goals, Other Values, and Resources

The problems with preparing a complete set of valid predictions of the different[5] real benefits and costs of each alternative policy are a function

---

[5] For deciding between alternatives, we are interested only in the differences in benefits and costs between them; identical benefits or costs are irrelevant for selecting the (relatively) best alternative. But they are important for other purposes, such as allocating resources to cover the costs, and preparing to use the benefits.

of three major variables: (1) the number of alternative policies; (2) the variety of the operational goals, other values, and required resources that are significant to the policymakers (that is, have a weight of more than zero); and (3) the degree to which the data, knowledge, and techniques needed for making predictions are available. The more alternatives there are, the harder it is to construct the predictions, because of the sheer labor involved. Similarly, the more relevant values there are, the harder it is to construct the predictions. Examining all the results of even one policy is impossible, because each one has an infinite chain of results. It is often very hard even to approximate such examination, by neglecting the more distant results, because the direct results are so many and so various. The job can be reduced to manageable proportions only by establishing a cutoff horizon, but correct use of this device presupposes a few clearly defined relevant values.

The third variable is more interesting, because it leads us to an internal contradiction in the pure-rationality model. Predictions are mainly based, directly or indirectly (that is, by means of intervening theories), on past experience. Reliable prediction generally becomes harder the more novel a policy is, and becomes nearly impossible for totally new alternatives. The contradiction is that the more complete the set of alternatives is, the less complete and reliable the set of predictions must be, and vice versa. This contradiction can be somewhat overcome by using prediction techniques, such as pilot projects, that depend less on past experience. But there are not enough such techniques to make prediction possible for many policies. Therefore this contradiction makes pure-rationality policymaking impossible in all but very simple situations where there are very few possible alternatives and prediction is easy.

Predictions of the real benefits and costs of the alternative policies must be stated in terms of the effects the various policies will have on the systems in which we are interested (an orientation reflected in the term "systems analysis"). Thus, when two alternative designs for tanks are considered, the correct question is not what the benefits and costs of the different tank designs are by themselves. The more correct question is what the different effects of the two tanks' designs on the total defense capacity will be. (The completely correct, but unmanageable, question is what the different effects of the two tanks' designs on the entire social system will be.) This is a totally different question, the answer to which depends on the interrelations between the tanks and the other components of the defense system. For instance, if combined land-air operations are potentially important, a slower tank may add more to overall fighting capability than a faster tank, which conclusion cannot be reached in terms of the characteristics of each tank by itself.

Phases 5 and 6. Calculating the Net Differential Expectation for Each Alternative, and Identifying the Best Alternative(s)

If the other phases of pure-rationality policymaking are fully developed, which implies that they have been quantified in commensurable terms, then calculating the net expectations of the alternatives in comparable units presents no difficulty. But insofar as any of the other phases are not fully developed, which they are not in almost all public policymaking, then carrying out phases 5 and 6 poses difficult problems, most of which arise because different kinds of benefits and costs cannot be compared. Phases 5 and 6 cannot be fully developed, quantitatively, for much the same reasons that the other phases of pure-rationality policymaking could not be, especially when the aggregative nature of public policymaking is taken into account.[6]

Furthermore, the selfsame policy will have different effects, and different benefits and costs, in different systems. Thus, applying the pure-rationality model to public policymaking is not only infeasible but also theoretically impossible, because the pure-rationality model presupposes a unified system in terms of which a policy's benefits and costs can be defined at least qualitatively.

Modern decision sciences permit some approximation of pure-rationality policymaking, when costs and benefits can be translated into money or some utility scale, when there are few alternatives, and when their different expectations can be very reliably estimated. These conditions hold for some problems of agricultural, transportation, and military policy, which are susceptible to such techniques of operations research as queuing theory, linear and dynamic programming, and simulation. The largest contemporary use of such techniques is illustrated, e.g., by the Penn-Jersey Transportation Study, which tried to approximate a

---

[6] A more sophisticated version of the pure-rationality model tries to cut down on the alternatives that must be fully worked out, by including "comparison by dichotomy" or some other type of decisionmaking by stages. However, defining goals, finding alternatives, etc., are just as hard in this version of the model, which must still be considered of limited significance for evaluating and improving policymaking. For a non-technical explanation of "search by dichotomy," see Stafford Beer, *Cybernetics and Management* (N.Y.: John Wiley, 1959), pp. 53ff.

pure-rationality transportation policy by means of a quantified simulation model of some aspects of the region. In the foreseeable future, the domain in which the pure-rationality model is valid may expand to cover more problems, but these will probably continue to be mainly: business-policy problems, where maximum profit is the overriding standard; some defense-policy problems, where "second-strike capability" and similar concepts provide overriding standards; water-resource policies, where net benefit can sometimes be calculated; and similar problems in very important but strictly limited areas. Most issues of public policymaking (including policies that condition subpolicies for which pure-rationality policymaking is partly feasible, once an overall policy has been determined, such as those mentioned above) seem destined to stay outside the domain of pure rationality.

This conclusion, based so far on the inherent limitations of and difficulties with the pure-rationality model, will be strongly reinforced when we take into account the importance of extrarational processes. But before I take up the extrarational model, I must examine a few models that derive from the pure-rationality model.

THE ECONOMICALLY RATIONAL MODEL

Recognizing how hard it is to achieve pure rationality in real policymaking, some authors who are interested in improving decisionmaking recommend that the various phases of pure-rationality policymaking should be developed in practice only insofar as it is economical to do so, that is, insofar as the cost of the input (in terms of what else could be done with the resources) into making policymaking more rational is less than the benefit of the output (in terms of the marginal improvement of the policy's quality). Since the idea of this model is to be only as rational as is economical, I will call this the "economically rational" model.

In the general terms stated above, the economically rational model seems beyond reproach to me, insofar as one accepts its basic assumption that rational processes are the highest form of problem solving. But insofar as one accepts extrarational processes, not as an unavoidable evil, but as a sometimes optimal way to solve problems, the economically rational model needs some important modifications.

Since my optimal model is largely a fusion of the economically rational model with the extrarational model, it would be redundant to explore the former's details and problems here. Instead, I will turn to two of its special cases, the sequential-decision model, and the incremental-change model.[7]

THE SEQUENTIAL-DECISION MODEL

The sequential-decision model was designed by Burton H. Klein of the RAND Corporation to handle decisions about development in military research and development, but the model is of general importance and can be applied to many other types of decisionmaking and policymaking. Its basic idea is that if some of the information needed to succeed in an activity can be learned only during the early stages of carrying out that activity, the more promising alternative ways to carry it out should be undertaken simultaneously, and the decision as to which is the best alternative should be delayed until the information has been learned.

As a simplified example, let's assume we must build a dam on a river. Building the dam will take five years, and will cost $1,000,000 per year. For every year over five years that it takes us to finish, we will incur a penalty of $2,500,000. Right now we know that there are two possible sites, A and B, at which we could build the dam, and that only one of the sites can support a dam. But we don't know which site is the good one, and the only way we can find out is by beginning to build the dam on the site and seeing whether the foundation remains stable after two years of work have been done.

There are two ways to approach this problem:

a. We can begin to build the dam on one site, which we select at random. We can compute the probable cost of the dam as follows: 50 per cent chance that we've picked the correct site, in which case the dam would cost $5,000,000; plus the other 50 per cent chance that we've picked the wrong site, in which case the dam would cost $12,000,000—that is, $5,000,000 to build, plus $5,000,000 penalties (since it will only be ready after seven years), plus $2,000,000 building expenses at the wrong site. The expected cost is therefore $\frac{1}{2}(5,000,000) + \frac{1}{2}(5,000,000 + 5,000,000 + 2,000,000) = \$8,500,000$.

---

[7] Another interesting model derived from the economically rational model is the so-called "theory of the second-best," which says that, when some conditions necessary for the "best" state of affairs (e.g., "free competition") cannot be met, a "second-best" state of affairs should be aimed at. However, allocating weights to the costs and benefits of different alternatives can also lead to the conclusion that the "second-best" has a higher expectation than the "best," since it is not saddled with the cost of not satisfying those particular conditions. We can therefore skip any separate consideration of this model.

b. We can begin to build the dam simultaneously at both sites, stopping work on the bad site after two years. In this case our total cost will be only $7,000,000 ($5,000,000 on the correct site plus $2,000,000 on the incorrect site).

The second approach is the better one, and would still be even if we knew at the beginning that site A had a 60 per cent chance of being the right one, since $6/10(5,000,000) + 4/10(5,000,000 + 5,000,000 + 2,000,000) = \$7,800,000$. Herein lies the innovation of Klein's sequential-decision model: textbook decision theory and common sense alike recommended building the dam on the site that has a 60 per cent chance of being right, but doing so has a higher expected value only if building on site A and building on site B are considered the only alternatives, as they usually are. Klein's model introduces a third alternative: to delay deciding between site A and site B until after we have learned which site is the right one by beginning to build on both of them at the same time.

The sequential-decision model can clearly be applied to weapon-systems development, where initial uncertainty is high, where most information is learned from the first stages of development, and where delay entails a very high penalty. Perhaps an even more important but unrecognized application of this model is to many policymaking situations. In making policy about foreign affairs, desegregation, and foreign aid, to mention a few major examples, sequential decisionmaking may provide a way out of having to either make policy under extremely uncertain conditions or not make policy at all. When initial uncertainty is high, when different paths can be tried out at the same time in order to learn important information from their first stages, and when time is at a premium, then the sequential-decision model can be an important guide on how to time experimental policies and delay decision on one definite policy so as to reduce both uncertainty and wasted time as much as possible. When these conditions are not met, for instance, when information is mainly learned during or after the final stages of executing the policy, or when alternative policies cannot be tried out simultaneously, then the sequential-decision model does not apply.

THE INCREMENTAL-CHANGE MODEL

Charles E. Lindblom, disturbed by the apparently widespread assumption in administrative-science literature that pure rationality is the best method for decisionmaking and policymaking, proposed a counter-model, that advocated "muddling through," slow evolution of policies by cautious incremental changes. As we shall see, such a model is not the opposite of the pure-rationality model; it is rather a special version of the economically rational model, and as such is closely affiliated with the pure-rationality model. Nevertheless, the incremental-change model is a fascinating innovation, and deserves close attention.

The basic idea of this model is that the more different an alternative is from past policies, the more difficult it is to predict its consequences, a fact I mentioned while discussing the pure-rationality model. Largely because of this fact, the more different an alternative is from past policies, the more difficult it is to recruit support for it, that is, the smaller its political feasibility is. Since radically innovative policies have a large chance of having unexpected and undesirable consequences and of being infeasible, this model says policymaking should be basically "conservative," and should limit innovation to marginal changes. In the terms of the economically rational model, a search for alternatives that covers only those that are incrementally different from past policies is the most reasonable approximation of pure rationality, because all other alternatives are much too likely to have undesirable and unforeseeable results and to be politically infeasible.

One point in this model's favor is that it describes actual decisionmaking behavior much better than either the pure-rationality model or the usual form of the economically rational model. Most public policy in modern (but not all contemporary) societies is made by incremental changes in older policies. Since this practice receives a theoretical approval from the elevation of incremental change into a normative model, and since conservatism is deeply ingrained in much human and organizational behavior, we can see why this model, which has many (though circumscribed) merits, has become rather popular. Two of its basic assumptions are respect for the past and skepticism about human ability to change the future. It thus meets the needs of a stable society, where slow evolution leads to institutions that embody the wisdom of generations and that should not be carelessly endangered. But ours is one of the most explosive periods ever experienced by humanity. The accelerating progress in science and technology, the emergence of a new type of developing state engaged in directed social change, the novel developments in most religions and ideologies, the population explosion—these are only the more obvious symptoms of an epoch that is characterized by rapid social change. Such change creates pressures and tensions that make men long for stability, that stimulate a new conservatism, and so create a climate favorable to incremental-change models, even while it makes such models continually less useful for deciding what to do.

The incremental-change model also meshes well with the basic ideas and concepts of the modern social sciences, especially in the United States, where social scientists' preference for "equilibrium models," "functional-structural analysis," and similar views of society as a complex balanced system predisposes them toward incrementalism, keeps them from making innovative policy suggestions, and so reinforces the policymakers' belief that radically innovative policies must necessarily be infeasible. The fact that there are social forces that create a predisposition toward accepting the incremental-change model makes it all the more necessary to scrutinize that model very carefully before accepting it as a policymaking strategy. If it is accepted uncritically, it can be very dangerous, since it offers a "scientific" rationalization for inertia and conservatism, can easily "prove" itself through self-fulfilling prophecy, and can thus block essential improvements, including improvements for public policymaking such as I am exploring in this book.

At the same time, the incremental-change model is often valid, and provides an invaluable guide for action if the domain in which it is valid is carefully defined. This domain is circumscribed mainly by: (1) the degree to which the results of past policies are considered satisfactory; (2) changes in the nature of the problem; and (3) the amount of innovation in the available alternatives.

When the results of past policies have been unsatisfactory, or have become so because of changes in what is wanted and in ideologies, incremental change is neither descriptive of actual behavior nor a valid normative model. Acute dissatisfaction leads to radical change, including revolution. From the normative point of view, when the results of past policies have been unsatisfactory, those results count for little in deciding what to do next, since incremental changes in them cannot produce significantly better results. Radical innovation is at least a way out of an intolerable situation, and there is always some chance that its unpredictable results will turn out to be an improvement. In other words, when one really has nothing to lose, radical innovations in policy may often be better than incremental change. In such circumstances, not every convulsive action is preferable to incremental policy change, but in general, the more the results of past policies are unsatisfactory, the more will optimal policymaking recommend radical innovations in policy.

The same conclusion follows from changes in the nature of problems. In many respects a new problem has no past, so that incremental change is not only not optimal but impossible. For instance, the problem of international control of nuclear armament is totally new, and analogies with earlier disarmament agreements, such as the Washington Naval Conference agreement of 1921 and the London Five-Power Naval Conference agreement of 1930, are almost completely misleading. Therefore, policymaking about nuclear disarmament must necessarily be innovative and consequently risky, but there are no satisfactory incremental-change alternatives.

When radically new means of action become possible, mainly because of new knowledge, the two major alternative strategies are: either (a) to continue making incremental changes in old policies, that is, to hold back on using the new knowledge; or (b) to use the new knowledge, that is, to make significant innovations in policy and take all the associated risks. The invention of programmed teaching machines is such a situation, in which an incremental-change strategy creates striking discrepancies between what is actually being done and what could be done by taking advantage of the accelerating rate of scientific discovery and technological invention. The successes of radical rebuilding of industry following destruction by war illustrates another case where radical innovation is desirable, but (alas) seldom voluntarily engaged in.

Most men live today under conditions they regard as increasingly unsatisfactory; they regard the results of past policies as less and less able to meet their needs and desires. Most contemporary societies, namely all non-modern ones, face an unprecedented challenge, that of accelerated and directed social change. In all modern societies, science provides many new alternatives, adoption of which requires that traditional policies be abandoned. The acute pressures of new problems also require new policies, whether about medicare for the fast-growing population over 65, or about space programs. Indeed, the earmark of enlightened leadership is it can overcome the incremental-change predisposition, and initiate innovative policies to achieve a significantly better society. Modern affluent societies also can afford to take the risks involved in innovative policies in certain areas, since they cover the costs of failure from their general resources.

The incremental-change model overemphasizes the importance of agreement between policymakers as a criterion for policymaking, neglecting the dynamic nature of "agreement" and the fact that political feasibility is only one of the requirements for a good policy. Also, the very concept of "incremental" change is vague, because the same change may be both "incremental" and "radical" in different systems and at different times.

The incremental-change model has, overall, much educational value, because it emphasizes the limits of human knowledge and so helps policy reformers and policy scientists avoid the cardinal sins of *hubris* and intellectual arrogance. It is especially significant for policymakers in avant-garde developing countries, because it draws their attention to the dangers of radically new policies and thus to the need to guard against uncertainty and risks as much as possible while introducing necessary innovations. The incremental-change model is valid for large areas of social action in which stability and predictability are the most important values, such as in judicial decisionmaking, where it provides an intellectual underpinning for the doctrine of precedents. It is also a valuable contribution to policy science, both because it explains a widespread mode of thinking and acting and so opens it up to conscious examination and critique, and because it stimulates efforts to construct normative models of policymaking. But the incremental-change model cannot be accepted as a universal or even widely applicable normative model for policymaking, despite its attractive formulation and despite (or because of) its compatibility with some of our deeply rooted biases.

THE SATISFYING MODEL

The satisfying model, as originally developed by Herbert A. Simon and James G. March, was more a behavioral model than a normative one, but since it has collected some normative trappings, I will deal with it here as another normative model.

For reasons derived from social psychology, the satisfying model claims that the satisfactory quality is also the best quality that decisionmaking can actually achieve. The central argument for this model says that a search for alternatives must in fact go through the following stages. First, policymakers identify obvious alternatives based on recent policymaking experience, and evaluate their expected payoffs in terms of the satisfactory quality. If they consider an expected payoff to be satisfactory, they carry out that alternative without trying to find additional alternatives that would have higher payoffs. Only when all the expected payoffs from the obvious alternatives fall below the satisfactory quality do policymakers try to find more alternatives, taking somewhat innovative alternatives and their expected payoffs into consideration. Alternatives are searched for in this manner until one with a satisfactory payoff is found, or until the policymakers despair of doing so and lower their standard for what they consider satisfactory. In either case, the end result is that policymaking tends to achieve satisfactory quality but not, in most cases, optimal quality.

For example, suppose we have a business organization looking for a suitable investment for $100,000, and that the informal consensus of the higher management is that a 6 per cent return is very nice, though the formal objective is more or less to maximize net earnings. What happens, according to the satisfying model, is that the staff will canvass first the investment opportunities it is familiar with from recent experience, and if it finds one that promises a 6 per cent return, it will adopt that alternative without trying to find out what better investment opportunities might be available.

Put in a more normative form, the satisfying model states that, because of human inertia and the strength of conservative forces in organizations, it is hard to achieve even the satisfactory quality, the big danger being that in fact the search for alternatives will stop earlier, and the standard for satisfaction be lowered accordingly. Therefore, satisfactory quality is quite an achievement, and policymaking should aim at it rather than at the optimal quality, which is in any case too utopian a goal to be a useful objective for organizational action.

The main strength of this model lies in its realistic tone and in its claim to be based on sound social psychological and organizational theory. It seems true that policymakers do not try very hard to improve their policymaking beyond what they consider satisfactory; in Chapter 6 I pointed out that this fact makes the satisfactory quality central for explaining policymaking. This fact also makes it clear that changing the satisfactory quality is a major lever for improving policymaking. The main weakness of the model is that it takes the satisfactory quality as given, and so ignores a main question it should be answering, namely, what the variables shaping the satisfactory quality are, and how much they can be consciously directed.

It is rather clear that different organizations have different propensities to innovate. In some cases, the satisfactory quality is close to the present quality and slows down innovation; in other cases, it is far beyond present quality, and thus stimulates innovation, though sometimes it overstimulates and leads to frustration and a reduced output.

From the behavioral point of view, the model brings out the important point that the distance between the satisfactory quality and the present quality (together with other variables) shapes the rate of innovation; this point seems to be supported by empiric evidence and by analytic reasoning for both microsystems and macrosystems. But as yet very little is known about the variables that determine the satisfactory quality.

From the normative point of view, the satisfying model makes an important, but indirect, contribution to policy science, in that: (a) it shows that the satisfactory quality must approximate the optimal quality if policymaking is to be anything like optimal; (b) it draws attention to the fact that the less elastic the satisfactory quality is and the less it can be adjusted to approximate optimality, the more it limits feasibility and thereby lowers the optimal quality itself; and (c) it points out how important knowledge about how to influence desired qualities is.

To say that the satisfactory rather than the optimal quality should be the main standard for evaluating and improving policymaking is meaningless unless we know both how the satisfactory quality is related to the survival quality and to the optimal quality, and how much the satisfactory quality, at least as held by the policymaking strata, could be changed (possibly also by making changes in those strata). The fact that policymaking cannot ordinarily be better than satisfactory does not transform every quality that policymakers believe satisfactory into a normative goal or an objectively reasonable achievement; rather it points out that the satisfactory quality itself must be considered a variable that shapes and is shaped by the requirements for optimal quality.

THE EXTRARATIONAL MODEL

All five of the normative models I have discussed so far share one basic assumption, namely, that pure rationality, when it can be achieved at a reasonable cost, is the best method for decisionmaking and policymaking. The differences between the pure-rationality model and the other four are not in their basic assumptions but in the way they estimate the practicality and justification for a pure-rationality policy in terms of benefits and costs. The economically rational model deviates from pure rationality because it accepts the restraints that limited resources put on trying to achieve pure rationality. The sequential-decision model in effect proposes a new type of policymaking strategy to be considered by pure-rationality and economically rational standards. The incremental-change model deviates from pure rationality on the grounds that innovative policies are necessarily risky and unpredictable, and that the unexpected results of such policies will likely be very costly. The satisfying model deviates from pure rationality on the grounds that, for social-psychological reasons, policymakers do not look for new alternatives after they have found one they consider satisfactory. But all these models are clearly derived from the pure-rationality model, are themselves justified in terms of "pure rationality," and are presented as realistic second-bests to the unachievable ideal, pure rationality. The model that is exactly opposite to the pure-rationality model is therefore not one of these four models. It is rather the extrarational model, whose various forms are based on some acceptance of extrarational processes as an optimal method for decisionmaking and policymaking.

Here I reach what is now one of the widest gaps between theory and practice. Experienced policymakers, who usually explain their own decisions largely in terms of subconscious processes such as "intuition" and "judgment," unanimously agree, and even emphasize, that extrarational processes play a positive and essential role in policymaking. Observations of policymaking behavior in both small and large systems, indeed, all available descriptions of decisional behavior, especially that of leaders such as Bismarck, Churchill, de Gaulle, and Kennedy, seem to confirm that policymakers' opinion. The importance of leadership, including its extrarational policymaking functions, is even now recognized in the more contemplative literature on social affairs and in much of the action-oriented literature on administration and management. However, there are many social scientists and decision scientists who bring in theoretical treatises and supposedly rigorous scientific analysis in order to paint a totally different picture: they reduce the functions of leadership to a skill in human relations; they regard environmental factors as the major reasons why certain leaders are chosen and why they operate as they do; and, most significantly, they either ignore the problem of the extrarational processes completely or try to finish it off by calling it "mysticism."

There are some major exceptions to this last sketch. Psychoanalytically oriented psychologists especially recognize some of the extrarational processes as basic, important components of human action, and try to undertake and support scientific (though often one-sided) study of them. But the contemporary behavioral sciences generally tend to ignore the whole issue. The modern decision sciences, except for isolated cases, either disregard extrarational processes or consider them an unavoidable evil to be minimized as much as possible.

The problem is not made any easier by the way in which most proponents of extrarational models present their cases. They usually argue in almost purely mystic terms that convey little to the non-believer. Such arguments, brought to an extreme in various theories of the "Superman," worded as accusations that human intelligence gets in the way of "real knowledge," and tied in (at least indirectly) with social catastrophes such as Nazism in Germany (and there are many such arguments in the extrarational literature), leave a bad taste in the reader's mouth that partly explains, but does not justify, the way extrarational models have been so totally rejected or at least ignored by the contemporary behavioral and decision sciences.

Anyone who tries to arrive at a balanced view, who tries to identify the domain in which the extrarational model could be a valid normative model for policymaking, or be at least part of one, must face a basic intellectual dilemma. Up to now, knowledge about extrarational processes has come mostly from intuition itself—clearly an unsatisfactory state of affairs. The fact that almost all policymakers cite "intuition," "judgment," etc., as their major way of arriving at decisions is also not very helpful, because we don't know how valid their self-images are, and because we have no way to compare the quality of a policy arrived at by means of intuition with the quality of one arrived at by means of a model based on rationality.

That science itself depends on non-scientific convictions is illustrated by the fact that experiments designed to find out whether there exist certain complex extrarational processes, such as extrasensory perception (ESP) and subception (effective but unconscious discrimination below the reflex level), have been given radically different interpretations. The literature leaves the reader, professional as well as amateur, more bewildered than before, and forces him to use his own a priori assumptions or "intuitions" to decide whether any of the contradictory "scientific" arguments are valid.

If we knew the characteristics of the extrarational processes, which perhaps include many different and separate processes with different specific features, we could allocate them defined roles in optimal policymaking, depending on whether their net output in a certain case is higher than that of "more rational" methods. Since we don't know even that much about extrarational processes, we have no way, even in theory, to decide what their optimal role in policymaking might be. But we should not, on that account, underestimate their importance in either actual or optimal decisionmaking and policymaking, which the decision-sciences literature often does. Instead I think the evidence about extrarational processes, unclear as it is, forces us to accept in part (after careful screening) the policymakers' introspective and observational impressions about the importance of extrarational processes in policymaking, and leave the burden of proof on those who argue that such impressions have no validity at all.

A thought-provoking and somewhat disturbing but clear-cut case in which extrarational decisionmaking processes are demonstrably better than pure rationality itself is the famous "Prisoner's Dilemma" in the theory of games. The story that sets up the game runs as follows. Two persons together commit a robbery and make their getaway in a stolen car. They are arrested and jailed in separate cells. The police have independent evidence that they stole the car but not that they committed the robbery. Therefore, if both keep quiet, each will be convicted only for stealing a car, and will receive a prison sentence of, say, five years. Now, the state attorney approaches each prisoner and suggests that he should make a full confession in writing, promising each prisoner that if he is the only one to confess by a given time, he will become the state witness and will be acquitted, while the other prisoner will be convicted on both counts and sentenced to twenty years. Each prisoner asks what happens if both of them confess; the state attorney explains that in this case there will be no state witness, so both will be convicted on both counts, but will receive lighter sentences because they admitted their deed, say, fifteen years' imprisonment each.

The payoff matrix for the game[8] is:

		PRISONER A	
		Confesses	*Does not confess*
PRISONER B	*Confesses*	A gets 15 years, B gets 15 years.	A gets 20 years, B gets 0 years.
	Does not confess	A gets 0 years, B gets 20 years.	A gets 5 years, B gets 5 years.

Assuming both prisoners make their decisions by means of pure rationality, they will both consider the alternatives as follows. "If the other guy confesses (or keeps quiet), should I confess or keep quiet? I should confess, never mind what he does, because no years in prison is better than five years, if he keeps quiet; and fifteen years in prison is better than twenty, if he confesses." As a result, both rational prisoners will talk, and will spend fifteen years in prison thinking about the limitations of pure rationality. If, on the other hand, each of the two prisoners follows a hunch that he should keep quiet, they will each spend only five years in prison, saving ten years each.

The intellectual significance of games like this is, in my opinion, tremendous. I find it all the more surprising that so little attention has been paid to their general implications in the decision-sciences literature, despite extensive discussion of their technical features. Here we have mathematical proof that pure rationality is inferior to extrarationality as a decisionmaking method for persons in certain situations. This should inspire either attempts to break up the game (which haven't worked) or attempts to draw conclusions within the decision sciences themselves as to where pure rationality ceases to be the ideal mode for decisionmaking and policymaking (almost none of which have so far appeared).

There are perhaps enough indications so far to make some sort of prima facie case for the claim that extrarational processes are sometimes a better method for policymaking (and have a higher net output) than

---

[8] This is a two-person, non-zero-sum, non-cooperative game.

pure rationality, even if the latter is feasible.[9] But there is no evidence yet as to what the cases are for which this holds true. Here is a very difficult and important set of problems for scientific investigation. However, remembering my conclusion that pure rationality cannot be achieved in most policymaking, I see that defining the role of extrarationality in optimal policymaking becomes much easier. Whether policymakers regard extrarational processes as being sometimes ideal or not, they have little choice but to rely greatly on them. The question thus becomes the less "sensitive" one of what is the best possible mix of rationality, extrarationality, and their various subtypes, and of how to create conditions that will allow these two different components of policymaking to work together.

This conclusion, which is rather different from those drawn from the various normative models I have described in this chapter, points out that we must construct a new normative model as a guide and tool for dealing with policymaking. My next step must now, finally, be to construct my optimal model, which can, I hope, fulfill these functions.

---

[9] Another, different illustration of the importance of extrarational elements for good solution of some types of problems are tacit bargaining signals in mixed conflict-cooperative situations. See Thomas C. Schelling, *The Strategy of Conflict* (Cambridge, Mass.: Harvard Univ. Press, 1963).

chapter 13 · The Major Characteristics of the Optimal Model

I will construct and present my proposed optimal model in three stages. I will explain and discuss its major characteristics in this chapter, present a detailed phase analysis of it in the next chapter, and analyze its structural framework and implications in the following chapter.

Presenting the major characteristics of my optimal model must necessarily involve me in certain subjective assumptions and premises, which I could try to justify by using positivistic terminology—that is, I could try to compensate for my model's lack of logical rigor by using value-laden terms, such as "scientific," by making up impressive esoteric terminologies, or by following the current fashion of using complex mathematical formulations. But I will do none of these. Instead, I will try to make my assumptions explicit during the course of this chapter, so that the reader can evaluate them on his own terms, and so adopt a consciously critical attitude toward my argument.

The major characteristics of the optimal model are: (1) it is qualitative, not quantitative; (2) it has both rational and extrarational components; (3) its basic rationale is to be economically rational; (4) it deals with metapolicymaking; (5) it has much built-in feedback.

QUALITATIVE, NOT QUANTITATIVE

An optimal quantitative model of policymaking can be constructed in terms of "marginal output," "opportunity cost," "aggregative net output," and similar concepts only in the abstract. However valuable it may be for other purposes, such a purely abstract model is of very little use for ours. Once we leave the world of pure abstractions and begin to deal with real conditions, we have to face the fact that the quantitative aspects of optimal policymaking depend in each case on the available inputs into, and on the stipulated outputs from, that specific case, which means we cannot construct a model that is universal, quantitative, optimal, and operational all at the same time.

The quantitative aspects of optimal policymaking depend on available inputs or stipulated outputs in three major ways:

1. In many cases, the desired or required gross output is specified, as it is for survival quality, and often is for satisfactory quality, since it may go hard on the policymakers if they do not achieve the latter. Insofar as the gross output is specified, it should be achieved with the lowest possible input; that is, optimal policymaking aims at the highest net output with that fixed gross output.

2. Sometimes the available input is fixed, or limited to a certain range. Here, optimal policymaking should aim at achieving the highest gross output, and thus the highest net output, possible with the given input.

3. In a situation where neither input nor output is fixed, that is, where both can be varied within certain limits, the relationship between the input, the best possible quality of policymaking, and the output will not generally be linear. Variations in input will result in disproportional changes in the achievable output, that is, in the best possible quality of policymaking (which is defined in terms of net output, that is, output minus input). Often the relationship will follow an S curve like that in Fig. 5.

Between points A and B changes in input will result in a more than one-to-one change in output and in the quality of policymaking. This relationship is very important because in most countries administrators often try to make the central public-policymaking system, especially the government machinery, more "efficient" by cutting input. Doing so may be a good way to motivate an administrative agency to improve its operations so as to keep up its output, and may also be justified if in fact the agency is between points C and D, where output is relatively independent of input. But often the agency is between A and B, where the correct way to increase net output is to increase the input (and to take steps to make sure that the input is being put to its fullest possible use) of such things as libraries, training, professional staff positions, special research and thinking units, periodic reexaminations of structure by management-science teams, and external consultants.

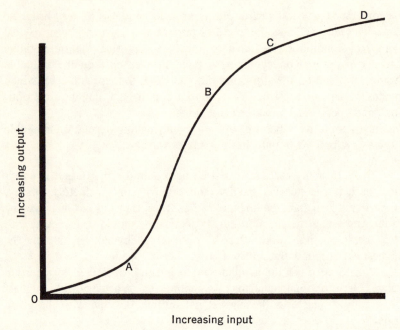

Increasing input

FIGURE 5. A TYPICAL RELATIONSHIP BETWEEN OUTPUT AND INPUT FOR
OPTIMAL POLICYMAKING

Because the quantitative aspects of optimal policymaking depend on feasible input (not only of general resources as expressed in money, but also of specific resources such as manpower and data) and on stipulated outputs, any universal, normative model must either be explicitly qualitative or use terms of the "marginal utility" type, which are in effect also qualitative rather than quantitative. At some time in the future it may perhaps be possible to construct an optimal model of policymaking (or at least of some parts of policymaking) that will be both operational and quantitative. It would have to be some sort of mathematical function, all of whose variables are operational, that would permit one to calculate the optimal degree to which each phase of policymaking, and policymaking as a whole, should be developed, once the numerical value of each variable had been fed into the function. However, such a quantitative optimal model cannot be constructed now or in the foreseeable future.

My solution to this problem is to distinguish between the qualitative and quantitative aspects of policymaking, and to construct a qualitative model that identifies and discusses the phases of optimal policymaking whatever the available inputs or stipulated outputs for them are. (This implies that in principle the model also applies to individual policymaking, though I will not discuss the model on that level.) The optimal intensity, that is, the degree to which each of the phases should optimally be developed, depends on the availability of inputs and on the stipulated outputs. I will use vaguely quantitative concepts, such as "as much as possible," so that the quantitative aspects will not be forgotten, even though I cannot give definite parameters for them.

In systems-analysis terminology, such a model is often called a "perferred" model, and the concept "optimal model" is reserved for quantitative models. I do not like this terminology because it assumes that optimality always requires quantification. Rather, one should distinguish between optimal-quantitative and optimal-qualitative models. The term "preferred," especially when it is used to refer to "preferred solutions," is also poor because it may create an impression that the validity of a normative-instrumental model, or of the solutions derived from it, depends primarily on its acceptability, whereas its acceptability (or potential acceptability) is only a necessary, not a sufficient (or even the most important), condition for it to be valid. Rather, the objective term "preferable" should be used.

BOTH RATIONAL AND EXTRARATIONAL COMPONENTS

I mentioned in the last chapter that we know almost nothing about extrarational processes or about their significance in decisionmaking and policymaking. Now I must explain my own view of them, since that view is one of the central assumptions on which I base my optimal model. I am neither extremely partial to nor extremely opposed to extrarational processes. On the basis of available evidence, I think they must play a significant, essential, and positive role in optimal policymaking, but as supplements to highly developed rational components rather than as substitutes for them. In other words, optimal policymaking needs both rational and extrarational components.

I base my opinion on three alternative arguments, the first being negative, the other two positive. First, limited resources, uncertain conditions, and a lack of knowledge place strict limits on the degree to which policymaking can feasibly be rational, so that policymakers must necessarily rely on a great deal on extrarational processes. Second, only extrarational processes will work in some phases of policymaking; for example, policymakers need "creativity" to invent new alternatives. Third, and this argument is more speculative and based on intuition, extrarational processes may solve some problems in some phases better than rational processes could, even though the latter by themselves could also solve the problems.[1] That is, where policymakers know of no usable algorithms (reliable techniques, such as linear programming, for arriving at solutions), they must rely on heuristics (non-routine, creative ways of arriving at solutions); and sometimes even when they know usable algorithms, heuristics are a better way to arrive at the same (or better) results. I leave open the question as to whether or not all heuristics could eventually be reduced to algorithms (or at least to heuristic programs), since, considering how little we know about heuristics now, that is a question of *Weltanschauung,* not of science.

Because there are so many barriers in the way of rational policymaking, policymakers usually tend in fact to rely too much on their "intuition," "judgment," or other extrarational processes, and to put the burden of making up for the weaknesses of the rational components on them. Policymakers are usually biased more toward "intuition" than "information" and more toward "guess" than "estimate," and must work very hard to achieve an "informed intuition" or a "guesstimate." One major way to improve policymaking is, therefore, to strengthen its rational components as much as possible. Another is to encourage and strengthen its extrarational components. This latter conclusion is all the more important because it has been neglected by most modern policymaking in theory and practice alike.

I could go into more detail about my view of extrarational processes, but I cannot "prove" it in any scientific sense, since there is so little data about them. The reader must accept it, reject it, or, hopefully, reserve judgment on it until he sees what implications I draw from it, although he should know by now that my conclusions will be very different from those of someone who believes that mystic feelings are absolutely superior to rationality and are only inhibited by it, or that decisionmaking should be mechanized by means of pure-rationality processes.

My general position, that optimal policymaking should have both rational and extrarational components, does not solve specific problems about how to divide the work between rational and extrarational components in concrete cases of policymaking. The solutions of these problems depend on the components of the various phases. It is relatively easy to construct an outline of what the phases of optimal policymaking should

---

[1] A good illustration is predictions of some types of behavior. An experienced lawyer may, by means of his tacit knowledge, predict the sentences that will be given by a certain judge, even though he has known the judge for only a very short time and therefore could not have been doing simple unconscious extrapolations. The same predictions can be arrived at by an elaborate and costly study, but will often be less reliable than those of the lawyer with good extrarational capacities for such predictions.

be, but such an outline does not determine what the internal construction of the phases should be, or what the relative weights of their rational and extrarational subphases should be.

Whereas the contents of the various phases of the pure-rationality model are clearly prescribed, we do not know enough yet to establish a similar prescription for the phases of optimal policymaking. Generally speaking, every phase has both rational and extrarational components, whose optimal relative weights depend on the particular phase, the available resources, the degree to which rational components can be constructed, and the degree to which extrarational components are effective in dealing with the particular issue, as well as on increases in knowledge, which permit a larger role for the rational components and changes in the extrarational components. Trying to assign a numerical ratio to the roles of rational and extrarational components in each optimal phase could therefore be of only limited validity, even if the issues and resources were kept constant. Nevertheless, I can give some qualitative indications of what those roles should be, and will do so in the next chapter.

BASIC RATIONALE IS TO BE ECONOMICALLY RATIONAL

Since policymaking needs many different and scarce resources, such as highly qualified personnel, time, intuition, knowledge, and equipment, it also needs a policy on how best to allocate these resources to different issues. On a broader level, this policy must decide how to allocate resources to policymaking, which competes with other activities that consume resources, and to public policymaking, which competes with private policymaking. A pure-rationality policy on this problem would theoretically lead to the highest aggregative net output of all policies (and other activities), and to equal marginal net outputs of the resources allocated to these policies and activities. However, such exact and elegant formulations are not very useful, because the problems that make pure-rationality policymaking impossible are many times worse for pure-rationality metapolicymaking. Even assuming that resources were allocated, overall, by pure rationality, their scarcity means that most policy issues could not receive enough resources that the policymakers can even try hard to approximate pure rationality. This is true even for the relatively simple problems where pure rationality can be achieved by using modern decisionmaking techniques, since the expected marginal net output of these techniques is often too low to justify allocating them the scarce resources (such as qualified manpower) needed to achieve pure rationality. What these considerations add up to is that optimal policymaking must allocate resources to the various stages of policymaking in a way that will use them most economically, as well as that the various stages of policymaking should optimally be improved insofar as doing so is justified by increases in their net marginal output. This is a basic rationale of the optimal model, which is thus affiliated with the economically rational model.

Realizing that policymaking resources partly determine the quality of policymaking has certain implications that must be developed in the model. One is the importance of developing resources for the long-term improvement of the policymaking system. Another implication, which deserves separate discussion because it determines the overall design of the model, is that the model must have a multiple-level structure. Since it is misleading to explore the phases of policymaking without considering the allocation of resources to policymaking, metapolicymaking and policymaking must be examined in conjunction, both being essential parts of the optimal model.

METAPOLICYMAKING PHASES

Policymaking, in the larger sense of the term, includes three main stages: (a) metapolicymaking, that is, policymaking on how to make policy; (b) policymaking in its usual sense, that is, making policy on substantive issues; and (c) re-policymaking, that is, making changes in policy based on feedback from the executing of policies. A comprehensive optimal model must include these three stages, which are dynamically interrelated. The distinction between them is often relative, though it is real; the same stage may, from the point of view of a higher level, be an executing of policy, whereas, from the point of view of a lower level, it may be metapolicymaking. Therefore, even though a policymaking system involves many stages and levels, this triple-stage structure of the model includes all of them.

The metapolicymaking phases manage the policymaking system as a whole, or at least manage significant sections of it. They (a) identify problems, values, and resources, and allocate them to different policymaking units; (b) design, evaluate, and redesign the policymaking system; and (c) determine the main policymaking strategies. They are a very important part of the optimal model, especially because they are neglected in most normative models. Thanks to them (and to the feedback phases), the model can be used to analyze, evaluate, and improve the policymaking system as a dynamic system, rather than as a collection of separate policymaking units and cases.

EXTENSIVE FEEDBACK PHASES

A pure-rationality policy implies a perfect strategy (in the game-theory sense), which includes, before any action is taken, a set of instructions for readjusting the actual policy to the extent that any or all of the predicted results require. It also implies a perfectly developed policymaking system. Pure-rationality policymaking thus needs no feedback. However, economically rational and mixed rational-extrarational policymaking (including optimal policymaking), where actual results will often be significantly different from expected results, do need feedback in order to revise policies, and in order to improve the policymaking system itself on the basis of the results of earlier policymaking.

In the optimal model, feedback is needed for two purposes: (1) for finding out whether discrete policies need to be revised, and (2) for enabling the policymaking system itself to "learn." These feedbacks take place both during and after policymaking on a particular issue. During the policymaking process, the results of the operation of each phase must be fed back to other phases. For instance, if evaluating the net predicted outputs of every examined alternative shows all of them to be unsatisfactory, more search for alternatives may be required, for which additional resources and other readjustments may be needed.

After policymaking on a specific issue ends,[2] feedback based on comparing actual output with expected output is essential to correct policymaking, to supplement the data on which future policymaking is to be based, and to improve the policymaking phases and structure themselves. Consequently, the optimal model of policymaking also includes post-policymaking phases, and a variety of communication and feedback mechanisms that interconnect all phases and make it possible to reactivate them at any stage of the public-policymaking process, should examination of any intermediate or post-policymaking results, or any unanticipated change in any of the phases or external conditions, so require. These feedbacks also permit systematic improvement of the policymaking system on the basis of its experience.

---

[2] The distinction between feedback during policymaking and feedback after some particular case of policymaking ends is one of convenience. Often policymaking, on some issues, is continuous and iterative. Some changes in terminology will easily adjust my optimal model to such cases.

In the next chapter I will present a detailed, phase-by-phase analysis of the optimal model, which I have designed to be (a) a framework for analyzing public policymaking; (b) a basis on which secondary criteria for ascertaining the quality of actual policymaking in terms of facets of process, output, structure, and input can be developed; (c) the main standard for appraising actual policymaking; and (d) a normative goal for improving policymaking. By its very presentation, the optimal model contains many proposals for improvements, but only as illustrations of more basic ideas. The main implications of the optimal model for needed changes in policymaking will be presented in Part V.

However, I should point out that the formulation of such a model can take different forms. The number of separate phases identified in it depends on how detailed one wants it to be. For example, one can regard "resource processing" as one phase, or one can distinguish between a "resource-perception phase," a "resource-specification-and-evaluation phase," and a "resource-allocation phase." My tendency to keep the number of distinct phases at a minimum and the model relatively simple results from much trial and error that proved to me a relatively simple model is the better operational tool for my purposes in this book. For other purposes, a differently constructed model would be better, and my model should be suitably transformed to meet those other needs. Keeping in mind these cautionings, and my earlier ones on how my model differs from a real public-policymaking system,[3] let us turn to the details of the model itself.

---

[3] See pp. 20–22. The reader might find it worthwhile to reread those reservations at this point.

chapter 14 · The Phases of the Optimal Model

The optimal model includes three major stages, metapolicymaking, policymaking, and post-policymaking, which are closely interconnected by communication and feedback channels. I break these stages down into 18 phases. The metapolicymaking stage includes seven phases:

1. Processing values.
2. Processing reality.
3. Processing problems.
4. Surveying, processing, and developing resources.
5. Designing, evaluating, and redesigning the policymaking system.
6. Allocating problems, values, and resources.
7. Determining policymaking strategy.

The policymaking stage also happens to include seven phases:

8. Suballocating resources.
9. Establishing operational goals, with some order of priority for them.
10. Establishing a set of other significant values, with some order of priority for them.
11. Preparing a set of major alternative policies, including some "good" ones.
12. Preparing reliable predictions of the significant benefits and costs of the various alternatives.
13. Comparing the predicted benefits and costs of the various alternatives and identifying the "best" ones.
14. Evaluating the benefits and costs of the "best" alternatives and deciding whether they are "good" or not.

The post-policymaking stage includes three phases:

    15. Motivating the executing of the policy.

    16. Executing the policy.

    17. Evaluating policymaking after executing the policy.

All these 17 phases are interconnected by a complex communication and feedback network, which can be considered a separate phase:

    18. Communication and feedback channels interconnecting all phases.

METAPOLICYMAKING STAGE

Metapolicymaking means policymaking on policymaking. The seven phases into which I divide this stage cover the major operations needed to design and manage the policymaking system as a whole and to establish overall principles and rules for policymaking. One unique feature of this optimal model is that it includes metapolicymaking phases, which I will therefore discuss in some detail. However, phases 5, 6, and 7 are more important than the others for what I am trying to accomplish in this book, since in actual public policymaking, which is aggregative, phases 1 to 4 are usually so dispersed and diffused that they are very hard to deal with meaningfully.

Phase 1. Processing Values

Every society (in terms of my concerns, every social stratum that influences policymaking) has a general reservoir of values that change constantly and that differ in the degrees to which they are conscious, intensely held, realistic, or backed up by power, in their structure and formality, and in the way they are distributed. These different "raw" values can be mutually independent, mutually reinforcing, contradictory, or anywhere in between. In their "raw" form, they are not very useful for evaluating problems or formulating goals for public policymaking; for such purposes they must be ordered and made specific.

Values can be specified and ordered to various degrees. At one extreme they are specified only by general terms such as "public interest," and are ranked only subjectively, often implicitly and inconsistently. At the other extreme they are reworked into fully operational goals that have a clear order of priority and even have some quantitative criteria for calculating their internal rates of exchange. What optimal metapolicymaking requires on this continuum depends very much on the particular policy that has to be made. Generally speaking, for optimal metapolicymaking, values should be specified at least enough to point out the main avenues of action and some rough priorities for them, including the basic values that must not be impaired (and so receive almost infinite weight).

Rational elements play an important, though limited, role in this specifying and ordering of values. Logical, semantic, and ethical analysis can help determine whether the various values are internally consistent; techniques from the behavioral sciences can help determine whether their social implications make them a consistent guide for policymaking. Also, rational techniques can provide information on the feasibility and opportunity costs of the different values. For example, a study done by the Central Planning Bureau in the Netherlands[1] calculated the total cost of achieving the main goals of all the various social groups in the Netherlands, and showed that it would surpass available resources twenty times over; this rational finding clearly has concrete implications for the value-processing phase of metapolicymaking. In principle, metapolicymaking should try to establish goals that are as close as possible to the greatest amount that policymaking could achieve. In other words, policymakers should feel satisfied only with achieving as much as they possibly can (as long as that also meets the standard of survival quality). Here, rational components can be very useful.

Final values and their order of priority can only be determined by value judgments, not by rational processes. For optimal metapolicymaking, value judgments should (as far as is "economical," including political costs) be made explicitly, and made only after the relevant data on the consistency and social consequences of the values, and on the feasibility of achieving them, have been carefully considered.

Sometimes specifying values can be dangerous to the very existence of the system. Insofar as the consensus necessary for maintaining the system depends on symbolic values that would be destroyed if they were made specific and explicit, these values must not be processed, even if not doing so may lead to poor policymaking on certain social problems, since maintaining the system is always one of the system's most important values (but not necessarily always *the* most important value). For

---

[1] Centraal Planbureau, Monografie no. 9, *Toeneming en besteding van het nationale inkomen in de komende vier jaren* (The Hague, 1963). Similar studies on the United States are Leonard A. Lecht, *The Dollar Cost of Our National Goals* (Washington, D.C.: National Planning Association, 1965), and *Goals, Priorities, and Dollars—The Next Decade* (N.Y.: Free Press of Glencoe, 1966).

instance, trying to specify the concrete referents of "free enterprise," "winning the war," or "Zionism" may sometimes reduce their ability to support a consensus, and thus endanger the effective operations and even the very existence of the party, war coalition, or voluntary organization that holds the value. On the other hand, not clarifying, for instance, the operational goals of "winning a war" may result in bad policies, with unnecessary costs and missed opportunities.

The value-processing phase is highly influenced by political processes, which determine the values that should be realized by public policy. Values are processed mainly by means of interactions and collisions between political bodies, public organizations, and interest groups. The outcome depends largely on the relative power, involvement, and commitment of the different interest groups, on the policymakers' image of the "public interest," and on the various personal and organizational characteristics of the main policymakers. (Some characteristics of this political structure are examined more closely in Chapter 15.)

Phase 2. Processing Reality

To understand policymaking, I think it is very important to distinguish between "objective reality" and one's "subjective image of reality." We can grant that any real object is rather a *Ding an sich,* in that we could go on describing it forever without exhausting all the facts about it. To deal with any real object, we must select a finite number of facts about it, give that set of facts a name, and let the rest of the information go. This set of facts is our "subjective image" of that real object. (If the human mind did not carry out this process almost automatically, we would not have language. We would not be able to select a class of animals from all the animals, select certain features that the unique individual members of the class have in common, label that set of common features by the term "dog," and thereafter recognize that both a Great Dane and a Pomeranian are particular cases of the abstract concept "dog.") The "subjective image" is always an abstraction from the "objective reality."[2]

Since policymakers, like all men, must operate in terms of their subjective images of reality, rather than in terms of objective reality, the quality of their policymaking must partly depend on how they select the facts from which they construct their subjective images. For one thing,

---

[2] The concept of "image" has many other epistemological and behavioral implications. For a stimulating and relevant discussion of some of them, see Kenneth E. Boulding, *The Image* (Ann Arbor: Univ. of Michigan Press, 1956).

the selecting process is influenced by values and preconceptions, by whether a particular fact seems significant in terms of the values and preconceptions one already holds. For example, many Kremlinologists have at times believed the rulers of the U.S.S.R. to be almost superhuman beings, whose every action furthers some devilishly clever master plan. These same Kremlinologists have interpreted the very same actions by the Kremlin much differently, when they have perceived at other times that the Russian rulers are merely human and fallible. These two different images of reality are based on the same objective reality, but they lead to very different policies.

The way individuals and organizations construct these subjective images depends not only on objective reality but also on the sets, structures, and values they already have.[3] Optimal metapolicymaking should pay attention to those facts that are or could be significant in terms of the values and goals established for policymaking during phase 1. Thus, geological formations are not significant for a society that is doing no mining, and are not relevant to its public policymaking. However, the situation is in fact more complex, because objective reality can in time create changes in a society's value system. Large, obvious deposits of ore may stimulate a culture to develop metallurgic techniques, and may lead to profound changes in its goals. I see here three interdependent variables: *objective reality* (which is itself changed by activities stemming from the other variables) is perceived in terms of *values* and other components of a person's "perception set" (that is, in terms of its potential significance for those values and other components) and is constructed into a *subjective image* of reality.

In every culture, certain subjective images of reality are held by different strata. These images may be more or less consistent, and more or less shared by other members of the society. I am concerned here only with the images of reality that are held by the members of the strata that make or influence policy. For optimal policymaking, the policymakers' subjective image of reality must approximate the aspects of objective reality that are relevant to their values as closely as possible, so that their policies will have the effects on objective reality they are intended to have. The policymaking system must therefore have highly developed sensory equipment and be able to learn. That is, it must deliberately

---

[3] The factors that shape individuals' perceptions of reality have been intensively studied. For a concise summary of findings, see William N. Dember, *The Psychology of Perception* (N.Y.: Holt, Rinehart, and Winston, 1961). Analogous social phenomena, including certain unique factors that shape the way organizations and other social units perceive reality, have not yet been similarly studied (except for small-group processes). The best treatment is still James G. March and Herbert A. Simon, *Organizations* (N.Y.: John Wiley, 1958), pp. 150ff.

collect data and intelligence, keep that information up to date, and change its image of reality in the light of feedback from the effects of its policies on objective reality. It must also create conditions that encourage the policymakers to know the situation "intuitively," by being personally involved in and acquainted with it.

For example, suppose the objective reality the policymakers must deal with includes a powerful antagonist. They must construct an image of him that approximates objective reality both by collecting and processing factual data about him and by learning about him directly, on a face-to-face basis; the latter method is essential for an intuitive evaluation of him, which cannot be achieved by rational processes alone. Relying too much on either one of these methods can cause the constructed image of reality to be dangerously distorted.[4]

Senior policymakers are often unavoidably distant from objective reality, must depend on multiply screened information, and often tend to process incoming information so as to make it fit their preconceptions and subjective expectations. These three factors, especially the last one, tend to distort their images of reality very badly. Because policymakers are very important for policymaking, any distorted images of reality they hold may cause very serious mistakes in policymaking. Therefore, one very important way to improve policymaking is to improve the way senior policymakers perceive reality; this improvement must be carried out on both the rational and the extrarational levels, by both information studies and personality development, for example.

The situation becomes more complicated when we take into account that our subjective reality includes an image not only of what reality is (and was), but also of what it will be. Since it is often easier to solve a problem while it is still in the making, optimal policymaking must have some reliable way to predict at least part of the future. Since how far ahead and in how much detail it should be able to predict depends on a number of variables, including the available resources, the nature and significance of the issues, and how useful the predictions are for present action, I cannot give any general rule for the optimal length of time or degree of detail; but the fact that optimal policymaking needs a reliable image of the future has an important implication for phase 2: it should include a developed subphase that scans the future as well as it can. Such

---

[4] Consider the results of President Roosevelt's relying too much on his face-to-face impressions of Stalin. See Hanson W. Baldwin, *Great Mistakes of the War* (N.Y.: Harper, 1944), pp. 4–5. On this aspect of Roosevelt's modus operandi, see Arthur M. Schlesinger, Jr., "Roosevelt and His Detractors," *Harper's Magazine* (June 1950), and George A. Lundberg's reaction in a letter to the editor, *Harper's Magazine* (Aug. 1950).

a subphase must use all available rational tools to the utmost, and then rely on informed intuition to settle the many uncertainties that are left after all data have been processed scientifically. Identifying and using persons with an unusual ability to deal with the future must also be a very important part of optimal metapolicymaking.[5]

The policymakers' subjective image of reality is one of the basic elements that condition metapolicymaking and policymaking; it determines what problems they will perceive and thus the general direction of their actions. This subjective image must be constantly improved (by feedback from objective reality, for instance) for policymaking to be optimal, and much attention and many resources (highly qualified manpower, time, research staffs, data-processing equipment) must be devoted to this task. Good illustrations of significant possibilities for improving the processing of reality would be to institutionalize a "social accounting system," which would supply a reliable view of social reality by using carefully established indicators and setting up "look-out institutes" to elaborate alternative possible states-of-the-future.

Phase 3. Processing Problems

The differences between the policymakers' values and their subjective images of reality are the subjective problems of a system. The more intensely the values are held and the bigger the difference between them and the image of reality is (especially when the image of reality falls below the satisfactory quality), the more serious are the problems considered to be.

Crucial problems with this phase are how much the "subjective problems" correlate with the "objective problems" and how much the satisfactory quality meets the standards of survival and optimal quality. The correlation between "subjective problems" and "objective problems" depends in turn mainly on the relationship between the subjective image and the objective reality. For instance, if an important dam is being weakened by floods, and keeping it in operation is valued, strengthening the dam will be a subjective problem insofar as the policymakers' subjective image includes information on the actual weakening of the dam and its future breakdown. If their subjective image does not include

---

[5] For a stimulating discussion of how hard it is to identify such persons, because of the probability that "accidental successes" will occur, see Karl W. Deutsch and William G. Madow, "A Note on the Appearance of Wisdom in Large Bureaucratic Organizations," *Behavioral Science,* VI, no. 1 (Jan. 1961), 72ff. I will return in more detail to relevant methods for improving predictions during my discussion of phase 12.

that information, then the dam will not be one of their subjective problems, and they will take no action. (Notice that being aware of the problem may or may not result in action. Being unaware of the problem necessarily means that no action will be taken.)

Neither processing reality (that is, constructing a subjective image of reality out of facts selected from objective reality) nor processing values leads spontaneously to subjective problems that correlate well with the objective problems. Instead, the subjective images of reality must be systematically compared with the values. Policymaking must therefore have explicit methods for making such comparisons and for translating their results into problems. Such problems should be stated in a way that helps the policymakers reduce the differences between their values and their image of reality (that is, helps them "solve the problem"), rather than in a way conductive to "pure" scientific inquiry. Such systematic comparison can, if the values are specified and ordered, be somewhat "programmed" as a fixed procedure for periodically processing both reality and values. Also, an intuitive awareness of "problems" can be consciously cultivated by introspection and by systematically surveying subjectively felt problems by means of, for instance, brainstorming sessions and panel discussions.[6]

The process of formulating problems also depends significantly on "hunches" about how the issue can be resolved, that is, largely on extrarational processes. For example, whether the policymakers formulate the problem of the dam as being one of "too much water pressure" or one of a "weakening of the dam structure" depends on how they first approach it; both formulations are equally "correct" in the way the policymakers derive them from comparing their subjective images and their values. Optimal policymaking should try not to be limited by the form in which a problem is stated, but must also recognize clearly how important extrarational processes are in formulating problems, and in getting an intuitive grasp on them, even under optimal conditions.

Processing problems involves not only trying to establish as "realistic" a set of subjective problems as possible, but also formulating them concretely and operationally, and ordering them according to their relative importance. For these two tasks to be carried out, the problems must be systematically and periodically surveyed, largely by rational procedures, and their importance must be evaluated in terms of the

---

[6] Some theories of democracy emphasize the "common man's" ability to "know where the shoe pinches" as a major reason for integrating him into policymaking. See A. D. Lindsay, *The Modern Democratic State* (London: Oxford Univ. Press, 1947), I, 269ff.

values that were specified and ordered values during phase 1, by both rational and extrarational procedures. A major difficulty here is that formulating the problem concretely and evaluating its importance depend on both (1) the particular values it is relevant to and (2) the policymakers' tacit assumptions about how they should start trying to solve it. That is, both tasks must get the full benefit of all available knowledge, but carrying them out successfully will still largely depend on extrarational judgments and "hunches." Optimal metapolicymaking must therefore be able to bring enough of both rational and extrarational processes to bear on these tasks that they can be carried out and their results made explicit.

Phase 4. Surveying, Processing, and Developing Resources

Surveying and processing resources involves examining subjective images of reality to see which parts of them can be used as resources to solve subjective problems. This phase differs from phases 1–3 in that a central component of the concept of "resources" is knowledge, which is much more susceptible to directed change than are values or objective reality. Systematic development of new knowledge that can be used to solve present and future problems is a major way to improve policymaking and is integral to this phase of optimal metapolicymaking. Because new knowledge is now developing quite rapidly, optimal policymaking should systematically examine newly available knowledge, mainly to identify those new bits of knowledge that could be used as resources for policymaking.

Optimal public policymaking must specify and evaluate its resources, just as it does its problems, but in terms of both those problems and other resource-consuming activities (such as pure research), and in terms of their potential uses for making and executing policies and for other activities. Under pure-rationality conditions, the "value" of each resource would be determined by marginal utility theory, which, together with dynamic programming, would also decide how best to allocate the resources to various tasks, including knowledge surveys and research on how to develop more resources. In actual public policymaking, the best that policymakers can hope for is to approximate the pure-rationality pattern very roughly. The potential payoff of most resources must be evaluated by means of informed intuition rather than scientific knowledge. Optimal metapolicymaking must (a) systematically and periodically scan present and future resources and problems; (b) estimate (or "guesstimate") the potential payoff of resources by using both knowledge and intuition; (c) explicitly evaluate the supply of and demand for each resource; and (d) specify needs for additional resources and further the development of new resources.

Phase 5. Designing, Evaluating, and Redesigning the Policymaking System

A very important phase of metapolicymaking is designing the policymaking system, including its structures and process patterns. Part of this operation can be carried out by suboptimization, that is, by subdividing policymaking into convenient parts, usually organizational structures whose various units specialize in different subpolicies. (This operation is also subject to values concerning the policymaking structure and process, such as those of democratic ideology.)

Policymaking must suboptimize to gain the benefits of specialization, and because so many policies, of many different types, must be made in all complex social units. At the same time, suboptimization has some serious negative consequences, especially the risk that subpolicies will not be properly integrated or synchronized, which could distort the aggregative effects of policymaking. For example, consider policymaking on foreign relations. Suboptimization requires that foreign-policy issues be allocated to territorial and functional subdivisions of the Department of State and of other departments and agencies (in particular, the Departments of Defense and Commerce, the Central Intelligence Agency, and the Agency for International Development). All these bodies, working separately, must inevitably make many contradictory subpolicies. The policymaking system must be constantly evaluated and, when necessary, redesigned so as to minimize these negative consequences of suboptimization, to establish and strengthen needed integrating mechanisms, and to allow for the constant changes in the problems, values, and resources fed into the system from its environment. Optimal policymaking must have a highly developed metapolicymaking phase for handling this task.

Trying to decide on the optimal strategy for this phase raises an interesting problem, indeed, a dilemma: at any point in time the main features of the policymaking system are given; should they be changed incrementally or radically? In principle, one could answer this question by seeing whether the conditions under which the incremental-change model is valid (see pp. 144–147) are met by the system. (This problem is of central importance for my thesis in this book, and I shall return to it from time to time.) Whatever the optimal strategy for redesigning the policymaking system may be, in this phase rational components clearly can and should play the central role. The knowledge now being contributed by research in systems management and organization theory must be put to its fullest possible use for improving the policymaking system. At the same time, extrarational components also have an important role to play, especially in inventing new designs for the system.

Because this phase is crucial for the quality of the policymaking system, it should receive a high input even if there are few available resources. Improving this phase is nearly always optimal because of its high payoff in improving future public policymaking as a whole. (The only exception is acute and critical crises, when all resources must be devoted to fighting an immediate and extreme danger. In affluent societies it is hard to imagine a crisis that would justify neglecting to improve the policymaking system, other than immediate danger of nuclear war.)

Phase 6. Allocating Problems, Values, and Resources

Allocating problems, values, and resources (or at least significantly improving their allocation—as in reality we do not engage in "zero-budgeting" in the sense of starting anew) is, like phase 5, a major phase of metapolicymaking, since it concerns the current management of the public-policymaking system. I will discuss its three subphases separately.

A. ALLOCATING PROBLEMS

The problems that are specified and ordered by phase 3 are allocated, often after they are broken down into subproblems, to different policymaking units and subsystems. This suboptimization makes better aggregate solutions of problems possible by keeping the problems to be solved by any one unit within manageable scope.

Public policymaking is only one way to deal with social problems.[7]

---

[7] The very definition of a problem as "social" is itself part and parcel of the same set of problems. I use the concept "social problem" to distinguish purely personal issues, such as individual frustrations, from problems that are more susceptible to collective action. This distinction approximates terminology that is accepted in all modern and most developing societies (Communist China is an exception in some ways) well enough for my limited purposes.

Deciding what should be handled by public policymaking and what by other methods of social policymaking is always a substantive problem for public metapolicymaking, and is beyond the scope of this book. I can point out that this issue must be dealt with by this subphase of public metapolicymaking, as well as by policy science.

Private policymaking and spontaneous adjustment are other important ways in which problems are solved. Furthermore, solving social problems is only one of many activities; society must also execute policies, engage in religious, contemplative, artistic, and recreational activities, and carry out pure research. At any point in time, deciding how to allocate all the problems (and resources) to these different activities is one of the basic problems faced by public policymaking.

In all contemporary societies (except the most "primitive"), public policymaking is the highest level at which authoritative decisions about allocating problems (and resources) are made. Despite its critical importance, this phase of metapolicymaking has not been studied. With a few exceptions, the only theories relevant to it are on whether the economy should be regulated by market mechanisms or by "planning." In general, discussions of the optimal role of "the state" are often purely ideological, rather than attempts to systematically compare the characteristics (including value input and value output) of different modes of dealing with social problems.

If problems are to be allocated in the best possible way, they must be distributed among the different policymaking subsystems in such a way as to give, with as little error as possible, the different kinds of problems to the subsystems that have the qualities needed to solve those problems. In the abstract this distribution could be carried out by linear or dynamic programming, but in practice it requires both rational and extrarational components because many of the important variables, such as the abilities of the various policymaking personnel, cannot be quantified, or even verbalized. If all existing, and newly arising, problems are to be allocated to subsystems that have the abilities needed to solve them, the metapolicymaking system must have the means, including feedback processes, to periodically reevaluate the way it allocates the problems.

B. ALLOCATING VALUES

For optimal policymaking, those values at which a problem is directed, and those most likely to be affected by the policymaking on that problem, must be allocated to the same policymaking unit that the problem is. This allocation requires, as most other phases do, both rational and extrarational components; knowing in advance which values are most likely to become involved in which case of policymaking depends on both information and intuition. This phase must also have feedback processes to improve itself.

The values are allocated mainly to four policymaking phases: establishing operational goals (phase 9), where values must help translate the allocated problems into operational goals; establishing other significant values (phase 10), which is based directly on the allocated values; comparing alternatives and identifying the best one (phase 13), and deciding whether the "best" alternative is "good enough" (phase 14), in both of which values provide the raw material for constructing the necessary criteria on which the decisions are based.

C. ALLOCATING RESOURCES

The resources identified and evaluated during phase 4 must be allocated in terms of where the problems and values have been allocated. Some resources are allocated to policymaking on a specific problem or set of problems; some to policymaking subsystems; some to other purposes, such as executing policies, pure research, and cultural activities; and some resources to surveys of knowledge, to research and development, and to evaluating and redesigning the public-policymaking system. This subphase must also have both rational and extrarational components to enable foreseeing as far as possible what the payoffs of different allocations will be, and systematic arrangements for reexamining the way it makes allocations and for learning from feedback.

Phase 7. Determining Policymaking Strategy

This metapolicymaking phase sets down the basic orientations and postures the policymakers will adopt in the discrete policymaking situations; for instance, whether they will tend to make incremental changes, which may sometimes provide maximum security for the system, or risky innovations, which provide maximum benefits. This phase also involves: (a) determining the extent to which pure-rationality policymaking is to be approximated in the areas where it is feasible; (b) establishing doctrines and methods, such as sequential decisionmaking and gaming, for dealing with uncertainty; (c) setting down basic premises, such as expected levels of economic activity and population that the various policymaking units are to rely on; (d) establishing other substantive and methodological instructions for policymaking (such as setting up a planning-programming-budgeting system).

The role of rational components in this phase depends on whether enough applicable knowledge, concepts, and analytic frameworks, whose development is a central concern of policy science, are available. More, though still not much, suitable knowledge is now becoming available, so that explicit strategies can and should partly replace "rules of thumb."

As in the other phases, extrarational components should play an essential and positive role in this phase, but they must supplement, not substitute for, full use of all available information and rational considerations.

POLICYMAKING STAGE

The phases of the policymaking stage are parallel in many ways to the metapolicymaking phases (as they are actually carried out by policymaking units in discrete policymaking situations) and to many phases in some of the normative models discussed in Chapter 12, so I will deal with most of them briefly.

Phase 8. Suballocating Resources

The resources allocated to a single policy issue or policymaking unit must be suballocated to the various phases of policymaking (including this one). The content of this phase is parallel to that of the resource-allocating subphase of phase 6, but since the competing demands are fewer and less complex, rational methods are relatively more developed (for example, modern budgeting techniques), and the domain of extra-rational components is proportionally smaller (but still very large).

Phase 9. Establishing Operational Goals, with Some Order of Priority

Phase 9 elaborates the problems and values allocated by the meta-policymaking stage. Although it does not aim at goals as concrete and quantified as in the pure-rationality model, optimal policymaking requires that goals be stated clearly and operationally (unless this would endanger basic values of the system, such as survival); that their consistency, both internal and with the other allocated problems and values, be explicitly examined; and that some order of priority, and some indication of how important achieving different degrees of the various goals is, be established. The problems with this phase are somewhat parallel to those of specifying values in phase 1, but since the operational goals are fewer, and are rather more concerned with means than with ends (especially after they have been suboptimized), more rational processes can be used to evaluate the comparative "values" of different operational goals and to examine their consistency. Insofar as different operational goals are based on different, unrelated final values, and so cannot be reduced to commensurable conceptual qualitative or quasi-quantitative terms (let alone fully quantitative terms), extrarational value judgments and intuitive evaluations will provide the main methods for developing this phase.

Phase 10. Establishing a Set of Other Significant Values, with Some Order of Priority

The content of this phase is like that of phase 9. It deals with other significant values, which do not constitute the direct operational goals of the policy (that is, are not directly part of the problem). Questions as to how operational and how ordered these other significant values should be, and how to make them so, are handled much as in phase 9.

Another problem here, and it is so difficult and complex it requires close examination, is what we mean by "significant" values. From the point of view of a political system as a whole, all results that affect any of that system's values are "significant," but to adopt such a broad view we would have to equate the values processed during phase 1 and the values of each policymaking subsystem with the values of the policymaking system as a whole. To do so would clearly overload each policymaking situation with so many values to be considered that most of the advantages of suboptimization would be lost, and effective policymaking made impossible. The values dealt with in phase 10 must in every case be limited to those that will probably be affected in some major way. In other words, suboptimization involves not only breaking up the problem, which task can be approached within a rational framework, but also delimiting the "other values" to be considered for each suboptimized problem. Since one can never be certain which actual values might become involved, such delimiting is very difficult. There is always the chance that the policy will seriously affect values that are regarded as "irrelevant" to a particular policymaking situation, but that are very important to the political system and the public-policymaking system as a whole. Explicit cutoff horizons must be established to help limit the values to be included in any set. Here extrarational processes can play an important role, especially when the policymakers have had no experience on which they could base their predictions.

There must be close feedback between this phase and phase 12 (establishing reliable predictions) to permit revision of the cutoff horizon and of the set of values established by this phase. Similarly, there must be close feedback between this phase and phases 1 (processing values) and 6 (allocating problems, values, and resources); when a policy affects values that are important for the system but are not within the cutoff horizon for that policymaking situation, the problem the policy concerns can be reallocated to a policymaking unit that is more sensitive to the values, or the cutoff horizon can be changed to include the values. Usually, reallocating the problem (for instance, to a unit higher in the hierarchy or to an interdepartmental unit) is more practical than trying to change a given policymaking unit's sensitivity to values.

Phase 11. Preparing a Set of Major Alternative Policies, Including Some "Good" Ones

Applying the concept of optimality to the set of major alternatives raises some interesting points. One way in which the optimal model differs from the pure-rationality model is that it considers many fewer alternatives. Yet, *optimal* implies more than "satisfactory," that is, more than a limited search for alternatives that continues only until one is found whose net benefits are considered "satisfactory."

One formal solution of this problem would be to stipulate that we should look for additional alternatives as long as the marginal benefits of doing so are higher than the marginal (opportunity) costs, that is, as long as we expect to turn up further alternatives whose additional net benefits justify the continued effort. The trouble with this solution, as with most economical formulations, is that it assumes we can foresee the results of additional search with a high probability of being right. This is too unrealistic an assumption to base an optimal model on. As soon as we begin to look for alternatives that are significantly different from past policies, we are engaging in creative innovation, and so will be little, if at all, able to predict either how many new alternatives we will find or what their net benefits will be.

We therefore need another way to circumscribe the optimal set of alternatives. We will stipulate that at least one of the alternatives should provide a net output that is not only "satisfactory" but "good." We should continue searching until we either find such an alternative or conclude that we can find no such alternative within the means at our disposal, in which case we must mobilize additional resources for the search or change our standard of "good."

These observations reveal that there is a dynamic interdependence between this phase and phases 8, 12, 13, and 14, but I prefer to cover those last three phases before I discuss this interdependence and the feedback loops involved in it. For now I can examine the role of rational and extrarational components in constructing the set of alternatives, taking the feedback process for granted.

Insofar as novel alternatives must be found, rationality can play only a limited though important role. In a few relatively simple cases, such as some military problems, pure-rationality techniques can identify new alternatives, for example, by programming computers to randomly synthesize new alternatives and to learn from feedback. One rational component is examining already known alternatives, which is by itself a formidable task often requiring extensive research and surveys of knowledge. Also, since we know a little about the conditions that stimulate or retard creativity, providing stimulating conditions is an important, rational means of action. For instance, organizational climate and styles of organizational leadership should be adjusted in light of what we know about how they affect creativity. Similarly, rational techniques (such as operational gaming and systematic followup) should be used to stimulate invention of new alternatives and to identify persons who have creative capacities, in order to put them into a stimulating environment and charge them with, among other functions, searching for alternatives.

Rational methods can also overcome a serious omission in much actual policymaking, namely, failure to examine the margins of proposed policies. In those many cases where incremental change is optimal, a correct way to formulate alternatives is to ask whether one should add to or subtract from current policies. Rational methods can be used both to identify such alternatives and to estimate their probable benefits and costs, and are also of some use in synthesizing new alternatives from parts of past policies.

All these rational techniques are auxiliary to creativity, which is the central way to invent new and better alternatives. Therefore, when innovative alternatives are desirable, the best way to acquire them is to use extrarational resources. This conclusion is the more important because it has often been neglected. To paraphrase one of the founders of modern systems analysis,[8] in a situation where technology and objectives change very swiftly, we must try to get on an entirely different curve, not look for a peak on a rather flat curve. Indeed, what we often need are changes in the appreciative system[9] and very novel ways to look at problems. One of the most critical phases for doing so (in addition to phases 1, 2, and 3) is phase 11, where much creativity in inventing new alternatives is essential.

---

[8] See Albert Wohlstetter, "Analysis and Design of Conflict Systems" in E. S. Quade, ed., *Analysis for Military Decisions* (Chicago: Rand McNally, 1964), p. 106.

[9] For the concept of "appreciative system" and its importance in public decisionmaking, see Sir Geoffrey Vickers, *The Art of Judgement: A Theory of Policymaking* (London: Chapman and Hull, 1965), Chap. 4.

Phase 12. Preparing Reliable Predictions of the Significant Benefits and Costs of the Various Alternatives

How hard it is to predict the benefits and costs of the alternatives depends on how many and how novel they are. More alternatives make the calculations more burdensome, and often there are no data or theories on which any predictions about the novel alternatives can be based. The more developed phase 11 is, the less developed phase 12 can be, and vice versa. It is therefore hard to determine generally how reliable the predictions should be, since setting too high a requirement for reliability would exclude too many innovative alternatives. "Playing safe" or "minimizing the risk" is justified only under certain conditions; under other conditions a policy that uses alternatives whose effects cannot be very well predicted may be better, for example, when the known alternatives have provided unsatisfactory net outputs.

This phase must meet two requirements to be optimal. First, the basic strategy choice between more innovative alternatives and more reliable predictions of benefits and costs (the more "radical" approach and the more "conservative" approach, respectively) should be made explicitly. This is a matter for metapolicymaking, namely, determining policymaking strategy (phase 7). When the strategy choice is left to the policymaking unit, as may sometimes be desirable, it involves the same components as it does in the metapolicymaking phase. Second, whatever strategy has been adopted, policymakers should try to construct as reliable a set of predictions as they can, within the limits set by economical allocation of resources, even if the predictions cannot be very reliable in any case.

Next we must consider what the optimal set of predictions, given a certain type and number of alternatives, should contain and how it should be constructed. It should include four main subelements for each alternative:

1. The foreseeable benefits and costs, in terms of operational goals and other values, with an explicit estimation of how probable their occurrence is.

2. An indication of how valid those predictions are, including a critical examination of the assumptions on which they are based and their sensitivity to mistakes in those assumptions.

3. An indication of how probable it is that unpredictable consequences will occur, with some informed guesses about the main direction

they might take, as well as an estimate of how valid the indication is and an explicit examination of its assumptions (including sensitivity estimation).

4. A clear demarcation of the cutoff horizon (in terms of time, territory, and spheres of social activity) on which each of the above predictions and estimates is based, some indication of what the long-range spillover and chain-reaction consequences might be, and an evaluation of how reliable this indication is and of the assumptions on which it is based (including sensitivity estimation).

The terminology used to describe these four subelements already indicates what the roles and relative importance of rational and extrarational components should be in constructing them. All available rational techniques and knowledge should be used to help reduce uncertainty. This is an area in which significant advances have been made in the decision sciences, for example, in developing methods for better predicting results of research and development. These advances can be used to reduce uncertainty in policymaking, after suitable adjustments have been made in them.[10] The most important rational techniques for reducing uncertainty about prediction sets include the following:

1. Theoretical analysis leads to prediction by way of a theoretical understanding of the involved phenomena. In essence, such analysis requires a behavioral model of the involved phenomena, which can be qualitative ("theory"), quasi-quantitative, or sometimes quantitative (as in econometrics). These models allow simulation of the alternative policies, and lead to predictions whose validity depends on the quality and validity of the models.

2. Extrapolation from the past, insofar as conditions are similar enough that differences can be compensated for and insofar as the alternatives are conservative, is a usable basis for prediction, even when the involved phenomena are not understood, in which case their future states cannot be predicted by analysis. These remarks also hold true for analogies with policies in the past or in other systems.

3. Focused research is a powerful tool for reducing uncertainty, though it is often time-consuming. It may be directed at providing data and knowledge that will allow the other techniques to be used. It may also be directly aimed at providing predictions, as in collating intelligence about international relations, or in public-opinion research about public reactions.

---

[10] See Thomas K. Glenman, Jr., *Issues in the Choice of Development Policies* (Santa Monica, Calif.: RAND Corp., 1965), pp. 17ff.

4. Pilot testing alternative policies is always hard and often impossible, but in many more situations than it has been used in, it is the only feasible way to arrive at reasonably reliable predictions, particularly for complex, basic social issues where the time needed is available; among such issues are birth control, housing patterns, and traffic-control systems. Gaming belongs here as a weak form of pilot testing by analogy.

5. In sequential decisionmaking, parallel approaches are adopted for as long as significant learning from them takes place. This is both a technique for reducing uncertainty that could be used as a component of this phase, and a basic strategy for dealing with uncertainty that could be set down in phase 7 (determining policymaking strategy).

6. An important method for making predictions that illustrates the possibilities for systematically using extrarational processes by means of explicit rational arrangements is canvassing the intuitive opinions and tacit knowledge of experts. A recent and promising method for doing so is the Delphi method developed at the RAND Corporation. In the Delphi method, selected groups of experts answer detailed questionnaires about their opinions on future developments (or other problems) and then receive feedback, in the form of summaries of their replies, to which they again respond.[11] In this way the effects of a group meeting that depress innovations and opinions are reduced, but the advantages of mutual stimulation and of give and take are largely retained. Some problems remain to be solved, such as how to identify, among equally famous experts, those who are especially capable at making predictions, and how to sum up non-converging opinions. But in principle the Delphi method shows how much room there is for better prediction methods that rely on both rational and extrarational processes. Some other possibilities would be to set up interdisciplinary teams that would work mainly on predictions, to encourage individual scholars to pay more attention to foreseeing the future (as done by de Jouvenel in France with his Futuribles group), and to use operational gaming to get better insight into possible future occurrences.

These and other rational methods can often significantly reduce uncertainty in predicting the benefits and costs of alternative policies. But they can rarely resolve uncertainty completely, and often leave a great deal of uncertainty unresolved. Extrarational processes, therefore, play a

---

[11] A good example of a Delphi study, one that is highly significant for long-range predictions about scientific breakthroughs, population control, automation, space progress, war prevention, and weapons systems, is T. J. Gordon and Olaf Helmer, *Report on a Long-Range Forecasting Study* (Santa Monica, Calif.: RAND Corp., 1964), also published as an appendix to Olaf Helmer, *Social Technology* (N.Y.: Basic Books, 1966).

very important part in constructing the prediction sets, both within the rational methods (review by specialists relies greatly on their "expert feel," to use the phrase of Mr. Justice Frankfurter) and as a separate source. Generally speaking, the more complex and novel the alternatives are, the less will rational methods be able to predict their effects, and the more must (and should) judgments, hunches, and similar extrarational processes be relied upon, after they have been nourished by the findings of the rational methods.

Even after everything possible has been done about it, policymaking continues to face much uncertainty. What its basic orientation in dealing with uncertainty will be is a strategy that must be established during metapolicymaking. How much uncertainty there is also largely determines what the optimal form of the policy should be, because different forms have different capacities for putting up with uncertainty. Among those with a large capacity are framework policies, conditional policies, and multiple-alternative policies. The high, residual uncertainty is also a major reason why intense feedback and repolicymaking are needed to adjust policies as their unpredictable effects are learned.

Phase 13. Comparing the Predicted Benefits and Costs of the Various Alternatives and Identifying the "Best" Ones

This phase combines the two phases for calculating and comparing net expectations in the pure-rationality model. Those two operations are so much less refined in the optimal model that distinction between them is unjustified. The balancing of benefits and costs between and within the various alternatives is carried out, whether separately or simultaneously, mainly by essentially similar mixtures of calculation and estimation, explicit comparison, and intuitive judgment.

The main problems with this phase are in trying to compare qualitatively different types of benefits and costs, which differ from one another not only in substance, but also in their chronological distribution and in how reliable the predictions that they will occur are. Identifying the best alternative is easy when there is one dominant alternative whose predicted benefits and costs are in all ways preferable to those of all the other alternatives. Although such alternatives are only rarely spontaneously identified, they can sometimes be synthesized by combining the best features of other alternatives, or can be created by imaginative innovation. Such a solution makes the complicated comparing of the benefits and costs of the alternatives unnecessary (or at least easier). Optimal policymaking requires a conscious effort to create such composite alternatives, and this task needs, among other things, intensive feedback between this phase and phase 11, where the alternatives are established.

Often no clearly dominant alternative can be created, in which case the predicted benefits and costs of the various alternatives must be compared and evaluated. The more the operational goals and other significant values are developed during phases 9 and 10, the easier this task is. Usually these two phases cannot be developed much beyond rough orders of priority, so that the comparative evaluation of the expected benefits and costs of the various alternatives will be based much less on rational processes than on extrarational processes, which often cannot even be stated explicitly. Recognizing this fact frankly seems clearly preferable to ex post facto "rationalizing" of decisions that were in fact based on intuition.

For optimal policymaking, the benefits and costs of the various alternatives must be stated explicitly, with special attention paid to their chronological distributions and to how reliable the predictions that they will occur are, so that the necessary value judgments can be made on clear-cut issues. The benefits and costs should be "measured" as much as possible, or at least classified on the same qualitative scale, with the non-comparable items listed separately on a qualitative balance sheet.

It is very important in optimal policymaking to allocate proper weights to the probabilities of various undesirable consequences. In policymaking we are usually not interested in *average expectations*. Often an alternative with a low average expectation that has little risk of undesirable results may be preferable to one with a high average expectation but with a possibility of negative results. Thus an economic policy that promises a sure 3 per cent annual growth may be preferable to one that promises 6 per cent annual growth with a 10 per cent chance of mere stagnation. The socially and politically naive (including some economic theorists) might calculate the average expectation of the latter policy to be a 5.4 per cent $(6 \cdot 9/10 + 0 \cdot 1/10)$ annual growth. However, the socio-political consequences of stagnation should in fact carry a significant negative weight to help overcome the recklessness that such naive calculations tend to inspire. For example, if we allocate stagnation a weight equivalent to -40 per cent annual growth, the value of the average expectation of the second policy will be 1.4 per cent $(6 \cdot 9/10 - 40 \cdot 1/10)$, and we see the clear superiority (under these assumptions) of the first alternative.

Optimal policymaking also requires that the decision criteria which are based on the allocated values be chosen explicitly, even if the choice is made extrarationally. This is a very important point, because it is more likely that judgments will be based on irrelevant or inconsistent criteria if those criteria have not been chosen explicitly. The decision during metapolicymaking on whether policymaking should try to minimize risks or maximize gain is especially important for making those criteria explicit. Another indispensable strategy decision is whether, in comparing uncertainties, policymaking should follow the "principle of insufficient reason" (based on a proposal by Jacob Bernoulli, which recommends treating uncertainties as if they have equal probabilities) or whether it should allocate "subjective probabilities" to uncertainties going by intuition, hunches, and feelings. Concepts from the decision sciences and from game theory can be very useful in establishing an optimal set of criteria for decisions, since they can provide a set of requirements that the criteria must satisfy even if they are based on subjective feelings and personal characteristics. Again, the requirement that the criteria be explicit does not apply if the criteria must be left vague in order not to upset a consensus needed to maintain the system. Various helpful techniques, such as backward induction by means of Bayesian algebra, are also available for dealing with the multiple alternatives of complex chains of predictions.

In choosing the "best" alternative, the policymakers must use the explicit criteria for decisionmaking to compare the advantages and disadvantages of the expected results of the various alternatives. They must also explicitly examine the various benefits and costs to see how much they are sensitive to differences in values between different systems or to mistakes in the predictions. (They could do so, for example, by means of a fortiori reasoning, in which serious mistakes in the predictions and in the value allocations could be assumed.) They should then give due (but not necessarily absolute) preference to alternatives that stand up better to such sensitivity testing. But after they have exhausted all relevant rational techniques, they must finally use intuitive judgments to choose the alternative whose set of consequences has the most preferable gestalt.

I mentioned that one could come up with two or more "best solutions" (with equal net payoffs) while I was discussing the pure-rationality model. Finding two or more equally "good" alternatives is much more likely with the optimal model, since its less refined criteria for comparing the evaluated alternatives make discriminating between different benefits and costs more difficult. As a result, one very often ends up with a number of alternatives whose advantages and disadvantages, though different, seem to balance out about the same, and which are therefore equally "good."

In the pure-rationality model, in which all alternatives and all benefits and costs are, by definition, fully considered, there are no rules for deciding among equally good alternatives, since it makes no difference which of the alternatives with equal maximum net benefits should be chosen. But the optimal model must have such rules, since it is open to improvement in all phases. In optimal policymaking, when policymakers end up with alternatives that seem equally good, they should try to reduce the number of such alternatives by synthesizing a better composite alternative, or by refining the way in which they evaluate benefits and costs. that is, by considering a longer period of time and more values in order to sharpen their predictions and their comparisons. If doing this job is not expected to create enough extra improvement in results to offset the resources it would use up, the final decision between the equally good alternatives should be made either randomly or by an intuitive guess.

Notice that a policy (or decision) should sometimes be selected from among the alternatives at random rather than by a detailed comparison of their predicted benefits and costs. This is especially the case for some competitive situations where one wants to keep the antagonists guessing, and for situations where available criteria give no single and clearly dominant solution and where questions of social justice and social acceptability militate against basing decisions on doubtful criteria (for example, jury service, granting of licenses, and selective service). Sometimes decisionmaking by means of loaded randomization is a major policymaking strategy that should be set down during the metapolicymaking stage; this is the case for conflict situations that fit game-theory models with a "mixed strategy" solution (for example, selecting targets in a limited war or deciding where to begin anti-discrimination operations).

Admittedly, randomization is a procedure that modern culture, which tends to be hostile to random factors, finds hard to swallow. Randomization also applies more to serial decisionmaking than to policymaking. Nevertheless, the possibility that a random choice may sometimes be the best way to select a public policy (and, even more so, a subpolicy) from a number of alternatives is interesting and sometimes important, and it should not be rejected because of a cultural bias.

Phase 14. Evaluating the Benefits and Costs of the "Best" Alternatives and Deciding Whether They Are "Good" or Not

In the pure-rationality model, identifying the best alternative ends the policymaking process. But in the optimal model, where the set of considered alternatives is incomplete, a search for more alternatives can be initiated if none of the ones first identified provide acceptable outcomes. Hence, phase 14, where the predicted benefits and costs of the best alternatives are evaluated in terms of the allocated problems and values to determine whether the expectation is "good" or not. The composition of phase 14 is like that of phase 13, but in phase 13 the benefits and costs of one alternative were compared with those of another, the result being a list of differential benefits and costs, whereas in phase 14 the complete benefits and costs of the best alternatives[12] are processed and compared to the "goodness" standard of the relevant policymaking unit. If the best alternative has a "good" expectation by this standard, it should be adopted as the policy, and the post-policymaking phases begun. If the alternative's expectations are "not good enough," feedback processes should set off a search for more alternatives or lead to changes in the standard; I will explain this process when I discuss the communication and feedback phase (18).

The "goodness" standard determines whether an alternative is accepted or rejected and a search for more alternatives begun. It is in fact a most important component of public policymaking. It largely determines how close policymaking gets to being optimal. If it is too "low," public policymaking will not be as good as it could be. If it is too "high," resources will be wasted on uneconomical searches for more alternatives, policymakers will become frustrated, and the quality of policymaking will be further depressed.

There is no universally valid formula for identifying the best "goodness" standard. Trying to create one would either lead to a grandiose formulation in terms of the expected net marginal output of additional search, which I discussed under phase 11, or return us to the analysis of main standards for appraisal that I presented in Chapter 6. On a more pragmatic level, I can give a few conditions, which involve the now familiar mix of rational and extrarational components, that an optimal "goodness" standard should almost always satisfy. It should require: (1) a high probability that the society will survive (in the larger sense); (2) a high probability that the policy will be politically and economically feasible; (3) continual improvements in the net expectation of policymaking in the same unit and of new policies as compared with similar policies in the past, unless the major environmental variables become worse; (4) better net expectations than in any comparable policymaking system; and (5) highly developed search for alternatives,

---

[12] In contrast to the pure-rationality model, optimality thus requires prediction and consideration of all relevant benefits and costs, not just of the inter-alternative differences between them.

with, at the least, extensive surveys of knowledge. It should also (6) pressure policymaking to be as good as possible, by requiring checking up on the policymaking phases through which the proposed alternative has passed, and by demanding independent simulating of some of them. Finally, it should (7) generally be explicit, and known during all earlier policymaking phases, whose activities it will influence because the various actors will anticipate its verdict. Establishing a "goodness" standard that satisfies these seven conditions, especially condition 6, will obviously impose certain structural requirements, such as that it be slightly redundant, on the policymaking system. I will discuss these requirements in the next chapter.

POST-POLICYMAKING STAGE

Phases that from a lower level look like policymaking often from a higher level look like a carrying out of policy. That is, these two stages are enough alike in composition and content that I can merely mention the main post-policymaking phase, the executing of policy, without discussing it in detail. I must pay somewhat more attention to the phases of post-policymaking that are unique to it; these are phase 15, motivating the executing of the policy, and phase 17, evaluating policymaking after executing the policy.

Phase 15. Motivating the Executing of the Policy

Identifying a "good" best policy and executing it are two different phases; the second does not necessarily follow from the first. Some "motivation" (in the organizational rather than psychological sense) must be introduced for executing the policy, which includes the formal approval of the policy, allocating resources to the executing, and "pushing" the executing. Motivating the executing of the policy is therefore an essential post-policymaking phase. Since public policymaking is action-oriented, that is, since policies are intended to be executed, the probability that an alternative will receive the motivation it needs to be executed is one of its most important outputs, and must be predicted when the alternative is evaluated during phase 12. This output is part of the alternative's feasibility, especially its political feasibility, as I explained in Chapter 4.

Giving or withholding such motivation is a main function of political power. Gaining the necessary support for a policy involves building a coalition of power centers that together control most of the power that is concerned with the problem the policy is about. Building coalitions is one of the basic political processes and should be a central topic of political science. The details of this process are beyond the scope of this book, but I can list some points that are directly relevant to optimal public policymaking.

1. The probability that a coalition strong enough to motivate the executing of a specific policy will form, depends partly on the characteristics of that policy, partly on the overall distribution of power, and partly on how the involved social and political institutions are structured and how much they tend to form coalitions.

2. Insofar as the probability that a sufficiently strong coalition can be formed depends on the characteristics of the policy, that probability should critically shape the policymaking process itself. Action-oriented policymaking allocates a considerable weight to the policy's chances of being supported by a coalition strong enough to motivate its execution, and this allocation distinguishes such policymaking from "utopian" policymaking (with the important exception of policies that are mainly intended to have long-range educational effects). This conclusion, as I have already pointed out several times, does not imply that establishing a coalition strong enough to motivate execution is proof that the policymaking process was successful and that the policy is good.

3. Policymaking should concern itself with strategies for forming coalitions, both while currently constructing policy alternatives and as a distinct problem to be dealt with by policies explicitly intended to form relatively permanent coalitions.

4. All policymaking phases should be influenced by the fact that a coalition must be formed if the policy is to be executed. For instance, values that are held by groups which might be in the coalition must be given a high weight and included within the cutoff horizon (phases 10 and 12). The need to form a coalition also sets some limits on how explicit the operational goals can be, and determines some structural characteristics of optimal policymaking, in that the groups which are most likely to be in the coalition often should be involved very early in the policymaking activity itself.

5. The need to form a coalition usually excludes some alternative policies, but the policymakers retain considerable freedom of choice, exactly how much depending on such variables as: (a) how many different coalitions might be formed from the various potential members; (b) how well the policymakers can sell policies to potential coalition

members, without respect to what the specific policies are about; (c) how strong the forces are that maintain coalitions even when certain members of the coalition oppose some specific policies; (d) how much the policymakers can buy support by means of inducements that do not depend directly on the policies in question; and (e) how much power the policymakers have (this partly overlaps some of the other variables).

That a policy must be politically feasible does *not* usually mean that there is one and only one feasible policy that must be adopted no matter what its other defects may be. In almost all contemporary societies, the official policymakers are not captive dolls manipulated by interest and pressure groups. In pluralistic democratic societies, the very multiplicity of the pressure groups and the complexity of the issues give the major official policymakers more discretion, not less. In complex dictatorial societies, belonging to the hierarchy gives the policymakers significant, though definitely limited, freedom in choosing policies. In avant-garde developing societies, the policymakers monopolize power more than in modern societies, and so have more freedom to act in many areas, but they are restrained by competing leaders, traditional elites, and especially the difficult requirement that the military remain loyal to the political leaders. The requirements of political feasibility thus impose limits on policymaking, but it still remains a process of making choices.

6. The major guidelines which ensure that policymaking meets the requirements imposed by the need to form coalitions must be set down during metapolicymaking, especially during the processing and allocating of values (phases 1 and 6). These guidelines are mostly concerned with the major, more or less permanent coalitions, and how they are formulated plays an important role in the bargaining process and the agreement needed to form a coalition.

7. The motivation for executing policy must operate constantly, although its intensity can vary. For instance, the motivation must be stronger to obtain legislative approval of the policy than it need be once the executing of it has become a more technical matter. Since what is needed to form and sustain a coalition varies from subphase to subphase, there must be intensive feedback between this phase, the policy-execution phase, and the various policymaking phases in order to make any changes that are needed in the policy itself. There are interesting differences in respect to coalition formation and coalition maintenance between various policy areas. For example, in foreign policy, initial support is often easily achieved, but support tends to break down when the policy provides undesirable results, even if foreseen. In internal policies, on the other hand, the main difficulty is often establishment of the initial coalition, which then will in many cases become a captive of the

policy and will be unable to desert it even if quite undesirable and unforeseen results develop.

8. Each potential coalition member decides whether he should join a coalition or not, and whether he should stay in it or not, by means of his own internal policymaking processes ("he" could of course mean a group). His decision will depend on, among other things, how well the proposed policy compares with his own "goodness standard," and on his own strategies for forming coalitions and gaining power.

9. Extrarational processes play indispensable roles in all the subphases. Familiarity with the field, a feeling for what is politically feasible, and skills at bargaining and forming coalitions are only a few of the extrarational abilities that are essential for those who practice the "art of the possible." At the same time, rational methods can be very helpful and therefore are essential to this phase if it is to be optimal. Intelligence operations, public relations, conflict theory, and propaganda techniques are examples of how important rational components are for this phase.

Phase 16. Executing the Policy

Analytically, the contents of this phase are similar to the various phases of policymaking. A policy is almost always executed by means of many subpolicymaking processes, as well as by "field operations" (such as building a dam, paying a pension, etc.) that involve relatively little decisionmaking. These processes not only add up to the executing of the policy, but are closely related to policymaking itself in two ways: (1) repolicymaking is needed during the executing of the policy; and (2) the way in which a policy is executed partly, and sometimes completely, determines what the actual contents of the policy are. Optimal policymaking must encourage whatever remaking of policies is shown to be necessary by the feedback from the executing of those policies. Optimal policymaking must also often leave the concrete definitions of the policy to be determined when it is applied to discrete issues during its execution. However, changes in the policy's contents that arise because the executing of the policy deviates from what the policymakers intended the policy to be are often undesirable and should be minimized.

These two phenomena are interrelated: the more efficiently the policy is readjusted as it is executed in light of feedback from that execution, the less will the executing tend to deviate from what the policymakers intend and so to create a new policy (as distinguished from proper subpolicies) of its own.

An altogether different situation is action without any policy. Here, single "execution" decisions may in time add up to an implicit policy. Such a method for formulating policies may be optimal in a good many cases, for which it should be explicitly decided upon during the metapolicymaking stage, but often it is merely a case of what I have called "zero-policymaking," that is, of not making policy.

Phase 17. Evaluating Policymaking After the Policy Has Been Executed

This phase and the next largely determine how well policies are remade as and after they are executed. Evaluating the policymaking begins when any executing of the policy begins, and continues until the executing, including any necessary remaking of the policy and executing of the remade policy, has been completed. This evaluation of policymaking has two subphases: (1) comparing the actual results of the executing, that is, the *actual* policymaking output, with the *expected* results; and (2) evaluating the differences between them. Actual policymaking results can fall into four categories: (1) expected and desired results; (2) expected and undesired results; (3) unexpected and desired results; and (4) unexpected and undesired results.

The purpose of the first subphase is to identify unexpected results, which include expected results that did not materialize. To this end, this subphase must include a clear cutoff horizon to limit the field within which results are looked for, scanning methods that will identify the policy's results, a clearly defined set of expectations for the executed policy, and a method for comparing the actual results with the expected ones.

The purpose of the second subphase is to evaluate the differences between the actual results and the expected results, that is, to identify the results that are both unexpected and undesired. Insofar as such results are present, which they almost always are, the policymakers must determine: (1) whether they call for any corrective action; and (2) if they do, whether they are caused (a) by incorrect executing of the policy, and so should be dealt with by changes in the way the policy is executed, or (b) by flaws in the policy or changes in relevant variables, and so should be dealt with by remaking the policy.

Since the details of this phase and its subphases are partly identical with those of earlier phases of policymaking, and are partly beyond the scope of this book, I will make only a few short observations on them to bring out the features that are most important for my purposes.

1. Policymakers, like other human beings, tend to readjust their expectations for a policy after its actual results are known, so as to diminish the gap between them. (This phenomenon has been explained

as being caused by a pressure to reduce post-decision dissonance.) However useful such readjustment may be in maintaining individual integrity and organizational morale, it badly distorts any post-execution evaluation of policymaking and destroys much of the usefulness of feedback, and must be kept under control if policymaking is to be optimal. The best ways to control it are to formulate the expectations for each of the alternative policies clearly and in writing during phase 12, and to charge special units with parts of the evaluation.

2. That a policy has unexpected results does not imply that policymaking was not optimal. Optimal policymaking, unlike pure-rationality policymaking, recognizes that a certain number of unexpected results is "normal." (How many are "normal" depends on the basic policy strategy, on the rate of change in the relevant conditions, etc.) This is a very important point, because the widespread tendency to blame policymakers for every unexpected result puts them under pressure to adopt the "safest" strategy, incremental change, and to purposely leave the policy's expectations ambiguous; both courses of action may lead to very much poorer policymaking.

3. Rational components play important roles in evaluating policymaking after the policy is executed, in identifying the actual results, and in comparing them with the expected results.

COMMUNICATION AND FEEDBACK

The last phase of the optimal model crosscuts and interconnects all the other phases, and is thus in a category by itself.

Phase 18. Communication and Feedback Channels Interconnecting All Phases

Evaluating policymaking while and after the policy is executed is important, not in itself, but in terms of the conclusions and feedbacks resulting from it, which include: (1) immediate feedback about the policy that is being executed aimed at stimulating remaking of the policy; (2) immediate feedback about the policy that is being executed aimed at stimulating changes in the way the policy is being executed; and (3) learning feedback, which is aimed at all the metapolicymaking, policymaking, and post-policymaking phases, and intended to improve their future operation in the light of current experience.

These feedbacks are only three of the many communication and feedback loops that connect all the phases and subphases of optimal policymaking with each other. Since all these phases are dynamically interdependent, and since most of them take place at the same time, policymaking must have highly elaborate and efficient communication and feedback channels and mechanisms in order to operate, especially to operate optimally. For optimal policymaking, not only should this network be elaborate and efficient, but noise in it should be strictly controlled, its thresholds should be carefully supervised, and its main components should be consciously designed and managed. I do not mean that every detail of the network should be planned, which is an impossible task, given the complexities of aggregative policymaking. But the communication of feedback loops should not be left to spontaneous self-direction; the more critical loops especially must be explicitly established and maintained. Learning feedback loops, on which the long-run quality of the policymaking system largely depends, and which inevitably disintegrate unless they are consciously maintained, are among the most critical.

Going into detail about all, or even the most important, of the communication and feedback loops would be tedious, and would add little to what I am trying to accomplish in this book. I will illustrate the contents of this complex phase by discussing one very important and so far oft-mentioned immediate-feedback loop, namely, the alternative-search feedback loop. Its purpose is to encourage searching for new alternatives until one is identified whose expectations satisfy the "goodness" standard. It begins from phase 14 when none of the predictions satisfy the "goodness" standard; leads to phase 11, where it sets off a search for additional alternatives; continues to phase 12, where the results of the new alternatives are predicted; and returns to phase 14, where the predicted benefits and costs of the new alternatives are compared with the "goodness" standard; if none of these alternatives are accepted, another cycle of feedback is set off. This main loop has some secondary loops. If not enough resources have been allocated to phase 11 to allow additional search, a feedback is set off to phase 8 to get a suballocation of more resources. If the additional resources are suballocated, the secondary loop returns to phase 11 and is closed; if not, one of two alternative feedbacks is initiated, a feedback to phase 6 for additional allocation of resources, or a feedback to phase 14 to change the "goodness" standard and adopt one of the earlier alternatives. If there is a feedback to phase 6, either the additional resources will be allocated to phase 8, thus closing a loop, or there will be a feedback to phase 14 to change the "goodness" standard and accept an earlier alternative. Phase 6 may allocate additional resources to phase 8 by withdrawing resources

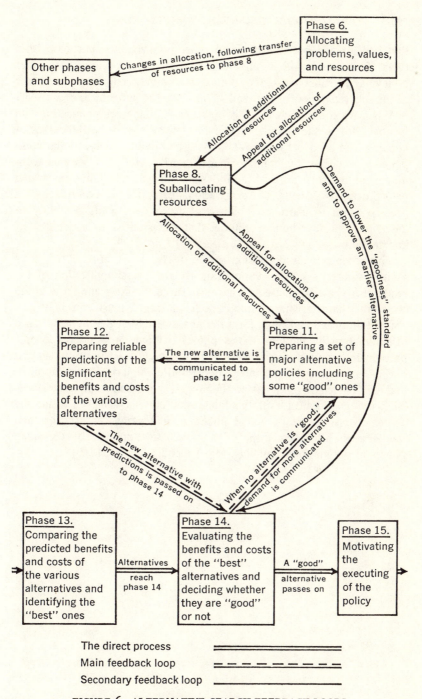

FIGURE 6. ALTERNATIVE-SEARCH FEEDBACK LOOPS

that had already been allocated to other policymaking purposes from them. This change will set off a complex network of feedback in other policymaking subsystems, and so may cause more feedback to the phases of the subsystem in question, and so on. (See Fig. 6 for these processes.)

When we consider that this is only one of many communication and feedback loops, the complexities of the network, and the difficulties of keeping it in adequate operation, should be obvious. The rational components needed to maintain such a network include the various techniques of network analysis and design, and of designing integrated data-processing systems. The extrarational components needed include a predisposition to learn, an ability to absorb data, and an ability to develop the positive human relations that are essential for a free flow of information.

This completes my discussion of the phases of the optimal model as such. My next task is to compensate for the oversimplification of the model this phase-by-phase analysis has caused, by integrating it with the structural characteristics of public policymaking. I must especially correct the atomized and static form the phases are in at the moment, since in optimal policymaking all the phases, subphases, and components participate in an iterative process and must be at least partly integrated into a single system. Such integration requires high-quality metapolicymaking (especially phase 5) and high-quality communication and feedback. On the practical level, this integration must be achieved within the aggregative structure of actual public policymaking that the optimal model must also deal with. (For a concise summary of the main phases of optimal policymaking, see Appendix B, pp. 311ff.)

chapter 15 · The Structure of Optimal Public Policymaking

So far I have been paying attention to the process patterns of optimal public policymaking. To complete the optimal model, I must consider the structural framework of public policymaking, and derive the implications the optimal model has for that structure. Applying the phases of the optimal model to the policymaking structure will make it an integrated systems model of optimal public policymaking, on which attempts to analyze, evaluate, and improve public policymaking can be based.

Putting forth one single policymaking structure as the best possible ideal model has always been a very attractive idea to Utopian writers, political commissars, abstract social philosophers, and others with a low tolerance for ambiguity, but in my opinion there is no such single optimal model. Many different structural combinations, operating according to various different principles, can be optimal, depending on such variables as: social values concerning the public-policymaking structure; available input; stipulated output; the nature and characteristics of the issues to be decided; the values and orientations of the major policymakers and policy-shapers, and their habitual work patterns; the existing policymaking structure; and how much the various power centers support, oppose, or are indifferent to various changes in traditional arrangements. We can describe the major characteristics of different social structures—of the hierarchy, of the free market, of groups that are antithetical, at cross-purposes, or willing to bargain, etc.—under various conditions. But there are too many variables, they can take on too many different kinds of values, and we know too little about them, for us to be able to set up a universal metamodel of social behavior, let alone derive from it a detailed and dynamic model of an optimal structure for public policymaking that will apply to all cases. Indeed, insofar as I am right in describing the public-policymaking system as exceedingly complex and partly "arbitrary," a detailed specification of all its structural elements is inherently impossible. The most the human mind can try to do, and it is more than enough for almost all meaningful purposes, is to provide some basic guides for designing the central features of the public-policymaking structure (or, to be more precise, for redesigning it).

Mankind may be able to undertake a formulation of such basic guides in the not-too-distant future with some confidence, especially if the task is only to construct the basic framework, not to predetermine details. The progress being made in administrative sciences and systems-design methods gives me cause to hope that policy science may come up with the knowledge needed to redesign the public-policymaking system, or at least some of its more important compact subsystems (such as government agencies and legislatures). But, to be frank, neither the facts nor the methods needed to set down a complete, basic guide for constructing optimal policymaking systems are yet available.

Nevertheless, with the help of my phase analysis of optimal policymaking, I can make a start at identifying some features that will be necessary for an optimal public-policymaking structure. I realize that both the nature of the task and our present state of knowledge join in making it impossible to specify all the details for all the cases of an optimal policymaking structure (or, perhaps, structures, each optimal for a different set of circumstances). Still, I think our present knowledge will allow me, without being too presumptuous, to enumerate at least some of the structural features that will in general be needed for optimal policymaking, and to describe them concretely and reliably enough that they can be used to analyze, evaluate, and improve contemporary policymaking structures.

THE AGGREGATIVE NATURE OF PUBLIC POLICY-MAKING

The reason why public policymaking is aggregative can be found in its inherent nature and genesis. Public policy is the product of a complex, dynamic interrelationship between many subpolicies, decisions, and subdecisions, each of which is itself reached by a complete decisionmaking process that is in turn composed of subdecisions, and so on, down to single decisions made by an individual acting nominally on his own. These multiple decisions are made by various social units and individuals who are distributed over many different social structures and points in time.

The nominal outcome of the interactions (insofar as they are relevant to policies) between these social units and individuals, that is, what they add up to, is the public policy, while the aggregating process is the public-policymaking process. The social units that participate in public policymaking constitute the structural framework of public policymaking; that is, they are the structural aspect of the public-policymaking system. The exact boundaries of this structure depend on what the policy is about, on how much time one considers, and on changes in the overall social system of which public policymaking is a subsystem. Nevertheless, in every society that is not right in the middle of a revolution, a relatively stable nucleus of units participates in most public policymaking, and is thus, by definition, the central public-policymaking structure of that society (and is generally identical with the "political structure").

The aggregativeness of public policymaking is not a result of historical accidents nor of ideologies that favor pluralism and decentralized authority. However such factors may have influenced the concrete shape of the public-policymaking structure in any one society, that structure is aggregative and complex because such characteristics are essential for public policymaking in almost all contemporary societies. Four major reasons why public policymaking must be aggregative are (1) so much public policy must be made that the work must be spread out among many policymaking units; (2) public policymaking is so complex, in terms of the information and skills needed for it, that the various issues it deals with must be handled by specialized bodies; (3) because the major centers of social power must support or at least acquiesce in policies, they must participate in the policymaking process; and (4) because public policymaking is so important in distributing social benefits and costs, many centers of social power are extremely interested in participating in public policymaking—in general, the broader the functions of the state are, the more such power centers are motivated to try to enter the political arena and participate in public policymaking.

Even the simplest model of public-policymaking structure must include the following four components:

1. The various units that participate in public policymaking (and interact with each other) and that can make different specific contributions to policymaking. How much and what each unit can contribute is determined by its different characteristics, such as its structure, values, interests, knowledge, and ability to process data.

2. A complex network of communication and feedback channels

that interconnect the different units. The interactions between the units take place by means of this network.

3. Some of the variables that determine how much and how importantly each of the different units actually contributes to various cases of public policymaking. We do not know enough yet to measure or even list all of these variables, but the ones we know about include: the resources that are at the disposal of the different units; the institutional or legal framework that sets down the formal procedure for public policymaking; the values of the social-cultural environment; and the images that the different units have of the significance of various kinds of policymaking, and of what the policy is about (such as whether it deals with "scientific" or "secret" matters).

4. The public policy that results from the interactions between the units. This policy can be analyzed in terms of various dimensions that parallel the dimensions of the contributions made by various units to policymaking and that constitute one of the basic conceptual taxonomies for analyzing public policy. They include: how long a range of time the policy is intended to cover; how sensitive it is to public opinion and interest groups; how much it is based on various kinds of expertness; how comprehensive it is; how consistent it is with previous decisions; and so on.

It is easy to state abstractly how the phases of the optimal model of public policymaking should fit into such a structural framework: an optimal structure for public policymaking should add up to all the phases of the optimal model at minimum cost (in terms of the resources that are consumed and the values that are made less achievable by the operating and maintaining of the structure itself). That is, the public-policymaking structure's output of "policy" should add up to the hypothetical output of a "pure" optimal public-policymaking process (one that is not distorted by the noise that is in fact inherent in all, and especially in complex, structures). This abstract statement can be made more usable by turning it into an additive matrix as in Fig. 7. This matrix tabulates the phases of the optimal model against the units that contribute to public policymaking. In each cell of the matrix is entered the contribution of that unit to that phase, and the contributions to each phase are then added up. The matrix can be broken down as far as convenient into subunits and subphases.

For optimal policymaking, four conditions must be satisfied: (1) there must be at least one unit that contributes to each phase; (2) the contributions of the various units to each phase must "add up" to that

Phases or subphases	Units or subunits									
	a	b	c	d	e	f	g	h	i	. . .
1	a_1	b_1	c_1	d_1	e_1	f_1	g_1	h_1	i_1	. . .
2	a_2	b_2	c_2	d_2	. . .					
3	a_3	b_3	. . .							
4	a_4	b_4	. . .							
5	a_5	. . .								
6	a_6	. . .								
7	. . .									
8										
9										
. . .										
Aggregative policy	a_i	b_j	c_k	d_l	e_m	f_n . . .				

FIGURE 7. AN ADDITIVE MATRIX OF POLICYMAKING STRUCTURE

phase's optimal operation; (3) the contributions of the various units to each phase must "add up" to that phase at low cost and with little distortion; and (4) the different phases must integrate into a dynamic process of public policymaking at low cost and with little distortion. (Conditions 3 and 4 strive for maximum efficiency, in the sense of maximum net output of the aggregation function. Strictly speaking, we cannot maximize benefits and minimize costs at the same time. Nevertheless, for our present limited purposes, special attention should be devoted to reducing costs and distortions, keeping in mind that we want to "optimize," not "minimize.")

The first condition permits one to draw a very important negative conclusion: if there is no unit contributing to one of the phases or subphases, then that phase or subphase is not being carried out. This conclusion sounds rather pedestrian, being quite simple, but it is therefore foolproof, and so is of great analytic and practical significance. If, for any phase, subphase, or component thereof, one can find no unit making any contribution to it after carrying out a careful search for latent, hidden, or camouflaged contributions, one can be sure that this lack reveals a significant shortcoming in the public-policymaking structure (that is, such a lack is a reliable secondary criterion). A matrix of policymaking structure, which cross-tabulates the different phases of policymaking and the contributions to them by the various units participating in policymaking, can be used to identify relatively easily essential components that are missing from a particular public-policymaking structure. Such a matrix is illustrated by the integrated scheme for evaluating public policymaking that I developed in Chapters 3 to 7 and used in Chapters 9 to 11.

It is more difficult to decide whether the various units contribute enough to the various phases and subphases, as required by the second condition. At present we cannot measure most of the contributions to the various phases or the optimal operation of the phases. It is even harder to decide how much a given distribution of contributions to a phase "adds up" to its optimal operation. Because the interactions between the various units are so complex, their contributions to a phase cannot be added up by any simple arithmetical method. For example, when searches for alternatives are being carried out by different, competing units at the same time, mutual stimulation can cause the total search to be more effective than the simple additive sum of searches carried out by each of the units individually. Or, the various operational goals contributed by different units may contradict, reinforce, or be irrelevant to one another, and the total operational goals must be quite different in each case. Or, different units that are engaged in predicting benefits and costs may under some conditions reinforce one another's mistakes, and the aggregate prediction will in this case be less valid than that of any one unit by itself. In general, the output of a system is not a simple sum of the outputs of its components. This is the basic rationale of systems analysis, systems management, systems engineering, systems simulation, etc., which are major components of modern management science and should become, although in more qualitative forms, major components of policy science.

The aggregate achievement by each different policymaking phase is always some mathematical function[1] of the specific contributions made to that phase by different units, but even what kind of function it is will

---

[1] For an explanation of different meanings of the term "function," see F. Parker Fowles, Jr., and E. W. Landberg, *Basic Mathematics for Administration* (N.Y.: John Wiley, 1962), pp. 81ff., and Robert K. Merton, *Social Theory and Social Structure* (Glencoe, Ill.: Free Press, 1949), pp. 23ff.

depend on the particular policymaking structure and its environment. Since we do not yet know enough to identify the forms of such functions even approximately, all I can do is outline some of the main types of relationships between units. For optimal policymaking, we are especially interested in relationships that can, under favorable conditions, approximate optimality, at low cost and with few distortions, by combining and reinforcing the best features of the contributions by the different units, while canceling out their bad features.

What we are looking for, therefore, are relationships between units that maximize their aggregative positive contribution to policymaking. One major task of policy science should be to outline such relationships for different policymaking phases, issues, and circumstances, but since it has not yet been carried out, I can only list some major types of relationships between units, and give some indication of what their aggregative effect on public policymaking is.

MAJOR TYPES OF RELATIONSHIPS BETWEEN UNITS

I shall briefly examine four major types of relationships between units; these are (a) the simple and (b) the complex hierarchies, and the polycentric structure with (c) many and with (d) few autonomous units.

The Simple Hierarchy

In a simple hierarchy, where different units prepare the data needed for optimal policymaking and where a small, central policymaking unit uses the data to determine policy, the contributions of the different units in part combine more or less additively and in part combine as in small-group decisionmaking (see pp. 80–81). But such a structure can deal adequately only with policy issues that require no extensive division of labor or specialization of roles and that need no support by groups which would otherwise have to be brought into the policymaking process. Some very important policies can (sometimes optimally) be made by a simple hierarchy. Thus, Presidential policymaking under conditions of stress and secrecy may best take place in a structure much like a simple hierarchy, that of the President and his main advisors. Such policymaking is influenced by a structure of many agencies that supply much of the relevant data, but the main making of policy must sometimes be done by a small structural nucleus.

This point, often neglected because of an emphasis on pluralism, has important theoretical and analytic implications, one of which is its reassertion of the often critical role of individual leaders in policymaking. Its major practical emphasis is on improving the structure surrounding the major policymakers, such as the President in the United States and the Prime Minister and Cabinet, collectively, in England. That the flow of information to such main policymakers should be as good as possible, that a balanced set of advisors should work closely with them, that standing procedures should ensure that the main agencies specializing in relevant areas (such as the Chiefs of Staff) participate in the policymaking in the "inner circle"—these points are well illustrated by the Presidential decisionmaking on armed intervention in Korea, on the Bay of Pigs invasion of Cuba, and on the Cuban missile crisis.

The Complex Hierarchy

In complex hierarchies, the policy issues are broken down into subissues and allocated to the different specialized units that make up the hierarchy. If these issues are subdivided in the best possible way and if every subissue is decided by the subpolicymakers in the best possible way, then the subdecisions will be mutually complementary, and the aggregate decision will approximate an optimal overall policy.

This is one of the most important types of structure. Being based on suboptimization, and so able to take advantage of extensive division of labor and specialization of functions, it is one of the most effective mechanisms for social management. But complex hierarchies have certain inherent limitations. Dividing labor among specialized units necessarily introduces a strong centrifugal element; each unit tends to adopt a narrow point of view that interferes with the integration of its contribution into an overall policy. As a result, either the relationships between the units will become more and more polycentric, or strong hierarchic controls will be established, but such controls reduce both the professional autonomy of the various units and thus the quality of their operation, consume more and more resources in order to coordinate and integrate the policymaking, and monopolize much of the available power. Such monopoly, besides being abhorred by democratic ideology, often leads to poor policies because individual idiosyncracies and lapses of attention can so easily distort policymaking in such circumstances.

Organizations seem to oscillate between these two types of response to the problems inherent in suboptimization. (Most of the professional literature discusses them in terms of "centralization vs. decentralization" and "concentration vs. deconcentration.") These problems and the resulting oscillation limit the capacity of complex hierarchies to deal with policy issues. In theoretical terms, the limit is reached as soon as the marginal costs of integrating policies are greater than the marginal benefits of additional division of labor and specialization. Changes in policymaking technologies, such as in operations research and in integrated electronic data processing, allow complex hierarchies to be larger, but do not eliminate their inherent shortcomings and the limit to their effectiveness.

The Polycentric Structure with Many Autonomous Units

The market model is a good example of a polycentric structure that has many autonomous units. Under certain conditions that are listed by economic theory, pure-rationality decisionmaking by many autonomous units can aggregate into pure-rationality solutions of complex problems, by means of the intervening and parametric functions of prices. Democratic theory can be somewhat based on a similar structural theory, the individual voter being regarded as the autonomous decisionmaker and the elections as the parametric functions.[2] The attractiveness of these theories is that they simplify the problem of optimal policymaking by not having it depend either on hierarchic suboptimization and aggregation or on leaders and their inner circle. However, in real life the "invisible hand" often does not operate, and societies must then resort to hierarchic structures. Furthermore, almost all such theories presuppose that individual men are purely or almost purely rational, which is too unrealistic a requirement.

Polycentric structures with many autonomous units are not very valid as models for public policymaking. They do apply fairly well to some types of economic policymaking. Indeed, the market mechanism is often regarded as a method for solving social problems that is an alternative to, rather than a type of, public policymaking. However, consciously designing a market mechanism can in principle be an explicit structural device, adopted during metapolicymaking as a preferred way to make

---

[2] This idea has been explored in several modern studies. See Robert A. Dahl, *A Preface to Democratic Theory* (Chicago: Univ. of Chicago Press, 1956); Anthony Downs, *An Economic Theory of Democracy* (N.Y.: Harper, 1957); and James M. Buchanan and Gordon Tullock, *The Calculus of Consent: Logical Foundations of Constitutional Democracy* (Ann Arbor: Univ. of Michigan Press, 1962).

policy about production, consumption, and prices, as it is when a market mechanism is proposed within a socialist economic regime,[3] and when the market mechanism is reinforced by such instrumental actions as, for example, anti-trust laws (but remember that in almost all political discussions of the free market, instrumental and self-valuable arguments and considerations are thoroughly mixed up). Looking at the major policymaking units, we find that polycentric structures with many autonomous units seem to apply to only a few special, though important, cases of policymaking. Most public policymaking requires structural arrangements that do not depend on the existence of such parametric mechanisms as market prices.

The Polycentric Structure with Few Autonomous Units

Polycentric structures with few autonomous units have a basic operational rationale that is radically different from that of polycentric structures with many autonomous units. The autonomous units in the former direct their operations not toward some anonymous intervening factor such as the price level, but toward one another. They operate in terms of "partisan mutual adjustment"[4] mainly by bargaining and forming coalitions with one another.

Mathematical functions that can partly indicate how policy contributions aggregate within a polycentric structure with few autonomous units, are provided partly by the theory of games and partly by the geometry of vectors: the power of the unit determines the length of the vector, and the policy the unit makes determines the direction of the vector. The sum of the vectors depends on the configuration of each field; different units can reinforce or neutralize one another, or have an aggregate effect that is quite different from what any one of them wanted. Because the field is dynamic and constantly changing, it cannot be adequately represented even by multidimensional vectors and matrices. But one overall generalization about it is justified: a vector not contributed by any unit at any time cannot affect the aggregate policy.

The way such aggregation functions operate is clearly illustrated by case studies of complex policymaking, such as on the Employment Act

---

[3] See Benjamin E. Lippincott, ed., *Oskar Lange and Fred M. Taylor: On the Economic Theory of Socialism* (Minneapolis: Univ. of Minnesota Press, 1938).

[4] See the provocative analysis of this concept in Charles E. Lindblom, *The Intelligence of Democracy* (N.Y.: Free Press of Glencoe, 1965).

of 1946 or on defense policymaking.[5] In these cases policymaking took place mainly within a polycentric structure with few autonomous units, and the resulting policy was in many ways such a vector product as I have described above. These general findings have two practical implications for optimal public-policymaking structure:

1. The better the policymaking is in the different units, the better (though not proportionately) the aggregate policy is, if the basic subjective interests and values of the various units approximate (or at least are not opposed to) the basic values and "rules of the game" of the overall policymaking system. To the extent allowed by this qualification, aggregative policymaking can be improved by improving the policymaking in each unit. The basic values and interests, at least concerning many significant issues, of most (but not all) public-policymaking units in an integrated, democratic society usually are similarly aligned.

2. In principle, a more or less optimal policy can result from the interactions of units that are themselves not operating optimally. This possibility, which has tremendous significance for both theory and practice, is implied by the idea of "checks and balances." *However,* although a polycentric structure *may* operate in this way, it does not necessarily do so spontaneously. Therefore, some overall systems management must reinforce those interaction patterns that aggregate in optimal policies and eliminate the interaction patterns that lower the quality of the aggregate policies.

For example, as long as questions involving opposed points of view were resolved by brute force, this was generally not the best way to solve a problem. But when an umpire was added, one of the most interesting types of polycentric structure was created: the judicial and semi-judicial hearing, which tries to establish an optimal policy (sometimes rather successfully) by having competing units make biased claims for opposing policies (e.g., in hearings before the independent regulatory commissions in the United States).

---

[5] For the classic study on the former, see Stephen K. Bailey, *Congress Makes a Law* (N.Y.: Columbia Univ. Press, 1950). For a generalized description and a general model based on such material, see Bertram M. Gross, *The Legislative Struggle* (N.Y.: McGraw-Hill, 1953), and David B. Truman, *The Governmental Process* (N.Y.: Knopf, 1951), respectively. On the latter, see, for example, Harold Stein, ed., *American Civil-Military Decisions: A Book of Case Studies* (University, Ala.: Univ. of Alabama Press, 1963).

There are a few more types of structure, most of which are subtypes of ones I have already discussed. For instance, there is the structure that has overlapping neighboring units, which is very important in policymaking on scientific issues;[6] the multipolar structure; small-group structures, which operate mainly in organizations but are also important for, say, public-opinion formation; various intra-organizational microstructures, such as the "staff" and "counterpart units"; and many more. Each one has its own particular characteristics, roles, and aggregation functions.

Although these and similar structures are very interesting, and very significant for political science, the study of public administration, and organization theory, a detailed examination of them would take me away from my specific objectives. I have discussed them enough to bring out the implications of the requirement that the contributions of the various units to each phase of policymaking should add up in such a way that the phase, and the policymaking system as a whole, operate optimally. My discussion has also been detailed enough that some concrete specifications about an optimal policymaking structure can be based on it. But before I present these specifications, I must make a few remarks on the third and fourth conditions for an optimal structure.

These conditions were that the structure should aggregate contributions into phases, and integrate the various phases into overall public policymaking, at low cost and with little distortion. The structural features that would accomplish this task cannot be designed in detail, not only for such reasons as I have already mentioned, but also because the cost depends on the specific values and resources of the society in question. For example, a society that has some manpower with great extrarational capabilities, but that has no academically trained manpower, must have a rather different policymaking structure than a society that has plenty of highly trained manpower. Consequently, the optimal structures whose aggregation function is designed to achieve optimal quality by, among other things, consuming the least resources must differ in many important ways from system to system (or subsystem).

Completely designing a public-policymaking structure with the necessary aggregative efficiency would require knowledge and methods much more advanced than any we have now. What we know at present can only impose a few conditions on such a design. For example, if time is at

---

[6] See Michael Polanyi, "The Republic of Science: Its Political and Economic Theory," *Minerva,* I, no. 1 (Autumn 1962), 54ff.

a premium, the phases and subphases of public policymaking must be so scheduled as to use the least total time, by having as many phases as possible take place at the same time. Scheduling designed to conserve other resources, such as high-quality manpower and equipment, can be similarly worked out. Some of the more promising techniques for doing so are some applications of critical-path scheduling, such as PERT (Program Evaluation and Review Technique) and, by derivation, PERT-COST. Some other concepts and techniques now being developed in the management sciences, which may perhaps apply to parts of the public-policymaking system, may permit us to construct, after we have more data, more sophisticated general models of public-policymaking structure that will reduce aggregative cost and distortion. But trying to do so now would wander too far off into abstract concepts or technical details. Although I therefore cannot give any universally valid specifications on how a policymaking structure could meet these conditions of aggregative efficiency, at least the conditions themselves can be used as secondary criteria for evaluating policymaking.

SOME SPECIFICATIONS FOR AN OPTIMAL STRUCTURE

Even though we do not know very much about what specific structures might satisfy the above four conditions for an optimal policymaking structure, I can translate the implications of my analysis into some fairly operational specifications for such an optimal structure. I can do so by combining the requirements of the optimal phases, the few conclusions I have drawn from the preceding analysis, and data from the administrative sciences and from political science, into a series of concrete organizational and structural requirements for optimal public policymaking.

To restate my present thesis: optimal structures can permissibly vary greatly in many ways, the details of which are not now known, but it is highly probable that unless they satisfy certain conditions, the public-policymaking process cannot come close to being optimal. The degree to which those structural conditions are satisfied can therefore be, at least partially, a secondary criterion for the quality of the public-policymaking structure; however, these structural conditions are necessary, but not sufficient, for optimality. They must be satisfied for the policymaking process to be optimal, but their being satisfied will not by itself automatically make public policymaking optimal; there are too many other relevant variables that may keep it from approximating optimality.

The essential structural requirements for optimal public policymaking seem to include the following:[7]

1. Many diverse units should participate in public policymaking as a whole, but not necessarily in every policymaking situation. Since the public-policymaking process is so complex and involves so many different kinds of phases, it must have a heterogeneous structure composed of a variety of specialized units. Quite apart from any ideological considerations, public policymaking cannot and should not be concentrated in one monolithic hierarchy. The public-policymaking system is and must be composed of many heterogeneous units, the relationships between which can belong partly to any of the polycentric, hierarchic, or other types of structure I have mentioned, depending on the political regime, the size of the country, the acuteness and nature of the policy issues, the available policy knowledge, and other resources and variables.

2. At least one unit must contribute to each phase, subphase, and component thereof. I have already explained why this requirement is so important: if no unit contributes to a phase or subphase, that phase or subphase cannot be carried out.

3. Some of the phases and subphases must have units that are formally charged with carrying them out. Some of the phases may be carried out almost spontaneously, by means of the inner dynamics and informally accepted roles of existing structures. For instance, motivating the executing of a policy (phase 15) is a "natural" process for political leadership. Similarly, many of the intuitive components of other phases arise "naturally," though they can often be improved by explicit action. But many optimal phases and subphases run counter to the "natural" behavioral tendencies of organizations and individuals. These include many of the rational components, such as the systematic aspects of resource suballocation (phase 6), establishing operational goals and orders of priority (phase 7), and the memory-storage element of learning feedback. I do not claim that operational goals and orders of priority are never established unless specific units are formally charged with doing so, but I do think that if such activity is to be systematic, some unit must be formally in charge of it. Similarly, specific roles and units must usually be formally established to take care of systematic thinking and planning, learning feedback, and other rational phases and subphases. Such formal units must also be established for some of the extrara-

---

[7] I will elaborate these suggestions and support them by empiric evidence in a forthcoming textbook on public administration to be published by Harper and Row.

tional components. For instance, searching for alternatives (phase 11) must, among other things, be subject to formal organizational pressures in order to somewhat overcome the forces of conservatism and inertia. Therefore, establishing a series of units explicitly in charge of developing specific phases of optimal policymaking is one of the most important specifications for an optimal policymaking structure.

4. One very interesting feature of an optimal policymaking structure is that it should be rather redundant: the contributions to the various phases should duplicate and overlap each other. I mentioned this feature in connection with the optimal "goodness" standard (phase 14), but it is of much broader usefulness. As elaborated in modern cybernetics, the basic idea of redundancy is one of "multiplexing," that is, of having many units perform the same operation and passing their outputs through a threshold level that ignores mistakes made by some of the parallel units.[8] This idea sheds new light on the positive functions performed by some structural characteristics of democracy, and by governmental organizations in general, which are often mistakenly regarded as "wasteful" because they are "duplicated." The correct criterion should be that the more critical a certain policy issue or one of its phases is, the more redundancy should be provided as a way to minimize the risk of mistakes. Checks and balances between different governmental units and the "Fail-Safe" procedure for nuclear bombers illustrate how multiplexing works on different levels. In applying this criterion to policymaking, one must keep in mind that not every redundancy is a "multiplexing" and that not all multiplexing is justified, just as every duplication is not to be condemned. Each case of redundancy must be examined in its own context.

5. Some of the units participating in policymaking should be isolated from certain other units, since they must have a certain structural (and perhaps social) distance from these other units in order to operate at high quality. Such isolation is usually needed between units that are mainly in charge of thinking and those that are mainly in charge of executing policies, and between the latter and those mainly in charge of evaluating policymaking. Thus, predicting outputs (phase 12) and evaluating the real results in terms of the expected ones (phase 17) must be kept separate in order to decrease the danger that expectations will be reinterpreted and so bias the evaluation of the real results. Also, some distance may be needed between, on the one hand, units that are mainly

---

[8] See John Von Neumann, "Probabilistic Logics and the Synthesis of Reliable Organisms from Unreliable Components," in C. E. Shannon and J. McCarthy, eds., *Automata Studies* (Princeton, N.J.: Princeton Univ. Press, 1950), pp. 83ff.

in charge of "analysis" (that is, comparing more or less given alternatives) and, on the other, units whose main function is imaginative invention of new alternatives. Similarly, the long-range elements of all phases must be kept separate from their short-range elements in order to prevent immediate pressures from undercutting long-range concerns. For instance, unless relatively independent units are responsible for identifying short-range and long-range problems (phase 3), the immediate pressures of the imminent problems will tend to drive the long-range problems out of the picture. Again, unless the units that allocate and suballocate resources (phases 5 and 6) are kept relatively isolated from most of the other units (but not from the unit that processes values), the whole allocation process loses its autonomy and becomes a mathematical function of the power of the various units.

6. Units that may be in the coalition whose power will motivate the executing of the policy must be included in the policymaking structure. The reasons for this specification have been fairly well covered by my discussion of phase 15 in the preceding chapter.

7. Some units that execute policy must be closely tied into the policymaking structure, in order to minimize the danger of an executing that distorts the policy and of policymaking that leads to infeasible policies. This requirement is rather the obverse of no. 5.

8. The units' outputs must be integrated by some method that tends to maximize their aggregative contribution to policymaking. It is not enough for each separate unit to contribute optimally to each separate phase. For optimal policymaking, the contributions must be combined optimally into the phases, and the phases into a policymaking process, by complex hierarchic and polycentric relations among various units. This integration may also require special integration units, predetermined communication channels, exchange mechanisms, integrated information storage, and so on.

9. The policymaking structure must be periodically reexamined and redesigned. There will always be constant changes in its environment, including the knowledge and resources available to it, in the problems that public policymaking must handle, and in the structure's own characteristics, and it must therefore be periodically readjusted in order to keep its operations optimal. Such readjustments seldom happen spontaneously. Usually a policymaking structure lags behind new needs until its increasing mistakes result in a crisis and then in more or less convulsive changes. Sometimes drastic overhaulings after longer intervals are preferable to keeping a structure in a state of perpetual reorganization. But whatever rate of readjustment is best, it must be decided on by optimal metapolicymaking, which should have special units in charge

of monitoring and redesigning the policymaking structure. This is a special case of requirement no. 3, but it deserves separate consideration because of its importance.

These specifications for an optimal public-policymaking structure are themselves subject to change, since they depend on our knowledge in policy science and on changing conditions and needs. Nevertheless they can be useful as tools for analysis, as secondary criteria and standards for evaluating the quality of actual public-policymaking structures, and as rough indicators of what improvements are needed in those structures.

part V

ON IMPROVING
PUBLIC
POLICYMAKING

chapter 16 · The Major Improvements Needed in Public Policymaking

Using both the optimal model and my evaluation and diagnosis of current public policymaking, I can set down the major areas in which contemporary public policymaking needs to be improved. These areas can be derived fairly easily from my descriptive listing of the ways in which current policymaking differs from optimal policymaking on pp. 121–122. By recasting these differences into a normative form, I arrive at the following list of major areas in which policymaking must be improved.

Contemporary public policymaking needs:

1. Much more metapolicymaking about basic characteristics of the policymaking system.

2. Much more learning feedback.

3. Much more systematic and explicit determining of policy strategies.

4. More elaboration of operational goals.

5. Much more searching for alternatives.

6. Much more explicit establishing of cutoff horizons, which should cover a longer period of time.

7. Much more development of rational components.

8. More development of extrarational components.

9. Many more specific units that are explicitly in charge of periodically and systematically evaluating and redesigning the policymaking system and its subsystems.

10. Many more specific units that are explicitly in charge of thinking, long-range policymaking, surveying knowledge, and carrying out research and development about policies.

11. A careful adjustment of the organizational and social distances between units that make policy, that execute it, and that motivate the executing of it.

12. Changes in the characteristics, roles, and contributions of the major units composing the policymaking structure.

13. Changes in the aggregation function.

14. Much higher qualifications for policymaking manpower and much more input of knowledge and information.

15. More equipment.

16. More energy and drive.

This list provides a framework on which operational and ordered suggestions for improvements in a real policymaking system can be based. I will present these suggestions in two main steps. The first step deals with the most important long-range condition for better public policymaking, namely, improvements needed in policy knowledge. These improvements will involve overcoming certain barriers that policy science is facing. It will also require some innovations in the way the knowledge-seeking institutions are organized and operate. (I will discuss both of these points in Chapter 17.) The second step requires various changes in policymaking itself, which I will discuss in four stages: changes in personnel in Chapter 18; changes in structure and process pattern in Chapter 19; changes in input and stipulated output in Chapter 20; and changes in environment in Chapter 21.

By adopting this order of presentation, I will arrive at cohesive suggestions for improvement, each of which covers several specific areas that need to be improved. For example, better policymaking personnel would help repair almost all of policymaking's shortcomings, and establishing units to conduct surveys of knowledge would help repair some of them. Table 4 (p. 310) shows the relationships between my suggestions and the specific areas that need improving, and so links them both with the earlier analyses on which I have based them.

I would like to make four more points about the suggestions I will present in the following chapters.

1. They are, I think, "realistically idealistic" for most societies. They neither are utopian nor describe a future situation that will come about in any case. Rather, I intend them to point out "good" alternatives that can be approximated if those concerned are willing to make a serious effort to do so.

2. They are only valid insofar as no radical changes in basic social structure or in knowledge take place. For instance, if high-capacity heuristic computers ("artificial brains") are developed, they

might permit and require larger parts of the policymaking system to be semi-automated, as has already been done for some secondary decision-making systems that deal with quantifiable data.

3. They are based on "guesstimates." That is, although they are based primarily on my analyses in this book, they also depend on the experiences that military, business, and other organizations have had; on what is currently known, especially in the behavioral sciences and decision sciences; on the opinion of professional policymakers and of students of policymaking as they are revealed by the many proposals for reform that can be found in the reports and hearings of public commissioners, in autobiographies, in political writings, and in the professional literature; and on my own subjective impressions and ideas, which have been shaped by my knowledge as a scientist, by my experience as a consultant, and by my personality.

4. They are so stated as to be neither too general nor too specific. I intend them to be specific enough to be used as a guide (and so demonstrate the significance of my analysis) for improving policymaking, but also general enough to apply to a variety of situations and to make it obvious that more data will be required to make them detailed enough to fit a particular system or subsystem. I have included the more specific proposals in the discussion only as illustrations, not as prescriptions good for whatever ails any policymaking system.

chapter 17 · Changes Needed in Knowledge

The optimal model makes it clear that knowledge is potentially of tremendous importance for public policymaking, both because the rational components are based on it, and because it can better define the roles of, and stimulate, the extrarational components. But for knowledge to actually perform these functions in public policymaking, three conditions must be satisfied: (1) the knowledge that can perform the function must exist; (2) there must be means for integrating it into actual public policymaking; and (3) powerful policymakers must want to improve public policymaking by using the knowledge strongly enough to overcome conservative ideologies and other forces of inertia. In this chapter I will see how much knowledge that is relevant to policymaking is available. The later chapters will in part discuss means for integrating knowledge into the public-policymaking process, and in Chapter 21 I will make some comments on the "will to innovate."

It is not easy to evaluate present and future knowledge in order to see what of it is relevant to policymaking, or to devise ways to find or create more of such knowledge. The available knowledge is dispersed among many disciplines, and hidden behind professional jargon and other barriers to communication. Its relevance to policymaking must be evaluated partly by informed guesses if no effort has ever been made to actually use that knowledge in public policymaking. It is even harder to foresee what knowledge might become available in the near future.

I do not think it is very useful to regard the future as an immutable, independent phenomenon that is completely external to man. I am much more interested in learning how man can change the future to make it what he wants. I therefore do not want merely to extrapolate the future state of our knowledge by assuming that present trends will continue; rather, I want to suggest ways in which we can accelerate some trends in order to develop knowledge that will be even more important for public policymaking. I will try to do this by identifying the barriers that are keeping us from developing such knowledge and by proposing means for overcoming them. If we can overthrow those barriers, or at least lower them, we may be able to stimulate discovery of the new and better policy knowledge we need.

In order to deal with the different, though interdependent, aspects of this project, I will take them on in the following order. First, I will undertake a more detailed examination of what kinds of knowledge optimal policymaking needs, in order to provide a standard for appraising knowledge, to find out what kinds of knowledge I should look for, and to indicate what new knowledge is needed. Next I will survey the knowledge we now have or are developing, and will evaluate it in terms of its significance for policymaking. Then I will examine the barriers that are keeping us from developing kinds of knowledge we need, considering the social sciences and the various interdisciplinary fields separately. Finally, I will present a proposal for establishing policy science as an integrated, distinct interdisciplinary field whose purpose is to systematically provide us with the knowledge we need for optimal policymaking.

THE KNOWLEDGE NEEDED FOR OPTIMAL PUBLIC POLICYMAKING

My first task must be to construct as accurate a picture as I can of the kinds of knowledge needed for optimal policymaking.[1] My conclusions so far indicate that such knowledge must meet two requirements: it should enable policymaking both to be as good as it can be and to become constantly better; and it should be available in the form that is most conducive to its actually being used in policymaking.

The first requirement has the following major implications:[2]

---

[1] Please notice that I am limiting myself to policy knowledge, as defined earlier (see p. 8). I am leaving aside so-called "pure" knowledge and technological knowledge about how policies can be executed, even though these are most important, since the knowledge I am concerning myself with is often based on the former, and since the latter influences many specific policies, especially by limiting the range of feasible alternatives. I will explore some problems caused by the somewhat artificial distinction between "pure" and "applied" policy knowledge later on.

[2] I arrived at this list by asking, for each optimal subphase and structural requirement in Chapters 11–13, "What knowledge is needed to put this into practice?" The specifications in it can be reformulated and classified into different degrees of generality and in a variety of ways.

1. We need to know how to establish and improve the rational components of optimal public policymaking. These components include: (a) examining the consistency of values and goals; (b) collecting intelligence; (c) predicting the probable results of different courses of action; (d) comparing benefits and costs; (e) constructing criteria for "best" and "good" alternatives; (f) constructing feedback systems; (g) programming systematic operations.

2. We need to know how to strengthen the extrarational components of optimal public policymaking. Specifically, we must know how to: (a) identify persons with great extrarational abilities and recruit them for central policymaking positions; (b) develop such extrarational abilities; (c) create conditions that will stimulate use of extrarational abilities.

3. We need to know how to integrate extrarational and rational components to best advantage. Specifically, we must know how to: (a) evaluate both the potential and the actual contributions of extrarational components to policymaking; (b) activate persons having developed extrarational abilities and integrate the abilities with rational components.

4. We need to know how to design and redesign the policymaking structure and its process patterns. For this we need to know, besides many things mentioned above, how to: (a) overcome inertia, conservative vested interests, and other factors that resist improvement; (b) improve individual, small-group, and organizational decisionmaking; (c) influence the contributions that different units make to policymaking; (d) discover and improve the aggregation functions of composite, inter-unit processes.

The second requirement, that knowledge should be available in the form that is most conducive to its being integrated into actual public policymaking, implies that it should be: stated in simple and communicable terminology; so organized and ordered as to be easily accessible; and teachable in a systematic and comprehensive way to persons who do or may participate in policymaking.

These specifications are the standard I will use to evaluate knowledge now being developed in terms of significance for policymaking. They also tell me what kinds of knowledge should be developed for better policymaking.

THE SIGNIFICANCE OF OUR CURRENT KNOWLEDGE FOR POLICYMAKING

Every textbook is a partial inventory of knowledge. There have also been some comprehensive efforts to survey the available knowledge in the behavioral sciences.[3] But there has been no inventory of knowledge that may be useful for policymaking, nor any comprehensive effort to predict the development of new policy knowledge.[4] The dearth of books intended to bring policy knowledge to the attention of policymakers is characteristic of the present state of affairs, especially when contrasted with the wealth of publications that supply relevant knowledge in a suitable form to business managers.

Any attempt to evaluate the significance for policymaking of knowledge that is currently being developed is hazardous. Nevertheless, my surveys of the literature and interviews with scholars in different disciplines seem to suggest the following points:

1. The disciplines of knowledge can, for our purposes, be roughly classified into four categories: traditional disciplines, such as history, law, engineering, and the life sciences; social-science disciplines, such as psychology (and educational psychology), sociology, anthropology, political science, public administration, international relations, and economics; new interdisciplinary fields, such as intelligence studies, conflict studies, regional studies, development studies, the management sciences, and the decision sciences; and abstract disciplines, such as logic, parts of semantics, mathematics, statistics, philosophy, and applied ethics.

There are vast differences between these disciplines in the nature, quantity, and form of the knowledge they could contribute to policymaking. The new interdisciplinary fields, being directly concerned with policy problems, can supply considerable relevant knowledge, though they are very young. Within the social sciences, economics is exceptional in being explicitly concerned with policy and able to supply a fair amount of policy knowledge. The other social sciences can contribute many relevant findings, but these findings are spotty and unsystematic. The traditional and abstract disciplines contribute little material that is di-

---

[3] E.g., see *A Current Appraisal of the Behavioral Sciences,* published as a supplement to *The American Behavioral Scientist* (1963–64), in cooperation with the Behavioral Research Council; and Bernard Berelson and Gary A. Steiner, *Human Behavior: An Inventory of Scientific Findings* (N.Y.: Harcourt, Brace, 1964).

[4] An important preliminary step toward a bibliography that will permit easier access to policy knowledge is *The ABS Guide to Recent Publications in the Social and Behavioral Sciences* (N.Y.: American Behavioral Scientist, 1965). *The Series of Computerized Bibliographies in Political Science, Government, and Public Policy,* published by the Universal Reference System, Inc., is also very promising.

rectly relevant to policymaking, except for a few areas of logic, mathematics, and, on a different level, philosophy.

2. Policy knowledge should be systematically organized so that one can identify the particular knowledge that is relevant to any particular policymaking issue, and should be stated in a form conducive to its being integrated into actual public policymaking, that is, in language that is as easy and clear as possible, with little esoteric terminology and no embroidery.

With a few exceptions, such as some of the literature in business administration and some integrated studies of a few "social problems" such as delinquency, these requirements are seldom met. The available policy knowledge is so dispersed among the different disciplines that it minimizes the significance of their contributions to policymaking both singly and altogether. For instance, knowledge about taxation policy or foreign aid is scattered among at least economics, sociology, and political science, and very few integrated studies of even such well-defined and recognized problems have been done.

Although a well-developed and precise terminology is necessary for scientific writing, and cannot be sacrificed to create an illusory simplicity of language that really only makes communication more difficult, nevertheless, the language in such writing is often far more complex than is strictly necessary. The current fashion of preferring mathematical formulations to prose statements, even when prose can express the desired relationships perfectly well, is equally worthy of contempt. Both of these bad habits contribute to the public's impression that "Science is incomprehensible," and keep even knowledge that is stated clearly from being applied to policymaking, because the language scares politicians and policymakers away from all such knowledge.

3. Except in business and public administration, and to a lesser degree in some interdisciplinary fields, those in the various disciplines have hardly tried to develop methods for teaching policy knowledge to policymakers, or to prepare their own students for active participation in policymaking. This state of affairs is particularly acute in the social sciences.

4. All the disciplines can reliably be expected to produce more policy knowledge. But, unless changes are made in their orientation, scope, methods, and interests, they will produce much less policy knowledge than they should at best be able to, and what they produce will be insufficient and unsuitable for optimal policymaking. Also, the knowledge they are currently developing has many blind spots, since many crucial issues of policymaking and metapolicymaking lie outside their fields of inquiry.

These general and somewhat abstract remarks are elaborated for each discipline in Appendix C (pp. 319ff), which surveys the types of knowledge each discipline is now developing and the types it may be able to come up with in the future. This survey demonstrates: (1) much policy knowledge is now available, and more such will become available in the foreseeable future; and (2) much more policy knowledge could and should be developed if conditions are optimal. These two conclusions point up the problems of how the knowledge we have can be integrated into policymaking, which I deal with in the next few chapters, and of how we can identify and overcome the main barriers that are keeping us from accelerating the growth of policy knowledge.

The two main sources of policy knowledge are the social sciences and the interdisciplinary fields. These two areas differ greatly in their characteristics and in the barriers they have against policy knowledge, which I will therefore discuss separately.

BARRIERS AGAINST DEVELOPING POLICY KNOWLEDGE IN THE SOCIAL SCIENCES

I see nine barriers that are keeping us from developing policy knowledge in the social sciences. Although they are interdependent and overlap to some extent, the most convenient way to discuss them is one by one.

1. The Characteristics of Their Subject Matter

The complexity of the social sciences' subject matter has often been cited as a major factor that prevents them from developing the kinds of knowledge needed for policymaking. It is true that society is complex, and that most of its phenomena are shaped by so many variables that a simple explanation of them is rarely possible. Nevertheless, this theme seems overworked. Complexity is too often blamed for ignorance that has other causes. The span of comprehension of the human mind is limited, even when it is reinforced by organizational and mechanical devices; therefore, a detailed understanding of a very complex system such as human society may be beyond our capabilities. But unless social behavior is a purely random phenomenon, there is no reason why we shouldn't be able to learn and understand its main regularities. Similarly, although we usually cannot consider all its variables at the same time, we can identify the major independent ones and see what their main effects on social behavior are; some such knowledge is already available, for example, in economics.

The characteristics of society without a doubt shape the form, exactness, and reliability of what we can know about social affairs. The research methods and theoretical structures we must have to deal with such characteristics will often differ from those that work best in other disciplines, such as, most particularly, the physical sciences. At the same time, there is nothing inherent in the characteristics of society that keeps us from developing policy knowledge, unless we adopt standards for recognizing and seeking such knowledge that are self-defeating, which leads to my next point.

2. Imitating the Physical Sciences

The unique characteristics of society become an insurmountable barrier against developing policy knowledge only when their study is encumbered with unsuitable tools and misleading expectations, as happens when social scientists suffer from a fixation on what they think are the methods of the physical sciences. The major symptoms of this peculiar disease, often exhibited by the more behaviorally oriented students of society, are: (a) they tend to seek relatively simple explanations, assume that Occam's Razor applies to social phenomena, and therefore tend to study only those issues to which it does apply; (b) they regard empirical research that can be subjected to statistical tests of validity and reliability as the only legitimate source of knowledge, and so ignore problems that are not susceptible to such methods; (c) they try very hard to come up with "factual" and "value-free" findings, and scorn normative recommendations as being incompatible with their status as "scientists"; (d) they regard all general theories with suspicion; (e) they therefore tend very strongly to concentrate on micro-issues, and to regard macro-issues of social structure and dynamics, including most of the problems that are important for policymaking, as subjects that "at present" are not susceptible to "scientific" examination, and that therefore ought not to be dealt with by contemporary social science. Such tendencies not only repress some sources of knowledge that are essential for policy science, such as introspection and impressionistic knowledge, but also prevent the social scientist from cooperating with the practical politician or policymaker, since they disparage the latter's experience-based knowledge.

3. Alienation from Policymaking

One barrier on which statistical evidence could be sought is how little social scientists participate in actual public policymaking as elected or appointed public officials or as consultants. That there is almost no significant empiric data on this critical problem is symptomatic of how little attention has been paid to the relation between social-science knowledge and policymaking. Personal involvement by social scientists in policymaking is essential not only for modern knowledge to be integrated into actual policymaking, but also for creating that knowledge by motivating suitable research and providing indispensable insights and understanding. The alienation of social scientists from actual policymaking is therefore a major barrier against developing a policy science. This conclusion is supported by the apparent fact that the more policy knowledge is available in a discipline, the more involved its students are in actual policymaking. For example, compare economics and sociology.

This relationship is self-reinforcing: scientists who have little to offer to policymaking have less chance to become involved in it, and therefore they continue to have little policy knowledge to offer. Most social scientists who recognize this closed circle apparently make no effort to break it. But in fairness I must admit that many expressions of a lack of interest in policymaking are probably a defensive reaction to not being asked to participate in it. The fault for social scientists' alienation from policymaking and their resulting neglect of policy knowledge therefore partly lies with the public-policymaking system, which does not co-opt enough psychologists, sociologists, political scientists, and other potential policy scientists.

4. Seeking for Certainty

A barrier that is implicit in many pronouncements by social scientists on their inability to provide policy knowledge is their seeking for certainty. An inability to provide foolproof solutions and the fact that social scientists give contradictory recommendations are often cited as reasons why no policy-directed recommendations should be made until knowledge "gets more mature and scientific." Such an argument is based on three mutually reinforcing premises, all fallacious, that lead to an equally fallacious conclusion. They are: (a) ultimately, we will have clear-cut solutions that will be agreed upon by all persons who have the necessary scientific knowledge; (b) until then, our knowledge cannot contribute much to policymaking; (c) scientists should avoid the public spectacle of giving contradictory advice, no advice at all being preferable; (d) therefore, until they can provide reliable recommendations on policy issues, scientists should devote all their energy to seeking knowledge, without getting sidetracked into making less-than-perfect contributions to policymaking.

These premises and their conclusion can be traced to the fixation on the physical sciences and to a desire to strengthen the reputation of the social studies as "real sciences." They are reinforced by the bewilderment and hostility many policymakers display when they are confronted with conflicting advice, which cannot but strengthen the tendency of many scientists to refuse to become involved in the public-policymaking process.

At this stage of the book it is redundant to explain the basic fallacy of this opinion; but since redundancy is sometimes useful, I will nevertheless do so, briefly, by applying the optimal model of policymaking to the problem. Optimal public policymaking involves using both all available knowledge and extrarational processes. Even if a bit of knowledge is not fully validated, it can contribute to better policymaking at least by making intuition better informed, provided its degree of validity is carefully explained so that it is neither over- nor under-valued. Similarly, contradictory opinions based on available knowledge can contribute to better policymaking at least by increasing the range of alternatives that are considered and by improving the information on which the extrarational processes are based; and surely this is better than policymaking that is based on no knowledge at all.

Overcoming this barrier will require a better understanding of the role social-science knowledge can play in policymaking, and of the nature of such knowledge, by both social scientists and policymakers alike. Economics again shows that such understanding can be achieved, and that limited validity and contradictory opinions should not discourage policy knowledge.

5. Favoring Incremental Change

One of the leitmotifs running through most theories and models of social science is that society is very complex. This in itself is certainly true. But one of the main conclusions drawn implicitly from this view of society, namely, that social change should always proceed by incremental steps, is certainly open to doubt. Recognizing the hazards of interfering with a complex system we do not adequately understand, contemporary social scientists tend to adopt a "safest" strategy and to develop a strong bias against large-scale directed social change. This bias in turn conditions the very questions they try to answer, the answers they arrive at, and the implications they draw from them.

This picture is oversimplified; it neglects the variety of viewpoints social scientists hold. It also does not look deep enough for the causes of this prevailing attitude, which may be largely a reflection of the fact that the culture of the United States conditions most modern social science everywhere. Nevertheless, the general picture seems clear enough; an extensive reading of American social-science writings leaves me with a firm impression that its main orientation is "conservative" and in favor of incremental change (which could very well be the policy that is often optimal in the United States). That social scientists are often considered "radicals" should not mislead us: the proposals of social scientists may look drastic from a very conservative viewpoint, but in fact nearly all of them are based on incremental change. Social scientists are usually, if at all, "radical" only on issues that are unrelated to their specialties; indeed, sometimes there is an interesting contrast between their professional knowledge and their amazingly emotional position on some public issues.

As long as social scientists do not add new policy alternatives to the repertoire of those already well-known to policymakers, there is little reason why the policymaker should recognize the importance of new policy knowledge or encourage its development. A bias in favor of incremental change helps retard innovation in knowledge, makes policy knowledge less useful, and thus decreases any motivation to find and use it.

6. "Pure" vs. "Applied" Knowledge

Another characteristic of most of the social sciences is that many of their students think there is a competition between "pure" and "applied" knowledge, and so tend to defend any and every quest for new knowledge willy-nilly. Apparently influenced by some quite outdated discussions about how resources were being allocated in the physical sciences, many social scientists feel that "pure" research is on the brink of being abandoned, and hence rely on slogans like "pure research is the best applied research" to justify their preoccupation with problems whose significance (theoretical and applied) approaches zero, and their retreat to facts that are banal, their argument being that such is the stuff of which "pure" knowledge is made.

The real danger from this argument is that it can easily be misused to prevent scarce resources from being allocated to research projects that can probably contribute significant theoretical or applied knowledge to policymaking. There is no question about the wisdom of studying fundamental issues or speculative theories that have no *direct* applications. It is a totally different thing to use the "pure knowledge" slogan to justify spending resources indiscriminately on investigations that have, in all probability, no significance, theoretical or applied. That is, what is dangerous is to argue that since all "pure" knowledge is highly important (which is not true) and since we can't predict at all which "pure" knowledge will have practical results (which is an exaggeration), therefore all additions to "pure" knowledge are potentially highly important and have a prior claim on available resources, and therefore all efforts to direct research toward socially significant issues endanger the "scientific endeavor."

Taking into account that available resources, especially highly qualified manpower, are limited, it is not enough even to demonstrate that a certain project will add to "pure" knowledge. The real issue is that we need to identify the projects that are most likely to provide significant knowledge, including knowledge that is relevant to policymaking. I do not mean at all that individual social scientists should be prevented from pursuing ideas that look promising to them alone, or that social research ought to be centrally planned. What I claim is (a) that the argument for "pure" knowledge must not be so interpreted that the search for policy knowledge is neglected; (b) that it does not provide a carte blanche for devoting large resources indiscriminately to investigations that have no reasonable chance of contributing either theoretical or applied significant knowledge; and (c) that acknowledging the vast importance of pure research can in no way conflict with a general desire to make knowledge serve human needs, and to encourage social science to seek knowledge that is likely to meet important human and social needs and contribute to better policymaking. The example of medicine provides much food for thought on the possibility and desirability of combining a scientific attitude with an orientation that favors action and of advancing applied knowledge hand in hand with basic research.

7. University Organization

The stuff out of which policy knowledge is made does not, for the most part, fall within the traditional boundaries between disciplines that are reflected by standard university organization. Knowledge from any one discipline is therefore often inherently unable to meet the needs of policymaking. Furthermore, the many traditional disciplines are organized into knowledge-tight departments that create many vacuums; certain problems are regarded by all the disciplines as being outside their proper domains. (On the other hand, where disciplines overlap, certain problems are investigated by more than one discipline; often this is a useful phenomenon, since it brings different, though unintegrated, points of view to bear on the same problem.)

There have been some attempts to overcome the limitations of the single disciplines, mainly by means of interdisciplinary teams and scholars. Such teams are a good idea in the abstract, but their actual operations at universities leave much to be desired, because it is hard to motivate a really interdisciplinary line of studies and because members from different disciplines have trouble communicating with each other. Individual interdisciplinary work is an increasingly important source of new knowledge, and many recent innovations in policy knowledge have been made by individuals who cross the boundaries between different disciplines; but present requirements for degrees and university advancement seldom encourage individuals to become interdisciplinary scholars.

This barrier against developing policy knowledge is still far from being adequately overcome. The present organization of universities prevents students from learning the basics of the disciplines that are most relevant to policy science, or even of the social sciences proper. Departmental jealousies and the anti-innovative bogeyman of "teaching less and less about more and more" join forces to prevent universities from designing interdepartmental curriculums that would give students a good grounding in the basics of all the social sciences and in their background subjects. Indeed, it seems that the attempts that have been made in this direction are now on the retreat, some interdisciplinary teaching programs having been abandoned or isolated. (On the other hand, the tendency to establish special Schools of Public Affairs may indicate some change in the needed direction.) The fact that individual scholars must depend on traditional, single-discipline departments for promotion, and lately have been depending more and more on national, single-discipline professional associations, also plays a large role in discouraging interdisciplinary research on policy knowledge.

Universities must establish interdisciplinary programs in the social sciences at the graduate level, and policy-science centers on the departmental level, if policy science is to become a recognized interdisciplinary field, and if we are to overcome this barrier (which, although, or perhaps because, it is partly administrative, is in fact one of the most insidious) against developing policy knowledge.

8. External Restraints

The various barriers I have mentioned so far exist within the community of social scientists. Since I do not wish to imply that the blame for the present underdevelopment of policy knowledge lies exclusively on them, I must emphasize the role of external restraints in that underdevelopment.

There are three major types of external restraint on the development of policy knowledge: (a) not enough resources; (b) restraints on selecting subject matter and methods of investigation; and (c) conventions about what findings are permissible. All these restraints exist in contemporary society, although the increase of funds for social-science research and the strong tradition of free scientific inquiry mitigate them somewhat in most western democratic states.

A. LACK OF RESOURCES

The argument that there are not enough resources for social research is often based on the fact that much less money is allocated to social research than to the physical and life sciences. This argument can be overstressed, because in fact large budgets do not always make for better social-science research; the comparison with the physical sciences, which do need very large budgets these days, is somewhat misleading. More money could certainly speed up social research, but only if the funds were carefully allocated in order not to strengthen the biases toward hyperempiricism and expensive, large-scale field studies whose significance is doubtful, and only if the funds were tied in with the entry of more high-quality manpower into such research.

A scarcity of high-quality manpower is much more serious in the long run than a scarcity of money. That many bright students tend to go into the physical sciences, engineering, and medicine if they are interested in scientific work or want to make a good and interesting living, and into law if they are interested in policymaking, is something of a barrier against advances in policy knowledge or in the traditional disciplines that potentially have the most to offer toward policy knowledge. The social sciences may be getting less and less of the first-class manpower, because of (1) widely accepted popular images and prestige ratings; (2) the contemporary social policy that encourages top students to go into physical sciences and engineering; (3) salaries; (4) the present methods of recruiting men for high-prestige jobs and policymaking roles, and (5) the limited demand for some types of highly qualified social scientists in the general labor market. If a careful study should indeed reveal a scarcity of top-quality students in the social sciences, we must rectify the situation immediately if we are to accelerate the development of policy knowledge.

B. RESTRAINTS ON SUBJECT MATTER AND RESEARCH METHODS

Such restraints are subtle, and operate largely through subterranean channels. Two well-known examples of such restraints are security restrictions on access to and exchange of information, and the Congressional reaction to the jury studies conducted by the University of Chicago. Security restrictions are less important a barrier in the social sciences than in the physical sciences, and do not seem today to be a major barrier against social-science knowledge. Indeed, the development of university-based civil strategists who have full access to top-secret material shows that security restrictions are not, in the United States, a major, insurmountable barrier against policy knowledge. The worst barriers against policy knowledge are social and political taboos that keep some matters from being studied. The jury studies are indeed a striking illustration of a social unit being declared off-limits for effective social-science research; Congress enacted a law that prohibits direct observation of the operation of a jury even if full precautions are taken to prevent damage to the involved parties.[5] The unique characteristics of the study that caused this legislative prohibition were that the researchers were enterprising enough to engage in their pioneering study, had the good fortune to meet lawyers and judges who were broadminded enough to cooperate, and so had at least a chance to penetrate into the working of juries. In most cases, such attempts are cut short much sooner, or are not even started, because negative results are anticipated.

Another interesting illustration is the Russell Amendment in 1958[6]

[5] See Waldo W. Burchard, "A Study of Attitudes toward the Use of Concealed Devices in Social-Science Research," *Social Forces*, XXXVI (Dec. 1957), 111ff, and "Lawyers, Political Scientists, Sociologists, and Concealed Microphones," *American Sociological Review*, XXIII (Dec. 1958), 686ff.

[6] Section 1602, Public Law 85760, 72 Stat. 864, H.R. 13450, approved Dec. 27, 1958.

which prohibited the government from carrying out or financing any study of "when to surrender." Although apparently the law was adopted because of a misunderstanding of a RAND study, the prohibition might still be reasonable. Supporting studies on whether surrender might be the best policy under certain conditions might undermine the credibility of United States defense policy, and thus could increase the risk of nuclear blackmail and war.

In most other countries, including the European democracies, restraints on subject matter and research methods are much stricter than they are in the United States, where there is no broad concept of "official secret." But even in the United States, such restraints are a significant barrier against research. Depth studies of actual policymaking are an essential step for developing policy knowledge. If indeed we want to understand the core processes of policymaking, and not just skirt its periphery, we must be able and encouraged to penetrate into the inner workings of the various policymaking units and processes, just as a physician is given complete liberty to examine his patients. Of course we must also develop a suitable code of ethics for social scientists, but the main burden is on members of the policymaking strata to open themselves up for study and to educate public opinion to accept the need for such study. There may be cases in which not knowing how an institution works is necessary for social survival; in such cases investigation should be prevented. But if we want to improve our policymaking processes and develop policy knowledge, then unless a clear danger to a basic social value is demonstrated, research on the central issues and units of policymaking should be encouraged, even if it is momentarily inconvenient and contrary to accepted attitudes and social taboos.

C. RESTRAINTS ON PERMITTED FINDINGS

External limitations on permissible findings, which not only prevent important policy knowledge from being developed, but hinder the essential functions of intellectuals in creating new policy alternatives, are the most dangerous of all. These restrictions operate endemically on various levels, from subconscious socialization, through informal social pressures, to outright prohibition. One of the most important advantages of western democratic societies is that they have no such formal prohibitions, and generally value freedom for scientific endeavors. It is hard to measure how much informal pressures operate to make research findings conform to generally accepted opinions. Some such pressures are unavoidable and do no harm, provided social scientists have a good measure of intellectual honesty and the courage of their convictions. But sometimes pressures for conformity are intense, especially on those problems that are most in need of innovative knowledge, such as those concerning the operation of the central policymaking institutions. Such pressure becomes stronger when controversial issues are involved, and cause many social scientists to tend to retreat into the safety of "validated facts" as distinguished crudely from "values," or, even more undesirably, to overreact and become highly emotional partisans.

Decreasing these restraints will require a joint effort by social scientists, the policymaking strata, and the public at large. Social scientists need much intellectual honesty and courage, a readiness to recommend drastic change when it is necessary, tact, and a sense of proportion, and must be able to avoid getting too personally involved in the issues. The policymaking strata and the public at large must learn to take a liberal attitude toward distasteful findings and apparently outrageous proposals. Only when both these conditions have largely been met will the way be open for real innovations in policy knowledge, for new ideas about the more critical and controversial policy issues, and for the emergence of real policy knowledge.

9. The Youth of the Social Sciences

It is often argued that the social sciences have not existed long enough to accumulate much knowledge. This argument applies less to law and political science than to sociology, for example. There is a large grain of truth in the claim that the scientific approach to social phenomena is relatively novel in all disciplines, and that, given enough time, they will come up with much more knowledge. Even so, I must ask whether the social sciences have developed as much policy knowledge as they could in the time they have had, and whether they are geared to develop as much as possible in the future. Insofar as I have diagnosed their situation rightly, I must answer "No"; they could have achieved more, and can achieve much more in the future if their barriers against developing policy knowledge can be overcome.

BARRIERS AGAINST POLICY KNOWLEDGE IN THE INTERDISCIPLINARY FIELDS

In their orientation and objectives, the interdisciplinary fields aim directly at improving policymaking, and so avoid some of the barriers found in the social sciences. But they have some unique barriers of their own, and share a few with the social sciences.

Assuming that most readers are less familiar with the interdisciplinary fields than with the social sciences, and thus with their significance as pioneers of policy science, I think I should discuss some major characteristics of the best-developed and more important ones, namely, the management and decision sciences.[7] I will combine the discussion with identifying the barriers that diminish their significance for policymaking, in order to elaborate somewhat the terse descriptions of them in Appendix C (pp. 319ff).

1. The management and decision sciences have a multidisciplinary base. They encompass parts of many traditional disciplines, including mathematics, engineering, economics, business administration, and (in principle though not in fact) the other social sciences. They take ideas, concepts, information, and techniques from such traditional disciplines, and try to integrate them into a new discipline distinguished by a unique subject matter and orientation. At the same time, their progress continues in part to depend on developments in their base disciplines, which must continue to supply components for them to integrate.

2. The management and decision sciences are very young. Some developments preceded World War II, but in the main these disciplines are a creation of the war, when operations-research units were set up, first in England and then in the United States, for studying military problems susceptible to mathematical analysis, such as search patterns for submarines and the optimal dispersal of radar units. After the war ended, operations research turned partly to civilian life, joining forces with quality control and some other techniques, to become one nucleus of the management and decision sciences.

3. The management and decision sciences are presently heterogeneous and unintegrated. One can distinguish several components in them, some of which are often regarded as distinct disciplines, including: (a) operations research (called "operational research" in England); (b) systems engineering (also known, with some changes in emphasis, as "systems approach," "systems management," or something similar);

---

[7] Even more interesting in many respects is systems analysis, which constitutes an important step from the management and decision sciences to policy science. However, its distinctive features are too diffuse, and its theory too underdeveloped, to permit me to treat it separately in this context. See Aaron Wildavsky, "The Political Economy of Efficiency: Cost-Benefit Analysis, Systems Analysis, and Program Budgeting," *Public Administration Review*, XXVI, no. 4 (Dec. 1966), 292ff, and Yehezkel Dror, "Policy Analysts: A New Professional Role in Government," *Public Administration Review*, XXVII, no. 3 (September 1967), 197ff.

(c) cybernetics; (d) information theory; (e) engineering economics; and (f) the decision sciences. On a more technical level, the management and decision sciences can be partly reduced to a series of techniques such as queuing theory; linear, mathematical, and dynamic programming; inventory theory; replacement theory; statistical decision-making; network analysis; rhochrematics (i.e., study of the flow of material); and simulation. These different techniques have not been reduced to a common denominator. Some are interrelated, but most are independent and stand by themselves.

4. These various subdisciplines and techniques share the following elements: (a) they are strongly oriented toward action, and view knowledge mainly as a tool for improving "operations" (in the sense of human and organizational activities directed at a goal); (b) they strongly value "rationality" and "efficiency" as the main norms to be furthered by the management and decision sciences, and disregard the positive contributions of extrarational components; (c) they depend mainly on quantitative models, and so are almost completely preoccupied with problems and variables that can be quantified; (d) they want to arrive at "holistic" views of investigated problems and systems that take all relevant variables into account. The last two elements contradict one another, and create an intellectual dilemma that limits unnecessarily the domain to which the management and decision sciences can be applied.

5. Those few who consciously perceive this dilemma usually think it can be solved by better integration with the social sciences, but they also lay down the condition that the latter must first be quantified. In other words, they ask the social sciences to adjust themselves to the self-perceived needs of the management and decision sciences, and do not think about the fact that the management and decision sciences need to change their own methods so as to be better able to accommodate data that cannot be quantified in the traditional measurement scales of their models. A statement by Russell L. Ackoff, one of the most important innovators in the management and decision sciences, is typical:

Unfortunately, there are relatively few behavioral scientists who are devoting their efforts to developing measures of psychological and social variables which permit the type of mathematical operations required in OR (Operations Research). . . . By combining pressures from within and without, it may be possible to accelerate the type of conceptual and metrical development in the behavioral sciences which is required by OR.[8]

---

[8] Russell L. Ackoff, "The Meaning, Scope, and Methods of Operations Research," in Russell L. Ackoff, ed., *Progress in Operations Research* (N.Y.: John Wiley, 1961), I, 27.

In fact, social-science materials, except from economics, are almost completely ignored in most of the management- and decision-sciences literature, despite some lip service to the "human element." Aside from paying some isolated attention to the "human variable," these interdisciplinary sciences have hardly tried to integrate psychological, sociological, and political-science material into their main body. In dealing with the human part of the "man-machine system," much of the management- and decision-sciences literature does not really assimilate modern findings on human motivations even when the writers are familiar with them. In this and other ways, such writers continue the tradition of Frederick Taylor on a much more complex and refined level, since they make too little use of the contributions of the "socio-psychological approach" and its more sophisticated critics and fellows,[9] and of the social sciences in general. This limited perspective is one of the main barriers that are keeping the contemporary management and decision sciences from developing policy knowledge.

6. Most of the applications of the management sciences are to the military and to industry. Specific problems in municipal management, educational administration, hospital management, town planning, and similar areas have been dealt with by the management and decision sciences, and methods for dealing with larger systems are being worked out. The largest applications of the management and decision sciences are apparently to complex weapons systems. The more thoroughgoing models for overall designing of organizations and for policymaking are well illustrated by the work of Jay W. Forrester and his team at Massachusetts Institute of Technology under the name of "Industrial Dynamics," and apply at most to the level of unitary business corporations.

7. The management sciences pay much attention to the problems of how they can become integrated into actual decisionmaking and policymaking. They recognize that they must "sell their goods" to the policymakers, and have devoted much thought to what the best organizational and personal relationships between management- and decision-sciences personnel and policymakers would be, as well as to the need to educate the policymakers so as to make them receptive to new knowledge and able to use it.

8. Although they say they want to influence the real world,

---

[9] The enterprising reader might compare two outstanding and pioneering books by faculty members of the School of Industrial Management of the Massachusetts Institute of Technology, namely, Douglas McGregor's *The Human Side of Enterprise* (N.Y.: McGraw-Hill, 1960), and Jay W. Forrester's *Industrial Dynamics* (N.Y.: John Wiley, 1961). The totally different (though not irreconcilable) orientations of these two books are all the more striking considering the physical proximity of the authors.

many of the management and decision sciences' practitioners and theoreticians tend to criticize it, to feel their mission is to remake reality (including human nature) completely, and to concentrate on radical "systems redesign."

9. The management sciences had to be given their own institutes in the university to be able to develop without being overwhelmed by the older departments. They regard close contact with real problems, mainly by serving as consultants, to be generally helpful, and even essential, for fruitful theoretical work in this field (though not so much for developing pure mathematical models).

This list of characteristics and barriers is not exhaustive. It would be especially interesting to have some data on the people that are active in the management and decision sciences. For instance, if most of the persons in this field have little tolerance for ambiguity, that trait may hinder the accommodation of this field to public policymaking, which contains many "political" elements. But my survey is broad enough that I can evaluate the contributions that the management and decision sciences have made or could make to policy knowledge, and their limitations. Their major potential contribution seems to be threefold: (1) knowledge, methods, and techniques that are directly relevant to some issues public policymaking must deal with; (2) an approach and frame of reference that is useful for public policymaking and metapolicymaking in general; and (3) much experience and ideas that are relevant to the development of a comprehensive policy science.

1. The knowledge, methods, and techniques the management sciences have now apply to only a few policymaking issues, namely, those that are susceptible to extensive quantification. Systems management has the broadest applicability to things like water-resources policies. The more specific techniques, such as linear programming or queuing theory, apply to specific aspects of problems, but not to much more.

2. On the other hand, the management sciences' basic approach and frame of reference, which is like that of most interdisciplinary fields, has very broad significance for public policymaking and metapolicymaking in general. Its significance lies in its holistic orientation, in the idea of using explicit simulation models as a tool in policymaking, in its conceptual equipment, and, most important of all, in its readiness to take a completely fresh look at the real world and to try to reform that world in the light of carefully constructed optimal "blueprints." In itself, this readiness and drive may be too much of a good thing, suffering as it does from overconfidence in pure-rationality solutions and in quantification. But, as a counterforce to some prevailing tendencies, it can fulfill an

essential and highly important role in developing policy knowledge and improving policymaking. In systems analysis the approach is more careful and therefore more useful: Preferable solutions are searched for, with somewhat less presumption of rationality and calculability.

3. Finally, the experience of the management sciences in getting established as a recognized interdisciplinary field (or fields), in combining a normative orientation with a scientific attitude, and in gaining partial acceptance by policymakers constitutes an important experiment and precedent. Feedback from this experience, and from its progress by trial and error, provides knowledge that is relevant to the problems involved in establishing a policy science. Their successful emergence itself shows that we can develop systematic policy knowledge and can apply it to actual policymaking, even though this has only been done on a small scale so far. Their precedent makes it more probable that parallel achievements on a larger scale can be made by establishing a policy science. The experience of systems analysis and its accelerated development serves as an even stronger precedent, in some respects, in this direction.

The management and decision sciences are the best-developed interdisciplinary fields, and are rather a model for some of the others, such as regional science. There are also some, such as development studies and EKISTICS (the study of human settlement founded by Doxiadis), that follow a different path, being interested in more qualitative phenomena. But they all share with the management and decision sciences a multidisciplinary base, an orientation toward action, and a need to be recognized as a distinct field of advanced study.

TOWARD A POLICY SCIENCE

So far I have pointed out some of the barriers that are retarding innovations in policy knowledge, and have indicated a few ways to overcome these barriers. Now I reach one of my major proposals for accelerating the discovery of policy knowledge and for increasing the actual use of such knowledge in policymaking: a new interdisciplinary field that focuses on these tasks should be established. Following Harold Lasswell's suggestion,[10] I call this new field "policy science," but the name itself is not important; the reader may call it anything that in his opinion better expresses its substantive contents as I describe them in this section.

---

[10] See Harold D. Lasswell, "The Policy Orientation," in Daniel Lerner and Harold D. Lasswell, eds., *The Policy Sciences: Recent Developments in Scope and Method* (Stanford: Stanford Univ. Press, 1951), pp. 3ff.

The essence of my suggestion is that a separate field is essential to speed up the development of policy knowledge and its being used for better policymaking. This field must constitute a distinct area for purposes of research and advanced teaching (and must be recognized as such by university administrations) and for recruiting and training professional policy scientists and policymakers. It should be patterned mainly on the modern interdisciplinary fields, applying their basic orientation and ideas more broadly to the policymaking system, and integrating them with assumptions, methods, and findings from the social sciences, while trying to avoid the shortcomings of both areas.

More specifically, some of policy science's characteristics should be as follows:

1. The central subject matter of policy science will be public policymaking, and will include knowledge on both policy issues and policymaking itself. It will try to answer such questions as: How do public-policymaking systems in fact operate? What are the main internal and environmental variables that influence their operation? What effects do changes in these variables have on the operations of public-policymaking systems? What main methods for solving problems are available to public policymaking, and what are their characteristics? How can the various rational and extrarational components of policymaking be improved? What major ways of dealing with social problems other than by public policymaking are there, and what are their important characteristics? How can changes best be made in policymaking systems?

2. Policy science will be oriented toward action. Its main aim will be to contribute to improving public policymaking, in both the short and the long run. Like medicine, economics, and the management sciences, its basic aim to contribute to real policymaking will color all its activities, but will not make relevant pure research and pure theory any less essential as a part of it.

3. Policy science will be an interdisciplinary field. It will depend heavily on the social sciences, on other interdisciplinary fields, and on such other branches of learning as history, philosophy, and mathematics for data and ideas, which it will reprocess, supplement, and integrate to meet the particular needs of the study of policymaking. Again, like medicine, it will not only consume knowledge, but also produce data and theories of significance for other disciplines.

4. The methodologies of policy science must be adjusted to its particular needs. It will not only make the fullest possible use of methods from contemporary social research, but, given the diffuse nature of much of its subject matter, will have to recognize explicitly the importance of

non-rigorous sources of knowledge including introspection, overall gestalt impressions, and intuitive understanding. It must pay special attention to the study of extrarational processes that are relevant for policymaking. It will prefer quantitative and rigorous research methods insofar as they are available, but must not delay considering essential phases of policymaking that are not susceptible to such methods.

Much knowledge of interest to policy science can come from the unformulated experiences of policymakers, both politicians and senior civil servants. At present, their knowledge is mostly lost to posterity; each generation must recover the same territory by expensive trial and error. This most wasteful state of affairs is not helped by most memoirs written by retired policymakers with an axe to grind (though there have been distinguished exceptions). One methodological challenge that policy science faces is to stimulate at least a partial explication of this experiential tacit knowledge, for instance, by providing selected policymakers with sabbaticals to enable them to write on subjects covered by their experience or to participate in research seminars. Such a program would be not only a very important way to enrich knowledge, but also a main avenue of contact between policy scientists and policymakers and a central means for educating public-policymaking personnel.

The Institute for Politics that has been set up under the direction of Richard E. Neustadt in the John Fitzgerald Kennedy School of Government at Harvard University as part of the Kennedy Memorial Foundation seems to be going in such a direction. The Center for Advanced Study in the Behavioral Sciences illustrates another perfect setting for such an experimental endeavor, which would bring together a mixed group of social scientists and senior policymakers. Two variations on this experiment should be tried out: having social scientists and policymakers cooperate in exploring a defined subject matter; and having them mix informally and at seminars, but without any structured project. Both may provide significant knowledge of many kinds.

5. Policy science will aim at instrumental knowledge that will improve policymaking regardless of the policymaking system's substantive values. This means that policy science could serve any goals, from increases in human happiness and self-fulfillment to genocide. Hopefully, policy science can help make policy goals more "reasonable" by exposing the psychopathological basis of some destructive goals, by helping to exclude persons who tend to accept such goals from policy-shaping positions, and by pointing out the boomerang effects of such goals. But there can be no certainty on this point; the uses to which knowledge is put do not depend on that knowledge itself.

Value and fact will be interrelated in policy science, in that policy scientists who accept western democratic values will strive to improve public policymaking in different ways from policy scientists who accept Communist ideology, who will select somewhat different problems for study and will operate with somewhat different explicit and implicit assumptions. Policy scientists who have fundamentally different values may share knowledge, terminology, methodology, technology and understand one another. At least, they should often be able to reduce disagreements to "second-order agreements" in which they agree on what it is that they disagree on. But their work and ideas will serve different goals, and their ideas will be conditioned by different, though partly overlapping, needs and preconceptions.

6. Policy science should try to achieve a holistic attitude, dealing with the policymaking system as a whole and considering the effect of changes in single variables on the overall quality of policymaking. Here is one of the important differences between policy science and the existing interdisciplinary fields, most of which focus on one sector of the policymaking system, such as the intelligence-collecting phases or the operations of unitary organizations. The management sciences aspire to a broader area, but are limited by their dependence on quantification. Policy science can be viewed, in some respects, as management science combined with social science and as systems analysis combined with political science, applied to the public-policymaking system. In the transformation it loses reliability and exactness, but gains broadness and significance.

7. Policy science will be action-oriented in two senses: (a) it will try to provide knowledge that can contribute to improving public policymaking; (b) it will actively promote the use of such knowledge in actual public policymaking. The second task will require a sensitivity to the fact that such knowledge must be presented in a way that gives it the highest probability of being used. The task will therefore require building channels of communication to policymakers, avoiding professional jargons, and developing a good measure of tact. More generally, it will require intensive research and thought on the problem of getting as much policy science used in public policymaking as possible. At the same time, there must be safeguards against the dangers of becoming too involved in actual public policymaking, of developing a vested interest in specific policies and policymaking units, and of distorting knowledge so as to make it more acceptable. Such safeguards might include professional organization, early formulation of a code of ethics, and not depending on single policymaking units, but the most important ones will be the strength of character of the individual policy scientists and the support they receive from the community of scholars.

8. Policy science should favor innovation and should try to achieve significant breakthroughs in designing policymaking systems. Searching for new alternatives for public policymaking requires imagination, and a recognition that hypothetical speculation is a legitimate pursuit of policy scientists, so long as it is clearly labeled as such. Manipulating normative "optimal models" of public policymaking will be an important part of policy science, like empirical study of actual public policymaking.

9. The available experience indicates that policy science must be established as a separate unit in the university structure, in addition to being developed at special policy-research institutes, if it is to develop properly. Unless it is recognized as a distinct area of study and teaching, it cannot have the freedom of action it must have to develop its own unique characteristics.

10. Policy science should be very aware of the importance of teaching and should pay much attention to training future policymakers and policy scientists. It must therefore develop a careful curriculum, new teaching methods, and new ways to reach active policymakers.

My suggestions for a policy science look so convincing (to me, anyway) that they must lead to the suspicious question, "If everything is so simple, why wasn't such a policy science established long ago?" After all, the concept of "social engineering" is well known, the idea of "applied social science" has been discussed ad nauseam, and the question "knowledge for what?" has already been asked and forgotten many times.

Parts of the answer to this question lie, I think, in the barriers against developing policy knowledge that exist in the social sciences. The subject matter of policy science is difficult, and the accepted predispositions and tendencies in the traditional social sciences have kept them away from it. Establishing a new field of science is always difficult, especially if it does not emerge naturally as a subdiscipline of an accepted branch of learning. Taking into account the strength of the barriers, there is no reason to be surprised that there is not yet any compact policy science. The increasing pressure of acute social problems, the increasing awareness by social scientists of these problems, the precedent of the new interdisciplinary fields, particularly the management sciences, and advances in knowledge that make a policy science feasible make it likely that the present is more ripe for establishing a policy science than was the past. Indeed, present developments in systems analysis are clearly more in the direction of policy science, though the development is occurring at too slow a rate and in too haphazard a way.

Establishing policy science as a separate field seems to be an important way to overcome some of the barriers against policy knowledge and to make policy knowledge that meets the needs I detailed at the beginning of this chapter as available as possible. Thus, I think, the cost of establishing a policy science would be justified, and the results well worth the price. But a strong push will be needed to mobilize the necessary resources, especially highly qualified manpower, and to overcome the barriers. In the abstract, one would expect such a push to originate with the actual public-policymaking system, which should eagerly encourage any possible source of help. In fact, one of the barriers against establishing a policy science is doubting whether any relevant knowledge it came up with would be used in actual public policymaking; such a doubt of course discourages devoting energy and time to an apparently hopeless task. Therefore, arrangements for integrating knowledge into actual public policymaking are essential not only for getting the available knowledge used, but also for encouraging an increase in the flow of policy knowledge and for establishing a policy science.

chapter 18 · Changes Needed in Personnel

The quality of its personnel is the single most important variable that determines the quality of public policymaking. Improving the personnel is therefore a major way to improve public policymaking. Furthermore, without changes in the qualifications and performance of the policymakers, most institutional improvements are doomed.

In general, we must be able to give the policymakers more policy knowledge, strengthen their rational and extrarational abilities, and adjust their performance and thinking to the needs of optimal policymaking. These changes will require significant innovations in the way that the various policymakers are recruited, trained, and promoted, but will not blur the basic division of labor between elected and appointed policymakers that is fundamental for the democratic form of government.

Most policymakers fall into three groups: politicians, senior civil servants, and experts. Because of the differences between these groups, I find it more convenient to examine them separately.

POLITICIANS

That we need better senior civil servants has been recognized in principle, and some steps have been taken to meet this need. Therefore, by extrapolation from the past, we can hope there will be further improvements in the quality of senior civil servants, even if there is no concerted drive to improve them. The situation is totally different for the most important of the public policymakers, namely, the politicians. With a few exceptions, especially in dictatorial countries, entering politics is mainly self-motivated, and advancement into the higher ranks is determined by a complex competitive process that emphasizes bargaining skills and, in democratic countries, the ability to recruit votes. Now that politics is increasingly bureaucratized, and public images are increasingly influenced by public-relations experts and organized publicity campaigns, bargaining skills may become even more important for the average politician in most countries, and charisma for the highest ranks. Whether or not these developments take place, one outstanding fact is that little if any systematic thought has been done on the quality of the politicians brought to the forefront by the present methods for recruiting and promoting them. Modern political theories have not progressed much beyond the opinions on the advantages of democratic elections that were so well expressed by British thinkers in the eighteenth and nineteenth centuries. Contemporary studies of political careers and leadership characteristics have not taken up this problem, since they have generally been limited to describing those characteristics that are easy to get at by statistical methods or case biographies. Although the psychological approach to political activity initiated by Graham Wallas and Harold Lasswell is not thus limited, it has not been developed enough that it could be used to improve the quality of politicians.

The simple fact is that this whole subject is taboo. Any suggestion for screening politicians is regarded as a violation of a basic value of democracy, and is therefore not a permissible alternative. This very dangerous axiom could very well cause democratic government to deteriorate relative to other types of regimes, unless it is carefully reexamined and circumscribed. The rising level of popular education in modern democratic countries might be accompanied by a concomitant improvement in the quality of politicians, but then it might not. There is a distinct risk that the quality of politicians will not keep abreast of either the more difficult problems or the new policy knowledge, so that either public policy will lag more and more behind what it should or could be or politicians will influence policymaking less. Comparing the roles of politicians in policymaking a few decades ago with their roles today does show that in modern countries most of them (but not the central political leaders) have less influence, especially on critical problems of military and scientific policy. Some of this decline in their influence may be desirable, or unavoidable, but some of it is caused by their being less and less qualified for their jobs, which trend may lead to an erosion of the principles and assumptions on which democracy is based.

Becoming a high-ranking politician is difficult in all societies; those who try it must work intensely to pass through a series of highly competitive screening mechanisms. Those who do successfully climb the ladder of politics therefore have highly developed skills that can be very valuable for optimal public policymaking, especially their extrarational skills in value judgment, in intuitively grasping situations, in sensing future needs, and in feeling "what the country will stand." Also, as "representatives" in democratic countries, or bearers of the dominant ideology in dictatorial countries, politicians are the main channel by which the values and goals of policymaking are determined. My optimal model of public policymaking recognizes the crucial importance of these contributions that politicians can make to public policymaking, whereas they are ignored or minimized by, for example, the pure-rationality and economically rational models, which at best tend to regard politicians as "a necessary evil" or "the price of democracy."

The typical career patterns of politicians in most contemporary societies reinforce their extrarational skills, but are not conducive to integrating knowledge into public policymaking. The politicians themselves have only limited policy knowledge, very few of them having received an education in any relevant discipline other than law. This by itself would not create a major difficulty, if politicians were able to use policy knowledge supplied by others, but often they cannot. Using complex knowledge requires much sophistication and knowledge, without which the policymakers tend to oscillate between relying on knowledge too much and rejecting it completely. In other words, to be able and willing to use a bit of knowledge, one must have a realistic image of what can be expected from it. Expecting too much leads in the long run to disappointment and overreacting against the knowledge, whereas underestimating what it could contribute means that it will be used too little.

Similarly, to deal with the fact that equally reputable scientists hold contradictory opinions, policymakers must have an understanding of the nature of scientific knowledge that will permit them to distill the useful portions from the contradictory opinions and have some basis for making a choice besides their purely personal impressions or the rhetorical skills of the various experts. Politicians have their own unique and essential roles in optimal public policymaking, and should not undertake the functions of policy-science experts. But politicians should be able to use knowledge to carry out their own roles, and should recognize the unique and essential role of policy knowledge in policymaking, in order to provide the climate and institutional arrangements that are needed to put knowledge to its best use. This best use depends on their having a correct view of the role of knowledge in public policymaking, which in turn depends on their being familiar with and sophisticated about policy knowledge. At present, the background and experience of most politicians does not give them such familiarity, let alone such sophistication.

The problem is mainly one of attitudes. Politicians could partly compensate for their own lack of knowledge by limiting their own roles, if they had a correct intuitive understanding of the autonomous role of knowledge in public policymaking. Or, as we have seen, the problem can be seen as one of balance and suitable symbiosis between politicians and experts; exaggeration in either direction leads either to relying too much on knowledge, or to not using it enough.

American politics has long been characterized by a strong belief in "common sense" and "practical knowledge" as the keys to social problems, and a strong suspicion that "experts" are "daydreamers" and "eggheads." These cultural traits, which go back to the Jackson-Jefferson controversy and earlier, seem closely related to egalitarian idealism and strong anti-elitism. They were reinforced by the image of the self-made practical man who successfully conquers the wilderness or establishes an industrial empire. Thanks to the country's size, richness, and isolation from European power struggles, the low-quality public policymaking that resulted in many cases from these beliefs was nevertheless good enough to handle the main problems. Results that were qualitatively catastrophic were never great enough to force such attitudes to change or to require any reform of the policymaking system other than in isolated institutions (such as in the army after the Spanish-American War debacle).[1] Following the crises of World War I, the Depression, World War II, and the Cold War, these attitudes slowly changed. First during the New Deal and then during the Kennedy administration, policymaking's reliance on knowledge was radically increased. The situation today is very different from what it was thirty years ago, and is continuing to change quite rapidly. Nevertheless, many, though always fewer, contemporary politicians are still strongly influenced by the traditional biases in favor of "common sense" and against "experts." These attitudes continue to be a strong barrier against using knowledge in public policymaking, especially when they are held by the many politicians who are unfamiliar with policy knowledge.

Developments have been different, for instance, in the Netherlands, where the constant pressures of critical hydraulic, social, political, and economic problems have required very good public policymaking merely for survival, and have made much use of knowledge essential.[2] These factors resulted in a self-limitation of the scope of "politics," and in institutional arrangements designed, quite successfully, to increase the

---

[1] The effect of this crisis on policymaking in the armed forces is well described in Otto C. Nelson, Jr., *National Security and the General Staff* (Washington: Infantry Journal Press, 1946).

[2] For a detailed discussion, see my forthcoming *National Planning in the Netherlands* (Syracuse: Syracuse Univ. Press, 1968).

effects of knowledge on public policymaking and on political delibera-
tions. Similarly, a strong tradition exists in Sweden of having most
proposals about public policy carefully examined by ad hoc public
commissions in which highly qualified experts participate; the minister
concerned must seriously consider the reports of these commissions,
because he is required to submit the commission's report to Parliament
with a detailed paper setting forth his own position. Such situations
clearly demonstrate that democracy is compatible with a large role for
knowledge in public policymaking.

There are several ways to improve the qualifications of politicians
without in any way violating the principles of democracy. For instance,
paying politicians who occupy third-rank positions more may attract
better candidates to such jobs, which ordinarily do not offer sufficient
rewards in terms of status to attract good candidates, but which are
important stepping-stones to higher office. Educational campaigns explaining the interest and challenge of politics may also help attract
high-quality manpower.[3] Much can be done in this direction on the
grass-roots level, where local politicians can rejuvenate the tradition of
encouraging bright young men to enter politics. Another painless possibility would be to introduce some policy-oriented courses into law-
school curricula, because many future politicians in many countries,
including the U.S.A., study law. Even without totally reconstructing the
teaching of law, as was proposed by Harold D. Lasswell and Myres S.
McDougal in a famous article,[4] something useful could be achieved by
introducing elective policy-science courses. Some examples are a Defense Policy Seminar initiated by some Harvard law professors and
courses in Legislation.

There have been some more innovative proposals, designed to encourage politicians to engage in "post-entry" training (as is done on a small
scale, for instance, for persons elected to municipal offices at the *Kom-
munskolan* in Sweden). What I have in mind are systematic arrangements that would allow politicians at several stages of their careers to get
away from day-to-day pressures and spend six months or a year on study
and thought. One way to do this is to offer special fellowships at
universities and research institutes, open to both junior and senior

---

[3] Quite unusual in this respect is a German book: Lothar Bossle, *Der junge
Mensch und die Politik* (*Young People and Politics*) (Osnabrück: A. Fromm,
1961). Similar literature on encouraging youth to enter politics and preparing
them to do so by presenting realistic expectations is urgently needed in English.

[4] Harold D. Lasswell and Myres S. McDougal, "Legal Education and Public
Policy: Professional Training in the Public Interest" (1943), reprinted in Lasswell, *The Analysis of Political Behavior* (London: Routledge and Kegan Paul,
1948), pp. 21ff.

politicians. A more institutionalized way would be to provide sabbatical leaves of absence, paid for by the state, to politicians who have served for a certain number of years in defined political positions, on the condition that they devote these years to self-developing activities, such as study, writing, or traveling abroad.

New knowledge may create additional steps we could take to improve the qualifications of politicians without in any way violating the principle of democratic elections. Special seminars in policy science could be organized, personality-development methods, such as Laboratory and T-Group methods, could be adjusted to the needs of politicians, etc. In the long run, we may have also to take steps to offset or even control public-relations techniques, which may create incorrect public images of political figures, and thus distort the democratic-election mechanism.

My main point here is that new knowledge requires new methods for developing politicians. The basic principle of democracy, that government should be elected by the people, is unconditional, and does not depend on knowledge; but the specific institutional mechanisms for carrying out this principle depend in their details on available knowledge and must be readjusted to new knowledge. There is nothing "undemocratic" about encouraging good persons to enter politics or about encouraging politicians to acquire policy knowledge and to engage in systematic self-development.

SENIOR CIVIL SERVANTS

The weaknesses of politicians, in not integrating enough knowledge into public policymaking, for example, could be largely, though not completely, compensated for by properly qualified senior civil servants, if the policymaking structure and process patterns were suitable. Compared with politicians, senior civil servants in most countries do indeed use knowledge more, but not enough more by any means. One of the main reasons why senior civil servants do not contribute enough to policymaking is that, like politicians, they lack the qualifications and attitudes that are needed for optimal policymaking. In no contemporary state are the formal qualifications for the senior civil service calculated to provide the overall understanding of policy knowledge and the patterns of performance and thought that would lead to optimal policymaking. The educational requirement for the senior civil service usually follows one of five patterns: (1) the European pattern, with emphasis on a legal education; (2) the British pattern, with emphasis on an unspecialized, advanced university education; (3) the United States pattern, with a narrow professional background, an unspecialized university education, or practical experience; (4) the pattern of many developing countries, where for lack of educated manpower, or for political reasons, high civil servants often have neither advanced formal education nor relevant experience; and (5) the U.S.S.R. pattern, with a narrow professional education or a political background. The one major exception is France, where the Ecole Nationale d'Administration provides a unique training for candidates about to enter the senior civil service. The training, though inadequate in terms of the modern social sciences, is excellent in many respects; it both gives them some preparation for using policy knowledge and trains them in extrarational policy skills by means of a system of internship.

The phenomenon among civil servants that parallels politicians' preference for "practical skill" is the idea that "experts should be kept on tap and not on top," which has been stated in its most convincing form by Harold Laski.[5] Although such an idea applies fairly well to narrow-minded, single-discipline experts, it is often understood to mean that "generalists" are always able to judge all matters better than experts, that all experts are suspect, and, most dangerous of all, that "generalists" need only "common sense" and high intelligence to face all problems and judge the relevance of all expert knowledge. This attitude characterizes especially the British civil service, though it is by no means uncommon in other countries, including the United States. The pressure of acute problems, the forces of routine and inertia, the lack of resources, and the strength of vested interests all reinforce the inadequate qualifications and attitudes of most senior civil servants in almost all countries to hinder the proper use of policy knowledge.

The importance of senior civil servants in shaping public policymaking is today generally recognized. So is the fact that a high-quality civil service is an essential precondition for good public policymaking and good executing of policies. The rise of the modern state was in every case accompanied by radical changes in the civil service that led, in the western democratic countries, to a central civil service of the career-merit type. This type of civil service successfully fulfilled its functions as long as the activities of the state were limited, but entered a period of crisis when government began to perform more and more varied functions and had to use more and more scientific knowledge. At present, this crisis is being dealt with mainly by such organizational palliatives as bifurcating the public service, which is creating a widening gulf between

---

[5] Harold J. Laski, "The Limitations of the Expert," *Harper's Magazine*, CLXII (Dec. 1930), 102ff. A convenient summary of Laski's arguments is provided in Robert Dubin, *Human Relations in Administration* (Englewood Cliffs, N.J.: Prentice-Hall, 1961), pp. 193–194.

the traditionally trained civil service and the single-discipline scientific experts who are active in government service.

That the United States has no clearly defined class of senior civil servants recruited from a narrow social base helps slow down the obsolescence of the federal public service by permitting it a degree of elasticity absent in continental Europe or England, but that fact has also kept the American system from enjoying the advantages of professional civil servants whose highly developed extrarational policymaking skills are based on long experience and on systematic indoctrination in the traditions of the service.

The radical changes in the academic preparation and post-entry training of business executives in the United States have as yet no parallel in the senior civil service, either in the United States (with the exception of the new City Manager profession) or in any other country (with the already mentioned exception of the Ecole Nationale d'Administration in France). Similarly, the careful training and retraining of military officers has no parallel in government service. The situation in business and military organizations shows clearly how far the qualifications of public-policymaking personnel lag behind those of military officers and professional business executives. This gap and the need for higher qualifications for senior civil servants have often been noted, for instance, by the Hoover Commission and the Committee on Foreign Affairs Personnel in the United States, and by the Boyer Committee in Australia.[6] Several ambitious proposals to overcome this gap have been made, but only a few of them have been acted on, mainly in the field of foreign-service personnel, where the need for improvement has been better recognized (in part because of more obvious failures of the traditionally trained diplomat). An important step was the Government Employees Training Act of 1958 in the United States, though until 1967 it has had few actual results.

The most important proposals for improving the civil-service policymakers can be summed up as follows:[7]

1. High-quality manpower should be drawn into the public service. In most western democratic countries, the best university graduates

---

[6] See The Committee on Foreign Affairs Personnel, *Personnel For the New Diplomacy* (N.Y.: Taplinger, 1962), and *Report of the Committee of Inquiry into Public-Service Recruitment* (Canberra: Government of the Commonwealth of Australia, 1959). The Fulton Committee has been appointed in England largely because of a similar uneasiness about the senior civil service.

[7] For detailed recommendations adjusted to the specific circumstances of one country and based on these general recommendations, see my forthcoming paper "A Senior Civil Service Policy for Israel: Preliminary Policy Analysis and Recommendations," prepared for Israeli Center for Policy Research (Jerusalem, 1968).

tend to go either into business or into the natural sciences. This has apparently always been the case in the United States, but is rather new in England and in some European countries, where the senior civil service has had a strong drawing power. England and most European countries, where the top persons still tend to want to enter the senior civil service, seem to be in little danger of not having good enough candidates, but in the United States this danger seems to be more acute, especially on the state level, which, in contrast to local government in most other modern countries, is in charge of some quite important policymaking functions.

Suggestions on ways to attract better manpower into government service tend to play up the monetary incentive, by proposing higher salaries for senior policymaking positions and, in the United States, by easing the laws about conflict of interest that may discourage business-men from entering government service. The available data on how people choose their occupations supports the idea that material incentives are one of the major variables influencing such choices, especially in the United States, where salaries are an important status symbol. At the same time, studies on occupational choice emphasize the sometimes greater importance of other variables, which include the image of the occupation, its social-prestige rating, and one's image of one's concrete chances for getting into it. The idealistic connotations of occupations must also be recognized as an important variable, which they are in avant-garde developing countries and in doctrinaire states, but often not in western countries, which ignore the strength of idealistic appeals to the ideal-starved youth of modern culture; consider how successful, at first, the recruiting of candidates for the Peace Corps was in the United States.

These remarks and findings suggest that increases in salary are only one, and not necessarily the most effective (and certainly not the cheapest), way to increase the flow of high-quality candidates into the senior civil service. Another way might be educational campaigns to explain the interests and idealistic connotations of public service, for instance, by lecture tours to universities and through the mass-communication media. Another highly effective and feasible way would be to establish special career patterns, designed to meet the interests and needs of high-quality university graduates and other promising candidates, by providing them with a variety of interesting experience and an assurance of fast progress into senior policymaking positions if they meet the requirements. Another might be to encourage people active in business, in professions, and in academic life to enter government service for a few years by offering them suitable fixed-term appointments. This method is used in the United States, though not enough, whereas in continental Europe, in England, and in most developing countries it is almost completely neglected.

Another problem is to determine what the optimal formal educational qualifications for entrance into the civil service are. For the general policymaking positions, the present educational system provides no one optimal field of study. Once policy science has been established as a discipline, it should become the preferred graduate academic background for the higher civil service; until then, a wide background with emphasis on the social sciences would have many advantages, and will have more, once some of the weaknesses (in terms of the skills and knowledge required for policymaking) in the way much social science is now taught are eliminated.

2. Optimal public policymaking requires senior civil servants who have a great deal of the knowledge and skills needed for policymaking. The less those who enter public service come equipped with such knowledge and skills, the more is it necessary to establish systematic and penetrating post-entry training. The only country that has made a serious attempt to solve this problem is France, with its Ecole Nationale d'Administration. Except for the military services, some foreign services and other special branches (such as the Department of Agriculture in the U.S.A.), and a few individual cases in the general senior civil service, post-entry training is minimal in all countries. Institutions like the Hochschule für Verwaltungswissenschaften at Speyer in Germany, the Administrative Staff College at Henley in England, and various similar institutions in Switzerland, Italy, Spain, and other countries are outdated in parts of their approach. Some of the developing countries make a more serious effort at such training, being more aware that they lack suitably qualified public officials, but as yet those efforts have had little effect, partly because the curricula of these training institutions are often quite technical and not geared to the needs of senior civil servants as policymakers in developing countries.

The best existing training programs are perhaps those provided at some universities, such as the special programs at Harvard, Princeton, and Syracuse. There are also some important programs mainly designed for senior civil servants from developing countries, such as at the University of Pittsburgh or at the Institute of Social Studies in The Hague. But all these programs are still very far from being good enough, reach only a few students, and have also had little effect.

A variety of proposals has been made for establishing special staff schools to which senior civil servants would go at various points of their careers. The more advanced proposals combine such intense training with overall career planning, including sabbatical leaves of absence, periods of training at regular universities, and job rotation. All such proposals have in fact been rejected (even after formal approval, as of the Government Employees Training Act in the U.S.A.), because of their expense, because of inertia or fear of "technocracy," because of difficulties in releasing the better officials from their current pressing duties, or for similar shortsighted reasons.

Career planning for senior public officials, designed to give them overall experience and a good education in policy knowledge, is one of the most convincing and relatively cheapest ways to provide better policymakers and contribute to better public policymaking. One could, therefore, reasonably expect that proposals in this line would meet with universal approval. That they have not testifies to the strength of the barriers against making improvements in public policymaking.

EXPERTS

Better civil servants and politicians will in no way make "experts," in the traditional sense of the term, superfluous. Rather, one of the main reasons for improving the knowledge of politicians and senior civil servants is to make them better able to work with experts and to use expert knowledge to the fullest, as they must for optimal policymaking. To put it differently, as policy knowledge increases, more experts of more different kinds must participate in policymaking if the knowledge is to be put to use. Such participation will require significant changes on the part of politicians and senior civil servants, as well as in the qualifications, attitudes, and orientations of the "experts."

The typical contemporary "expert," be he in the physical sciences, engineering, social sciences, or operations research, has been educated in a single discipline (even if an interdisciplinary field) and is biased in his outlook. He tends to be overimpressed by those facts that fit into his specialty, and to ignore all others. If his specialty is in the natural sciences, he is likely to have very naive images of policymaking, to overrate the potentialities of rationality and physical-science methodologies, and to hold a very simplified view of human nature and social institutions. The same, surprisingly enough, holds true for some social-science "experts," at least when they are fresh out of college, and especially for economists. Experience helps overcome these handicaps, but at a high price, and often not enough. Most social scientists must ultimately work on a team in an organizational setting, often cooperating with experts in other fields and with various types of managers or administrators, but their university training does almost nothing to prepare them for such roles. Most other disciplines do even less to prepare the future expert for his role as a contributor of specialized knowledge to policymaking.

Considering the growing importance of single-discipline experts in contributing different kinds of specialized policy knowledge to policymaking, the burden of integrating this knowledge is too heavy even for the best-trained politicians and civil servants, unless they are helped by the experts themselves. To give such help, the experts must be trained rather differently and must follow rather different career patterns within the policymaking system.

First, all students of narrow specialties must learn the basic concepts about human and social behavior, especially about those phenomena most likely to be misunderstood by the uninformed. Also, on the graduate level, work on comprehensive policy projects as members of interdisciplinary teams and in survey courses on policy science should be obligatory for students whose professional careers may involve work in policymaking structures, such as traffic engineers, public-health experts, city planners, economists, and statisticians.

Such academic preparation can be very helpful, but is insufficient by itself. The student's lack of time and experience must keep him from doing much more than broadening his horizons, which would still be a big advance over the present situation. Additional steps must be taken to permit better integration of experts into policymaking after they actually begin participating in units that contribute to policymaking. These additional steps might include rotation designed to give single-discipline experts some experience in solving problems comprehensively, planned participation in interprofessional teamwork and in the general training programs for senior civil servants, and, for the more important experts, special advanced training courses.

Special attention must be paid to developing new types of experts who specialize in the applications of various interdisciplinary fields to policymaking, especially policy scientists who will serve as professional policy analysts in new staff positions. The new professions of civil strategist and systems analyst demonstrate rather well what I have in mind on a broader scale. Preparing policy scientists for staff positions as policy analysts will be one of the most important functions of policy science, and is a major reason why policy science must be established as a distinct area of research and advanced study.

SOME ADDITIONAL OBSERVATIONS

The recommended development for all types of policymaking personnel must be multidimensional. It must deal with all aspects of knowledge and personality, including: (a) intellectual capacities; (b) explicit knowledge; (c) tacit knowledge; (d) patterns of behavior; (e) orientations and propensities; and (f) basic personality structures. Developing such aspects for better policymaking would involve developing such things as: (a) capacities for conceptualization, abstract thinking, and considering problems in terms of probabilities; (b) knowing methods of prediction and ways of dealing with uncertainty; (c) a "feeling for the possible"; (d) a habit of listening to what others have to say; (e) an ability to tolerate ambiguity and a propensity to innovate; and (f) creativity, a store of energy, and integrity. Each of these various dimensions would have to be developed differently, by means of formal lectures and exercises, gaming and simulation, T-Group sessions, carefully planned career patterns and rotation, or whatever else is useful.

So far I have examined some proposals for improving public policymakers by means of better recruiting and better post-entry development and training. Another important, though indirect, way to get better policymakers would be to provide a reserve of suitable candidates by means of changes in the educational system. General changes in the curriculum of public education can significantly improve it in the qualities needed for better policymaking personnel. However, such an influence would be so diffuse I had better discuss it in Chapter 21, under changes needed in the environment.

Here again I should mention my more limited proposal that policy science be set up as a separate interdisciplinary field for advanced university teaching. At present, a person wishing to enter politics is, in most countries, best advised to study law, not only because law is a convenient stepping-stone, but because skills in law are the nearest to policy skills that one can be trained in at a university. Similarly, persons interested in the higher government service have little to choose from. The social sciences in general, and political science and public administration in particular, are the best available alternatives, but are at present very inadequate ones in terms of what is needed for optimal policymaking. If instruction in policy science were available, many persons aspiring to policymaking positions would likely pick parts of this course of study and would thus come at least somewhat better prepared to their roles, insofar as they do go into politics, government service, or some other policymaking position for which of course they also need other types of knowledge, and certain personality characteristics, especially moral integrity. Even if they do not get into any policymaking position, such persons would improve the environment of the policymaking system, and would thus make a meaningful contribution to better policymaking and to better democratic control over it.

chapter 19 · Changes Needed
in Structure
and Process Patterns

C hanges in structure and process patterns are, like changes in personnel, input, and output, a major way to improve a policymaking system. There is an extremely large number of changes in structure and process patterns that might be feasible and beneficial, from minor changes in subcomponents to radical redesign of the entire system. Some of the changes that are needed I have already pointed out in earlier discussions of the policymaking system, especially in Chapter 15. Others can easily be deduced from comparing actual policymaking with the optimal model. The contemporary literature of public administration and political science also discusses various reforms that would partly meet the requirements for optimal policymaking I developed in Part IV.

Listing here all the changes that are needed in structure and process patterns is both almost impossible and unnecessary. Instead, to illustrate the practical significance of my analysis, I will discuss eight major types of changes that are needed in structure and process patterns. I have selected these types to be a representative sample of feasible and significant suggestions of medium generality.

ESTABLISHING AND REINFORCING SPECIAL
ORGANIZATIONS FOR POLICY ANALYSIS

One of the main recommendations that emerge from comparing the optimal model with actual policymaking is to establish and reinforce special organizations for policy analysis. Optimal policymaking requires systematic thinking that is based on knowledge and oriented toward innovation on medium- and long-range policy issues. Not enough of such thinking can generally take place in action-oriented organizations because of both the pressure of acute problems and the way that a pragmatic organizational climate, based on experience and oriented toward executing policies, depresses innovation. Establishing special organizations that are charged with taking a fresh look at basic policy issues is a necessary (though not sufficient) step toward approximating optimality in public policymaking.

Such organizations should provide a continuous flow of comprehensive "policy papers" on the more important and basic policy issues to the regular administrative and political policymaking units. Such papers should, for instance, reformulate the issues on the basis of better analysis and better predictions of what the future will bring, elaborate the available knowledge in a way conducive to its being applied to the issue, list innovative alternative policies on the issue, and explicitly explore their probable consequences. In addition, and in some ways more importantly, such organizations should influence the whole tone of public policymaking, increasing its rational contents and causing it to operate in terms of longer periods of time.

I will mention two such organizations, in order to emphasize their extreme importance for raising the quality of policymaking and to illustrate both their feasibility and their problems. One is the RAND Corporation, which was set up at the initiative of the U.S. Air Force. The other is the Central Planning Bureau in the Netherlands.

After several evolutions, the RAND Corporation emerged as an independent, non-profit research institute, working mainly for the U.S. Air Force but enjoying a significant degree of autonomy, which was reinforced by some foundation support and by high professional esteem. Besides the analysis of more technical problems the RAND Corporation does for the Air Force, it does independent thinking on both high- and medium-level policy problems, including significant work on metapolicymaking. Some of the more important advances in knowledge about better methods for public policymaking, such as using systems analysis, have been made at the RAND Corporation.[1] The RAND Corporation

---

[1] One of the main initiators at RAND of such better methods, Charles J. Hitch, became the Comptroller of the Department of Defense under Mr. McNamara, and carried out many innovations in methods of decisionmaking and policymaking. Some of his chief assistants were also brought over from the RAND Corp. This rotation of personnel from a separate policy-analysis unit to a policymaking staff unit in the central policymaking organization is an important method for integrating knowledge and policymaking.

has also made very important substantive contributions to basic policies, such as the crucial idea of "second-strike capacity," which seems to have originated largely in the Strategic Bases Study.[2]

Though its work is limited in scope and in its effects, the RAND Corporation illustrates how much public policymaking could be improved by establishing non-profit advising corporations, operating as autonomous organizations and applying great scientific sophistication to policy issues. Other, comparable bodies in the United States that deal with security problems are, for instance, the Research Analysis Corporation (RAC), the Institute for Defense Analysis (IDA), the Hudson Institute, and Analytic Services, Inc. (ANSER, which was established by the RAND Corporation to deal with short-range problems, and so take that pressure off RAND itself). Defense problems have also stimulated the establishing of various special organizations for policy analysis in several European countries, such as Sweden, Denmark, England, and the Federal Republic of Germany.

Despite its name, the Central Planning Bureau in the Netherlands is not a "planning" unit that sets down targets and means for achieving them, but a central economic staff and research agency, whose main function is to contribute to better economic policymaking. It operates by feeding into the policymaking process data, alternatives, predictions, and methods based on much knowledge and a significant input of resources into research and thought. It is an integral part of the governmental machinery, but is independent in its main operations, and is accepted by the main policymaking units and the public at large as a highly expert and non-partisan institution. There are various channels that tie its work into economic and socio-economic policymaking; some of them are formal, others informal. The more formal ones include a biannual publication of reviews and predictions about the state of the economy, staff papers submitted to economic policymaking bodies, and the membership of its personnel in many bodies that contribute to economic policymaking. The more informal ones include the many personal contacts between its members and members of the latter bodies. The overall, long-term influence of its work in improving policymaking by educating the policymakers to use knowledge and by means of explicit methods of

---

[2] RAND Study R-226, Apr. 1, 1954. See Bruce L. R. Smith, *The RAND Corporation: Case Study of a Non-Profit Advisory Corporation* (Cambridge, Mass.: Harvard Univ. Press, 1966), Chap. 6. Since that book was written, the RAND Corporation has been moving in the direction of policy analysis of non-military social problems, as illustrated by its undertaking (in 1967) a comprehensive study of problems of New York City and its proposal (of October 1967) to set up as part of RAND a Policy Research Institute on the Problems of Society.

analysis is very significant, as is its immediate influence on specific policies. For these reasons the Central Planning Bureau is a very successful illustration of the sort of research organization I have in mind.

The particular features of the RAND Corporation, the Central Planning Bureau, and other such units depend on their particular environments. A body trying to operate like the Dutch Central Planning Bureau would have a difficult time in the U.S.A., as is illustrated by the history of the National Resources Planning Board and by the factors that limit the role and impact of the National Security Council. The operations of the President's Council of Economic Advisers have been more successful, though it has been hampered by inadequate resources, by having to depend on many established administrative agencies and on the personal preferences of the President, and by the pressures of acute problems, all of which have kept it from becoming the type of center for innovative and penetrating systematic thought that it should be.

There are several ways in which organizations for policy analysis can be institutionalized and located with respect to other organizations. They can be: (a) independent organizations operating in rather close contact with parts of the government, such as the RAND Corporation; (b) government organizations enjoying much independence in their current work, such as the Central Planning Bureau in the Netherlands and the Swedish Defense Research Institute; (c) inter-university organizations maintained by several institutions of higher learning, such as the Institute for Defense Analysis; (d) organizations which are distinct units within a university, such as the Syracuse University Research Corporation; and (e) independent, profit or non-profit organizations working for a broad range of clients, such as the Stanford Research Institute. The optimal choice among these and other alternatives depends on the specific features of real situations; I shall therefore restrict myself to laying down three main criteria for evaluating the alternatives and for selecting the preferable institutional setup for the proposed organization. First, the institutional setup must ensure professional independence, in order to minimize the danger that findings and recommendations might be adjusted according to the wishes of the client or to pressures from other interests. Second, the setup must ensure that there will be relationships of mutual trust between the organization and the various bodies that make and execute policy, so that the former will have access to necessary data and will be more likely to affect actual policymaking. Third, the setup must ensure close mutual relationships and cooperation with other scientific and research institutions, in order to not only permit but encourage the bringing of the fullest scientific potential to bear on the various policy-analysis projects.

These criteria may be partly inconsistent. It is therefore important to give careful thought to the institutional setup for the proposed organization, in order that it will satisfy an optimal mix of these three criteria. At the same time, it is clear that the success of such an organization will in many respects depend more on the quality of its staff than on the formal institutional arrangements. An essential condition for its success, therefore, is meticulous care in selecting the staff members.

It is not easy to establish useful organizations for policy analysis, considering how many interests and traditions are involved and how hard it must always be to establish the carefully balanced relationship that is needed, but the examples of the RAND Corporation, the Dutch Central Planning Bureau, and similar units show that such research organizations can be successfully established, and that whatever they achieve is usually a distinct improvement over the earlier state of affairs. Establishing such organizations is therefore, despite the difficulties, one of the most important ways to improve public policymaking.

ESTABLISHING AND REINFORCING UNITS FOR SYSTEMS MANAGEMENT, METAPOLICYMAKING, AND COMPREHENSIVE PUBLIC POLICYMAKING

Another main recommendation that emerges from comparing the optimal model with actual policymaking is to establish and reinforce units for overall systems management, metapolicymaking, and comprehensive policymaking. Detailed systems management is neither possible in a complex society nor permissible in terms of democratic values because it is overcentralized. It is also unnecessary, thanks to the aggregative nature of policymaking, which permits many issues to be taken care of by the continuous mutual adjustment that goes on between the multiplicity of units which participate in public policymaking. But a significant amount of systems management, metapolicymaking, and comprehensive policymaking is nevertheless needed to approximate optimality; some of it is needed for the public-policymaking system as a whole, and most of it is needed for the main structural components of the public-policymaking system. In particular, systems management and metapolicymaking are needed to accelerate changes in the policymaking system that will allow it to take advantage of new knowledge and to adjust itself to novel problems and conditions, and comprehensive policymaking is needed to counterbalance the dangers of suboptimization.

At present there are almost no units that fulfill these functions for the overall system, and very few that do so for single organizations. Some units, such as parts of the Bureau of the Budget in the United States or the central Organization and Methods Division of the British Treasury, deal with some aspects of systems management and sometimes even metapolicymaking, but they do so within narrowly defined boundaries and with limited success.

Efforts to set up comprehensive policymaking units, such as the Ministry for Economic Affairs under Sir Stafford Cripps in England in 1947, have also failed in most cases. Nevertheless, there have been some partial successes in comprehensive planning (such as in Puerto Rico), in metapolicymaking (such as the decision to establish a planning-programming-budgeting system in U.S. federal government agencies), and in systems management (such as the North American Air Defense Command) that indicate some progress is being made in such directions.

The major reasons why most systems-management, metapolicymaking, and comprehensive-policymaking units (including national planning bodies) are weak include: (1) such units often lack power and resources, which are monopolized by agencies having executive authority and concrete tasks; (2) such units are right now of little real use, since they lack the knowledge, data, personnel, and orientations that are essential for them to function properly; and (3) the political and social environment is not favorable to them, there being little acceptance of, and even less demand for, the contributions such units may be able to make to policymaking.

These reasons are interdependent, and mutually reinforce one another. Thus, that such units are not now useful further depresses their power; their low power further reduces their input, which diminishes their usefulness even more; and so on. Happily, this interdependence of the variables also provides a key for improving the situation: a change in any one of the variables can partly reverse the trend and so become a takeoff stage for significantly improving such units. New knowledge that may permit better systems management, metapolicymaking, and comprehensive policymaking must be available as a spark to set such a process off. Such new knowledge may also increase the power of such units, and may cause the environment to become more accommodating and favorable toward them. The increasing work by the Bureau of the Budget on important aspects of systems management and metapolicymaking, and some of the changes in defense policymaking that have been made under Secretary of Defense McNamara, are very relevant to this whole problem.

Special organizations for policy analysis can make some significant contributions to public policymaking even if there are no immediate and visible changes in the structure of the main public-policymaking organizations. But units in charge of systems management, metapolicymaking, and comprehensive policymaking must often be integrated into the central public-policymaking structures. Their establishment immediately changes the internal power map and influences all the major aspects of organizational behavior, and is therefore opposed by all the forces of conservatism and inertia that are operating in the structure.

Some of the other suggestions I will present in this chapter, particularly the next two, are closely related to this one. The concepts and functions of systems-management, metapolicymaking, and comprehensive-policymaking units will therefore be made concrete in the following sections, which I present separately for convenience and because they are important in themselves, but which elaborate various ideas that (although they could be partly carried out one by one) are in principle essential features of systems management, metapolicymaking, and comprehensive policymaking.

ESTABLISHING AND REINFORCING SPECIALIZED STAFF UNITS FOR POLICY KNOWLEDGE IN PUBLIC-POLICYMAKING ORGANIZATIONS

Improving public policymaking requires, among other things, improving the various major organizations that make up the public-policymaking system, which in turn requires, besides everything else I've already talked about, establishing and reinforcing special staff units to be in charge of policy knowledge. I can discuss this recommendation most easily by distinguishing between three types of such units, though they may (and often should) be fused together in practice.

1. Professional Staff Units

Establishing specialized staff positions for policy analysis and decision analysis is essential (though not sufficient) for better policymaking. The major function of such professional staff units is to contribute to better policymaking and decisionmaking by considering alternatives more thoroughly and by imaginatively creating new alternatives. (These two roles may need separate organizational locations.) In essence, these units should do—from the inside, in close contact with current activities, and on a more limited and concrete scale—what special policy-analysis organizations do. Other functions of the professional staff units will include: (1) continuous education of the policymakers on the uses and limitations of the different disciplines, and of policy knowledge in general; (2) contributing, on a current basis, relevant knowledge to policymaking; and (3) liaison with universities, special policy-analysis and research organizations, and central systems-management, metapolicymaking, and comprehensive-policymaking units. Only as integral components of the various main policymaking organizations, such as executive departments, party headquarters, or legislative committees, can such staff positions exert any real influence on the inner processes of policymaking. Non-profit advisory corporations, consultants, central offices of science and technology, contracting research institutes—all such outside agencies need the specialized staff positions within the main policymaking organizations to act as their counterparts, without which their own effects on policymaking must remain superficial.

The professional staff units should in principle be composed of two types of personnel: policy analysts, and professionals from the various disciplines that can contribute to better decisionmaking and policymaking. Limiting myself to the major disciplines, I think the minimum requirement for improved public policymaking right now is that an economist, a management and decision scientist, a political scientist, a sociologist, a social psychologist, a systems analyst, and experts in whatever interdisciplinary fields are relevant to the operations of the particular organization should participate in all current decisionmaking on all but purely technical issues. As progress is made in new disciplines, additional experts will have to be added to this list, for instance, "futurists," who specialize in predictions and taking account of the future. These professionals should work as a team that is headed, when possible, by policy analysts. Organizationally, such teams should be attached to the heads of the main policymaking structures as professional staff units.

Care must be taken to avoid the possible boomerang effects that could result from setting up, with much fanfare, units whose composition and qualifications fall below the critical mass needed to make significant contributions to policymaking and decisionmaking. For example, "systems analysis" units staffed by inexperienced men trained only in quantitative economic methods may in many areas harm the cause of improving policymaking, because they will try to apply unsuitable tools to complex and largely non-quantifiable policy issues. For the proposed professional staffs to make effective contributions to policymaking, the changes in the training of experts, senior civil servants, and politicians I have suggested must be carried out, and policy analysts must be available. There is no need to wait until all these changes have taken place, but some special training for the central position of policy analyst will usually be essential if the professional staff unit is to operate successfully.

Within the pressured atmosphere of most policymaking units, there is only limited room for comprehensive depth studies on policy problems, though there is much need and room for better policy analysis to be carried out by suboptimization. The proper place for comprehensive depth studies is mainly in special organizations for policy analysis. The role of the professional staff units located in the regular policymaking organizations themselves is to bring their specialized viewpoints and knowledge to bear on the ongoing policymaking process without trying to go deeper than conditions and resources permit. In order to do so, these units should be closely interwoven into the policymaking process.

It is not enough that selected problems related, in the opinion of a politician or senior official, to sociology be referred to the sociologist, and so on. Rather, every significant policy issue should pass through all the main staff experts as individuals and as a team, so that all of them have a full opportunity to apply their specialized knowledge to it. For instance, assuming some problems of taxation policy are under consideration, it is up to the economist to discuss the different fiscal, monetary, and economic implications of the various alternatives; the sociologist should point out their probable consequences for social mobility and social stratification; the political scientist should deal with the chances the alternatives have of being approved by the legislature and with their expected political consequences; the social psychologist should point out the importance of arriving at a method of taxing that will motivate people to pay the tax less unwillingly; and the management scientist should deal with administrative aspects, for instance, the possibility that several changes in taxation policy could be combined to permit simpler tax assessment and integrated data processing. Working as a team, directed if possible by a policy analyst, the professional staff will integrate their different opinions into a number of major alternatives, with a prediction of benefits and costs and an analysis of its sensitivity to values for each alternative. Both the individual comments and the collectively worked-out alternatives should be fed into the policymaking process, in the form of position papers, of comments during oral discussions, of individual briefings with policymakers, etc.

The monetary cost of such professional staff units will be very small compared with the total budgets of the main policymaking and executing structures. The social and organizational costs in terms of human friction, communication difficulties, and so on are higher, but they too are very small compared with the high net benefits the improvements in policymaking can be expected to create, considering which, it is symptomatic that little has been done toward establishing such units in any country, and nothing whatsoever in most countries. True, the professional training received nowadays by many social scientists often makes them a nuisance in policymaking units until they catch on and relearn a lot, but this too is a small price to pay for what they could contribute.

2. Units to Survey and Retrieve Knowledge

The rapid multiplication of knowledge makes it almost impossible for professionals to keep up with new theories and findings. Certainly policymakers, whether academically trained or not, are unable to follow new developments in knowledge and to identify those items that are directly relevant to their problems. That the knowledge relevant to single policy issues is scattered throughout a rapidly increasing number of periodicals, reports, and books makes the task even more difficult. For instance, knowledge relevant to policymaking on the control of drugs is published in literature belonging to sociology (social factors influencing the propensity to use drugs), law (constitutionality of legal restraints, effects of law on behavior), organization theory and economics (feasibility and cost of control mechanisms), psychology (individual factors influencing the propensity to use drugs), political science (political feasibility of various control mechanisms), and more; in each one of these fields relevant data may appear in a large range of periodicals, books, reports, field studies, etc.

No single staff officer can hope to survey all the relevant material in his specialty. Furthermore, much important material is often available in sources that nominally belong to another discipline. Therefore, special units must be established to survey new knowledge, identify those bits of knowledge presently or potentially relevant to the activities of the organization, and communicate the relevant data from current and accumulated indexes to appropriate staff officers and policymakers. Such units can sometimes best serve several organizations.

For such units to carry out their functions optimally, there must be a transformation in our present systems of storing knowledge. In particular, we need a new classification of knowledge geared to policymaking needs and automation of storage, indexing, and retrieval. Techniques already in use in the United States, for instance, at the National Library of Health or the Central Intelligence Agency, can and should be applied to policy knowledge. But even when such units are not working optimally, they can still significantly improve the flow of relevant knowledge into policymaking.

3. Units for Policy-Oriented Research and Development

Research and development, in the sense of a systematic activity directed at discovering new knowledge (research) and applying it (development), is nowadays recognized as a major strategy for improving the quality of operations. Highly developed in some sectors of private industry (such as electronics and organic chemistry) and government (such as defense and agriculture), research and development is an increasingly important activity, consuming much money and a large proportion of the available high-quality human resources.

This picture seems at first glance to be a bright one, at least as long as we neglect its internal management problems. But when we go into details, it soon becomes clear that research and development is being concentrated on certain clusters, and that many important policy issues are being completely ignored. If this situation were the result of conscious policymaking and a calculated allocation of priorities, or of a reliable spontaneous mechanism for allocating priorities, it might perhaps be regarded as satisfactory. But in fact the absence of research and development on many policy issues seems to be the result of preconceptions and historical accidents. When we take into account the relatively low cost of some types of such research and development, such as social-science research, and the high marginal utility of even limited surveys and investigations on issues dealt with nowadays only by means of "common sense" and "obvious facts," it seems pretty clear that every medium-size or larger policymaking agency should have at least a small research and development unit of its own, which should engage in three main functions: (a) small-scale research; (b) developing available knowledge to be applied to the problems and policy issues faced by the agency; and (c) contact with outside research and development bodies, which would execute larger projects for the organization under contract.

Establishing research and development units, specialized staff positions, and units to survey and retrieve knowledge (usually some combination of all three) is essential not only for integrating knowledge into policymaking, but also for increasing policy knowledge. Hence the special importance of this suggestion.

DEVELOPING EXPLICIT POLICYMAKING METHODS

I have already mentioned the interesting fact that, except for the military "estimate of the situation," no explicit methods designed to assure systematic decisionmaking have until recently been developed for administrative and political organizations. One of the few steps toward such a method are the planning-programming-budgeting system and program-analysis techniques used at the Pentagon, which are being introduced throughout the federal government, following Presidential instructions of August 25, 1965. This is an important move, which should be followed up by developing and using a more comprehensive and more general explicit method for policymaking.

This suggestion is not without its dangers. If the explicit method established as a guide for operations is either too unrealistic, as methods based on the pure-rationality model are, or if it follows too closely patterns established by the past, as illustrated by the incremental, muddling-through model, it will do more harm than good.

These dangers must be avoided. Methods should be elaborated that move toward optimality. These methods should meet three conditions: (a) they should be close enough to the realm of the possible to be a meaningful guide for action; (b) they should be sufficiently idealistic when compared with the real world to stimulate significant improvement in policymaking; and (c) they should be broad enough and flexible enough to work in many different sets of circumstances. Such explicit methods can make significant contributions to improving actual policymaking, once they are recognized and accepted as general guides by the major policymaking personnel and units.

A simplified version of the optimal model of policymaking as presented in Chapter 14 can illustrate the potentials (and perhaps also the dangers) of such a method. For purposes of current policymaking, the following elements (not necessarily in any fixed order) should be standard features of a preferable policymaking method:

1. There should be some clarification of values, objectives, and criteria for decisionmaking.

2. The method should include identifying the alternatives, with an effort to consider new alternatives (by surveying comparative literature, experience, and available theories) and to stimulate creation of novel alternatives.

3. The method should include preliminary estimating of expected payoffs from the various alternatives, and deciding whether a strategy of minimal risk or of innovation is preferable.

4. If the first, the incremental-change model should be followed. If the latter, the next step is establishing a cutoff horizon for considering the possible results of the alternative policies, and identifying the major expected results, relying on available knowledge and on intuition.

5. Analysis of the alternatives should deal with both quantitative ("economic") and qualitative ("political") factors, in order to over-

come the limitations of current systems analysis and advance toward policy analysis.

6. The method should include an effort to decide whether the issue is important enough to make more comprehensive analysis worthwhile.

7. Theory and experience, rationality and extrarationality, will all be relied upon; the composition of the mix must depend upon their various availabilities and on the nature of the problem.

8. Explicit techniques, such as simulation and the Delphi method, should be used as far as they are appropriate, and knowledge from various disciplines should be brought to bear on the issues involved.

9. The method should include explicit arrangements to improve the policymaking by systematic learning from experience, stimulating initiative and creativity, developing the staff, and encouraging intellectual effort.

This is only one version of the elements of an explicit policymaking method. Many variations could be possible and useful in various spheres of activity. Also, I must repeat and reemphasize that any optimal model, and any normative "policymaking method" based on it, depend on available knowledge and understanding. The model and the method must always be adjusted to the newly available information, ideas, and resources. Provided arrangements are made for periodically revising the policymaking method, and provided the method clearly sets down its own domain of validity and recommends other methods when they are more suitable (as pure rationality may be for limited and fully quantified issues), then explicitly establishing policymaking methods as guides, outlines, and checklists to be followed in practice would appear to be an important means for improving policymaking.

TRANSFORMING THE POLICYMAKING APPARATUS INTO A "MANPOWER-MACHINE" SYSTEM

The changes recommended up to now share one effect: they would all put more highly trained and qualified persons into the main policymaking organizations. To get the maximum benefit out of this change in manpower, one must at the same time use significantly more automatic and integrated data-processing equipment.

That equipment will in no way serve as a "governing machine," as has been suggested in some popular literature on computers and in some of the less-sophisticated science-fiction novels.[3] Policymaking is based on complex heuristic processes that are beyond the capacity of any foreseeable machines. But integrated data processing can play an important and increasing auxiliary role in policymaking, in at least three respects:

1. Policy-knowledge processing, storage, and retrieval, which I have already mentioned.

2. Quantitative decisionmaking on subpolicies that can be dealt with by pure-rationality techniques, which I have already discussed.

3. Better and quicker communication and feedback, permitting more integrated and more data-based policymaking. This possible use of integrated data processing is well illustrated by the modern Communication and Command systems developed in the armed forces, e.g., the Strategic Air Command, or the new NORAD combat-operations center in Colorado.

These techniques, carefully applied, could significantly improve policymaking on many issues, for instance, on economics, on registering Negro voters in the South, on public security in big cities, or on some segments of the anti-poverty program.

Both adding more professionals to policymaking organizations and using more automatic data processing will reduce the auxiliary and clerical staff, most of whose activities will be transferred to computers. As a result, two features of a policymaking unit that is operating close to optimality will be: (1) most of the personnel will be highly trained professionals; and (2) data-processing equipment will play an important role in their work. Putting these two features together, we can see that improving the policymaking apparatus involves transforming it into a system that embraces both the highly qualified manpower and the machines. Although this characterization applies mostly to the special policy-analysis organizations and to the systems-management, metapolicymaking, and comprehensive-policymaking units, it also applies, in a more diluted form, to the various policymaking organizations as a whole (and indeed most modern organizations).

This view has important implications for both the patterns of interpersonal relations and the formal structure of authority within policymaking organizations. The dominant principle in contemporary

---

[3] The idea of a "machine à gouverner" based on cybernetics seems to have been seriously discussed for the first time in a review by Père Dubarle in *Le Monde* of Dec. 28, 1948. See Norbert Wiener, *The Human Use of Human Beings* (Garden City, N.Y.: Doubleday, 2d, rev. ed., 1954), pp. 178ff.

organizations is that of hierarchy, as tempered by the internal balance of power and by the influence of the "human relations" school. Although they have been modified by modern findings on motivation, as well as by egalitarian and democratic values, the principles of hierarchic structure and formal relationships seem nevertheless to continue to fit large organizations that have many levels staffed by persons of diverse qualifications and training. But most available indications are that significant changes in structure and interpersonal relations are needed in other types of organizations. For instance, laboratories and universities seem to operate best given patterns of organization and motivation that differ very much in certain ways from the standard hierarchy-authority prototype. Once transformed into manpower-machine systems, policymaking organizations will have to adjust their patterns of organization and motivation to the needs of the changed system, in order to stimulate interprofessional teamwork and creativity. Such changes include: (1) motivations based on self-fulfillment and personal development, as well as on material and social rewards; (2) encouraging novel ideas and daring innovations, by means of a permissive organizational climate, group techniques, such as "brainstorming," and perhaps establishing special "new ideas" subunits;[4] (3) encouraging the communicating and exchanging of ideas and opinions along both formal and informal channels; and (4) encouraging egalitarian behavior, by means of changes in status symbols and in the ranking system.

Since contemporary research in administrative science tends to neglect organizations that are such creative "manpower-machine" systems, such as planning units, radio and television corporations, or publishers, the available data do not permit formulation of more concrete recommendations. Rectification of this ignorance is urgently needed. Even without the findings of much more intense studies, the available material clearly indicates that many traditional concepts and habits of behavior, such as "unity of command," "formal channels," and "decision by precedent," must be gotten rid of.

SYSTEMATIC LEARNING FEEDBACK

One of the amazing weaknesses in much contemporary public policymaking is that there is no systematic learning from experience. Very few evaluations of the real outcome of complex policies are made, and there are even fewer on which improvements of future policymaking

---

[4] E.g., see William J. J. Gordon, *Synectics* (N.Y.: Harper, 1961).

can be based. The interested reader can easily verify this fact for himself by asking some political or administrative policymaking unit about the results of a specific past decision. Even if that decision was embodied in an easy-to-identify form, such as a law, in only relatively few cases will the results have been studied in earnest, and in almost no cases will the results of such study have been translated into explicit conclusions for future policymaking. In spite of the common tendency to justify action in terms of "experience," the simple fact is that learning from experience is accidental and sporadic. Institutional arrangements that encourage processing policymaking experience and learning from it are quite scarce, and spontaneous learning often does not operate well, because organizational defense mechanisms often distort the expectations and results of policymaking, which are hard to identify anyway.

Correcting this omission can be an important wedge for improving public policymaking. Systematic learning feedback can often be introduced, at least in part, by requiring an explicit audit of a policy's results after a definite period of time has elapsed. The details of such arrangements must vary with the scope and character of the policy and the involved units. For instance, having a special research institute study the main effects of basic legislation every five years would provide important information for the various lawmaking units. The same is true for other formal policies, such as municipal master plans. For other types of policies, annual studies conducted within the various policymaking units themselves may be preferable. Universities might be asked to prepare case studies of past policies, their results, and their implications for better policymaking in the future.

The point here is that one of the more neglected phases of optimal policymaking, systematic learning feedback, can be improved relatively easily and at low cost by means of explicit reforms, namely, formal arrangements for periodically processing the results of policies. Such formal arrangements will often include establishing special analytical units in charge of learning feedback in larger organizations (a function which can often be combined with the policy-analysis units mentioned earlier). Such units should avoid trying to pin the blame for past mistakes on someone, and should instead focus on positive recommendations for the future. Such recommendations can be both general and specific. The general recommendations will deal with the policymaking method and the metapolicymaking phases, the specific with concrete policy issues.

Establishing such units will raise many problems concerning their organizational location, their relationships with the line and staff units, techniques for storing their specific findings so that they can be retrieved when similar policy issues arise, and so on. These are secondary administrative problems, and are outside the scope of this book. What I do want to emphasize here is that many weaknesses in actual policymaking seem to be caused by rather elementary mistakes. An important way to stop repeating the same mistakes is to encourage learning from experience by institutionalizing learning feedback.

INTEGRATING SCIENTISTS INTO PUBLIC POLICYMAKING BETTER

How much policy knowledge is used in actual policymaking depends very much on the social distance between policymakers and scientists. The existence of the "two cultures," to borrow C. P. Snow's concept, which seems somewhat true of most societies, poses formidable barriers to communication between policymakers and scientists. It might be even more correct to speak about "a multiplicity of cultures," since communication is scarce not only between scientists and policymakers, but also between different groups of scientists and between different groups of policymakers.

Reducing this distance directly is difficult; it would require radical changes in the educational system designed to give all strata of the population a shared nucleus of culture and knowledge, including the basics of the humanities, the natural sciences, and the social sciences. Besides such a far-going and long-range transformation, several formal and informal mechanisms are needed for better integrating scientists into policymaking. Many of these mechanisms, though not all of them, have been developed and tried out as part of an effort to affiliate the natural sciences more closely with policymaking. As yet only a very few efforts have been made to use these mechanisms for integrating social scientists into policymaking.

The available experience with knowledge from the natural sciences, from some interdisciplinary fields, and from organization theory permits me to discuss two more ways that scientists might be better integrated into public policymaking, in addition to the organizational and educational arrangements I have already discussed.

1. Improving Personal Contacts between Policymakers and Scientists

The usefulness of formal mechanisms for improving communication between policymakers and scientists depends very much on informal factors, especially on the personal contacts between policymakers and scientists. Even with the differences in training and orientation referred to (somewhat incorrectly) by the concept of the "two cultures," much can nevertheless be done to improve their personal contacts. Social meetings, common workshops, shared training courses, mixed working teams—these are some of the available devices for trying to achieve better personal contacts between experts, politicians, and senior civil servants. Experience with common clubs for politicians and scientists in some of the Scandinavian countries demonstrates the feasibility and usefulness of such activities.

On a more fundamental level, the involved groups should recognize that they must get together to better integrate knowledge into policymaking. The tendency of many scientists to be aloof, which is reinforced by their professional self-images, on the one hand, and by their differences from policymakers in personality, orientation, and pattern of behavior, on the other hand, is distinctly dysfunctional for such integration. Similarly, the uneasiness of many policymakers in the presence of scientists is both a symptom of and a cause of the social distance. Self-analysis, and a determined effort by all the involved groups to overcome the barriers, are necessary before any institutional devices can do much good.

2. Integrating Universities into Public Policymaking Better

Universities and special research institutes are the main centers for scientists and knowledge. Therefore, integrating them into policymaking better is a major way to integrate both scientists and knowledge into policymaking. Much is done in this direction in the United States, both by contracting research projects to universities and by co-opting university personnel into policymaking forums, and perhaps even too much, since too close an integration may lessen the independence of universities and disturb the undirected flow of ideas that is essential for some types of innovation and for considering "taboo" subjects. The large amount of government-sponsored research at universities in the United States may already have had a detrimental long-range effect on some disciplines, mainly by diverting their limited manpower into problems for which government research funds are available, but which are not necessarily always the most important long-range problems. (This danger need not contradict my recommendation in Chapter 7 that research funds be allocated to encourage policy knowledge, if sufficient care is taken. Neither does it contradict the finding that insufficient involvement of social scientists in public policymaking hinders development of policy knowledge, as much of the present extensive university involvement is too limited in disciplines and subject matters.)

This policy involvement is a rather unique characteristic of university life in the United States. In most other countries, universities are very detached from policy problems. Such underusing of a potential source of policy contributions is especially disturbing in the developing countries, where the scarcity of resources necessitates a maximum effort to use all the available ones. In many developing countries a strong case can also be made for giving priority at universities to applied research on concrete policy issues and operational problems. In many disciplines, including the social sciences, action-directed studies of local problems would also be a most important way that the universities located in developing countries could contribute to the general body of scientific knowledge.

CHANGES IN THE AGGREGATION FUNCTION

Improving public policymaking also requires some changes in its aggregation function. Primarily, we must be able to identify and approximate an aggregation function that maximizes the aggregate quality of policymaking. More concretely, we need methods for influencing the contributions that the various participating units make, for varying the relative influence of different units, and for establishing new types of units that will improve the aggregate results.

It is very difficult (and often undesirable) to carry out significant changes in the aggregation function. Such changes touch upon deeply rooted "rules of the game" and upon very strong interests. More importantly, the values that the function implies often prohibit instrumental changes in the institutional arrangements, which can be very sensitive to values. Significant changes in the aggregation function thus usually take place only during revolutions or other convulsive forms of social change, which are not conducive to rational and calculated redesigning of systems. But there are exceptions to this generalization; minor changes are sometimes feasible during periods of controlled social change. To illustrate, I will take up two problems that can be partly handled by deliberate change. The first problem involves the contributions that elected legislatures make to public policymaking. The second problem involves the roles of interest and pressure groups, and especially the fact that widespread and diffuse interests, such as those of consumers, are underrepresented in the power structure.

The proper role of the legislature is in many ways decided by basic values of the political ideology, which as such are part of the given environment of public policymaking and are beyond the proper scope of instrumental reform. But many specific features of the ways legislatures operate are not entitled to such protection from critical scrutiny.

I cannot formulate recommendations of any general validity, since the possible weaknesses in the way the U.S. Congress operates are very different from those in how the British House of Commons operates, which in turn can hardly be compared with the weaknesses of the Italian bicameral Parliament or the Japanese Diet. But there are two rather universal characteristics which I can use as illustrations of improvements that are needed in the policymaking roles of legislatures in western democratic countries; these concern medium-range policies and the consistency of policies. In general, legislatures contribute little to shaping medium-range policies, largely because most such policies, if there are any, usually are informal and so do not need legislative approval. In fact, legislatures often keep medium-range policies from crystallizing, since they are reluctant to give up the power involved in making policies in small bits and year by year. The U.S. Congress refuses to approve multiple-year foreign-aid programs. Its operations, like those of most other legislatures, would be improved by multi-year budgeting, at least for defined projects.

Similarly, legislatures often treat various facets of a policy as independent variables and change single items in it without considering the effects of such changes on the consistency of the policy as a whole. Most countries have learned to protect themselves against such disturbances of the overall consistency and balance of their annual budgets by formally or informally limiting the authority of the legislature, or by taking advantage of peculiarities in the legislature's distribution of power. The U.S. Congress enjoys unusual power to change individual items in the budget, and this power may well need some limitations in order to strengthen the role of the budget as an instrument for integrating policy.

A similar problem exists for "plans," whose internal consistency requires that incompatible changes not be made in their details. One way to solve the problem would be to limit the authority of the legislature to accepting or rejecting a plan as a whole, as it is, thanks to Rexford G. Tugwell, in Puerto Rico.[5] Under this arrangement, the overall influence and supremacy of the legislature is insured by its authority to reject the plan as a whole; the plan must and should be adjusted to meet the anticipated reaction of the legislature, but at the same time, its details are fairly safe from being distorted by "pork barrel" politics.

With the second set of problems, which concern the role of pressure groups in aggregative public policymaking, a major difficulty stems from

---

[5] See Rexford G. Tugwell, *The Place of Planning in Society* (San Juan: Puerto Rican Planning Commission, 1954).

the fact that how much influence a pressure group enjoys depends on how organized it is and on how many resources it has at its disposal, but not necessarily on how many persons will benefit from its activities. Although democratic ideology emphasizes that the larger group should have the larger influence on policy, pressure groups, being highly active, tend to have more influence than their size merits. In theory, politicians and civil servants are expected to balance the situation by "representing the common people," but in fact interest groups often (though by no means always) exercise such tremendous influence on them that they sometimes fail to consider the "general good," especially when most of the interest groups are pressing in the same direction, in which case the politician and the executive lose much of the freedom for decisionmaking they enjoy when the pressure field is pluralistic, with many interest groups pushing in different and contradictory directions.

Let us consider, for instance, the problem of smoking and cancer. There is almost unanimous agreement among medical experts that there is a very high probability that smoking significantly increases the incidence of lung cancer. If by means of some magic device all persons due to die in a rather unpleasant way from smoking-induced cancer were suddenly to become really aware of this fact, they would surely become an irresistible pressure group that would immediately agitate for restraints on smoking, at least for total prohibition of all advertising of tobacco and for intensive anti-smoking propaganda sponsored by the government, and perhaps for more strict legal restraints. Right now, we can be very sure that many such persons exist, but they do not know their individual destinies. The intense pressures from the few groups that have a material interest in cigarettes outweigh in most countries the unorganized interests of the many candidates for cancer, and in fact prevent governments from taking action against smoking. Another illustration in most countries is the agricultural block, which, thanks to its organization, often has an undue influence on agricultural and economic policymaking.

The free operation of pressure groups, within certain limits as to legitimate tools (direct bribery, for instance, is prohibited in all modern countries), is an important feature of democracy. The drawbacks of unbalanced pressure groups should therefore not be minimized by radical restraints on their activities. (Such restraints are also quite ineffective, although requiring pressure groups to publish more information on their activities than is demanded by present lobbying-regulating laws may be useful.) What is needed is positive action to strengthen the power of groups that are underrepresented in policymaking. Efforts have been made in various countries to organize consumers as a counterbalance to the compact pressure groups, especially during periods of rationing in World War II. In some cases, special administrative units have been set up to "represent" the consumers (the Consumers Council of the National Bituminous Coal Commission in the United States is one such unit), but none of these devices have been very successful.

Another way to approach the problem is through some form of "functional representation," to supplement political representation and pressure-group activities. The idea of having some kind of "economic parliament" to deal with socio-economic problems was once quite popular in Europe, going back to the tradition of the Guilds, the Corporate State, and Syndicalism. Although the idea was brought into disrepute by Fascist Italy's misuse of it, it may nevertheless be very useful. Consider the successful operation of the Social Economic Council in the Netherlands; it is a sort of "economic parliament," in which employers, employees, and the government are represented equally, and which deals with a multitude of social and economic problems. This particular arrangement would probably not fit the United States, although on the municipal level comparable advisory bodies, designed to represent the main social and economic interests, often can play an important role in redevelopment and similar projects. Active government operations designed to educate the "mass consumers" to their interests and make them more active, and to form new pressure groups to counterbalance the established ones, may perhaps be another available solution in the U.S.

I could give many more illustrations of deliberate changes that might be made in the aggregation function. These might include changes in the electoral system, in legislative procedures, and in the division of functions between central and local governments. Because the concept of "aggregation function" is so broad, it could cover all improvements in political institutions that might influence policymaking, and therefore is in danger of losing any operational meaning. Nevertheless, suggestions for improvements in a system's aggregation function are important and useful and should be considered explicitly, because they (a) draw attention to the need for improving the interaction patterns that are an important element of the aggregative public-policymaking process; (b) stress the importance of evaluating specific proposals for improvements in single political institutions in terms of their effects on the quality of aggregative policymaking (as well as in terms of other yardsticks, such as how well they implement democratic values); and (c) point out that both imaginative building and incremental improving of institutions can be important avenues for significantly improving aggregative public policymaking.

chapter 20 · Changes Needed
in Input
and Stipulated Output

Almost none of the changes I have suggested in policymaking, nor any other proposals for consciously improving policymaking, can be carried out unless both the input into policymaking and its stipulated output are increased.

CHANGES NEEDED IN INPUT

Some major changes that are needed in input have already been discussed in Chapter 18, in connection with the need to draw better manpower into the main policymaking occupations. Since the quality of manpower is critical for the quality of policy, improvements in the first are necessary for improvements in the second. From an overall social point of view, high-quality manpower is the most scarce of resources. Malthus' famous paradigm might well be rewritten to state that, whereas *the complexity of social problems increases geometrically, the manpower able to deal with those problems increases arithmetically.* The gap between these two may become therefore more and more a critical factor limiting human development.

Because high-quality manpower is growing scarcer in many occupations (due to growing demand), policymaking-personnel quality can be improved in the short run only by transferring human resources which might go into science, business, or some free profession, into politics and the civil service. If this recommendation is carried out for municipal, local, and national government, the involved numbers will not be insignificant. Improving public policymaking may therefore be costly in terms of the other ways the necessary high-quality manpower could be used, even after changes in the environment increase the total supply of highly qualified human resources. In many western democratic countries, comparing the quality of contemporary public policymaking with that of scientific endeavors and private business justifies these costs, especially when we consider that both science and business are becoming more and more dependent on public policymaking.

In general, because public policymaking is ever more socially significant, a higher input into public policymaking promises large net social benefits, even when the opportunity costs of the input are relatively high. This applies both to high-quality manpower and to all other types of resources.

All proposals for improving public policymaking require general resources (that is, money). These resources are very small compared with the total budgets of administrative agencies, but that immediate, visible, and tangible fruits do not follow increases in input into policymaking decreases its appeal to the budgetmakers, politicians, as well as budget examiners. The tendency to concentrate on small items, so well satirized by Parkinson in his ironic description of budgeting, also makes the small items involved in policymaking a favorite subject for overscrutiny. A proposal to invest $3,000,000 in better play facilities for children is apt to be accepted by a municipal council with little examination and much expression of pleasure, whereas a proposal to spend $100,000 on a study of how youth uses its leisure time, or to add two sociologists to the staff of the planning commission, is sure to be discussed at length and in detail to see if it can be cut. This happens even when such proposals will fairly soon significantly increase the benefit of the municipality's youth programs and even though the expenses are of no real significance for the budgetary situation of the municipality.

Overcoming barriers against allocating sufficient resources to policymaking itself requires better metapolicymaking, especially on allocating resources. Because the resource-allocating phases are so critical, they are strategic points for introducing improvements into public policymaking. Judging by verbal expressions, reforms in budgeting are popular, though most proposals tend to be somewhat one-sided, with overemphasis on measurable items and on the monetary aspects of the world.

The proposals of the Subcommittee on National Policy Machinery of the U.S. Senate (Jackson Committee) illustrate an increasing awareness of the importance of the budgeting process for policy improvement, and certain developments in budgeting knowledge show how this crucial metapolicymaking activity can be improved.[1] But in the real world budgeting is largely a political process shaped by power struggles, in which improvements in policymaking are often the underdog.[2] Even worse, from our point of view, are the findings of a study in 1965 which show that "the budgetary process of the United States government is equivalent to a set of temporally stable linear decision rules" and "a set of simple decision rules can explain or represent the behavior of participants in the federal budgetary process in their efforts to reach decisions in complex situations."[3]

Improving budgeting units and processes is therefore critical for better policymaking. Some of the main improvements should be directed at alerting the budgetmakers to the dependence of better policymaking on more resources and to the importance of allocating enough attention and even more than enough resources to improving policymaking. Improving budgeting will require steps to offset the tendency of most budgetmakers to concentrate too much on the fiscal aspects of budgeting, and of many systems analysts to concentrate too much on quantifiable variables. For instance, budgeting units should preferably be located in the office of the Prime Minister or President rather than in the Ministry of Finance; the senior officials of the government budgeting unit should be familiar with the issues of substantive policymaking; economists and lawyers should not dominate the governmental budgeting unit; systems analysts should also be trained in the "soft" social sciences and be subordinated to policy analysts; and close contact should be maintained between budgeting, operations planning, programming, and policymaking.

CHANGES NEEDED IN STIPULATED OUTPUT

Increases in policymaking input are neither feasible nor often useful unless changes also take place in the stipulated output. Raising the

---

[1] See *Organizing for National Security* (Washington: U.S. Govt. Printing Office, 1961), III, 87ff. On the new, but still much too narrow and technical knowledge, see, e.g., David Novick, ed., *Program Budgeting* (Cambridge, Mass.: Harvard Univ. Press, 1966), of which an abridged advance version was published by the U.S. Govt. Printing Office in 1965.

[2] E.g., see Aaron Wildavsky, *The Politics of the Budgetary Process* (Boston: Little, Brown, 1964).

[3] Otto A. Davis, M. A. H. Dempster, and Aaron Wildavsky, "A Theory of the Budgetary Process," *The American Political Science Review*, LX, no. 3 (Sept. 1966), 537, 543.

stipulated output can often do a lot of good, even without much increase in input, by stimulating the policymaking system to greater efforts.

I base these conclusions on the tendency of the satisfactory quality to be the best any operation, including policymaking, can achieve (as explained in Chapter 12). Because of this phenomenon, improving policymaking requires raising the satisfactory quality by stipulating in quantitative and qualitative terms an output that is based on simulation, estimation, or guesstimation of the optimal output, that is, the output among all the feasible ones (taking a realistically idealistic view of "feasibility") that satisfies most of the policymakers' values. That stipulated output should then replace the earlier satisfactory quality, which is usually based on past experience, historical accidents, personal predispositions, and organizational biases. That is, the stipulated output, based on some attempts to simulate optimality, should be a basis of the "goodness" standard.[4] To have the most beneficial effect on the real world, the stipulated output should: (1) meet the objective survival needs, and (2) be significantly higher than the present output. But it should in most (but not all) cases not be too much higher, or it will be considered unrealistic and will lose its motivational effect.

A main political-administrative process that tries to stipulate outputs is planning. Planning should involve, in general, at least two steps: (1) establishing a stipulated output that approximates optimality, and (2) finding means for achieving that output. Planning, in its correct meaning, must be kept distinct from detailed control and interference; the latter might sometimes be the right way to act, but planning can just as well arrive at the conclusion, for instance, that a free market is the best way to achieve a particular stipulated output (e.g., a certain rate of annual economic growth).

Used in such a sense, planning is nowadays regarded favorably even in countries where the verbal symbol "planning" has unfavorable political and emotional connotations because it has been associated with one particular type of "planned economy."[5] One of the important transformations taking place in contemporary business management is the growing acceptance of intermediate- and long-range planning, including establishing stipulated goals, as a key to development and success. Improving public policymaking may often require a similar move, since establishing

---

[4] See pp. 187–188.

[5] For example, planning as defined above is acceptable to the author of a very important, though definitely outdated, anti-planning tract, namely, Friedrich A. Hayek, who explicitly limited his anti-planning argument to "planning in the sense of a directed economy." See F. A. Hayek, *The Road to Serfdom* (Chicago: Univ. of Chicago Press, 1944), p. 26.

carefully determined stipulated outputs is an essential means for stimulating the policymaking (and executing) system to a greater effort.

But there are other reasons for regarding the establishing of suitable stipulated outputs as an important requirement of better policymaking. Not less, and perhaps more, significant is that stipulated outputs are essential as operational goals, whose importance, in addition to their motivating greater efforts, I have discussed at some length (in Chapters 12 and 14). From those analyses, the conclusion emerges that establishing stipulated outputs improves policymaking by providing more-developed and better-considered operational goals, which in turn condition most other phases of policymaking.

chapter 21 · Changes Needed in the Environment

The public-policymaking system is only a subsystem of society, and interacts constantly with culture, public opinions, social groups, economic, religious, and educational institutions, and all other components of society. Various types of societies differ significantly in how much autonomy the public-policymaking system enjoys and in how strong the society-shaping effects of public policymaking are compared with the policy-shaping effects of society. At one extreme, we have the avant-garde developing states, in which directed social change is the main aim of specific policymaking cadres. At the other extreme, we have the modern western democratic state, in which policy is presumed to be guided by the wishes of the population and does very much reflect the values and relative strengths of a heterogeneous set of social power centers. Even in the pure avant-garde developing state, the operation of the public-policymaking system is circumscribed and basically shaped by the social ecology. Diffuse social characteristics, as well as the activities of widespread power centers, determine the features of public policymaking even more in other types of countries and particularly in modern western democratic states.

It would be a serious mistake to underestimate how much autonomy the public-policymaking system enjoys and how much that system shapes society even in modern western democratic states, where, for instance, modern government establishes social policies and research and development policies that in the long run significantly influence important characteristics of society.

Even after taking into account certain variables that somewhat increase the autonomy of the public-policymaking system, such as the growing complexity of the issues and the strength of national leaders who can use mass-communication media, the influence of the environment on public policymaking remains tremendous. This state of affairs is both unavoidable and desirable according to democratic ideology (and some analyses of the instrumental advantages of aggregative policymaking by mutual adjustment). Consequently, improving policymaking necessarily depends on changes in the environment.

The main changes needed are in the ways that public opinions are formed, which I will therefore discuss briefly. I will then mention changes that are needed in the demands made on the public-policymaking system, in the willingness to change, and in the rational content of culture, all of which are closely associated with the changes needed in opinion formation. Finally, I will touch on some required changes that are needed in individual patterns of thinking and behavior and in resources.

CHANGES NEEDED IN THE WAYS PUBLIC OPINIONS ARE FORMED

Public opinions (I use the plural to emphasize the multiplicity of the publics and the heterogeneity of their opinions) exert much influence on public policymaking in all societies. In western democratic countries this influence is particularly intense and pervasive because elections are a major mechanism for selecting and legitimizing parts of the main policymaking elite, and because the feasibility of many policies depends on public support. Consequently, as well as for ideological reasons, wanting to invoke favorable public opinions is an important leitmotif of public policymaking. Furthermore, the ways public opinions are formed exert a tremendous indirect influence by shaping the attitudes of policymakers and by coloring the whole atmosphere of the policymaking system. Thus, when public opinions tend to judge policies by their halo effects, their short-term results, and the degree of catharsis they provide for aggressive drives, policies will tend to have halo effects and short-term results, and to be aggressive and emotionally loaded. Similarly, insofar as public opinions are significantly influenced by single spectacular mistakes, policymaking tends to "play safe" by following precedents and avoiding innovation.

Many thinkers have pointed out that democracy depends on enlightened public opinion: what they have in mind, in general, is that citizens should be familiar enough with public issues to be able to arrive at intelligent opinions on which to base their votes. Certainly, we expect this condition to be fulfilled in Utopia. But if the success of democracy indeed depended on the people's ability to judge the main policy issues on their merits, then democracy would surely have perished by now. In a simpler world a privileged few could be familiar with all the main policy issues and know all there is to know on them. But in a complex modern society, the main problems are so diverse and so much difficult knowledge is needed to deal with them, that no one can form an enlightened opinion of his own on more than a few policy issues. Certainly the "common man" is highly dependent on information and opinions that are supplied for him, even if he is well educated and highly intelligent, as often he is not.

It seems, therefore, that our ideal of an "enlightened public" must be revised; what we should aim at is not a public able to form independent, valid opinions on main policy issues, but a public able and willing to evaluate and judge (a) main policymaking styles and the values on which they are based; (b) the soundness of the process by which policies are arrived at; and (c) the integrity and capacity of the various leaders who are competing for electoral support.

Point (a) permits the public to choose between candidates A, B, and C, or parties A and B, who in their behavior and pronouncements present different basic values and policymaking styles. For instance, the choice between Goldwater and Johnson in the United States, and between Labor and Conservative in England, should (and largely does) depend on a preference for different values, policymaking styles, and personalities.

Point (b) is more related to our main concern. It provides a basis for valid public critiques and public pressures on specific policy issues; it also provides a rational underpinning for preferring one style of policymaking to another. For instance, we should not expect the citizen to judge various proposed policies on how to control inflation, though the population at large should be able to judge certain more clear-cut and value-dependent policies, such as whether to abandon Viet Nam or fight it out there, though not such finer points as whether to bomb Hanoi or not. But most persons in a democracy should be able to judge how much a proposed policy is based on acceptable basic values and leadership styles, and (at least in general) how much a policy is based on exploring new alternatives, examining probable results by means of available knowledge, establishing explicit cutoff horizons, setting down operational goals, etc. Toward this end changes must be made in what policies are presented to the public and in how they are presented, and much attention given to explaining how the policy was arrived at and what values it was based on. But first and foremost, there must be changes in how public opinions are formed; opinions must be based more on evaluating how a policy is arrived at and what its value components are (as well as on personalities and policymaking styles) than on trying to judge specific policies on their merits.

CHANGES NEEDED IN THE DEMANDS MADE ON THE PUBLIC-POLICYMAKING SYSTEM

The changes that are needed in the demands the environment makes on public policymaking are partly related to the changes that are needed in how public opinions are formed and to those needed in stipulated output. Since organizations tend toward self-satisfaction and inertia, they need continual prodding. The demands made on the public-policymaking system by various parts of its environment, such as public opinions and interest groups, provide an important part of such prodding, and make for better policymaking insofar as they lead in the same direction as the requirements for better policymaking.

Another very important source of prodding is competition with other policymaking systems. Thus, an improvement in military policymaking in one country often stimulates similar improvements in another. Competition between policymaking subsystems within one country can also result in important improvements—changes in policymaking in the United States Navy and Army often follow innovations in policymaking in the Air Force, and improvements in state government often follow improvements in federal government. The competition for larger shares of the budget between different departments may also sometimes result in better policymaking in the departments, if the "rules of the game" are appropriate. It follows that it might be possible to improve policymaking by establishing more competing policymaking agencies. Another benefit to public policymaking from establishing a significant number of special policy-analysis organizations may be the innovative impetus they could provide by competing with the traditional policymaking units. This expectation is well supported by the effects that the competition with newer organizations engaged in analysis of defense policy has on the military.

The idea of increasing competition between central public-policymaking units and other social units located in their environment (and between various public-policymaking units) so as to improve aggregative policymaking is fascinating. But many pitfalls stand in its way, such as that the public-policymaking system might become overly involved in fighting competition instead of making better policy. Formulating relevant, operational suggestions for more far-going steps in this direction will require more knowledge than is available at present, and so must wait until policy science becomes more adequate for its tasks.

CHANGES NEEDED IN THE WILLINGNESS TO CHANGE

Social tendencies toward conservatism about political institutions, partly as an overcompensation for the accelerating change in technological institutions, are in most societies a serious barrier against reforming public policymaking, and must be overcome before significant improvements can be made in public policymaking. Society must want changes in the policymaking system and be willing to make those changes. It must be willing to give up its ritual anomie, in which particular institutional arrangements are regarded as expressing basic values and are therefore immune to critical reexamination. The basic values of democratic ideology are outside the domain of science and other types of instrumental rationality, but the detailed shapes and operations of various political bodies are merely a means for achieving the basic democratic values, and should be readjusted, on the basis of rational considerations, to meet the needs of new problems and knowledge.

True, the widespread acceptance of such "revisionist" ideas is another step toward disenchantment with modern society, and so might increase social and individual alienation. We must take steps to reduce these dangers, steps whose effectiveness, in turn, depends on the quality of public policymaking. The possibility that social institutions will not adjust to new knowledge because of social conservatism carries with it the greater danger that the regimes which are more sensitive to public opinion, particularly democratic regimes, might lose their long-term struggle with ruthless types of regimes, in which such barriers are not as important in preventing improvements in policymaking.

CHANGES NEEDED IN THE RATIONAL CONTENT OF CULTURE

One of the critical differences between modern countries and developing countries is in certain of their cultural values and symbols. These differences are hard to pin down, and are not very susceptible to rigorous study. Nevertheless, the available material tends to indicate that at least some of these differences involve the "rational content" of culture. This concept covers such diverse items as how much naturalism or mysticism is used to explain reality; how positively oriented the culture is toward goal-oriented activity or how fatalistic and passive; or whether the culture has ritualistic fixations or is more ready to adjust its actions according to feedback.

Although my term "rational content" may not be the best name for what I have in mind, such differences between cultures do seem to exist, according to the best available evidence. The overall culture exerts a tremendous influence on the tone of policymaking, and a low rational content is therefore one of the greatest environmental barriers against high-quality public policymaking. Rational content must be increased if policymaking is to be improved.

This problem is most acute in developing countries whose culture has a relatively low rational content. Overall directed cultural transformation is at best a slow and difficult process, which itself requires very high-quality public policymaking. The only feasible interim solution in those countries, however repugnant it is to western democratic ideology, is to isolate public policymaking somewhat from the traditional culture. This situation holds for the avant-garde developing states, where at least two cultures exist: the culture of the new elites and the traditional culture. One problem is that, for unavoidable historical reasons, the avant-garde culture also often includes many items with a low rational content, such as an unrealistic view of the feasible rate of socio-economic development. However, the culture of the new elites is usually significantly more rational than the traditional culture in these countries. The task of making the avant-garde culture (which is limited to a very small segment of the population) more rational is probably, in at least some of the countries, a manageable social task.

In the so-called modern countries, the rational content of culture also needs strengthening so as to encourage better public policymaking. But here fewer changes are needed, and they are mostly in the ways public opinions are formed and in the ways individuals think and behave.

CHANGES NEEDED IN INDIVIDUAL PATTERNS
OF THINKING AND BEHAVING

Many of the changes discussed in this and earlier chapters will involve changes in the way individuals think and act. In an important sense, all social operations, including policymaking and improving it, are finally reducible to what individuals do. This is not just an abstract observation; to improve policymaking in all the directions my various suggestions have pointed out will require using means that change individual patterns of behavior, such as formal education, training, personality development, and changing the premises of groups.

Just as a "democratic personality" is needed for democracy,[1] certain personality traits and skills must become widespread in the population before human society can fully accommodate itself to the present transformation in knowledge. These personality traits and skills involve, in particular, the higher mental activities, especially high problem-solving capacities, habits of rigorous thinking about instrumental problems, a high propensity for creative thinking, tough-mindedness about forming independent opinions, abilities to relearn and to change conclusions in the light of feedback and new data, and an ability to think in terms of sophisticated concepts. We also need better education in human values and democratic ideals, lest instrumental knowledge be misused and result in technological barbarism.

Achieving such changes in individual patterns of thinking and acting will require extensive changes in the educational system, in both the subjects that are taught and the methods of learning. For instance, various forms of simulation games, such as the *Dispatcher* game developed by Avalon Hill Company, prediction games, such as *Future,* developed by Keiser Company, and logic games, such as *WFF'N PROOF: The Game of Modern Logic,* developed by Layman E. Allen, illustrate important new tools for better training of thinking processes.

This call for changes in the educational system is long-range. Improving the public-policymaking system need not, and should not, wait until the changes in individuals take place. But in order to avoid too narrow a view of the effect of new knowledge on policymaking, and on society in general, one must bear in mind that, in principle and in the long run, adjusting patterns of social organization and operation to new knowledge depends on making important changes in the knowledge, skills, and personalities of individual men.

CHANGES NEEDED IN RESOURCES

To round off the list of the changes that are needed in the environment, I must mention again that we need more and better resources for better policymaking, mainly knowledge, drive, and high-quality manpower (equipment is mainly a result of knowledge). Most of the changes

---

[1] See Karl Mannheim, *Freedom, Power, and Democratic Planning* (London: Routledge and Kegan Paul, 1951), pp. 228ff.

needed in knowledge, drive, and manpower I have already discussed, but I must still point out that the educational system must be directed specifically at identifying and preparing potential high-quality policymakers, especially in the developing countries, but in modern countries as well.

An often-mentioned proposal is to enlarge the base from which potential high-quality policymakers are recruited, by overcoming social barriers that exclude women and often members of various social groups from many policymaking positions. Society may have more trouble swallowing some of the other changes in the structure and content of the educational system that will be needed to increase the supply of high-quality manpower for policymaking, private as well as public. Frankly recognizing that one of the main functions of education is to prepare future social elites, including the scientific and policymaking elites, does not negate its other goals, such as egalitarian values and broadening the educational base, but it does involve a readiness to pay *some* price in terms of those other goals, such as the social differentiation that is caused by establishing homogeneous classes or schools for the very gifted. The study of education must provide institutional arrangements that minimize such costs, for instance, comprehensive high schools which provide social mixing and shared activities for youth with different aptitudes. The need to gear the educational system to training an elite is nowadays increasingly recognized for scientific and technological subjects; thus there is already a modern basis for a broad view of the educational system as being responsible, among other goals, for providing high-quality manpower for elite positions, and such changes should meet less resistance than in the 1940's.

The changes that are needed in education illustrate very well the interdependence of the public-policymaking system and its environment; establishing an educational policy is one of the important functions of the public-policymaking system. But the quality of public policymaking, including its educational policies, depends on the characteristics of the educational system. Also, the quality of both systems depends on certain environmental variables they share, such as the way public opinions are formed or the culture. Because of this interdependence, one actor by himself cannot transform the characteristics of the whole field, but any one actor can exert some influence on all the other actors, and on the field as a whole.

It follows that although the environment limits the degree to which the public-policymaking system can improve itself, the latter can influence the former and can thus create some of the conditions it needs for better public policymaking. Therefore, it is up to the public-policymaking system, and all its components, to assume the initiative for improving itself, both directly and by trying to influence its environment. Simultaneously, it is up to every component of the environment, including individual citizens, to take the initiative to improve public policymaking both directly, by some effect, however minor, on the public-policymaking system, and indirectly, by influencing the components of the environment.

part VI

THE CHOICE:
SHAPING THE FUTURE
OR
MUDDLING THROUGH

chapter 22 · The Significance of Society's Major Alternatives

Overdramatizing problems is a poor way to deal with them. Society is not really at a crossroads where it must choose between muddling through and optimal policymaking. There is no one intersection between these two avenues of social action that would permit either one of them to be chosen once and for all, and the problem to be definitely resolved. The real world is much more complex, dynamic, and difficult than that; its infinitude of problems are always scattered over a long time. Also, the distinction between different methods of public policymaking is not always very sharp in specific cases; there are usually many alternatives rather than a clearly dichotomous choice. Society's situation, therefore, is not much like being at a crossroads where two obvious highways both pose the need and provide the opportunity for one clear decision. Rather, society is in many ways moving in a wilderness; it must select some method for deciding which general direction it should go in, as far as the topographical conditions and the available resources permit, and must change its method and direction when the terrain or new circumstances so require.

Choosing a guideline for the direction public policymaking should take involves answering three major questions:

1. Is public policymaking to follow the traditional pattern of evolving by slowly adjusting to new conditions and knowledge by means of incremental changes and convulsive changes following crisis, or is public policymaking, in part at least, to be consciously subjected to a new and explicit systems redesign that aspires to improve policymaking as much as possible?

2. What optimal design for public policymaking can serve as an instrumental goal toward which real policymaking should be directed?

3. Are there feasible strategies for changing actual policymaking so as to better approximate optimal public policymaking?

I have devoted most of this book to trying to provide a scientific basis for analyzing, evaluating, and improving public policymaking and to laying a foundation for policy science. I shall conclude it by trying to pull some of my more applied arguments together into short answers to the above three questions.

SLOW AND SPONTANEOUS ADJUSTING OR DIRECTED CHANGE

Explaining conservative attitudes about political institutions in terms of "overreaction," "fixation," "compensation," etc., does not validly rebut their content. The argument on "institutional wisdom" is especially cogent, and insofar as it is valid, it presents an off-limits sign to the would-be improver. It would be presumptuous to adopt, in the face of all the contrary evidence that is available, a far-going optimistic view of how much a conscious application of human knowledge and action can accomplish. Such an optimistic view must always be tempered by a realistic image of human nature, which should be based both on a survey of what human action has accomplished in the past and on the findings of modern psychology, especially psychoanalysis. One should also bear in mind that the tremendous progress in social arrangements that culminated in the modern democratic state did take place rather spontaneously, without benefit of optimal policymaking. The case is very strong for respecting traditional institutions and their ability to adjust themselves and for taking a reserved attitude toward the scientistic gospel, which preaches that "rationality," "science," and "knowledge" are the new saviors of humanity; we should pause before we embark on an irreversible redesigning of institutions.

I say "pause," and not "stop," on purpose. Although we must not ignore the limits human intelligence and knowledge are subject to, nor the wisdom of generations that has been embodied in the present forms of many social institutions, while we are seeking a way to improve public policymaking, neither should we exaggerate their conservative implications. Accepting the limits of knowledge and recognizing the wisdom built into traditional institutions do not imply that knowledge should not be used to improve and redesign social institutions, provided that: (1) the knowledge is reasonably validated; (2) the improvement is really based on the knowledge, after all its implied values have been made explicit; and (3) the involved risks are accepted only after the payoffs involved in adopting or not adopting the proposed improvements have been carefully considered.

It is the third condition that holds the key to the problem as it is faced today. Insofar as I am right in my thesis that contemporary public policymaking is not good enough to deal with the increasingly complex, difficult, and critical problems that are being generated by the constantly accelerating technological and social revolution, and insofar as my diagnostic evaluation of the contemporary quality of public policymaking in Part III is correct, then the conclusion to be drawn is quite clear. Even if it is true that "the growing intelligence of mankind seems not to be growing rapidly enough to achieve mastery over the social problems, which the advances of technology create,"[1] and even if knowledge is only one limited way among many for perceiving reality more fully, nevertheless it is also true that "systematic reasoning is something we could not, as a species or as individuals, possibly do without."[2]

Insofar as knowledge that is relevant to human action becomes available, it is our moral duty, as well as our best bet, to use it as much as possible, with due humility but without giving in to the conservative biases so deeply rooted in most individuals and social institutions. However bizarre the implications of such knowledge may look to our conservative minds, we must not be distracted from carefully considering those implications on their own merits. Consider how different most contemporary public-policymaking units and processes are from the ones that were accepted as universally valid only a few generations ago. It is reasonable to expect that future public-policymaking systems will differ even more from ours. The choice we face is either to try to change the public-policymaking system in the light of what we know and thus increase our chances of realizing our basic values more fully and of dealing better with the problems faced by society, or to leave the shaping of the future to the short-sighted (though not blind) forces of spontaneous historical evolution. Put in these terms, it seems to me that careful but determined and purposeful redesigning of the public-policymaking system must be our best strategy.

---

[1] Reinhold Niebuhr, *Moral Man and Immoral Society* (N.Y.: Scribner's, 1960), p. 50.

[2] Aldous Huxley, *The Doors of Perception* (London: Chatto & Windus, 1960), p. 62.

THE CHARACTERISTICS OF OPTIMAL PUBLIC POLICYMAKING

The optimal model of public policymaking I presented in some detail in Part IV will certainly not be received with universal acclaim. My assumption that optimal public policymaking is not a pure-rationality process, that it involves many extrarational components, will make this model distasteful to believers in "pure rationality," who will prefer to devote their energies to following their fata morgana. On the other hand, the many rational components of my optimal model will make it unacceptable to those who regard extrarational processes as the more valid ones. The model's strong predisposition toward innovation will also disturb those who believe tradition is the major embodiment of human wisdom.

The argument I have developed and presented in this book is that, despite the partial truths embodied in each of these positions (and partly because of them), we must try to so improve public policymaking that it moves, with time, toward the optimal model (which itself changes continually). Incremental change often does not fit new problems, since new knowledge and quickly changing conditions often make the past a poor, largely irrelevant, and even misleading guide for the future. Pure rationality is both impossible in practice and theoretically doubtful in its complete rejection of any possible advantages of extrarational components; whereas the more mystic approaches underrate the significance of rationality.

Admittedly, these assumptions are not susceptible at present to reliable proof. It is not inconsistent with our present scientific knowledge to believe that ultimately all problems can be reduced to parameters that will permit them to be solved by means of pure rationality (though it is completely clear that at present they cannot be so reduced), or to believe that mystic identification with the universe leads to a fuller perception of reality and the complete resolution of problems, or to believe that slowly evolving traditional patterns are in the long run best for mankind. Such assumptions cannot now, or perhaps ever, be "scientifically" proved or disproved, but they seem unreasonable to me in the light of both experience and knowledge and of their implications for human action.

Even if the reader holds some of these beliefs, I can defend my idea of optimal policymaking, as I elaborated it in Part IV, by a second and more pragmatic argument. Assuming pure rationality is ultimately possible and desirable, would not approximating optimal policymaking be the greatest step we can presently take in that direction? Or assuming "intuition" is the ultimate means for realizing human destiny, would not approximating optimal prolicymaking be the best possible way we can deal with social problems in the world as it is, since such policymaking tries to encourage extrarational components? These arguments will not satisfy the purists, but may convince the reader who is not quite sure of what the ultimate truth is, but in the meantime is looking for a way to improve humanity's abilities to deal with its problems, and is therefore provisionally willing to adopt optimal public policymaking as an instrumental-normative model that actual policymaking should aim at. But this still leaves open the question about what strategy we should follow to change society so as to approximate optimal policymaking better.

STRATEGIES FOR IMPROVING SOCIETY

Many persons, including perhaps most sophisticated policymakers, may be ready to accept my arguments so far as "theoretically sound," but will regard them as "impractical." Their main argument will probably be that, human nature being what it is, muddling through is still the only possible method for improving society.

This claim has a considerable factual basis. Conservative forces are very strong indeed, and human history, ancient as well as modern, refutes any easy optimism on the possibility of social reform by a stroke of the pen, or even by a closely reasoned book. Nevertheless, considerable progress has been made by applying available knowledge, and when sufficient support was forthcoming, the improvements did sometimes prevail over inertia. A career civil service based on merit, the city-manager form of municipal government, and planning-programming-budgeting methods illustrate that conscious improvements can be and have been made in the policymaking system. Parts of the military establishment and certain industrial enterprises demonstrate, at the same time, that more improvements in the policymaking system can come from presently available knowledge, if we have enough determination and incentive to put it to use.

A sudden transformation of the public-policymaking system is not possible; neither am I advocating one. Improving public policymaking must be a continuing endeavor, requiring sustained effort over a long period. The most harmful effect of the incremental-change argument (which denies the possibility that significant improvements could be made in public policymaking by some innovative jumps) is that it paralyzes efforts, and thus tends to be a self-fulfilling prophecy. Granted the difficulties exist, what we need is an even stronger effort to overcome them. The difficulties of the problems faced by public policymaking make improvements in it necessary, and the knowledge we are now developing makes such improvements possible; we must therefore mobilize the energy needed to carry out those improvements. Even if the strength of conservative factors and the scarcity of available resources limit the rate and scope of the improvements, we may still be able to make some innovative improvements. The wisdom-of-generations and incremental-change arguments are in this respect a sleeping pill, whereas the optimal model should stimulate maximum efforts to improve actual public policymaking.

Improving public policymaking is a lengthy and difficult process, but a feasible one. Using all available resources (including social support) in order to introduce those improvements that are feasible under contemporary conditions, and to build up conditions and resources (again including social support) for accelerated improvement of the public-policymaking system in the future, the actual characteristics of public policymaking can slowly but surely be changed, from relying almost entirely on muddling through to optimal policymaking (which itself includes a significant, but limited, amount of muddling through). To do so, we must first of all know that policymaking needs to be improved and know the ways we can improve it, then we must recruit the support we need and take up the job itself.

APPENDIXES

appendix A · Tables

TABLE 1. AN INTEGRATED EVALUATION OF PUBLIC POLICYMAKING IN MODERN DEMOCRATIC COUNTRIES

Criteria for ascertaining the quality of public policymaking / Main policymaking units	Primary criterion: Net probable real output	A. Process patterns: 1. Metapolicymaking about basic characteristics of policymaking system	2. Learning feedback	3. Determination of policy strategy	4. Elaboration of operational goals	5. Extent of search for alternatives	6. Establishment of cut-off horizon and its characteristics	7. Development of rational components	8. Development of extra-rational components	B. Outputs: 1. Nominal output	2. Feasibility	3. Probable real output	C. Structural elements: 1. Units explicitly in charge of periodic, systematic evaluating and redesigning of the policymaking structure	2. Units explicitly in charge of thinking, long-range policymaking, surveying knowledge, and policy-relevant R and D	3. Organizational and social distance between units making policy, those executing it, and those motivating the executing	4. Characteristics, roles, and contributions of different main units composing the policymaking structure	5. Main forms of the aggregation function	D. Inputs: 1. Qualified manpower	2. Knowledge and information	3. Equipment	4. Energy and drive
(Individuals) a. Private individuals	low	low	low	low	low	low	low	low	low or medium	low	low or medium	low	—	—	—	small or medium contribution		—	low or medium	low	low or medium
b. Intellectuals	low or medium	low or medium	low or medium	low or medium	low	mixed	low	mixed	mixed	low or medium	low	low or medium	—	—	—	medium contribution		—	medium or high	mixed	low or medium
c. Political leaders	mixed	low	low or medium	low or medium	low or medium	low or medium	low	low or medium	mixed	low or medium	medium or high	mixed	—	—	—	medium or large contribution		—	medium	low or medium	mixed
(Organizations) d. Legislative bodies	low or medium	low	low	low	low	low	low	low	medium or high	low or medium	medium or high	low or medium	low	low	—	medium contribution		medium or high	low or medium	low	mixed
e. Political executive	mixed	low	low or medium	low or medium	low or medium	low or medium	low or medium	low or medium	high	medium or high	high	mixed	low or medium	low	—	large contribution		medium or high	mixed	low or medium	mixed
f. Civil service	mixed	low	low or medium	low or medium	low or medium	low or medium	low or medium	medium	medium	medium	medium	mixed	low	low	—	large contribution		mixed	medium or high	medium	low or medium
g. Courts	high but narrow	low	low or medium	low	low or medium	low	high but narrow	high but narrow	high but narrow	high	medium	high but narrow	low	low	•	small or medium contribution		high but narrow	high but narrow	low or medium	medium
h. Parties	low or medium	low	low or medium	low or medium	low or medium	low	low	low or medium	medium or high	low or medium	medium or high	low or medium	low	low	—	medium or large contribution		medium	low	low	low or medium
i. Universities	high but narrow	low or medium	medium	low	low	mixed	low	high	low	medium or high	low	high but narrow	low or medium	medium or high	—	small or medium contribution		high	high	medium or high	mixed
j. Interest groups	low or medium	low	low or medium	low	low or medium	low or medium	low or medium	low or medium	medium or high	low	low or medium	low or medium	low	low or medium	—	medium contribution		mixed	mixed	low or medium	mixed
k. Other relevant units: special thinking units, e.g., RAND and planning bodies	high but narrow	medium	high but narrow	medium or high	medium	medium or high	medium	high	low	mixed	low or medium	high but narrow	low or medium	high	—	small or medium contribution		high	high	high	mixed
Aggregate quality of policymaking for each criterion	medium	low	low	low	low	low or medium	low	low or medium	medium or high	low or medium	high	medium	low or medium	low	medium	mainly from c, d, e, f, h, j	mainly polycentric with medium number of units	mixed	mixed	low or medium	low or medium
Main standards for appraising ascertained qualities																					
(1) Past qualities: last 20 years	slightly or medium above	little change	little change	slightly above	little change	slightly above	little change	slightly above	little change	little change	little change	slightly or medium above	little change	slightly above	little change	less contribution by d; more by e, f, i, k	little change	little change	medium above	much above	little change
(2) Qualities of other systems: modern Communist countries	slightly or medium above	similar	similar	slightly below	much below	slightly above	slightly below	slightly above	similar or slightly above	much below	much above	slightly or medium above	similar	?	slightly above	different	slightly or medium above	similar	similar	similar or slightly below	slightly or medium below
(3) Satisfactory quality	approximating	approximating	approximating	approximating	approximating	slightly below	approximating	slightly below	approximating	slightly below	approximating	approximating	slightly below	slightly below	approximating	slightly below	approximating	slightly below	slightly below	slightly below	approximating
(4) Professional standards: not developed	—	—	—	—	—	—	—	—	—	—	—	—	—	—	—	—	—	—	—	—	—
(5) Survival quality	Note 1	Note 1	Note 1	Note 1	Note 1	Note 1	Note 1	Note 1	Note 1	approximating	slightly or medium above	Note 1	Note 1	Note 1	slightly or medium above	Note 1	slightly above	Note 1	Note 1	Note 1	Note 1
(6) Planned quality: not developed	—	—	—	—	—	—	—	—	—	—	—	—	—	—	—	—	—	—	—	—	—
(7) Optimal quality	medium or much below	much below	much below	much below	much below	much below	much below	much below	slightly below	slightly below	approximating	medium or much below	much below	much below	approximating	medium or much below	approximating	medium or much below	much below	slightly or medium below	medium below

Note 1: approximating today; below in extrapolated future

TABLE 2. AN INTEGRATED EVALUATION OF PUBLIC POLICYMAKING IN MODERN COMMUNIST COUNTRIES

Main policymaking units	Primary criterion: Net probable real output	A1. Metapolicymaking about basic characteristics of policymaking system	A2. Learning feedback	A3. Determination of policy strategy	A4. Elaboration of operational goals	A5. Extent of search for alternatives	A6. Establishment of cut-off horizon and its characteristics	A7. Development of rational components	A8. Development of extra-rational components	B1. Nominal output	B2. Feasibility	B3. Probable real output	C1. Units explicitly in charge of periodic, systematic evaluating and redesigning of the policymaking structure	C2. Units explicitly in charge of thinking, long-range policymaking, surveying knowledge, and policy-relevant R and D	C3. Organizational and social distance between units making policy, those executing it, and those motivating the executing	C4. Characteristics, roles, and contributions of different main units composing the policymaking structure	C5. Main forms of the aggregation function	D1. Qualified manpower	D2. Knowledge and information	D3. Equipment	D4. Energy and drive
(Individuals) a. Private individuals	low	low	low	low	low	low	low	low	low or medium	low	low or medium	low	—	—		small contribution	—	—	low or medium	low	low or medium
b. Intellectuals	low or medium	low	low	low	low	low or medium	low	mixed	low or medium	low or medium	low or medium	low or medium				small or medium contribution			medium or high	mixed	mixed
c. Political leaders	mixed	low	low or medium	low	medium	low or medium	low	low or medium	mixed	medium or high	low or medium	mixed	—	—		large contribution	—	—	mixed	mixed	medium or high
(Organizations) d. Legislative bodies	low	low	low	low	low	low	low	low	medium	high	medium	low	low	low		small contribution		medium	low	low	medium or high
e. Political executive	mixed	low	low or medium	medium	medium	low or medium	low or medium	low or medium	medium or high	medium or high	mixed	mixed	low	?		large contribution		—	mixed	mixed	medium or high
f. Civil service	mixed	low	low or medium	low or medium	low or medium	low or medium	low or medium	low or medium	medium	medium or high	medium	mixed	low	?		medium or large contribution		—	mixed	medium or high	medium
g. Courts: do not contribute to public policymaking	—	—	—	—	—	—	—	—	—	—	—	—	—	—		no contribution		—	—	—	—
h. Parties: Communist party	mixed	mixed	low or medium	mixed	medium or high	low or medium	low or medium	low or medium	medium or high	medium or high	low or medium	mixed	low	?		large contribution		mixed	medium	low or medium	high
i. Universities	medium	low	low or medium	low	low	low or medium	low	mixed	low	mixed	medium	medium or high but narrow	low	mixed		small or medium contribution	—	medium or high	medium or high	medium or high	mixed
j. Interest groups	low or medium	low	low	low	low or medium	low or medium	low	low or medium	medium or high	operate through hidden channels	low or medium	low or medium	low	low		?	—	mixed	mixed	low	mixed
k. Other relevant units: special thinking and research units	?	?	?	?	?	?	?	?	?	?	?	?	?	?		?	—	?	?	?	?
Aggregate quality of policymaking for each criterion	medium	low	low	low	mixed	low or medium	low or medium	low or medium	medium or high	high	low or medium	medium	low		low or medium	mainly from c, e, f, h, j	mainly polycentric with medium number of units	mixed	mixed	low or medium	medium or high
Main standards for appraising ascertained qualities																					
(1) Past qualities: last 20 years	medium or much above	little change	little change	slightly above	little change	slightly above	little change	slightly above	little change	little change	slightly above	medium or much above	little change	?	slightly above	some more influence by a, b, j,	little change	little change	slightly or medium above	medium or much below	slightly below
(2) Qualities of other systems: modern democratic countries	slightly or medium below	similar	similar	slightly above	much above	slightly above	slightly below	slightly above	similar or slightly below	much above	much below	slightly or much below	similar	?	slightly below	different	slightly or medium below	similar	similar	similar or slightly above	slightly or medium above
(3) Satisfactory quality	medium or much below	?	?	?	?	?	?	?	?	approximating	much below	medium or much below	?	?	?	slightly below	slightly below	slightly or medium below	slightly or medium below	slightly below	slightly below
(4) Professional standards: not developed	—	—	—	—	—	—	—	—	—	—	—	—	—	—	—	—	—	—	—	—	—
(5) Survival quality	Note 1	Note 1	Note 1	Note 1	Note 1	Note 1	Note 1	Note 1	Note 1	much above	slightly below	Note 1	Note 1	Note 1	Note 1	Note 1	Note 1	Note 1	Note 1	Note 1	slightly or medium above
(6) Planned quality	medium or much below	—	—	—	medium or much below	—	—	—	—	medium or much below	medium or much below	medium or much below	—	—	—	—	—	medium or much below	?	medium or much below	medium or much below
(7) Optimal quality	much below	much below	much below	much below	much below	much below	much below	much below	much below	much above	much below	much below	much below?	much below	medium below	slightly or medium below	slightly or medium below	medium or much below	much below	slightly below	approximating or slightly below

Note 1: approximating today; below in extrapolated future

TABLE 3. AN INTEGRATED EVALUATION OF PUBLIC POLICYMAKING IN AVANT GARDE DEVELOPING COUNTRIES

Criteria for ascertaining the quality of public policymaking / Main policymaking units	Primary criterion: Net probable real output	A.1. Metapolicymaking about basic characteristics of policymaking system	A.2. Learning feedback	A.3. Determination of policy strategy	A.4. Elaboration of operational goals	A.5. Extent of search for alternatives	A.6. Establishment of cut-off horizon and its characteristics	A.7. Development of rational components	A.8. Development of extrarational components	B.1. Nominal output	B.2. Feasibility	B.3. Probable real output	C.1. Units explicitly in charge of periodic, systematic evaluating and redesigning of the policymaking structure	C.2. Units explicitly in charge of thinking, long-range policymaking, surveying knowledge, and policy-relevant R and D	C.3. Organizational and social distance between units making policy, those executing it, and those motivating the executing	C.4. Characteristics, roles, and contributions of different main units composing the policymaking structure	C.5. Main forms of the aggregation function	D.1. Qualified manpower	D.2. Knowledge and information	D.3. Equipment	D.4. Energy and drive
(Individuals) a. Private individuals	low	low	low	low	low	low	low	low	low or medium	low	low or medium	low	—	—	—	small contribution	—	—	low	low	low or medium
b. Intellectuals	low	low	low	low	low	low	low	low or medium	low	low	low or medium	low	—	—	—	small contribution	—	low or medium	low or medium	low or medium	low or medium
c. Political leaders	mixed	low	low or medium	low	medium	low or medium	medium or high	low	mixed	medium or high	low	low or medium	—	—	—	large contribution	—	—	medium	low or medium	medium or high
(Organizations) d. Legislative bodies	low	low	low	low	low	low	low	low	low or medium	mixed	low or medium	low	low	low	—	small contribution	—	low or medium	low	low	medium or high
e. Political executive	mixed	low	low or medium	medium	medium or high	low or medium	medium or high	low or medium	mixed	mixed	low	mixed	low	low	—	large contribution	—	mixed	low or medium	low	high
f. Civil service	low or medium	low	low or medium	low or medium	mixed	low or medium	low	low	low or medium	mixed	low or medium	low or medium	low	low	—	medium contribution	—	low or medium	low or medium	low or medium	mixed
g. Courts: do not contribute to public policymaking	—	—	—	—	—	—	—	—	—	—	—	—	—	—	—	no contribution	—	—	—	—	—
h. Parties (ruling party)	low or medium	low	low or medium	low or medium	medium	low or medium	low or medium	low	mixed	medium or high	low	low or medium	low	low	—	large contribution	—	mixed	low	low	high
i. Universities	low	low	low	low	low	low	low	medium	low	mixed	low	low	low	low	—	small contribution	—	mixed	low or medium	low or medium	mixed
j. Interest groups	low	low	low	low	low or medium	low	low	low	mixed	low or medium	low	low	low	low	—	medium contribution	—	low or medium	—	low or medium	mixed
k. Other relevant units: the army	mixed	low or medium	mixed	mixed	mixed	mixed	mixed	mixed	mixed	medium or high	medium	mixed	low or medium	low or medium	—	large contribution	—	mixed	low or medium	low or medium	medium or high
Aggregate quality of policymaking for each criterion	low or medium	low	low	low	medium or high	low or medium	low or medium	low or medium	mixed	medium	low or medium	low or medium	low	low	low or medium	mainly from c, e, h, j, army	hierarchic and polycentric with few units	low or medium	low or medium	low	medium or high
Main standards for appraising ascertained qualities																					
(1) Past quality: independence movement and first years of statehood	much above	slightly above	slightly above	slightly above	slightly above	slightly above	slightly above	slightly above	slightly or medium above	much above	slightly above	much above	similar	similar	slightly above	slightly above	some more influence by army, sometimes below	slightly above	slightly above	slightly or medium above	similar or slightly and medium below
(2) Qualities of other systems: modern western societies	much below	medium below	medium below	slightly below	much above	different	slightly above	much below	similar or slightly below	medium or much above	much below	much below	slightly below	slightly below	slightly or medium below	much below	slightly below	much below	much below	much below	medium or much above
(3) Satisfactory quality	much below	—	—	—	slightly below	slightly below	slightly below	slightly below	slightly below	much below	much below	much below	—	—	much below	much below	much below	slightly below	slightly below	slightly below	much below
(4) Professional standards: not developed	—	—	—	—	—	—	—	—	—	—	—	—	—	—	—	—	—	—	—	—	—
(5) (Physical) survival quality	much above	much above	much above	much above	much above	much above	much above	much above	much above	much above	much above	much above	much above	much above	much above	much above	much above	much above	much above	much above	much above
(6) Planned quality	much below	—	—	—	—	—	much below	—	much below	much below	slightly below	much below	—	—	—	—	—	much below	much below	much below	much below
(7) Optimal quality	medium below	medium below	medium below	medium below	slightly or medium below	medium below	slightly below	medium below	slightly below	medium above	much below	medium below	medium below	medium below	slightly or medium below	medium below	slightly below	medium below	medium below	approximating or slightly above	approximating or slightly below

TABLE 4. RELATIONSHIP BETWEEN SUGGESTIONS FOR IMPROVEMENTS AND SPECIFIC IMPROVEMENTS THAT ARE NEEDED

Suggestions for improvement \ Improvements needed	Much more meta-policymaking about basic characteristics of policymaking system	Much more learning feedback	Much more systematic and explicit determination of policy strategy	Some more elaboration of operational goals	Much more search for alternatives	Much more explicit establishing of cutoff horizon covering a longer period of time	Much more development of rational components	Some more development of extrarational components	Many more specific units explicitly in charge of periodic, systematic evaluating and redesigning of the policymaking system	Many more specific units explicitly in charge of thinking, long-range policymaking, surveying knowledge, and policy-relevant Rand D	Careful adjustment of organizational and social distance between units making policy, those executing it, and those motivating the executing	Some changes in the characteristics, roles, and contributions of the major units composing the policymaking structure	Changes in the aggregation function	Much higher qualifications for policymaking manpower and much more input of knowledge and information	Some more equipment	Some increases in energy and drive
a. Concerning knowledge: Establishing a policy science and developing more policy knowledge in all disciplines	XX	XX	XX	X	X	XX	XXX	X	XX	XXX	X	XX	X	XXX	X	
b. Concerning personnel: Improving politicians	X	X	X	X	XX	X	XX	XX	X	X	X	XX	X	XXX		X
Improving senior civil servants	XX	XX	XX	XX	XX	XX	XXX	X	XX	XX	XX	XX	X	XXX		X
c. Concerning structure and process patterns: Improving experts (including developing analysts)	XX	XX	XX	XX	XX	XX	XXX	X	XXX	XXX	X	XX	X	XXX	X	X
Establishing and reinforcing special research organizations	XXX	XX	XX	XX	XXX	XX	XXX	X	XXX	XXX	X	XX	X	XX	X	X
Establishing and reinforcing units for systems management, metapolicymaking, and comprehensive public policymaking	XXX	XX	XXX	XX	XX	XX	XX		XXX	XXX	X	X	X	XX	X	
Establishing and reinforcing professional staff units	XX	XX	XX	XX	XX	XX	XX	X	XX	XX	X	XX	X	XX	X	
Establishing and reinforcing units to survey and retrieve knowledge	X	XX	X	X	XX	X	XX	X	X	XXX		X		XX	XX	
Establishing and reinforcing units for policy-oriented research and development	X	X	X	X	XXX	X	XX	X	X	XXX	X	X	X	XX	X	
Developing explicit policymaking methods	X	XX	XX	XX	XX	XX	XX	X	X	X		X	X	XX	X	
Transforming policymaking apparatus into a manpower-machine system	X	XX	X	X	X	X	XX	X				XX	X	X	XXX	
Introducing systematic learning feedback	X	XXX	X	X	XX	X	XX	XX	X	X		X	X	XX	XX	X
Improving personal contacts between policymakers and scientists	X	X	X		X		X	X		X	XX	X	X	XX		X
Better integration of universities in public policymaking	XX	XX	XX	X	XXX	X	XX	X	XX	XXX	X	XX	X	XX	X	X
Changes in the aggregation functions	X	X	X	X	X	X	X	X	X	X	XX	XX	XXX	X	X	X
d. Concerning input and stipulated output: Increase in resources put into policymaking	XX	XX	XX	X	XX	X	XX	X	XX	XX				XX	XX	X
Establishing a stipulated output that approximates optimality	X	X	X	X	X	X	X	X	X	X	X	X	X	X	X	XX
e. Concerning the environment: Improving the ways public opinions are formed	X	X	X	X	X	X	X	X	X	X	X	X	X	X	X	XX
Improving public demands on the policymaking system	X	X	X	X	X	X	X	X	X	X	X	X	X	X	X	XX
Increasing the propensity to change	XX	XX	XX	XX	XX	XX	XX	XX	XX	XX	XX	XX	XX	XX	XX	XX
Increasing the rational content of culture	X	X	X	X	X	X	XX		X	X	X	X	X	X	X	X
Improving individual patterns of thinking and behavior							X	X						XX		X
Increasing overall policymaking resources	X	X	X	X	X	X	X	X	X	X	X	X	X	X	X	X

Symbols: X = makes some contribution satisfying this need for improvement.
XX = makes significant contribution satisfying this need for improvement.
XXX = makes large contribution satisfying this need for improvement.

appendix B · A Summary
of the Phases of Optimal
Public Policymaking

Phase	Main functions of the phase	Rational subphases	Extrarational subphases
Metapolicymaking stage			
1. Processing values	Specifying and ordering values to be a general guide for identifying problems and for policymaking	Examining the internal and functional consistency of values; gathering information on feasibility and opportunity costs; determining the optimal degree to which values should be specified; creating favorable conditions for extrarational processes	Value judgments; tacit bargaining and coalition-formation skills
2. Processing reality	Perceiving objective reality and constructing a subjective image of present and expected future reality that approximates those aspects of objective reality which are relevant to policymaking	Systematic intelligence and scanning operations; using knowledge to predict future reality; learning explicitly from feedback; creating favorable conditions for extrarational subphases; identifying persons with extrarational capacities	An intuitive grasp of reality; a feeling for future developments
3. Processing problems	Stating problems in an action-oriented form, and with an order of priority based on comparing subjective reality with the processed values	A programmed and systematic method for comparing subjective reality with the processed values; cultivating and surveying extrarational subphases	An intuitive feeling for situations; hunches about possible solutions, and formulating problems accordingly; a feeling for "where the shoe pinches"

4. Surveying, processing, and developing resources	Perceiving and evaluating resources; developing new resources, especially "knowledge"	Systematically scanning reality; determining the opportunity costs of various resources; conducting research on how to transform available materials into resources; systematic surveys of knowledge; and research and development on decisionmaking	Hunches about the possible payoffs of different uses of resources; inventiveness and scientific creativity
5. Designing, evaluating, and redesigning the policymaking system	Establishing the structure and process patterns of policy-making; suboptimizing; redesigning the system as required by feedback and changes in relevant variables	Systematically applying knowledge from systems analysis, organization theory, etc.; encouraging a predisposition to change; encouraging conditions that will facilitate creativity	Creatively inventing new policymaking designs
6. Allocating problems, values, and resources	a. After suitably suboptimizing problems, allocating the subproblems to the various policymaking units and subsystems (or to other problem-solving processes) b. Allocating values parallel to the allocation of problems, so that the major values involved in a certain problem go to the same policymaking unit	a. Using knowledge to select the optimal allocation; systematically comparing the aggregate of allocated problems with the total problems before allocation; creating favorable conditions for extrarational subphases b. Using knowledge to predict the values that will be involved in the policymaking on a certain problem; creating favorable conditions for extrarational subphases	a. Hunches about the possible payoffs of different allocations b. Intuitive judgments as to what problems will involve what values

Phase	Main functions of the phase	Rational subphases	Extrarational subphases
Metapolicymaking stage (Continued)			
	c. Allocating resources to the various policymaking units and subsystems (and to other activities that consume resources) in such manner as will maximize the aggregate net output	c. Using knowledge to select the optimal allocation; creating favorable conditions for extrarational subphases	c. Hunches about the possible payoffs of different allocations
7. Determining policymaking strategy	Establishing basic doctrines and premises for policymaking; selecting major strategies on whether to favor incremental change or innovation, on how to deal with uncertainty, etc.	Making greatest possible use of the decision sciences; creating favorable conditions for extrarational subphases	Creative thinking about and inventing of new strategies; hunches about the possible payoffs of different strategies; an ability to face ambiguity and uncertainty
Policymaking stage			
8. Suballocating sources	Allocating resources to the phases of public policymaking in such manner as will maximize their probable aggregate real output	Using knowledge to select the optimal suballocation; creating favorable conditions for extrarational subphases	Hunches about the possible payoffs of different suballocations

9. Establishing operational goals, with some order of priority for them	Stating goals in an operational form; examining their consistency; establishing some priority and some approximate rate of exchange among them	Examining the internal and functional consistency of the goals both by themselves and as compared with the allocated problems and values; using semi-quantified methods to establish some appropriate rate of exchange and order of priority among them	Hunches about the values likely to become involved with the various goals; value judgments; intuitive evaluations
10. Establishing a set of other, major significant values, with some order of priority for them	Identifying other relevant values likely to become involved in policymaking; establishing relative weights	Explicitly establishing a cut-off horizon; using prediction techniques to identify values likely to become involved; examining their internal and functional consistency; using semi-quantified methods to establish some appropriate rate of exchange and order of priority among them	Hunches about the values that are likely to become involved; value judgments; intuitive evaluations

Phase	Main functions of the phase	Rational subphases	Extrarational subphases
Policymaking stage (Continued)			
11. Preparing a set of major alternatives, including some "good" ones	Searching for possible alternative policies until at least one "good" one is identified	Examining known alternatives, by means including surveys of literature and comparative studies; research on how to construct composite alternatives and invent new ones; identifying and recruiting creative manpower; establishing conditions that stimulate creativity; using knowledge to decide whether continuing the search is worthwhile	Hunches about the likely results of a continued search for alternatives; creativity needed to invent new or composite alternatives
12. Preparing a set of reliable predictions of the significant benefits and costs of the various alternatives	Predicting the probable benefits and costs of the alternatives, with some estimation of how reliable the predictions are and of their sensitivity to changes in various variables	Using prediction techniques; experimenting; creating favorable conditions for extrarational subphases; developing a checklist of conditions to be satisfied by the set of predictions	Hunches and intuitive judgments

13. Comparing the predicted benefits and costs of the alternatives, and identifying the best ones	Establishing criteria for choice based on the allocated problems and values; processing the predicted benefits and costs in terms of the criteria; comparing the processed benefits and costs of the different alternatives; identifying the alternative(s) with the highest probable net real benefit	Value judgments and intuitive evaluations about both specific benefits and costs and the whole gestalt of benefits and costs
14. Evaluating the benefits and costs of the "best" alternative and deciding whether it is "good" or not	Appraising the benefits and costs of the "best" alternative by means of the "goodness" standard	Intuitive judgment on "goodness" standard and appraisal of alternatives in its terms

Post-policymaking stage

15. Motivating the executing of the policy	Deciding to execute the policy; mobilizing support; continuing to allocate resources and "push" to the executing	Surveying the relevant distributions of power; using political science, communication theory, opinion-formation theory, and conflict theory; selecting persons with appropriate extrarational skills	A feeling for the "art of the possible," skills at forming coalitions and at bargaining

317

Phase	Main functions of the phase	Rational subphases	Extrarational subphases
Post-policymaking stage (Continued)			
16. Executing the policy	Executing of the policy, and thereby also significantly shaping the policy	All the rational phases and subphases of policymaking, but with some variations; substantive operational activities	All the extrarational phases and subphases of policymaking, but with some variations; substantive operational activities
17. Evaluating the policy after executing it	Comparing the actual results of executing the policy with the predicted results; evaluating the deviations	Carrying out an explicit, systematic, programmed comparison of the real results with the predicted results; using knowledge to identify the reasons for the deviations	Impressionistic evaluation of the significance of the deviations and their causes, both individually and as an entire gestalt
Feedback stages			
18. Communication and feedback channels multiply interconnecting all phases	Intercommunication between all phases, and feedback of the results of each phase, to enable dynamic changes to be made at each and every stage of the policymaking process; improving the policymaking process by means of learning feedback	Systematically programming and constructing feedback channels; establishing explicit threshold levels; establishing and maintaining learning processes; storing the findings from feedback	Impressionistic evaluation of the outputs of the different phases, to determine whether feedback should be initiated; tacit learning from feedback

318

appendix C · Policy Knowledge
and the Disciplines
of Knowledge

Discipline	Present and foreseeable contributions	Possible future contributions
A. Traditional		
1. History	Raw material for all social sciences; perspective; stimulating the search for alternatives	Raw material for policy science; material to develop some extrarational policymaking skills
2. Law	Some information on the probable consequences of various forms of legislation; a variety of legislative and judicial techniques as alternative forms for policies	Reliable information on potentials and limits of law as a means for directed social change; new modes of lawmaking and law enforcement as alternative forms and contents for policies
3. Engineering	An increasing range of feasible policy alternatives and more reliable predictions of benefits and costs; some concepts for the decision sciences; tools for data processing and programmed decisionmaking	Significant concepts and methodologies (e.g., ideas of systems engineering and systems management); better tools for data processing and programmed decisionmaking; tools for improving some types of heuristic decisionmaking
4. The life sciences	Some knowledge on the influence of ecological and biophysical variables on decisionmaking	Psychoactive drugs to improve rational and extrarational processes and to increase energy; new policy alternatives; conscious efforts, based on genetics, to improve qualities that are, in the long run, relevant to decisionmaking
B. Social sciences		
5. Psychology	Identifying persons who have some decision-making capacities; some knowledge on the variables that shape the quality of individual and small-group decisionmaking and policy-making; a little knowledge on the nature and conditions of "creativity"; some improvement of decisionmakers by means of various types of psychotherapy	Improvements on all its present and foreseeable contributions; some knowledge on "intuition" and other extrarational processes, and perhaps on extrasensory perception and its uses for better decisionmaking

6. Educational psychology	Some improvements in the rational and extra-rational capacities of policymakers by means of teaching methods oriented toward problem solving; developing special training techniques, such as simulation games, oriented toward decisionmaking	Systematic training of policymakers, and significantly improving their rational and extra-rational capacities, by integrated use of novel techniques and special curricula; improving decisionmaking habits in the population, by means of new methods for teaching traditional subjects (e.g., mathematics); better informing the population at large, and the policymaking and policy-evaluating strata in particular, by means of new techniques and equipment (e.g., programmed teaching machines)
7. Sociology and anthropology	Frames-of-reference and concepts of some help for understanding society and social problems; some ideas on limits and main avenues of social change, which help delimit the range of feasible policy alternatives and help "guesstimate" probable benefits and costs; some applied knowledge on a few social problems; a general orientation that is very helpful for sensitizing policymakers to the complexities of policy issues and their social dimensions	Fuller understanding of societal dynamics and of the main variables that shape society; some reliable knowledge on possibilities for shaping society by conscious action; significant data on an increasing number of social problems, permitting fuller control of more social phenomena
8. Political science	Some information on the characteristics of policymaking and the variables that shape it; some understanding of the relationships between different political ideologies and types of policymaking structures; some evaluation of policymaking and some proposals for reforms; some information on the limits of political feasibility and the variables that shape them	Great improvements on present and foreseeable contributions, which would be a sound basis for increasing political feasibility by understanding its main variables and (in conjunction with policy science) systematically evaluating policymaking, and searching extensively for, and evaluating, ways to improve it

Discipline	Present and foreseeable contributions	Possible future contributions
B. Social sciences (Continued)		
9. Public administration and business administration	Some knowledge on organizational behavior and the variables that shape it; techniques for improving organizational operations, especially on the low and middle levels; in conjunction with the decision sciences, some information on organizational decisionmaking behavior and some normative models	Great improvement on present and foreseeable contributions; means for improving organizational operations on the higher level, with special attention to policymaking and "thinking" processes; reliable knowledge on "creative organizations"
10. International relations	A little information and knowledge on international behavior and the variables that shape it; some conceptual frameworks and preliminary data on policymaking on foreign relations; in conjunction with theory of games and conflict studies, some behavioral and normative models on policymaking on foreign relations and military strategies	Great improvements on present and foreseeable contributions
11. Economics	Reliable policy-oriented knowledge on macroeconomic phenomena in highly developed societies and the variables that shape them; some ideas on the economics of growth and strategies for accelerated and planned economic development; many concepts, methods, and techniques for improving decisionmaking and some normative models for decisionmaking and policymaking that are applicable mainly to quanti-	In conjunction with development studies, reliable policy-oriented knowledge on economic phenomena in developing societies and the variables that shape them; in conjunction with the decision sciences, normative models for decisionmaking and policymaking applicable also to unquantifiable phenomena; methods for better quantification of more variables; methods for making the concept of "social welfare"

		more operational
	fiable phenomena; some clarification of the concept of "welfare"	Improvements on present and foreseeable contributions
C. New interdisciplinary fields		
12. Intelligence and information studies	Analysis of information needs; designs for intelligence collection, information storage, and information retrieval; methods for data processing	Improvements on present and foreseeable contributions
13. Communication studies	Some information on and understanding of, and some methods for influencing, the ways public opinions are formed	Great improvements on present and foreseeable contributions; in conjunction with educational psychology, methods for educating public opinions to meet the needs of optimal policy-making
14. Conflict studies	In conjunction with international relations, some knowledge about international conflicts; beginnings of a general theory of conflict, providing qualitative concepts applicable to certain situations and quantitative models applicable to a very few situations; some training tools for policymakers (e.g., simulation games)	Extensive, reliable information on and understanding of conflict situations and dependable methods for minimizing resorts to violence in some types of conflicts; general and particular theories of conflict providing concepts and normative models for policymaking on potential or actual conflict situations; developed tools for training policymakers to make better decisions about conflict situations
15. Regional studies	Comprehensive approach to regional problems, by means of rigorous analysis and quantitative simulation models	Broader applicability by including more variables in models; adjustment of regional studies to apply to larger and more complex areas

Discipline	Present and foreseeable contributions	Possible future contributions
C. New interdisciplinary fields (Continued)		
16. Comprehensive planning	Comprehensive approach to planning; some knowledge on the environmental requisites, structural arrangements, and personnel qualifications needed for comprehensive planning; some normative models and strategies for comprehensive planning	In conjunction with systems management and decision sciences, information and knowledge on requirements and optimal characteristics of comprehensive planning, in the sense of multifaceted, complex, future-oriented policymaking about systems
17. Systems management and systems analysis (tends to converge with no. 19)	An orientation and conceptual framework for simultaneous control and direction of an interacting set of variables; some methods and techniques for managing relatively simple systems whose main variables are susceptible to quantification, for designing and redesigning such systems and for examining alternatives in terms of such systems	Conceptual tools for analyzing complex systems; methods and techniques for designing, redesigning, and managing complex systems, including systems whose main variables are not susceptible to quantification and for examining alternatives in terms of such systems
18. Development studies	Some information on and understanding of the processes of social change and the variables that shape them; some suggestions for influencing and accelerating a few aspects and phases of social change, in terms of both basic strategies and certain details	Improvements on present and foreseeable contributions
19. Decision and management sciences, and operations research (tends to converge with no. 17)	Rigorous methods for quantitative decisionmaking on a few problems; some suggestions for improving heuristic decisionmaking on relatively simple issues; a basic approach and frame of reference that is conducive to better	Further development of present and foreseeable knowledge; orientations, concepts, methods, and techniques basic to all facets of policy science; increased applicability of methods for more rigorous treatment of qualitative variables

		policymaking, because it emphasizes explicit processes, holistic orientations, a readiness for innovation, and using multidisciplinary knowledge; some knowledge on organizational and psycho-sociological problems of multidisciplinary work-teams and of integrating novel types of "thinking" units into conventional organizations; some experience with the difficulties of and requirements for establishing a new action-oriented interdisciplinary field at universities; some experience with training practicing decisionmakers and decision-science staff officers
20. Policy science	Beginning of an orientation and some conceptual frameworks; some suggestions for studying and improving policymaking	Analytical concepts, quantifiable (metric and non-metric) parameters, qualitative frameworks, and methodologies for investigating and evaluating policymaking; reliable and extensive knowledge on policymaking; systematic normative models for policymaking, both for the public-policymaking system as a whole and for limited policymaking situations; detailed specifications for, and suggestions on how to make, the improvements that are needed in various facets of policymaking and its environment; a general theory of policymaking; curricula and methods for training various types of policymakers, policy scientists, and policy analysts.

D. Abstract

21. Logic and semantics	Rules for correct reasoning; symbols for rigorous thinking; language for programming some	Further development of present and foreseeable knowledge; conversion of some heuristic

Discipline	Present and foreseeable contributions	Possible future contributions
D. Abstract (Continued)	thinking processes into computers; **teaching tools to improve reasoning**	processes into algorithms; **methods and tools for programming some heuristic thinking processes; ideas for novel intelligence-amplifying machines**
22. Pure and applied mathematics, and statistics	Abstract models that are suggestive for analyzing some policy issues and identifying some main strategies; rigorous models applicable to a few decision issues; concepts and techniques for improving some elements of decisions, especially the prediction sets; methodologies for investigating and simulating some aspects of society; concepts, methods, and exercises for teaching and developing problem-solving skills	Further development of present and foreseeable knowledge; quantitative models of wider applicability, allowing reliable simulation of complex non-deterministic systems with some unquantifiable variables
23. Applied philosophy and ethics	Sensitizing policymakers and policy scientists to the limits of "scientific knowledge" and to the critical importance of ideologies, beliefs, and pure value judgments; value theory, helping to classify and order values, and to develop criteria for examining the internal consistency of values; clarifying the problems involved in applying ethics to policy issues	Further development of present and foreseeable knowledge; better methods for increasing operationality of ethics in policymaking; designing curricula and teaching methods for policymakers and policy scientists to counterbalance dangers that better instrumental knowledge could be misused and to fight tendencies toward trained incapacity and intellectual arrogance

appendix D · Bibliographic Essay

My purpose in this essay is only to help the reader who wishes to pursue further some of the problems, issues, and ideas I discussed in the text. I have tried to provide not a complete list of relevant books and articles covering all subject matters, but only a list of selected basic and more recent books (and a few articles) that are available (with single exceptions) in English.

CHAPTER 1

Many of the ideas mentioned in Chapter 1 are developed in detail later on, and will be covered by the bibliographic notes for those chapters.

The general thesis that actual policymaking does not use available knowledge is presented in Carl L. Becker, *Progress and Power* (Stanford: Stanford Univ. Press, 1936). An already classic exposition of the view that social-science knowledge should serve policymaking is Robert S. Lynd, *Knowledge for What?* (Princeton, N.J.: Princeton Univ. Press, 1948), especially pp. 1–3. A somewhat unsophisticated and overstated claim for the potential contributions of knowledge to solving social problems is George A. Lundberg, *Can Science Save Us?* (N.Y.: Longmans, Green, 2d ed., 1961), especially pp. 18ff. A more careful analysis is Alexander H. Leighton, *Human Relations in a Changing World* (N.Y.: Dutton, 1949).

For a view emphasizing the limited usefulness of science, see Hans J. Morgenthau, *Scientific Man vs. Power Politics* (London: Latimer House, 1947). C. Wright Mills, *The Sociological Imagination* (N.Y.: Oxford Univ. Press, 1959), is very stimulating in this context.

On the problems of integrating natural-science knowledge into policymaking, see Don K. Price, *Government and Science* (N.Y.: New York Univ. Press, 1954); J. Stefan Dupre and Sanford A. Lakoff, *Science and the Nation: Policy and Politics* (Englewood Cliffs, N.J.: Prentice-Hall, 1962); especially Robert Gilpin and Christopher Wright, eds., *Scientists and National Policymaking* (N.Y.: Columbia Univ. Press, 1964); Sanford A. Lakoff, ed., *Knowledge and Power: Essays on Science and Government* (N.Y.: Free Press of Glencoe, 1966); and Don K. Price, *The Scientific Estate* (Cambridge, Mass.: Harvard Univ. Press, 1965). Stimulating, though somewhat naive, is Marcus C. Goodall's *Science and the Politician* (Cambridge, Mass.: Schenkman, 1965). An interesting case study is Robert Gilpin, *American Scientists and Nuclear Weapons Policy* (Princeton, N.J.: Princeton Univ. Press, 1962).

Nearly all of these books ignore the social sciences. A distinguished exception is an important book in German: Klaus Lompe, *Wissenschaftliche Beratung der Politik* (*Scientific Consultation of Politics*) (Göttingen: Otto Schwartz, 1966). Another interesting discussion in German is Heiner Flöhr and Klaus Lompe, eds., *Wissenschaftler und Politiker—Partner oder Gegner?* (*Scientists and Politicians—Partners or Adversaries?*) (Göttingen: Otto Schwartz, 1967).

The novels of C. P. Snow include some of the most stimulating expositions of the difficulties of integrating science and policymaking. His basic thesis is that there are two different "cultures" between which bridges are hard to build; see his *The New Men* (1954), *The Affair* (1960), and *Corridors of Power* (1964). His *Science and Government* (London: Oxford Univ. Press, 1961) is especially important; it is based on the Bodkin Lectures he presented at Harvard in 1960, and in it he presents his thesis while discussing two critical scientific policy issues that Winston Churchill faced before and during World War II. A representative anthology of Snow's work is Stanley Weintraub, ed., *C. P. Snow: A Spectrum* (N.Y.: Scribner's, 1963). For critics of Snow, see the Earl of Birkenhead, *The Professor and the Prime Minister* (Boston: Houghton Mifflin, 1963), and Albert Wohlstetter, "Scientists, Peers, and Strategy," *Foreign Affairs,* Apr. 1963.

Useful introductions to the sociology of science are Bernard Barber, *Science and the Social Order* (Glencoe, Ill.: Free Press, 1952), and Bernard Barber and Walter Hirsch, eds., *The Sociology of Science* (N.Y.: Free Press, 1962). On the contemporary relevance of scientific knowledge for an acute problem, and especially its limitations, see Quincy Wright, William M. Evan, and Morton Deutsch, eds., *Preventing World War III: Some Proposals* (N.Y.: Simon and Schuster, 1962).

For illustrations of "dangerous" knowledge that is developing, see Seymour M. Faber and Roger H. L. Wilson, eds., *Man and Civilization: Control of the Mind* (N.Y.: McGraw-Hill, 1961), pp. 77ff. The idea of "intelligence amplifiers" is presented by W. Ross Ashby, "Design for an Intelligence Amplifier," in C. E. Shannon and J. McCarthy, eds., *Auto-*

mata Studies (Princeton, N.J.: Princeton Univ. Press, 1956); see also Arthur L. Samuel, "Artificial Intelligence: A Frontier of Automation," *Annals of the AAPSS,* CCCXL (Mar. 1962), 10ff, and James T. Culbertson, *The Minds of Robots* (Urbana: Univ. of Illinois Press, 1963). A provocative anti-Utopia about nuclear blackmailing by "private" groups is Mordecai Roshwald, *A Small Armageddon* (London: Heinemann, 1962). A comprehensive preview of one of the most difficult problems facing policymaking is provided in the two volumes of the collection by H. Wentworth, ed., *Taming Megalopolis* (Garden City, N.Y.: Doubleday, Anchor Books, 1967). A preview of the critical problems posed by future arms developments, going far beyond the well-known issues of nuclear weapons, is given in Nigel Calder, ed., *Unless Peace Comes: A Scientific Forecast of New Weapons* (London: Allen Lane, 1968). A completely different and very worthwhile illustration of a public-policy problem, which also illustrates a "systems-analysis approach" to it and thus indicates the potential benefits of a more refined policy-analysis method, is Richard R. Nelson *et al., Technology, Economic Growth, and Public Policy* (Washington, D.C.: The Brookings Institution, 1967).

For the concept of a "policy science," see Harold D. Lasswell, "The Policy Orientation," in David Lerner and Harold D. Lasswell, eds., *The Policy Sciences: Recent Developments in Scope and Method* (Stanford: Stanford Univ. Press, 1951), which should be read by anyone interested in this subject. Some pioneering modern treatments of the idea of shaping the future of mankind by means of conscious action based on knowledge are Dennis Gabor, *Inventing the Future* (N.Y.: Lechner & Warburg, 1963) and Bertrand de Jouvenel, *The Art of Conjecture* (N.Y.: Basic Books, 1967), first published in French in 1964. An interesting and rather unique collection of teaching-examples of analysis of some social problems is Heinz-Dietrich Ortlieb and Friedrich-Wilhelm Dörge, *Wirtschafts- und Sozialpolitik: Modellanalysen politischer Probleme* (*Economic and Social Policy: Exemplary Analyses of Political Problems*) (Opladen: C. W. Leske, 1964, 3d ed., 1967). A comprehensive theory of societal guidance, basic to policy science, is presented in Amitai Etzioni, *The Active Society: A Theory of Societal and Political Processes* (N.Y.: Free Press of Glencoe, 1968, forthcoming).

CHAPTER 2

The concept of "public policy" is often used but seldom adequately discussed. A distinguished exception is Morton Kroll, "Hypotheses and Design for the Study of Public Policies in the United States," *Midwest*

Journal of Political Science, XI (Nov. 1962), 363ff. Some interesting and relevant articles are concentrated in the various volumes of *Public Policy: Yearbook of the Graduate School of Public Administration,* Harvard University (Cambridge, Mass.: Graduate School of Public Administration). An important new periodical dealing with relevant issues is *The Public Interest.* For an important distinction between policymaking (or "strategic planning") and other types of planning, see Robert N. Anthony, *Planning and Control Systems: A Framework for Analysis* (Boston: Harvard Graduate School of Public Administration, 1965).

A comprehensive though overcritical discussion of the concept of "public interest" is Glendon Schubert, *The Public Interest: A Critique of the Theory of a Political Concept* (N.Y.: Free Press of Glencoe, 1960). For an essay supporting some aspects of the concept of "common interest" against the group approach of Arthur F. Bentley and his school, see Leo Weinstein, "The Group Approach," in Herbert J. Storing, ed., *Essays on the Scientific Study of Politics* (N.Y.: Holt, Rinehart, and Winston, 1962). See also Carl J. Friedrich, ed., *The Public Interest* (N.Y.: Asherton Univ. Press, 1962), and Richard E. Flathman, *The Public Interest* (N.Y.: John Wiley, 1966).

A convenient survey of philosophies of history, which clearly brings out the different opinions on free will vs. determinism, is Patrick Gardiner, ed., *Theories of History* (N.Y.: Free Press of Glencoe, 1959). My own position is very near to Isaiah Berlin's in *Historic Inevitability* (London: Oxford Univ. Press, 1954), especially pp. 30ff. See also Haralit Ofstad, *An Inquiry into the Freedom of Decision* (London: Allen and Unwin, 1961).

One of the best discussions of models as a tool for analysis is Karl W. Deutsch's *The Nerves of Government: Models of Political Communication and Control* (N.Y.: Free Press of Glencoe, 2d ed., 1966), especially Part I. The book includes many stimulating ideas on government as a policymaking system and repays careful study. On models see also Herbert A. Simon and Allen Newell, "Models: Their Uses and Limitations," in Leonard D. White, ed., *The State of the Social Sciences* (Chicago: Univ. of Chicago Press, 1956).

On the importance of tacit knowledge in scientific discovery, see the literature cited in the footnote on p. 20.

CHAPTERS 3–6

The most comprehensive, systematic theory and framework for evaluating action is presented in Bertram M. Gross, *The Managing of Organi-*

zations (N.Y.: Free Press of Glencoe, 1964), II, 467ff. Some parts of the literature aim at a systematic theory of evaluation, with the help of concepts and ideas taken mainly from economic theory. It is most developed for evaluating investments, and is generally quite technical. Good, relatively non-technical introductions to relevant subjects are E. L. Grant, *Principles of Engineering Economics* (N.Y.: Ronald, 1958); F. Paul de Garmo, *Engineering Economy* (N.Y.: Macmillan, 3d ed., 1960); William Warren Haynes, *Managerial Economics: Analysis and Cases* (Homewood, Ill.: Dorsey, 1963); Raymond J. Chamber, *Accounting, Evaluation, and Economic Behavior* (Englewood Cliffs, N.J.: Prentice-Hall, 1966); R. N. McKean, *Efficiency in Government Through Systems Analysis* (N.Y.: John Wiley, 1958); and Arthur Maass *et al., Design of Water-Resource Systems* (Cambridge, Mass.: Harvard Univ. Press, 1962), Part I. A good theory of criteria for evaluations which is oriented toward policymaking is in Charles J. Hitch and Roland N. McKean, *The Economics of Defense in the Nuclear Age* (Cambridge, Mass.: Harvard Univ. Press, 1960), Part II.

Some problems of quantification in administrative operations are discussed in Bureau of the Budget, *Measuring Productivity of Federal Government Organizations* (Washington, D.C.: U.S. Govt. Printing Office, 1964). A more general discussion is Eliot D. Chapple and Leonard R. Sayles, *The Measure of Management* (N.Y.: Macmillan, 1961). A detailed discussion of a specific tool is Spencer A. Tuckner, *Successful Managerial Control by Ratio-Analysis* (N.Y.: Macmillan, 1961). On the possibility of measuring real outputs of social welfare, see Jerome Rothenberg, *The Measurement of Social Welfare* (Englewood Cliffs, N.J.: Prentice-Hall, 1961); Ronald G. Ridker, ed., *Economic Costs of Air Pollution: Studies in Management* (N.Y.: Praeger, 1966); and Robert Dorfman, ed., *Measuring Benefits of Government Investments* (Washington, D.C.: The Brookings Institution, 1965).

The literature dealing with the evaluation of weapon-systems development, which tries to identify reliable secondary criteria for selecting contractors and for incentives is very stimulating. See Merton J. Peck and Frederic M. Scherer, *The Weapons Acquisition Process: An Economic Analysis* (Boston: Harvard Graduate School of Business Administration, 1962), and Frederic M. Scherer, *The Weapons Acquisition Process: Economic Incentives* (Boston: Harvard Graduate School of Business Administration, 1964).

A good, though outdated, annotated bibliography covering most of the literature is Paul Wasserman, *Measurement and Evaluation of Organizational Performance* (Ithaca, N.Y.: Cornell Graduate School of Business and Public Administration, 1959).

On the tendency to adjust activities so as to achieve the highest output in terms of those items that are measured, see Peter M. Blau, *The Dynamics of Bureaucracy* (Chicago: Univ. of Chicago Press, 2d, rev. ed., 1963), pp. 33ff. On the tendency to adjust the image of desired outputs to match the actual outputs, see Leon Festinger, *A Theory of Cognitive Dissonance* (Stanford: Stanford Univ. Press, 1957), esp. pp. 32ff; Jack W. Brehm and Arthur R. Cohen, *Explorations in Cognitive Dissonance* (N.Y.: John Wiley, 1962); and Leon Festinger, *Conflict, Decision, and Dissonance* (London: Tavistock, 1964).

CHAPTERS 7 AND 8

For a good annotated bibliography on decisionmaking, see Paul Wasserman and Fred S. Silander, *Decisionmaking: An Annotated Bibliography* (Ithaca, N.Y.: Cornell Graduate School of Business and Public Administration, 1958), and the supplement to it published by Cornell in 1964.

On individual decisionmaking, see W. Enger Vinacke, *The Psychology of Thinking* (N.Y.: McGraw-Hill, 1952), and D. M. Johnson, *Psychology of Thought and Judgment* (N.Y.: Harper, 1955). For illustrations of some modern field studies, presented within a systematic theoretical and conceptual framework, see Jerome S. Bruner *et al., A Study of Thinking* (N.Y.: John Wiley, 1956), and Orville G. Brim, Jr., *et al., Personality and Decision Processes* (Stanford: Stanford Univ. Press, 1962). A concise summary of findings and methods is provided in Donald W. Taylor, *Thinking* (Technical Report 7, Dept. of Psychology and Dept. of Industrial Administration, Yale Univ., Sept. 1962). A convenient collection is Ward Edwards and Amos Tversky, eds., *Decision Making* (Middlesex, Eng.: Penguin, 1967). For a different approach, see M. L. J. Abercrombie, *The Anatomy of Judgment* (London: Hutchinson, 3d ed., 1965).

On small-group decisionmaking, a good up-to-date survey in Barry E. Collins and Harold Guetzkow, *A Social Psychology of Group Processes for Decisionmaking* (N.Y.: John Wiley, 1964). For a collection of research reports and theoretical papers, see Darwin Cartwright and Alvin Zander, eds., *Group Dynamics: Research and Theory* (N.Y.: Harper, 2d ed., 1960). On family decisionmaking see Nelson N. Foote, ed., *Household Decisionmaking* (N.Y.: New York Univ. Press, 1961).

On organizational decisionmaking, see Herbert A. Simon's classic *Administrative Behavior: A Study of Decisionmaking Processes in Administrative Organizations* (N.Y.: Macmillan, 2d ed., 1957); William J. Gore and J. W. Dyson, eds., *The Making of Decisions: A Reader in*

Administrative Behavior (N.Y.: Free Press of Glencoe, 1964); William J. Gore, *Administrative Decisionmaking: A Heuristic Model* (N.Y.: John Wiley, 1964); Marcus Alexis and Charles Z. Wilson, *Organization Decision Making* (Englewood Cliffs, N.J.: Prentice-Hall, 1967); and two papers in James G. March, ed., *Handbook of Organizations* (Chicago: Rand McNally, 1965), namely, Donald W. Taylor, "Decisionmaking and Problem Solving" (pp. 48–86), and Julian Feldman and Herschel E. Kanter, "Organizational Decisionmaking" (pp. 614–644). An innovative monograph is Anthony Downs, *Bureaucratic Structure and Decisionmaking* (Santa Monica, Calif.: RAND Corp., 1966). Relevant also are two very modern treatments of public-administration behavior, namely, Gordon Tullock, *The Politics of Bureaucracy* (Washington, D.C.: Public Affairs Press, 1965), and Anthony Downs, *Inside Bureaucracy* (Boston: Little, Brown, 1967).

For collections of public-administration case studies, see Harold Stein, ed., *Public Administration and Policy Development* (N.Y.: Harcourt, Brace, 1952); Emmette S. Redford, ed., *Public Administration and Policy Formation* (Austin: Univ. of Texas Press, 1958); F. M. G. Willson, *Administrators in Action* (London: Allen & Unwin, 1961), vol. I; and Gerald Rhodes, *Administrators in Action* (London: Allen & Unwin, 1965), vol. II. For a decision-focused case study, see Richard M. Cyert et al., "Observation of a Business Decision," *Journal of Business,* XXIX (1956), 237ff. Interesting also is the collection by Kent Roberts Greenfield, ed., *Command Decisions* (N.Y.: Harcourt, Brace, 1959). On organizational decisionmaking, see also James G. March, "Some Recent Substantive and Methodological Developments in the Theory of Organizational Decisionmaking," in Austin Ranney, ed., *Essays on the Behavioral Study of Politics* (Urbana: Univ. of Illinois Press, 1962). A sophisticated theory of organizational decisionmaking is presented in Richard M. Cyert and James G. March, *A Behavioral Theory of the Firm* (Englewood Cliffs, N.J.: Prentice-Hall, 1963).

On community and municipal decisionmaking, see Martin Meyerson and Edward G. Banfield, *Politics, Planning, and the Public Interest: The Case of Public Housing in Chicago* (Glencoe, Ill.: Free Press, 1955); Robert A. Dahl, *Who Governs?* (New Haven, Conn.: Yale Univ. Press, 1961); Edward C. Banfield, *Political Influence* (N.Y.: Free Press of Glencoe, 1961); Roscoe C. Martin et al., *Decisions in Syracuse* (Bloomington: Indiana Univ. Press, 1961); Wallace S. Sayre and Herbert Kaufman, *Governing New York City* (N.Y.: Russell Sage Foundation, 1960); Oliver P. Williams and Charles R. Adrian, *Four Cities: A Study in Comparative Policy Making* (Philadelphia: Univ. of Pennsylvania Press, 1963); and Alan A. Altshuler, *The City Planning Process:*

A Political Analysis (Ithaca, N.Y.: Cornell Univ. Press, 1965).

Case studies on national policymaking are Stephen K. Bailey, *Congress Makes a Law* (N.Y.: Columbia Univ. Press, 1950); Earl Latham, *The Group Basis of Politics: A Study in Basing-Point Legislation* (Ithaca, N.Y.: Cornell Univ. Press, 1962); Jason L. Finkle, *The President Makes a Decision: A Study of Dixon-Yates* (Ann Arbor: Univ. of Michigan, Institute of Public Administration, 1960); Aaron Wildavsky, *Dixon-Yates: A Study in Politics* (New Haven, Conn.: Yale Univ. Press, 1962). Allison Griffith, *The National Aeronautics and Space Act: A Study of the Development of Public Policy* (Washington, D.C.: Public Affairs Press, 1962), and Raymond A. Bauer, Ithiel de Sola Pool, and Lewis Anthony Dexter, *American Business and Public Policy* (N.Y.: Asherton, 1963), provide much information on actual policymaking, in particular on why pressure groups have smaller effects than they are expected to. Good case studies on military policymaking can be found in Harold Stein, ed., *American Civil-Military Decisions: A Book of Case Studies* (University, Ala.: Univ. of Alabama Press, 1963). Also interesting are Vernon Van Dyke, *Pride and Power: The Rationale of the Space Program* (Urbana: Univ. of Illinois Press, 1964), and Richard Worcester, *Roots of British Air Policy* (London: Hodden and Stoughton, 1966). A case study within a decisionmaking framework is Robert A. Levine, *The Arms Debate* (Cambridge, Mass.: Harvard Univ. Press, 1963).

A general framework for the study of decisionmaking, applied to foreign policymaking, is presented in Richard C. Snyder, *et al., Foreign Policy Decisionmaking* (N.Y.: Free Press of Glencoe, 1962); the first part of this collection, which includes the suggested framework, was published in 1954. For a systematic set of research proposals covering most facets of some central decisionmaking processes, see Richard C. Snyder and James A. Robinson, *National and International Decisionmaking* (N.Y.: The Institute for International Order, 1961). Important also is Burton M. Sapin, *The Making of United States Foreign Policy* (Washington, D.C.: The Brookings Institution, 1966).

On the usefulness and dangers of journalistic impressions as a source of data and ideas, see Anthony Sampson, *Anatomy of Britain* (N.Y.: Harper, 2d ed., 1965). The importance of writings by participant observers is best demonstrated by Arthur M. Schlesinger, Jr., *A Thousand Days: John F. Kennedy in the White House* (N.Y.: Houghton Mifflin, 1965), and Theodore C. Sorenson, *Kennedy* (N.Y.: Harper, 1965). Much less revealing, and more typical of this type of literature, is Herbert Morrison, *Government and Parliament* (Oxford: Clarendon Press, 1959). A good discussion of political autobiographies is G. P. Gooch,

Studies in Diplomacy and Statecraft (N.Y.: Longmans, Green, 1942), pp. 227–290.

CHAPTERS 9–11

Most books and articles dealing with social and political behavior include some material on policymaking, but, as yet, only a few books have focused on policymaking as a central political-social organizational process. A unique attempt in this direction is William C. Mitchell, *The American Polity* (N.Y.: Free Press of Glencoe, 1962). Very relevant also is Zbigniew Brzezinski and Samuel P. Huntington, *Political Power: USA/USSR* (N.Y.: Viking, 1964), and Peter H. Juviler and Henry W. Martin, eds., *Soviet Policymaking* (N.Y.: Praeger, 1966). Unique in many respects is John R. Raser, "Personal Characteristics of Political Decision-Makers: A Literature Review" (La Jolla, Calif.: Western Behavioral Science Institute, 1965). See also W. H. G. Armytage, *The Rise of the Technocracy: A Social History* (London: Routledge and Kegan Paul, 1965).

Case studies and monographs also include much relevant data. Besides those mentioned for Chapters 7 and 8, a recent one dealing with the U.S.S.R. is Sidney I. Ploss, *Conflict and Decisionmaking in Soviet Russia: A Case Study of Agricultural Policy, 1913–1963* (Princeton, N.J.: Princeton Univ. Press, 1965). An important study of the role of the courts in public policymaking in the United States is Glendon Schubert, *Judicial Policy-Making* (Glenview, Ill.: Scott, Foresman, 1968).

Relatively more attention is devoted to economic policymaking and planning. See Albert O. Hirschman, *Journeys Toward Progress: Studies of Economic Policymaking in Latin America* (N.Y.: Twentieth Century Fund, 1963); most of the papers in Everett E. Hagen, ed., *Planning Economic Development* (Homewood, Ill.: Irwin, 1963); J. Hackett and A. Hackett, *Economic Planning in France* (Cambridge, Mass.: Harvard Univ. Press, 1963); J. C. R. Dow, *The Management of the British Economy, 1945–1960* (Cambridge, Eng.: Cambridge Univ. Press, 1964); Albert Waterston, *Development Planning: Lessons of Experience* (Baltimore: Johns Hopkins Press, 1965); A. H. Hanson, *The Process of Planning: A Study of India's Five-Year Plans, 1950–1964* (N.Y.: Oxford Univ. Press, 1966); and the *National Planning Series* edited by Bertram M. Gross and published by Syracuse Univ. Press. Highly readable and illuminating is Edward S. Flash, Jr., *Economic Advice and Presidential Leadership* (N.Y.: Columbia Univ. Press, 1965).

The myth of authoritarian efficiency is exploded by Burton H. Klein,

Germany's Preparations for War (Cambridge, Mass.: Harvard Univ. Press, 1959), and Alan S. Milware, *The German Economy at War* (London: Athlone, 1965).

With a few such exceptions, the interested reader has no choice but to wade through masses of general books and collect the scattered items relevant to policymaking.

CHAPTERS 12–14

For a simple exposition of some of the elements of pure-rationality decisionmaking, and a good introduction to some related concepts and techniques, see Irwin D. J. Bross, *Design for Decision* (N.Y.: Macmillan, 1953). For comprehensive and advanced treatments, see C. W. Churchman, *Prediction and Optimal Decision* (Englewood Cliffs, N.J.: Prentice-Hall, 1961), and Peter C. Fishburn, *Decision and Value Theory* (N.Y.: John Wiley, 1964). The ideal of pure rationality is basic to operations research and the modern management sciences; see David W. Miller and Martin K. Starr, *Executive Decisions and Operations Research* (Englewood Cliffs, N.J.: Prentice-Hall, 1960). For a critic from within, see C. West Churchman, "Decision and Value Theory," in Russell L. Ackoff, ed., *Progress in Operations Research* (N.Y.: John Wiley, 1961), I, 35ff.

For different views on the ultimate possibility of reducing all problems to algorithms, or at least to heuristic computer programs, compare Allen Newell and Herbert A. Simon, "Heuristic Problem Solving: The Next Advance in Operations Research," *Operations Research,* VI (Jan.–Feb. 1958), 1ff, and Herbert A. Simon, *The New Science of Management Decision* (N.Y.: Harper, 1960), on the one hand, with Harold D. Lasswell, "Current Studies of the Decision Process: Automation versus Creativity," *The Western Political Quarterly,* VIII (Sept. 1955), 381ff, on the other hand. A nice illustration of the far-reaching possibilities of pure-rationality calculation is Victor E. Smith, *Electronic Computations of Human Diets* (East Lansing: Michigan State Univ. Graduate School of Business Administration, 1964).

On the problems of measuring and aggregating social values, see Kenneth J. Arrow, *Social Choice and Individual Value* (N.Y.: John Wiley, 2d ed., 1963) and Jerome Rothenberg, *The Measurement of Social Welfare* (Englewood Cliffs, N.J.: Prentice-Hall, 1961).

The economically rational model is elaborated in Charles J. Hitch and Roland N. McKean, *The Economics of Defense in the Nuclear Age* (Cambridge, Mass.: Harvard Univ. Press, 1961). It is implicitly, and often explicitly, accepted in operations research as the "optimal" (but not ideal) model. For its application to problems of research decisions, see Russell L. Ackoff, *Scientific Method: Optimizing Applied Research Decisions* (N.Y.: John Wiley, 1962), especially Chapter 2. It is also the basis of systems analysis. See the collection by E. S. Quade, ed., *Analysis for Military Decisions* (Chicago: Rand McNally, 1964); Thomas A. Goldman, *Cost-Effectiveness Analysis: New Approaches in Decision-making* (N.Y.: Praeger, 1967); and Stephen A. Margolin, *Public Investment Criteria: Benefit-Cost Analysis for Planned Economic Growth* (Cambridge, Mass.: M.I.T. Press, 1967). An interesting case study is Robert E. Kuenne, *The Polaris Missile Strike: A General Economic Systems Analysis* (Columbus: Ohio State Univ. Press, 1966).

The "theory of the second-best" was developed in R. G. Lipsey and Kelvin Lancaster, "The General Theory of Second-Best," *Review of Economic Studies,* XXIV (1956–57), 11ff.

The sequential-decision model was developed by Burton H. Klein. See his "The Decisionmaking Problem in Development," in National Bureau of Economic Research, *The Rate and Direction of Inventive Activity* (Princeton, N.J.: Princeton Univ. Press, 1962).

The incremental-change model is discussed in the various writings of Charles E. Lindblom. It was presented in a most provocative form in his "The Science of 'Muddling Through,'" *Public Administration Review,* XIX (1959), 79–88, and is further developed in David Braybrooke and Charles E. Lindblom, *A Strategy of Decision* (N.Y.: Free Press of Glencoe, 1963). A worthwhile paper bringing out the shared basis of the sequential-decision model, the incremental-change model, and Hirschman's recommendation for an unbalanced development strategy is Albert O. Hirschman and Charles E. Lindblom, "Economic Development, Research and Development, and Policymaking: Some Converging Views," *Behavioral Science,* VII (Apr. 1962), 211ff. For an earlier criticism of the incremental-change model, see my "Muddling Through—Science or Inertia?" *Public Administration Review,* XXIV (Sept. 1964), 154ff.

There are some interesting possibilities for mathematical models based on gradualism and on using experience and intuition. One such model of "approximation in policy space" is presented by Richard Bellman, "Dynamic Programming and Markovian Decision Processes, with Particular Application to Baseball and Chess," in Edwin F. Beckenbach, ed., *Applied Combinational Mathematics* (N.Y.: John Wiley, 1967), pp. 221ff.

Some very interesting papers on decisionmaking can be found in Carl J. Friedrich, ed., *Nomos VII. Rational Decision* (N.Y.: Atherton, 1964), and the volumes of *Papers on Non-Market Decision Making*

(Charlottesville: Thomas Jefferson Center, Univ. of Virginia, starting in 1966). See also the new periodical *Socio-Economic Planning Sciences.*

The satisfying model originated in the writings of Herbert A. Simon. See Herbert A. Simon, *Models of Man* (N.Y.: John Wiley, 1957), pp. 291ff; James G. March and Herbert A. Simon, *Organizations* (N.Y.: John Wiley, 1958), pp. 136ff; and the introduction to the second edition of Herbert A. Simon, *Administrative Behavior* (N.Y.: Macmillan, 1957). It is presented in a more advanced form in Richard M. Cyert and James G. March, *A Behavioral Theory of the Firm* (Englewood Cliffs, N.J.: Prentice-Hall, 1964). An interesting normative analysis based on the satisfying concept is presented in Oliver E. Williamson, *The Economics of Discretionary Behavior: Managerial Objectives in a Theory of the Firm* (Englewood Cliffs, N.J.: Prentice-Hall, 1964).

On extrasensory perception (ESP), see: George R. Price, "Science and the Supernatural," *Science,* CXXII (Aug. 26, 1955), 359ff; S. G. Soal, "On 'Science and the Supernatural,'" *Science,* CXXIII (Jan. 6, 1956), 9ff; J. B. Rhine, "Comments on 'Science and the Supernatural,'" *loc. cit.,* pp. 11ff; Paul E. Meehl and Michael Scriven, "Compatibility of Science and ESP," *loc. cit.,* pp. 15ff; and George R. Price, "Where Is the Definitive Experiment?" *loc. cit.,* pp. 17ff. All these articles are in reprint P-279 in the Bobbs-Merrill Reprint Series in the Social Sciences. For a good anthology on that subject, see Fabian Gudas, ed., *Extrasensory Perception* (N.Y.: Scribner's, 1961).

On subception, see R. S. Lazarus and R. A. Mclearly, "Automatic Discrimination Without Awareness: A Study of Subception," *Psychological Review,* LXIII (1956), 74ff; and R. S. Lazarus, "Subception: Fact or Artifact? A Reply to Eriksen," *loc. cit.,* pp. 343ff.

A convenient illustration of extremely pro-intuition literature is Virginia Burden, *The Process of Intuition* (N.Y.: Greenwich, 1957). For a discussion of Thomas Carlyle's position on the danger that "rationality" can "corrupt" leadership, see Eugene Jennings, *An Anatomy of Leadership: Princes, Heroes, and Supermen* (N.Y.: Harper, 1960), p. 74.

For a different classification of modes of decisionmaking, including both descriptive and normative elements, see Harold D. Lasswell, *The Decision Process* (College Park, Maryland: Bureau of Governmental Research, College of Business and Public Administration, Univ. of Maryland, 1956).

For a discussion of the Prisoner's Dilemma, see R. Duncan Luce and Howard Raiffa, *Games and Decisions* (N.Y.: John Wiley, 1958), pp. 94ff. See also Anatol Rappaport, *Strategy and Conscience* (N.Y.: Harper, 1964), pp. 48ff, and Anatol Rappaport and A. M. Chammah, *Prisoner's Dilemma* (Ann Arbor: Univ. of Michigan Press, 1965).

An important pioneering attempt by decision scientists to at least face the possibility that extrarational processes may sometimes be optimal is Maynard W. Shelly and Glenn L. Bryan, eds., *Human Judgements and Optimality* (N.Y.: John Wiley, 1965). For very balanced discussions of complex decisionmaking, see Louis H. Mayo and Ernest M. Jones, "Legal-Policy Decision Process: Alternative Thinking and the Prediction Function," *The George Washington Law Review,* XXXIII (Oct. 1964), 318–456; and Sir Geoffrey Vickers, *The Art of Judgment: A Study of Policymaking* (London: Chapman & Hall, 1965). A good example of rational research on the variables which influence extrarational processes, in this case productivity, is Donald Pelz and Frank M. Andrews, *Scientists in Organizations* (N.Y.: John Wiley, 1967).

On the possibility and desirability of inventing new and dominant solutions, see Henry Metcalf and L. Urwish, eds., *Dynamic Administration: The Collected Papers of Mary Parker Follett* (N.Y.: Harper, n.d.), especially pp. 30ff, and Max C. Otto, *Science and the Moral Life* (N.Y.: New American Library, 1949), pp. 65ff. Sir Frederic Bartlett, *Thinking: An Experimental and Social Study* (N.Y.: Basic Books, 1958), makes an important distinction between thinking within closed systems and adventurous thinking. Compromise, in its positive sense, may also implicitly involve constructing an overall dominant alternative; see T. V. Smith, *The Ethics of Compromise and the Art of Containment* (Boston: Starr King, 1956), pp. 45ff.

On social-system accounting, see Raymond A. Bauer, *Social Indicators* (Cambridge, Mass.: M.I.T. Press, 1966), and the separate version of Bertram M. Gross, *The State of the Nation: Social-System Accounting* (London: Tavistock, 1966). See also the essays on "Social Goals and Indicators for American Society," Vol. I and II, *The Annals of the American Academy of Political and Social Science,* May and September 1967.

For some interesting observations on the history of quasi-randomization as a decisionmaking technique, see F. N. David, *Games, Gods, and Gambling* (N.Y.: Hafner, 1962), pp. 13ff. See also Richard Lewinsohn, *Science, Prophecy and Prediction* (N.Y.: Harper, 1961).

For a discussion of bases for predictions, see Daniel Bell, "Twelve Modes of Prediction," in Julius Gould, ed., *Penguin Survey of the Social Sciences, 1965* (Middlesex, Eng.: Penguin, 1965). A very extensive survey of prediction methods is Erich Jantsch, *Technological Forecasting in Perspective* (Paris: OECD Working Document DAS/SPR/66.12, 1966). Modern prediction methods, such as Delphi and operational gaming, are discussed in Olaf Helmer, *Social Technology* (N.Y.:

Basic Books, 1966). A stimulating article on predicting political be-havior is Benjamin Akzin, "On Conjecture in Political Science," *Political Studies,* XIV, no. 1 (Feb. 1960), 1–14. Also very important is William F. Butler and Robert A. Karesh, *How Business Economists Forecast* (Englewood Cliffs, N.J.: Prentice-Hall, 1966).

Very interesting is the substantive work of futuristics, as presented, for instance, by the American Academy of Arts and Sciences' Commis-sion on the Year 2000. See "Toward the Year 2000: Work in Progress," *Daedalus,* Summer 1967. See also Robert Jungh and Johan Galtung, eds., *Mankind 2000* (Oslo: Norwegian Univ. Press, 1968), and Herman Kahn and Anthony J. Wiener, *The Year 2000* (N.Y.: Macmillan, 1967). A new periodical devoted to this subject is *Futures,* to be started in 1968 by Iliffe Sciences and Technology Publications, London.

CHAPTER 15

The reader interested in a comprehensive frame of reference for viewing the policymaking system should familiarize himself with the concepts and frameworks of the systems approach. The most comprehensive textbook is Arthur D. Hall, *A Methodology for Systems Engineering* (Princeton, N.J.: Van Nostrand, 1962). The reader who dislikes engineering jargon may prefer Richard A. Johnson *et al., The Theory and Management of Systems* (N.Y.: McGraw-Hill, 1963), espe-cially Part I, and the less technical papers in Donald P. Eckman, ed., *Systems: Research and Design* (N.Y.: John Wiley, 1961), and in Mihajlo D. Mesarovie, ed., *Views on General Systems Theory: Proceed-ings of the Second Systems Symposium at Case Institute of Technology* (N.Y.: John Wiley, 1964). An annual collection of papers on various facets and levels of systems theory are *General Systems: Yearbook of the Society for General Systems Research* (Ann Arbor, Mich.: Society for General Systems Research, starting in 1950).

Neither modern political theory nor the contemporary management sciences engage in critical examinations or normative prescriptions about the macro-structure of the political system. Indeed, nowadays even analytical literature on the advantages and disadvantages of different kinds of regimes under various conditions is out of fashion, perhaps because the present research patterns in the behavioral sciences encour-age preoccupation with micro-issues, on the one hand, and because the tense international situation and the ideological nature of the cold war discourage critical examination and exposition of the relative nature of basic social institutions, on the other hand. In any case, very little literature is available on the basic structural problems of the political order. A trail-blazing work is Robert A. Dahl and Charles E. Lindblom, *Politics, Economics, and Welfare* (N.Y.: Harper, 1953). Most important is Charles E. Lindblom, *The Intelligence of Democracy: Decisionmaking Through Mutual Adjustment* (N.Y.: Free Press of Glencoe, 1965), and Paul Diesing, *Reason in Society: Five Types of Decision and Their Social Conditions* (Urbana: Univ. of Illinois Press, 1962). These books deal with different types of system structures and aggregation functions, comparing their effectiveness under various circumstances.

Of more limited scope, but valuable in exposing the basic functional-structural assumptions of different versions of democracy, is Robert A. Dahl, *A Preface to Democratic Theory* (Chicago: Univ. of Chicago Press, 1956). Also important is Karl W. Deutsch, *The Nerves of Government: Models of Political Communication and Control* (N.Y.: Free Press of Glencoe, 2d ed., 1966), which views government as a cybernetic system. David Easton, *A Systems Analysis of Political Life* (N.Y.: John Wiley, 1965), also views the political system mainly as a policymaking structure. A shorter version of the latter book is David Easton, *A Framework for Political Analysis* (Englewood Cliffs, N.J.: Prentice-Hall, 1965).

A general formulation of polycentricity as a principle for managing social tasks is in Michael Polanyi, *The Logic of Liberty* (Chicago: Univ. of Chicago Press, 1951), pp. 111ff. Applications of market models to the political system include Anthony Downs, *An Economic Theory of Democracy* (N.Y.: Harper, 1957), and James M. Buchanan and Gordon Tullock, *The Calculus of Consent* (Ann Arbor: Univ. of Michigan Press, 1962). Interesting is the application of this approach to public finance, in James M. Buchanan, *Public Finance in Democratic Process: Fiscal Institutions and Individual Choice* (Chapel Hill: Univ. of North Carolina Press, 1967). As a counterbalance to the assumptions of the last three books, the reader might do well to read William Kornhauser, *The Politics of Mass Society* (N.Y.: Free Press of Glencoe, 1959). Marcus Olson, Jr., *The Logic of Collective Action: Public Goods and the Theory of Groups* (Cambridge, Mass.: Harvard Univ. Press, 1965), is also relevant here.

The modern bargaining approach to politics is in many ways a continuation of the group approach presented in Arthur F. Bentley, *The Process of Government* (Chicago: Univ. of Chicago Press, 1908). A modern version of this approach is David B. Truman, *The Governmental Process* (N.Y.: Knopf, 1951). An illuminating analysis of Congress in terms of pressures and bargaining is Bertram M. Gross, *The Legislative Struggle: A Study in Social Combat* (N.Y.: McGraw-Hill, 1953).

An explicit bargaining model of the political process is developed in

Charles Lindblom, *Bargaining: The Hidden Hand in Government* (Santa Monica, Calif.: RAND Corp., 1955). Rigorous theories of bargaining, based on the theory of games, are presented in Duncan Black, *The Theory of Committees and Elections* (Cambridge, Eng.: Cambridge Univ. Press, 1958), and William H. Riker, *The Theory of Political Coalitions* (New Haven, Conn.: Yale Univ. Press, 1962).

On PERT, see Robert W. Miller, "How to Plan and Control with PERT," in Edward C. Bursk and John F. Chapman, eds., *New Decisionmaking Tools for Managers* (Cambridge, Mass.: Harvard Univ. Press, 1963). See also Albert Battersby, *Network Analysis for Planning and Scheduling* (N.Y.: Macmillan, 1964).

CHAPTER 16

Very many proposals for reforms are scattered throughout professional and popular books, periodicals, and newspapers. Since no analysis of such proposals' contents nor any comprehensive survey of them is yet available, the interested reader must pick up on his own the proposals scattered in his regular reading, and browse through readily available sources to identify additional ones. Whatever his regular reading diet may be, he is sure to come up with proposals that illustrate contemporary trends well.

Besides being in such dispersed sources, many proposals are included in the applied political-science and public-administration literature, and even more in the reports of committees of inquiry and sometimes of semi-private study groups. Four books devoted to proposals for reforming national policymaking are: Arthur C. Millspaugh, *Toward Efficient Democracy* (Washington, D.C.: The Brookings Institution, 1949); James MacGregor Burns, *Congress on Trial* (N.Y.: Harper, 1949); Charles S. Hyneman, *Bureaucracy in a Democracy* (N.Y.: Harper, 1950); and W. W. Rostow and Max F. Millikan, *A Proposal: Key to an Effective Foreign Policy* (N.Y.: Harper, 1957). Many of the books in the new interdisciplinary fields also include proposals on policymaking in general, as well as on specific policies. For a proposal to set up a National Security Research Organization, see Herman Kahn, *On Thermonuclear War* (Princeton, N.J.: Princeton Univ. Press, 1960), pp. 579ff. For some interesting proposals in an article, see Michael D. Reagan, "Toward Improved National Planning," *Public Administration Review,* XXIII (Mar. 1963), 10ff. For some reports of official committees of inquiry, see U.S. Senate Subcommittee on National Policy Machinery, *Staff Reports and Recommendations* (Washington, D.C.: U.S.

Govt. Printing Office, 1961); Government of Canada, *Report of the Royal Commission on Government Organization* (Montreal: Government Printer, 1962), especially vol. I; and the Parliament of the Commonwealth of Australia, *Report of the Committee of Inquiry into Public-Service Recruitment* (Canberra: Commonwealth Government Printer, 1959). For some good reports by private study groups that include significant proposals for reforming policymaking, see H. Field Haviland, Jr., ed., *The Formulation and Administration of United States Foreign Policy* (Washington, D.C.: The Brookings Institution, 1960); The Committee on Foreign Affairs Personnel, *Personnel For the New Diplomacy* (Washington, D.C.: Taplinger, 1962); and some of the research and policy reports of the Committee for Economic Development.

On problems of lobbying and its control, compare, for example, R. Joseph Monson, Jr., and Mark W. Cannon, *The Makers of Public Policy: American Power Groups and Their Ideologies,* with James Deakin, *The Lobbyist* (Washington, D.C.: Public Affairs Press, 1966). On the reform of Congress, see, for example, American Enterprise Institute, *Congress: The First Branch of Government* (Washington, D.C., 1966), and Arthur D. Little, Inc., *The Management Study of Congress* (N.Y., 1965).

These are only a few examples from a very rich field, but glancing over them will provide the reader with some picture of the present tendencies in the reform literature.

CHAPTER 17

In order to help the interested non-professional reader gain some direct impression of the material on which Appendix C is based, I will mention some selected readings on some of the disciplines in the following notes.

The direct contributions of engineering and the life sciences are illustrated by two books: Arthur D. Hall, *A Methodology for Systems Engineering* (Princeton, N.J.: Van Nostrand, 1962), is an excellent example of the significance of engineering of machine systems for systems design in general, including human and man-machine systems; and Leonard Uhr and James G. Miller, eds., *Drugs and Behavior* (N.Y.: John Wiley, 1960), surveys psychopharmacological research.

The contributions of computer engineering deserve special attention. Good non-technical discussions are John A. Postley, *Computers and People* (N.Y.: McGraw-Hill, 1960), and Edmund C. Berkeley, *The*

Computer Revolution (Garden City, N.Y.: Doubleday, 1962). Stimulating discussions of the future of organizations in the age of computers and decision sciences are H. J. Leavitt and T. L. Whisler, "Management in the 1980's," *Harvard Business Review,* XXXVI (Nov.–Dec. 1958), 41ff; and Herbert A. Simon, "The Corporation: Will It Be Managed by Machines?" in Melvin Anshen and G. L. Back, eds., *Management and Corporations, 1985* (N.Y.: McGraw-Hill, 1960). For a broader perspective, see Norbert Wiener, *The Human Use of Human Beings: Cybernetics and Society* (Garden City, N.Y.: Doubleday, 2d, rev. ed., 1954). The field of engineering economy, which combines economics, decision theory, and some aspects of engineering, should also be mentioned here. See F. Paul Degarmo, *Engineering Economy* (N.Y.: Macmillan, 3d ed., 1965).

On history, see A. L. Rowse, *The Use of History* (London: Hodder & Stoughton, 1946), Chap. 1, and Patrick Gardiner, ed., *Theories of History* (N.Y.: Free Press of Glencoe, 1959).

In law, a distinct school of jurisprudence has emphasized for a long time that there should be a study of law directed at the needs of policymaking. The classic work in this direction is Jeremy Bentham's *The Principles of Morals and Legislation.* The applied approach received a specifically American form in a famous article by Roscoe Pound, "The Need of a Sociological Jurisprudence," *The Green Bag,* XIX (1907), 607ff. For an exhaustive survey and discussion of applied approaches to the study of law, see Julius Stone, *The Province and Function of Law* (Cambridge, Mass.: Harvard Univ. Press, 1950), pp. 406ff, and *Social Dimensions of Law and Justice* (Sydney, Aus.: Maitland, 1966). For contemporary proposals in this area, see Frederick K. Beutel, *Some Potentialities of Experimental Jurisprudence as a New Branch of Social Science* (Lincoln: Univ. of Nebraska Press, 1957). A comprehensive proposal to direct the teaching of law toward preparing policymakers is Harold D. Lasswell and Myres S. McDougal, "Legal Education and Public Policy: Professional Training in the Public Interest," first published in *The Yale Law Journal,* Mar. 1943, and reprinted in Harold D. Lasswell, *The Analysis of Political Behavior* (London: Routledge and Kegan Paul, 1948). Some other relevant works are Richard A. Wasserstrom, *The Judicial Decision: Toward a Theory of Legal Justification* (Stanford: Stanford Univ. Press, 1961); Carl A. Auerbach *et al.,* eds., *The Legal Process: An Introduction to Decisionmaking by Judicial, Legislative, Executive, and Administrative Agencies* (San Francisco: Chandler, 1961); Walter P. Murphy, *Elements of Judicial Strategy* (Chicago: Univ. of Chicago Press, 1964); and Gideon Gottlieb, *The Logic of Choice* (London: George Allen,

1968). These books discuss various aspects of judicial decisionmaking, from which more general findings on decisionmaking and policymaking can be drawn.

An overview of the applicability of the social sciences as a whole to policy problems is provided by a symposium on "Applied Social Research in Policy-Formation," in *Philosophy of Science,* XVI (1949), 161ff. Many illustrations are provided by articles in two periodicals, *The Journal of Social Issues* and *Social Problems.* A thorough treatment is provided in the various parts of *The Use of Social Research in Federal Domestic Programs,* A Staff Study for the Research and Technical Programs Subcommittee of the Committee on Government Operations, House of Representatives, U.S. Congress (Washington, D.C.: U.S. Government Printing Office, 1967).

In psychology, one area contributions are coming from is differential psychology and testing techniques. See Anne Anastasi, *Differential Psychology* (N.Y.: Macmillan, 3d ed., 1958), and *Psychological Testing* (N.Y.: Macmillan, 2d ed., 1961). For a pioneering treatment of how to best use tests for personnel decisions, see Lee J. Cronbach and Goldine C. Gleser, *Psychological Tests and Personnel Decisions* (Urbana: Univ. of Illinois Press, 1957). The biggest barrier against developing and using good tests is the widespread use of bad tests, which lead to such abuses and dangers as are described in an exaggerated way in Martin L. Gross, *The Brain Watchers* (N.Y.: Random House, 1962). Such abuses, while self-reinforcing, are largely the result of the "social ethics" described by William H. Whyte in *The Organization Man* (N.Y.: Simon and Schuster, 1956), and are not inherent in the testing technique itself.

The psychology of creativity, which helps identify variables that are conducive to creativity, is very important for policymaking. A very good annotated bibliography is Morris I. Stein and Shirley J. Beinze, *Creativity and the Individual* (N.Y.: Free Press of Glencoe, 1960). For a representative collection of essays, see Harold D. Anderson, ed., *Creativity and Its Cultivation* (N.Y.: Harper, 1959). A single coherent approach is presented in the enlarged edition, edited by Michael Wertheimer, of Max Wertheimer's *Productive Thinking* (N.Y.: Harper, 1959), in which, on the basis of various theories of creativity and productive thinking, he formulates recommendations for improving these phenomena. A good summary of findings on the improvement of thinking is provided in Donald M. Johnson, *The Psychology of Thought and Judgement* (N.Y.: Harper, 1955), pp. 481ff. The idea of "brainstorming" is proposed in Alex F. Osborn, *Applied Imagination* (N.Y.: Scribner's, rev. ed., 1957). For experimental work on the usefulness of brainstorming, see Donald W. Taylor, Paul C. Berry, and Clifton H. Block, "Does Group Participation When Using Brainstorming Facilitate or Inhibit Creative Thinking?" *Administrative Science Quarterly,* III (June 1958), 23ff. Other suggestions for better thinking can be found in Eliot Dole Hutchinson, *How to Think Creatively* (N.Y.: Harper, 1955); William J. J. Gordon, *Synectics: The Development of Creative Capacity* (N.Y.: Harper, 1961); Harold J. Leavitt, *Managerial Psychology* (Chicago: Univ. of Chicago Press, Phoenix ed., 1962), pp. 216ff; and Norman R. F. Maier, *Problem-Solving Discussions and Conferences* (N.Y.: McGraw-Hill, 1963).

Educational psychology's main contribution lies in methodologies for better teaching and training in skills and knowledge that are relevant to policymaking. Most of the relevant literature is about grade-school students and about using new methods for teaching traditional subjects such as mathematics. See Edward M. Glaser, *An Experiment in the Development of Critical Thinking* (N.Y.: Teachers College, Columbia Univ., *Contribution to Education,* no. 843, 1941); George Polya, *How to Solve It* (Garden City, N.Y.: Doubleday, 2d ed., 1957) and *Mathematical Discovery: On Understanding, Learning, and Teaching Problem Solving,* (N.Y.: John Wiley, 1962), vol. I; and T. G. Thurstone, *Teacher's Manual for the Green Book* (Chicago: Science Research Associates, *Learning to Think Series,* 1949). Another relevant part of the literature deals with methods for better executive training, such as the Case method. See Kenneth R. Andrews, ed., *The Case Method of Teaching Human Relations and Administration* (Cambridge, Mass.: Harvard Univ. Press, 1953), and Frank P. Sherwood and William B. Storm, *Teaching in Public Administration: Essays on the Case Approach* (Los Angeles: School of Public Administration, Univ. of Southern California, 1962). Simulations games are very interesting and promising; they were first developed as war games and then applied to business situations. See Clayton J. Thomas, "Military Gaming," in Russell L. Ackoff, ed., *Progress in Operations Research* (N.Y.: John Wiley, 1961), I, 421ff; Stanley Vance, *Management Decision Simulation* (N.Y.: McGraw-Hill, 1962); and Sidney F. Griffin, *The Crisis Game* (Garden City, N.Y.: Doubleday, 1965). An annotated bibliography on war games is available: Vera Riley and John P. Young, *Bibliography on War Gaming* (Chevy Chase, Maryland: Operations Research Office, Johns Hopkins Univ., 1957). More recent developments in simulation as a tool for teaching and research are covered in Harold Guetzkow, ed., *Simulation in Social Science: Readings* (Englewood Cliffs, N.J.: Prentice-Hall, 1962); Harold Guetzkow *et al., Simulation in International Relations: Developments for Research and Teaching* (Englewood Cliffs,

N.J.: Prentice-Hall, 1963); and Andrew M. Scott, *Simulation and National Development* (N.Y.: John Wiley, 1966). In the long run, new teaching methods may provide an important method for training in policymaking skills; consider *WFF 'N PROOF: The Game of Modern Logic,* developed by Layman E. Allen of Yale Law School and based on the approach to learning of Alan R. Anderson and Omar K. Moore of Yale University. For a general non-technical introduction to programmed teaching techniques, see Wendell I. Smith and J. Williams Moore, eds., *Programmed Learning* (Princeton, N.J.: Van Nostrand, 1962).

Particularly interesting is the potential contribution of psychoanalysis, from both individual techniques and group techniques such as T-Groups and sensitivity sessions. See A. Margaret, "Generalization in Successful Psychotherapy," *Journal of Consulting Psychology,* XIV (1950), 64ff, and Robert Tannenbaum *et al., Leadership and Organization: A Behavioral Science Approach* (N.Y.: McGraw-Hill, 1961), Chap. 9. On T-Group methods, see L. P. Bradford *et al., T-Group Theory and Laboratory Method* (N.Y.: John Wiley, 1964), and Edgar H. Schein and Warren G. Bennis, *Personal and Organizational Change Through Group Methods: The Laboratory Approach* (N.Y.: John Wiley, 1965).

The applied uses of sociology are discussed in P. Lazarsfeld, W. Sewell, and H. Wilensky, eds., *The Uses of Sociology* (N.Y.: Basic Books, 1967). See also Arthur B. Shostak, *Sociology in Action* (Homewood, Ill.: Dorsey, 1966). For a careful evaluation, see Gunnar Myrdal, "The Relation Between Social Theory and Social Policy," *The British Journal of Sociology,* IV (Sept. 1953), 210ff. For surveys of applied sociological knowledge on problems of social deviation and racial discrimination, on internal problems of formal organizations, etc., see Dennis Likert and Samuel P. Hayes, Jr., eds., *Some Applications of Behavioral Research,* (Paris: UNESCO, 1957); Robert K. Merton and Robert A. Niebet, eds., *Contemporary Social Problems: An Introduction to the Sociology of Deviant Behavior and Social Disorganization* (N.Y.: Harcourt, Brace, 1961); and S. N. Eisenstadt, ed., *Comparative Social Problems* (N.Y.: Free Press of Glencoe, 1964). The latter two have a larger scope than most "social problems" texts. A good, though outdated, example of the applicability of sociological knowledge to policy problems is Alexander H. Leighton, *The Governing of Men* (Princeton, N.J.: Princeton Univ. Press, 1946). A very readable description of applied anthropology at work is George M. Foster, *Traditional Cultures and the Impact of Technological Change* (N.Y.: Harper, 1962).

In some respects, the literature on political science is the most disappointing of all, perhaps because of my high standards for the study of policymaking, which should, I think, be a major topic for political-science research and theory. In the footnotes and other bibliographic notes I mention some of the relevant substantive writings. Let me mention here some writings on political science that clearly bring out, either explicitly or by default, the lack of concerned efforts to develop policy knowledge.

An international survey of methods, research, and teaching in political science is UNESCO, *Contemporary Political Science* (Paris: UNESCO, 1950). Systematic discussions are B. Cricks, *The American Science of Politics, Its Origin and Conditions* (London: Routledge and Kegan Paul, 1959); D. Easton, *The Political System* (N.Y.: Knopf, 1953); C. S. Hyneman, *The Study of Politics* (Urbana: Univ. of Illinois Press, 1959); V. Van Dyke, *Political Science: A Philosophical Analysis* (Stanford: Stanford Univ. Press, 1960); Harold Lasswell, *The Future of Political Science* (N.Y.: Atherton, 1963); and Albert Somit and Joseph Tannhaus, *The Development of American Political Science: From Burgess to Behavioralism* (Boston: Allyn and Bacon, 1967). The collision of views is best brought out by contrasting Easton's opinion that efforts to arrive at a policy science are "premature" (*op. cit.,* pp. 78ff) with Harold D. Lasswell, *The Policy Sciences* (Stanford: Stanford Univ. Press, 1951), pp. 3ff. A very readable, personalized discussion is W. J. M. Mackenzie, *Politics and Social Science* (Middlesex, Eng.: Penguin, 1967). A book that brings out what little contemporary political science has contributed to an understanding of some basic social issues is Leslie Lipson, *The Great Issues of Politics: An Introduction to Political Science* (Englewood Cliffs, N.J.: Prentice-Hall, 3d ed., 1965).

Economics is the most policy-oriented of all the traditional social sciences; almost all its theories have clear, and in most cases explicit, implications for policymaking. See the classic statement in Alfred Marshall, *Principles of Economics* (London: Macmillan, 8th ed., 1920), Chap. 4, especially paragraph 4. A classic survey of economic thought that clearly shows a direct concern with policy is Charles Gide and Charles Rist, *A History of Economic Doctrines* (London: Harrap, 1915). For a non-technical survey, see Pierre Mendes-France and Gabriel Ardant, *Economics and Action* (Paris: UNESCO, 1955). For a critical discussion, see Sidney Schoeffler, *The Failure of Economics: A Diagnostic Study* (Cambridge, Mass.: Harvard Univ. Press, 1955). The special subject of managerial economics, which applies economic concepts to managerial issues, illustrates that much of the modern management sciences and decision sciences is based on economics. See Milton H. Spencer and Louis Siegelman, *Managerial Economics: Decisionmaking and Forward Planning* (Homewood, Ill.: Irwin, rev. ed., 1964).

Passing on to some of the new interdisciplinary fields, I recommend the following:

On intelligence studies, see Sherman Kent, *Strategic Intelligence for American World Policy* (Princeton, N.J.: Princeton Univ. Press, 1951; Roger Hilsman, *Strategic Intelligence and National Decisions* (Glencoe, Ill.: Free Press, 1956); and Harry Howe Ransom, *Central Intelligence and National Security* (Cambridge, Mass.: Harvard Univ. Press, 1958). The literature on the politics of intelligence organizations should also be mentioned here, though no reliable study is available. See, for instance, David Wise and Thomas B. Ross, *The Invisible Government* (N.Y.: Random House, 1964).

Conflict studies are based on the theory of games. The best text is R. Duncan Luce and Howard Raiffa, *Games and Decisions: Introduction and Critical Survey* (N.Y.: John Wiley, 1957). A delightful, almost non-mathematical introduction is J. D. Williams, *The Compleat Strategyst* (N.Y.: McGraw-Hill, rev. ed., 1966). For some applied uses, see Martin Shubik, ed., *Readings in Game Theory and Political Behavior* (Garden City, N.Y.: Doubleday, 1959).

The major approaches and interests in modern conflict studies are illustrated by the following books, some of which are already classics: Henry A. Kissinger, *Nuclear Weapons and Foreign Policy* (N.Y.: Harper, 1957); Morton A. Kaplan, *Systems and Processes in International Politics* (N.Y.: John Wiley, 1957), especially pp. 169ff; Anatol Rappaport, *Fights, Games, and Debates* (Ann Arbor: Univ. of Michigan Press, 1960); Kenneth E. Boulding, *Conflict and Defense: A General Theory* (N.Y.: Harper, 1962); Thomas C. Schelling, *The Strategy of Conflict* (Cambridge, Mass.: Harvard Univ. Press, 1960), and *Arms and Influence* (New Haven: Yale Univ. Press, 1966); and Herman Kahn, *On Thermonuclear War* (Princeton, N.J.: Princeton Univ. Press, 1960), *Thinking About the Unthinkable* (N.Y.: Horizon, 1962), and *On Escalation: Metaphors and Scenarios* (N.Y.: Praeger, 1965). The books by Kissinger and Kahn are more oriented toward policymaking, the others more toward theory. Kahn's *On Escalation: Metaphors and Scenarios* also demonstrates the importance of strategic studies as a breeding ground for new methods of analysis and thought, which are very important for policymaking in general.

A collection that tries to apply some of the new knowledge from conflict studies to concrete issues and areas, and thereby shows off many of the weaknesses of these studies, is David M. Abshire and Richard V. Allen, eds., *National Security: Political, Military, and Economic Strategies in the Decade Ahead* (N.Y.: Praeger, 1963). *The Journal of Conflict Resolution,* started in 1956, is the main periodical for conflict studies, though an increasing number of relevant articles appear in other journals, especially *World Politics.*

On the importance of the new "strategy experts" on the one hand and their danger on the other hand, compare Bernard Brodie, "The Scientific Strategists," in Robert Gilpin and Christopher Wright, eds., *Scientists and National Policymaking* (N.Y.: Columbia Univ. Press, 1964), pp. 240ff, with Irving L. Horowitz, *The War Game: Studies of the New Civilian Militarists* (N.Y.: Ballantine, 1963), especially pp. 11ff. An interesting survey of the main schools of strategy at universities and some of their effects is Gene M. Lyons and Louis Merton, *School for Strategy* (N.Y.: Praeger, 1965).

On regional studies, see Walter Isard, *Methods of Regional Analysis* (N.Y.: John Wiley, 1960).

Good introductions to development studies are Benjamin Higgins, *Economic Development* (N.Y.: Norton, 1959); Everett E. Hagen, *On the Theory of Social Change* (Homewood, Ill.: Dorsey, 1962); Lucian W. Pye, *Aspects of Political Development* (Boston: Little, Brown, 1966); and S. N. Eisenstadt, *Modernization: Protest and Change* (Englewood Cliffs, N.J.: Prentice-Hall, 1966).

Good, non-technical introductions to the management and decision sciences, each covering part of the field (besides those already mentioned) are: Leonard W. Hein, *The Quantitative Approach to Managerial Decisions* (Englewood Cliffs, N.J.: Prentice-Hall, 1967); Joseph F. McCloskey and Florence N. Trefethen, eds., *Operations Research for Management* (Baltimore: Johns Hopkins Press, 1954), vol. I; Stafford Beer, *Cybernetics and Management* (N.Y.: John Wiley, 1959), and *Decision and Control* (N.Y.: John Wiley, 1966); Herbert A. Simon, *The New Science of Management Decision* (N.Y.: Harper, 1960); David W. Miller and Martin K. Starr, *Executive Decisions and Operations Research* (N.Y.: John Wiley, 1961); Edward C. Bursk and John F. Chapman, eds., *New Decisionmaking Tools for Managers* (N.Y.: Mentor, 1965); A. R. Prest and R. Turvey, "Cost-Benefit Analysis: A Survey," *The Economic Journal,* LXXV (Dec. 1965), 683ff; and Richard A. Johnson, Fremont E. Kast, and James Rosenzweig, *The Theory and Management of Systems* (N.Y.: McGraw-Hill, 1963). There is no one book which adequately covers the field on either a technical or a general level. The main periodicals in English devoted to the management and decision sciences are *Operations Research, Management Science,* and *Management Technology.* A critical discussion of some recent tendencies is Robert Bogaslaw, *The New Utopians: A Study of Systems Design and Social Change* (Englewood Cliffs, N.J.: Prentice-Hall, 1965). Easy non-technical introductions are Stanford L. Optner, *Systems Analysis for*

Business Managements (Englewood Cliffs, N.J.: Prentice-Hall, 2d ed., 1968), and Guy Black, *The Application of Systems Analysis to Government Operations* (Washington, D.C.: National Institute of Public Affairs, 1961). A very useful list of papers in systems analysis by the institution which pioneered its development is *A Bibliography of Selected Rand Publications: Systems Analysis* (Santa Monica, Calif.: The RAND Corp., November 1967, SB-1022).

A broader collection, covering material on the borderline between management sciences and organization theory, is William W. Cooper *et al.,* eds., *New Perspectives in Organizations Research* (N.Y.: John Wiley, 1964). A good collection on organization theory is Albert H. Rubenstein and Chadwick J. Haberstoch, *Some Theories of Organization* (Homewood, Ill., Dorsey, rev. ed., 1966).

Of interest here is a discussion on the possible role of operations research in national planning; see Russell L. Ackoff, "Operations Research and National Planning," *Operations Research,* V (Aug. 1957), 457ff; Charles Hitch, "Operations Research and National Planning—A Dissent," *Operations Research,* V (Oct. 1957), 718ff; and Fred Haussmann, "Operations Research in National Planning of Underdeveloped Countries," *Operations Research,* IX (Mar.–Apr. 1961), 230ff. On possible uses of operations research for public problems, see Philip M. Morse, *Operations Research for Public Systems* (Cambridge, Mass.: M.I.T. Press, 1967). An unusual collection of essays dealing with an even broader application of an "operations-research attitude" at its best is J. R. Lawrence, *Operations Research and the Social Sciences* (N.Y.: Tavistock, 1966).

On possibilities for arriving at theories of values, which can serve as applied ethics, see Nicolai Hartman, *Ethics, Vol. II: Moral Values,* trans. by Stanton Coit (N.Y.: Macmillan, 1932); Donald Davidson *et al.,* "Outlines of a Formal Theory of Value, I," *Philosophy of Science,* XXII (Apr. 1955), 140ff; Nicholas M. Smith, Jr., "A Calculus for Ethics: A Theory of the Structure of Value, Part I," *Behavioral Science,* I (Apr. 1956), 111ff; and C. West Churchman, *Prediction and Optimal Decision* (Englewood Cliffs, N.J.: Prentice-Hall, 1961). For more direct efforts to apply philosophy to policymaking, see Arthur E. Murphy, *The Uses of Reason* (N.Y.: Macmillan, 1943); Rupert C. Lodge, *Applied Philosophy* (London: Routledge and Kegan Paul, 1951); and Wayne A. R. Leys, *Ethics for Policy Decisions* (Englewood Cliffs, N.J.: Prentice-Hall, 1952).

The potential contributions of logic and semantics are illustrated by R. W. Morell, *Managerial Decisionmaking* (Milwaukee: Bruce, 1960), and Albert Upton, *Design for Thinking* (Stanford: Stanford Univ. Press,

1961); the latter could be a good introductory text for the interested reader.

On mathematical models for social sciences, see James S. Coleman, *Introduction to Mathematical Sociology* (N.Y.: Free Press of Glencoe, 1964), and H. R. Alkers, Jr., *Mathematics and Politics* (N.Y.: Macmillan, 1965). More advanced treatments of mathematical models for decisionmaking are R. M. Thrall *et al., Decision Processes* (N.Y.: John Wiley, 1954), and Peter C. Fishburn, *Decision and Value Theory* (N.Y.: John Wiley, 1964). For a rigorous mathematical theory underlying many mathematical models of decisionmaking, see Emanuel Parzen, *Stochastic Processes* (San Francisco: Holden-Day, 1962). The reader who wants to brush up his mathematical thinking capacities, with special attention to mathematics that is relevant to decisionmaking, should study either John G. Kemeny *et al., Introduction to Finite Mathematics* (Englewood Cliffs, N.J.: Prentice-Hall, 1956), or F. Parker Fowler, Jr., and E. W. Sandberg, *Basic Mathematics for Administration* (N.Y.: John Wiley, 1962).

Concerning the barriers to policy science, see P. F. Lazarsfeld and Wagner Thielsens, *The Academic Man: Social Scientists in a Time of Crisis* (Glencoe, Ill.: Free Press, 1956); C. Wright Mills, *The Sociological Imagination* (N.Y.: Oxford Univ. Press, 1959); Theodore Caplow and Reece J. McGee, *The Academic Marketplace* (N.Y.: Basic Books, 1959); and Harold Guetzkow, "Conversation Barriers in Social Science," *Administrative Science Quarterly,* IV (June 1959), 68ff.

On the tendency of the social sciences to imitate the natural sciences, see Friedrich A. Hayek, *The Counterrevolution of Science* (Glencoe, Ill.: Free Press, 1952), Part I. The continuing influence of this tendency, though in a somewhat more guarded way, is illustrated by E. J. Meehan, *The Theory and Method of Political Analysis* (Homewood, Ill.: Dorsey, 1963). Some difficulties of interdisciplinary research are discussed in Margaret Barron Luszki, *Interdisciplinary Team Research: Methods and Problems* (N.Y.: New York Univ. Press, 1958), and some of problems with policy-oriented research are discussed in Milton D. Graham, *Federal Utilization of Social-Science Research: Exploration of the Problems* (Washington, D.C.: The Brookings Institution, 1954), and in the Brookings Institution's *Research for Public Policy* (1961). Talcott Parsons presented some provocative arguments against giving advice on policymaking in a paper, "Role of the Behavioral Scientist in the International Situation," at the annual meeting of the ASA in Washington, D.C., in March 1963. A pioneering effort to bridge the gulf between social-science literature and social action is the periodical *Trans-action.*

CHAPTERS 18–21

I have already given many references to literature relevant to the ways policymaking should be and could be improved in the footnotes in the text and in the bibliographic notes for Chapter 16, so I will give only a few supplementary references dealing with specific issues here.

On the role of experts in government, see W. A. Johr and H. W. Singer, *The Role of the Economist as Official Advisor* (London: Allen & Unwin, 1955). The professional staff of Congress is discussed in Kenneth Kofmehl, *Professional Staff of Congress* (West Lafayette: Purdue Univ. Studies, 1962). Some of the problems of introducing highly qualified staff experts into organizations run by rule of thumb are explored in a fascinating study by Harold L. Wilensky, *Intellectuals in Labor Unions* (Glencoe, Ill.: Free Press, 1956). Worth reading also is a more recent book by Harold L. Wilensky, *Organizational Intelligence: Knowledge and Policy in Government and Industry* (N.Y.: Basic Books, 1967). Much less reliable is Loren Baritz, *The Servants of Power* (Middletown, Conn.: Wesleyan Univ. Press, 1960). A most important study of the interaction between a professional staff agency and the executive is Edward S. Flash, Jr., *Economic Advice and Presidential Leadership: The Council of Economic Advisers* (N.Y.: Columbia Univ. Press, 1965). Some of the difficulties of adjusting to new knowledge are brought out in Morris Janowitz, *The New Military: Changing Patterns of Organization* (N.Y.: Russell Sage Foundation, 1964).

Published literature on the RAND Corporation is meager. Two overall surveys are John McDonald, "The War of Wits," *Fortune* (Mar. 1951), pp. 99ff, and R. D. Specht, "RAND—A Personal View of Its History," *Operations Research*, VIII (Nov.–Dec. 1960), 825ff. Official releases and reports are *The Rand Corporation* (1963), *The Rand Corporation: The First Fifteen Years* (1963), and the *Rand Annual Reports*. A thorough and pioneering study on the RAND Corporation that also discusses the broader ramifications of non-profit advisory corporations is Bruce L. R. Smith, *The RAND Corporation: Case Study of a Non-Profit Advisory Corporation* (Cambridge, Mass.: Harvard Univ. Press, 1966).

On the Central Planning Bureau in the Netherlands, see my *National Planning in the Netherlands* (Syracuse: Syracuse Univ. Press, 1968).

A conservative treatment of civil-service training is the United Nations' *Handbook of Training in the Public Service* (N.Y.: United Nations, 1966). A detailed proposal for leadership training is discussed in my article "The Improvement of Leadership in Developing Countries," *Civilizations,* XVII (1967), 72ff.

Doctrines for better decisionmaking are illustrated by military "estimates of the situation" and "judicial doctrines." The first are discussed in William J. Harris, "Decision," *Military Review,* XXXIII (Apr. 1956), 33ff, and John E. Schremp, "Military Problem Solving," *loc. cit.,* pp. 28ff. The second is discussed in William A. Robson, *Justice and Administrative Law* (London: Stevens, 3d ed., 1951), pp. 360ff.

On the planning-programming-budgeting system, see Department of Defense, *Study Report on the Programming System for the Office of the Secretary of Defense* (Washington, D.C.: Directorate for Systems Planning, 1962), and David Novick, ed., *Program Budgeting: Program Analysis and the Federal Government* (Cambridge, Mass: Harvard Univ. Press, 1965). A somewhat different system is proposed in Robert N. Anthony, *Planning and Control Systems: A Framework for Analysis* (Boston: Graduate School of Business Administration, Harvard Univ., 1965). These materials should be read in conjunction with the "Statement on National Policy by the Research and Policy Committee of the Committee for Economic Development," in *Budgeting for National Objectives: Executive and Congressional Roles in Program Planning and Performance* (N.Y.: Committee for Economic Development, 1966). A thorough study of innovations in the U.S. Department of Defense is S. Enke, *Defense Management* (Englewood Cliffs, N.J.: Prentice-Hall, 1967). Convenient is Samuel A. Tucker, ed., *A Modern Design for Defense Decisions: A McNamara-Hitch-Enthoven Anthology* (Washington, D.C.: Industrial College of the Armed Forces, 1966).

The reader can well identify the problems posed by PPBS and its introduction by comparing a proposal to introduce PPBS in the State Department with a description of ineffectiveness in the Department of State. Compare Thomas C. Schelling, *PPBS and Foreign Affairs,* memorandum, Subcommittee on National Security and International Operations, Committee on Government Operations, U.S. Senate (Washington, D.C.: U.S. Government Printing Office, 1968), with Chris Argyris, *Some Causes of Organizational Ineffectiveness Within the Department of State* (Washington, D.C.: Department of State, 1967).

On the potentialities of machine systems, see Edward F. R. Hearle and Raymond J. Mason, *A Data-Processing System for State and Local Governments* (Englewood Cliffs, N.J.: Prentice-Hall, 1963); and Edward Bennett *et al., Military Information Systems: The Design of Computer-Aided Systems for Command* (N.Y.: Praeger, 1964). For a preliminary discussion of the characteristics of new forms of organizations, see Victor A. Thompson, *Modern Organization* (N.Y.: Knopf, 1961).

Two good discussions of reforms in England, of the Cabinet and the Legislature respectively, are Hans Daalder, *Cabinet Reform in Britain, 1914–1963* (Stanford: Stanford Univ. Press, 1964), and Bernard Crick, *The Reform of Parliament* (London: Weidenfeld and Nicolson, 1964).

On policymaking's dependence on environmental variables, see Zbigniew Brzezinski, "Totalitarianism and Rationality," *The American Political Science Review,* L (Sept. 1956), 751ff, and John Friedman, "Introduction to the Study and Practice of Planning," *International Social Science Journal,* XI (1959), 327ff, especially pp. 337–338. An original discussion of characteristics of political elites that are essential for effective bureaucracy is S. N. Eisenstadt, "Bureaucracy and Political Development," in Joseph La Palombara, ed., *Bureaucracy and Political Development* (Princeton, N.J.: Princeton Univ. Press, 1963). The dependence of institutions on principles is discussed in Brian Barry, *Political Argument* (N.Y.: Humanities Press, 1965).

That achievements and efforts depend on stipulated output is the main thesis of David C. McClelland, *The Achieving Society* (Princeton, N.J.: Van Nostrand, 1961). The limits of human changeability are explored in Benjamin S. Bloom, *Stability and Change in Human Characteristics* (N.Y.: John Wiley, 1964). The importance of political culture is thoroughly discussed in Gabriel A. Almond and Sidney Verba, *The Civic Culture* (Princeton, N.J.: Princeton Univ. Press, 1963).

Some problems of better teaching of policy-relevant information are brought out in J. U. Michaelis, *Social Studies for Children in a Democracy* (Englewood Cliffs, N.J.: Prentice-Hall, 4th ed., 1968). The urgency of adjusting government information to the needs of better policymaking evaluation by the population is brought out by Marjorie Ogilvy-Webb, *The Government Explains: A Study of the Information Services* (London: Allen and Unwin, 1965).

CHAPTER 22

Obstacles to change and some methods for overcoming them are discussed in George Ives, *Obstacles to Human Progress* (London: Allen & Unwin, 1939); Ronald Lippitt *et al., The Dynamics of Planned Change* (N.Y.: Harcourt, Brace, 1958); and Warren G. Bennis *et al.,* eds., *The Planning of Change* (N.Y.: Holt, Rinehart, 1961). The factors influencing innovation are explored in H. G. Barnett, *Innovation: The Basis of Cultural Change* (N.Y.: McGraw-Hill, 1953).

A good study of a political institution that shows these obstacles at work is Neil MacNeil, *Forge of Democracy: The House of Representatives* (N.Y.: McKay, 1963). Good studies that show these obstacles at work in organizations are: Tom Burns and G. M. Stalker, *The Management of Innovation* (Chicago: Quadrangle, 1961); Ashley L. Shiff, *Fire and Water: Scientific Heresy in the Forest Service* (Cambridge, Mass.: Harvard Univ. Press, 1962); Morris Janowitz, ed., *The New Military Changing Patterns of Organization* (N.Y.: Russell Sage Foundation, 1964); Michael Crozier, *The Bureaucratic Phenomenon* (Chicago: Univ. of Chicago Press, 1964); and Chris Argyris, *Organization and Innovation* (Homewood, Ill.: Irwin and Dorsey, 1965).

On various reform strategies and their difficulties, see David Braybrooke and Charles E. Lindblom, *A Strategy of Decision* (N.Y.: Free Press of Glencoe, 1963), and Albert O. Hirschman, *Journeys Toward Progress* (N.Y.: Twentieth Century Fund, 1963), pp. 227ff. Limitations on political reform are discussed in two highly significant books, M. Oakeshott, *Rationalism in Politics* (London: Methuen, 1962), and Aaron Wildavsky, *The Politics of the Budgetary Process* (Boston: Little, Brown, 1964), pp. 128ff.

Finally, the reader is invited to read Michael Young, *The Rise of the Meritocracy, 1870–2033* (London: Thames and Hudson, 1958), which brings out some of the dangers of oversystematic social arrangements, and two books by John Kenneth Galbraith, *The Affluent Society* (Cambridge, Mass.: Riverside, 1958), which gives a very stimulating discussion of "conventional wisdom" and change as applied to economic ideologies, theories, and policies, and *The New Industrial State* (London: Hamish Hamilton, 1967), which poses some of the main dilemmas faced by future-oriented public policymaking.

INDEX